EL SALVADOR:

CENTRAL AMERICA
IN THE
NEW COLD WAR

EL SALVADOR:

CENTRAL AMERICA
IN THE
NEW COLD WAR

Edited by
Marvin E. Gettleman
Patrick Lacefield
Louis Menashe
David Mermelstein
Ronald Radosh

GROVE PRESS, INC./NEW YORK

792 4006

"Cold War, Cold Comfort," by Ronald Steel, reprinted by permission of *The New Republic*, © 1981, The New Republic, Inc. "Dictatorships and Double Standards," by Jeane Kirkpatrick, reprinted from *Commentary*, November 1979, by permission, all rights reserved. "Totalitarianism vs. Authoritarianism," by Michael Walzer, reprinted by permission of *The New Republic*, © 1981, The New Republic, Inc. "Reagan's Latin America," by Tom J. Farer, reprinted with permission from *The New York Review of Books*. Copyright © 1981 Nyrev, Inc. "Class Struggle and Civil War in El Salvador," by Harald Jung, reprinted by permission of *New Left Review*. "The Politics of Salvadoran Christian Democracy," by Stephen Webre, reprinted by permission of Louisiana State University Press, from *Jose Napoleon Duarte and the Christian Democratic Party in Salvadoran Politics: 1960-1972*, by Stephen Webre, copyright © 1979. "The Salvadoran Left," by Latin America Regional Report, reprinted, with permission, from *Latin America Regional Report*, Mexico and Central America, August 15, 1980. "Salvador's Plight Tears a Famous Family Apart," by Warren Hoge, © 1981 by The New York Times Company. Reprinted by permission. "The *Frente's* Opposition: The Security Forces of El Salvador," by Cynthia Arnson, reprinted with permission from The Institute for Policy Studies, 1901 Que Street, NW, Washington DC 20009. "Have You No Sense of Decency, Sir?" by Anthony Lewis, © 1981 by The New York Times Company. Reprinted by permission. "The Need for Agrarian Reform," by Laurence R. Simon and James C. Stephens, Jr., reprinted with permission from © OXFAM-America. "The False Promise—and Real Violence—of Land Reform in El Salvador," by Peter Shiras, reprinted with permission from *Food Monitor*, 350 Broadway, New York, NY 10013. "El Salvador's Land Reform—The Real Facts and the True Alternatives," by Roy L. Prosterman, reprinted with permission from *Food Monitor*. "El Salvador's Land Reform: A Real Promise, but a Final Failure," by Leonel Gomez, reprinted with permission from *Food Monitor*. "El Salvador's Land Reform: The Relationship of Reform to Repression," by Peter Shiras, reprinted with permission from *Food Monitor*. "Salvador Land Reform Aids Few," by Raymond Bonner, © 1981 by The New York Times Company. Reprinted by permission. "The Cross and the Sword in Latin America," by Alan Riding, reprinted with permission from *The New York Review of Books*. Copyright © 1981 Nyrev, Inc. "Oscar Romero: Archbishop of the Poor," by Patrick Lacefield, reprinted with permission from the November, 1979, *Fellowship*, the magazine of the Fellowship of Reconciliation, Box 271, Nyack, NY. "Beefing-Up the Salvadoran Military Forces: Some Components of U.S. Intervention," by Cynthia Arnson, reprinted with permission from The Institute for Policy Studies. "Blots on the White Paper: The Reinvention of the 'Red Menace,'" by James Petras, reprinted by permission from *The Nation*, March 28, 1981, copyright 1981 The Nation Associates. "Further Blots on the White Paper: Doubts About Evidence and Conclusions," by Robert G. Kaiser, reprinted by permission, © *The Washington Post*. "El Salvador: Which Vietnam?" by William E. Colby, reprinted with permission, © *The Washington Post*. "The Last War, the Next War, and the New Revisionists," by Walter LaFeber, reprinted with permission from the January, 1981, issue of *Democracy*, copyright © 1980 by the Common Food Foundation. "El Salvador: Why Not Negotiate?" by Robert E. White, reprinted with permission from The Carnegie Endowment for International Peace. "Crumbs and Shattered Illusions," by Guillermo Ungo, reprinted with permission from *Newsfront International*. "Freedom and Unfreedom in Nicaragua," by Shirley Christian, reprinted by permission of *The New Republic*, © 1981, The New Republic, Inc. "Guatemala: The Coming Danger," by Marlise Simons, reprinted with permission from *Foreign Policy* magazine #43 (Summer, 1981), Copyright 1981 by the Carnegie Endowment for International Peace. "We Have 12 Helicopters in Honduras—Is It the Next El Salvador?" by Peter Shiras and Leyda Barbieri, reprinted with permission from *Democratic Left*. "Debate Over U.S. Policy on Human Rights," by Jeane Kirkpatrick and Patricia M. Derian, reprinted with permission from *U.S. News & World Report*.

First Evergreen Edition 1981
Second Printing, 1982
ISBN: 0-394-17956-0
Library of Congress Catalog Card Number: 81-82119

Library of Congress Cataloging in Publication Data
Main entry under title:

El Salvador, Central America in the new Cold War.

  Bibliography: p.390
  Includes index.
  1. El Salvador—Politics and government—
1944-   —Addresses, essays, lectures.
2. Communism—El Salvador—Addresses, essays,
lectures.   3. El Salvador—Foreign relations—
United States—Addresses, essays, lectures.
4. United States—Foreign relations—El Salvador—
Addresses, essays, lectures.   I. Gettleman,
Marvin E.
F1488.E4   972.84′052   81-82119
ISBN 0-394-17956-0   AACR2

Manufactured in the United States of America

GROVE PRESS, INC., 196 West Houston Street, New York, N.Y. 10014

ACKNOWLEDGMENTS

IN the course of putting this book together, we received advice and help for which we are grateful. First of all, we thank our editor at Grove Press, Lisa Rosset, whose enthusiasm for our project from the very start has been heartening. We are also appreciative of the efforts of our literary agent, Betty Anne Clarke.

Special thanks go to Cynthia Arnson, John Dinges and Michael Parenti, all of whom are affiliated with the Institute for Policy Studies in Washington, D.C., an organization recently much maligned by the political right wing in the United States; and to Anne Nelson, who helped us select from among her many moving photographs those most appropriate and who also assisted in designing their layout.

In addition, we wish to acknowledge the assistance of the following: Zena Jacobs, Vera Marek and Hana Stranska of the Spicer Library, Polytechnic Institute of New York; the helpful if anonymous librarians at the Herbert H. Lehman Library, Columbia University, and the Government Documents Division, New York Public Library; Deborah Levenson and Marilyn Young, both of New York University; Nancy Lieber, Institute for Democratic Socialism; Walter LaFeber, Cornell University; Cindy Hounsell, Ellen Schrecker and Allis Wolfe, all of Manhattan; Hobart A. Spalding, Jr., Brooklyn College, City University of New York; Robert Armstrong and Stephen Volk, North American Congress on Latin America; Fred Siegel, Jan Rosenberg, Sheila Menashe, Claudia Menashe, Daniel Radosh, Laura Radosh, Linnea Capps Lacefield and Rachel Fruchter, all of Brooklyn, New York; Penny Schantz, Democratic Socialist Organizing Committee; Rick Kunnes, New American Movement; John A. Womack, Jr., Harvard University; I. Leonard Leeb and Frederick C. Kreiling, Department of Social Sciences, Polytechnic Institute of New York; Hermione McLemore and Darline Vincent, office of the Department of Social Sciences, Polytechnic Institute of New York; Albert L. Brusakos, the Polytechnic Institute of New York print shop; Pete Seeger; David Curzon and Gonzalo Martner, of the office of Planning, Programming and Evaluation of the United Nations; Michael Barry, Dot Gregory, Tom Bleha, Carl Matthews, Peter Knecht and David Simcox, all of the U.S. Department of State; Victoria Rideout, office of Congressman Gerry Studds; Mark Pinsky, office of Congressman Ted Weiss; Julius Topol, District Council 37, Municipal Employees Legal Services Plan, New York; Marvin Ciporen, Amalgamated Clothing and Textile Workers' Union, New York; Richard E. Feinberg, Woodrow Wilson International Center for Scholars; and Carlos Torres, a Salvadoran student at the Polytechnic Institute of New York. Finally, a special note of gratitude to a Salvadoran friend who was of invaluable assistance to Patrick Lacefield during a visit to El Salvador in 1979.

CONTENTS

GENERAL INTRODUCTION

Coffee growers should not anguish over the situation in El Salvador today; there was a similar one in 1932, and if it was solved then it can be now.

> —Representative of the
> Frente Unido Cafetalero
> (coffee plantation owners),
> March, 1980

IN late 1980, after the assassination of six leaders of the Salvadoran opposition, a radio broadcast from the capital city declared that "with this action the Salvadoran social process has become an unyielding confrontation." [1] This confrontation has not been confined to the tiny country of El Salvador; it has taken on regional and even global significance, and has become a matter of growing public concern in the United States. The outgoing administration of President Jimmy Carter, and especially the new Ronald Reagan regime, have committed the U.S. to involvement in this confrontation. The possibility of involvement of U.S. armed forces is real—already over fifty acknowledged "advisers" are in El Salvador.

It is in this dangerous situation that we offer this volume of documents, historical essays and analyses of current developments, hoping to stimulate more informed public debate and careful consideration of policy alternatives. Such a debate has already begun in the United States, but voices calling for reasoned and peaceful solutions to the problems of El Salvador, Central America, and the rest of the Third World generally will have to be amplified and mobilized in order to counter the tendency on the part of authorities in Washington to view upheavals and insurgencies as exercises in externally directed "Communist expansion." We have included official speeches, remarks at press conferences, government briefing reports and "White Papers," for authoritative statements of the government's position. We include in its entirety Jeane Kirkpatrick's famous November, 1979, essay, which anticipated the Reagan administration's viewpoint so well that it earned its author a high government position. [2] For reasons of space we have generally limited our focus to the political aspects of the situation and their implications for policy, but this should not be interpreted as an intent to downplay long-term economic factors, which underlay popular discontent in El Salvador, as well as other areas. [3]

---

[1] Radio San Salvador, December 1, 1980 (Foreign Broadcast Information Service, Daily Reports, December 3, 1980).

[2] See Reading 3.

[3] Considerations of space have also meant that we have had to eliminate most footnotes. Those wishing to pursue the issues raised in this book further should refer to the original source material as well as the bibliography we have provided.

But finding the most accurate and forceful statement of the U.S. government's position is not quite the same as finding out the true state of affairs in El Salvador. The United States has become a party to the confrontation in the region, and its position has to be counterposed to those of other interested parties. Hence, we present documents and views of the current Salvadoran ruling junta, as well as its rebel opponents. These documents produced in the actual struggle, little known to the general public, constitute an important part of our book. With them, readers can have a better basis for understanding the sources of conflict in El Salvador. Do they stem from Russian-Cuban-Nicaraguan efforts to destabilize a society that otherwise would be making genuine progress toward social justice and harmony, as Washington authorities say? Or is there another level of reality, one in which local, historically based grievances far outweigh external, conspiratorial factors in explaining the insurgency in El Salvador?

Historical influences can be traced back to the Spanish conquest, if not before. By 1524 Pedro de Alvarado, one of the cruelest of the *Conquistadores* had subdued the indigenous population of Central America with legendary brutality. Under Spanish colonial domination, El Salvador was part of the Captaincy-General of Guatemala, and for some time after independence continued to be part of a federated Republic of Central America.[4] Although this union dissolved in factional struggles among the post-independence local tyrants, these indigenous leaders could occasionally unite in response to a common situation, as in 1855–56 when Central American armed forces came together temporarily to defeat the U.S. *filibustero*, William Walker.[5] For the remainder of the nineteenth century and on into the twentieth, El Salvador was plagued by frequent interference by the dictators of neighboring countries, as well as the depredations of its own. The most notorious modern dictator, whose name has been adopted by a leading right-wing "death squad," [6] was General Maximiliano Hernández Martínez. Believer in the esoteric doctrines of Theosophy, as well as in the tenets of Fascism, Martínez (as he was universally called in El Salvador) took over the state by a *coup d'état* in 1931,[7] just as the full force of world depression was reaching Central America, dramatically affecting the already vulnerable economies of the region.

Introduced in the early nineteenth century, coffee rapidly came to dominate not only the economy but the social structure of El Salvador. The coffee plantations which flourished on the country's fertile volcanic soil depended upon a fluctuating world market, and demanded intensive mobili-

---

[4] J. Fred Rippy, *Latin America: A Modern History* (Rev. ed., Ann Arbor, Mich., 1968), Chap. XV.

[5] Alastair White, *El Salvador* (London, 1973), pp. 76–77.

[6] See reading 16, below.

[7] David Lena, "Análisis de una Dictadura Fascista Latin-Americana: Maximiliano Hernández Martínez," *La Universidad*, XCIV (Sept.–Oct., 1969); Thomas P. Anderson, *Matanza: El Salvador's Communist Revolt of 1932* (Lincoln, Neb., 1971), Chaps. III–IV.

zation of the labor force. Thus, there developed both a coffee growers' oligarchy, virtually a state within a state, and a rapidly growing rural proletariat.[8] (Already the most densely populated country in Central America, El Salvador experiences the staggering population growth rate of 3% per year.) Leftist organizations and propaganda began to appear by the 1920s, appealing not only to the landless workers but to segments of the middle class as well. The major figure in the Salvadoran left in this period was Augustín Farabundo Martí, scion of one of the leading oligarchic families, who, when the international price for coffee dropped, and the growers attempted to pass on at least part of their losses to the peasants, organized resistance in the rural areas. In January, 1932, just as El Salvador's major volcano, Izalco, erupted, the peasants in many regions attacked villages and cities, aiming at the local oligarchs, military outposts and telegraph stations. This has been called the first Communist revolution in Latin America.[9] Accounts of it, and of the massacre (*Matanza*) carried out by General Martínez, may be found in a major work of scholarship by the U.S. historian Thomas P. Anderson. According to Professor Anderson, the heritage of military dictatorship, and "Indeed, the whole [subsequent] political labyrinth of El Salvador can be explained only in reference to the traumatic experience of the uprising and the *Matanza*." [10]

Dealt a crushing blow in 1932, the left in El Salvador has risen again in response to the persistence of misused oligarchic power and military brutality. The leading insurgent organization has taken the name of the martyred leader of the 1932 uprising while a right-wing death squad took the name of the dictator who ordered his execution. The current contest of such forces as the Hernández Martínez death squad against the Farabundo Martí National Liberation Front illustrates the importance of historical factors in shaping the present day confrontation in El Salvador.

* * *

Motivated by a conviction of the need to learn from history, and to do what we can to prevent U.S. power from being enlisted on the side of an oppressive antipopular force in El Salvador (in short, to prevent the transformation of El Salvador into another Vietnam), the editors of this book pretend no agnostic impartiality, and do not attempt to present any mechanical balancing of readings on various "sides" of the questions. Yet, we believe we have presented a multisided book. Anyone seeking the best, authoritative statements upholding Washington's view of the conflict in El Salvador will find them here; but those looking for convincing and impressive arguments opposing further U.S. intervention will also find them in these pages.

——The Editors

---

[8] David Browning, *El Salvador: Landscape and Society* (London, 1971), pp. 155–73, 222–23; Alejandro D. Marroquin, *Latin America and the Caribbean* (Belfast, 1968), pp. 188ff.

[9] Anderson, *Matanza*, p. 2 and passim.

[10] Anderson, *Matanza*, p. 159.

PART ONE

SEEING RED: THE REAGAN ADMINISTRATION LOOKS AT THE WORLD

EDITORS' INTRODUCTION

Being confident of our future, we are now free of that inordinate fear of Communism which once led us to embrace any dictator who joined us in that fear.

—Jimmy Carter, 1977

First and foremost, let me emphasize . . . that our problem with El Salvador is external intervention in the internal affairs of a sovereign nation in this hemisphere—nothing more, nothing less. That is the essential problem we're dealing with.

—Alexander M. Haig, 1981

THE decade of the 1980s has begun with an unusual historical turnabout. A mutually agreed-upon policy of global relaxation between the great powers—détente—has given way to the tensions of renewed Cold War. What seemed like the good sense to put a lid on weapons of mass destruction, as negotiated in the Strategic Arms Limitation Treaty (SALT), has been replaced by the demented logic of a renewed arms race. After an interval when it appeared that the U.S., wiser for the experience of the Vietnam war, was willing to come to terms with the turbulent quest for social and economic justice in the Third World, El Salvador was converted into a flashpoint of East-West confrontation in a bizarre re-enactment of the old policy of "containment" of Soviet power.

It is as if the ghosts of Harry Truman and John Foster Dulles have reappeared in the forms of Ronald Reagan and Alexander Haig.

The reasons for the turnabout are subtle and complex, but one element is apparent: the change was not sudden, but gradual and cumulative; it began well before the coming of the Reagan presidency, although it is the present administration in Washington that has articulated the outlook of the New Cold War most clearly.

The U.S. emerged from the Second World War with seemingly unlimited power to impose its will globally. That power was challenged from two directions. One was the reluctance of the U.S.S.R. to surrender its primary war gain, the domination of Eastern Europe, and its willingness, under harsh Stalinist and post-Stalin rule, to match U.S. military technology in nuclear and conventional spheres. A second was the colossal restlessness of the Third World, from simple nationalist movements against colonialism to profound transformations of inherited social structures and political forms. The Cuban revolution was an example of the latter right at our doorstep.

Washington's method for dealing with the two challenges was to combine and equate them: to explain away Third World rebelliousness as a manifestation of Soviet power and expansionist ambitions. The equation was acceptable to a generation of Americans who supported the grand strategy of Containment.

The Vietnam War fractured the equation. While Soviet military assistance played an important part in Vietnamese resistance to American force, the war came to be seen by many inside and outside of the U.S. government as an indigenous struggle of long duration for national independence against external powers.

Seen in proper perspective, the Vietnamese experience should have been understood as another instance of a Third World people's national awakening. Whether the Vietnamese won or lost, the Soviets would have gone on building their military arsenal to the point of reaching a rough parity with the U.S. The Nixon-Kissinger strategy seemed to accept U.S. defeat in Vietnam and the reality of Soviet military power. U.S. withdrawal from Vietnam and the initiation of SALT were the results.

Others saw it differently. President Reagan was later to say that U.S. armed forces were not defeated in Vietnam; *they were not allowed to win*. Vietnam was seen as another U.S. failure, against a backdrop of Soviet military growth and activity in Africa and the Middle East. (*Soviet* failures in such places as Somalia and Egypt are often overlooked in these inflated estimates of Moscow's achievements.) When a popular revolution swept away the seemingly impregnable throne of the Shah of Iran in 1979, the sense of failure deepened—it turned to humiliation and outrage when U.S. embassy personnel were held hostage by Iranian student militants for over a year.

Late in 1979 the U.S.S.R. sent troops into Afghanistan to protect a tottering client regime. The Carter administration, deeply ambivalent in its attitudes toward the U.S.S.R. and the role of U.S. power in the Third World—its "Trilateralist" rhetoric of refocusing East-West attention to North-South concerns, and forging a bloc made up of the U.S., Western Europe and Japan, amounted to very little in foreign policy operations—now used Soviet intervention in Afghanistan as the occasion to retool for a new era of global confrontation with the U.S.S.R. SALT II was allowed to languish in the Senate. A

"Rapid Deployment Force" was established for quick U.S. military action in the Third World. Steps were taken to re-establish the draft. Vast increases in U.S. and NATO military budgets were projected. (One of the last acts of the Carter administration was to resume shipments of lethal weaponry to the Salvadoran junta.) As George Kennan warned, a climate of war hysteria settled over Washington in the aftermath of Soviet intervention in Afghanistan.[1]

If Carter took the first measures in the New Cold War, it was left for Ronald Reagan to revive the old fundamentalist mood and language.

---

[1] Kennan wrote: "Never since World War II has there been so far-reaching a militarization of thought and discourse in the capital. An unsuspecting stranger, plunged into its midst, could only conclude that the last hope of peaceful, nonmilitary solutions had been exhausted—that from now on only weapons, however used, could count." *The New York Times*, February 1, 1980. Kennan's words carry a special kind of weight: a former ambassador to Moscow, he was also one of the architects of the original Containment policy and his "The Sources of Soviet Conduct," signed "X," was a basic document of Cold War I. See *Foreign Affairs*, Vol. XXV, July 1947, pp. 566–82.

Chapter I

THE RUSSIANS ARE COMING, AGAIN

---

1. Soviet Ambitions, Soviet Immorality *

BY RONALD REAGAN AND ALEXANDER HAIG

Preoccupation with the Soviet Union as the main global danger to U.S. interests has been a major theme—with many variations—of the Reagan administration's foreign policy. From the President on down, administration spokesmen have sounded that theme repeatedly at important public forums, as the following statements show. President Reagan denounced the U.S.S.R. at his first press conference and amplified his charges in a nationally televised interview conducted by Walter Cronkite; and Secretary of State Haig emphasized the Soviet danger in his first public speech after taking office.

Q. MR. PRESIDENT, what do you see as the long-range intentions of the Soviet Union? Do you think, for instance, the Kremlin is bent on world domination that might lead to a continuation of the cold war? Or do you think that under other circumstances détente is possible?

A. [*Pres. Reagan*] Well, so far détente's been a one-way street the

---

* From the President's Press Conference, January 29, 1981, transcript in *The New York Times*, January 30, 1981, and from "Interview with Walter Cronkite," March 3, 1981, *Department of State Bulletin*, Vol. 81, No. 2049, April 1981, p. 9. Haig's address before the American Society of Newspaper Editors, April 24, 1981 is from United States Department of State, *Current Policy*, No. 275, April 1981.

Soviet Union has used to pursue its own aims. I don't have to think
of an answer as to what I think their intentions are: They have repeated it.

I know of no leader of the Soviet Union, since the revolution and
including the present leadership, that has not more than once repeated in the various Communist Congresses they hold, their determination that their goal must be the promotion of world revolution
and a one world Socialist or Communist state—whichever word you
want to use.

Now, as long as they do that and as long as they, at the same time,
have openly and publicly declared that the only morality they recognize is what will further their cause: meaning they reserve unto themselves the right to commit any crime; to lie; to cheat, in order to
obtain that and that is moral, not immoral, and we operate on a
different set of standards, I think when you do business with them—
even at a détente—you keep that in mind. . . .

———————

Q. [*Walter Cronkite*] Your hard line toward the Soviet Union is in
keeping with your campaign statements, your promises. But there are
some who, while applauding that stance, feel that you might have
overdone the rhetoric a little bit in laying into the Soviet leadership
as being liars and thieves, etc.

A. [*Pres. Reagan*] Let's recap. I am aware that what I said received
a great deal of news attention, and I can't criticize the news media for
that. I said it. But the thing that seems to have been ignored, well,
two things: one, I did not volunteer that statement. This was not a
statement that I went in and called a press conference and said:
"Here, I want to say the following." I was asked a question. And the
question was: What did I think were Soviet aims? Where did I think
the Soviet Union was going? And I had made it clear to them, I said:
"I don't have to offer my opinion. They have told us where they're
going over and over again. They have told us that their goal is the
Marxian philosophy of world revolution and a single one-world Communist state and that they're dedicated to that." And then I said:
"We're naive if we don't recognize in their performance of that, that
they also have said the only morality"—remember their ideology is
without God, without our idea of morality in the religious sense.
"Their statement about morality is that nothing is immoral if it furthers their cause, which means they can resort to lying or stealing or
cheating or even murder if it furthers their cause and that is not

immoral. Now, if we're going to deal with them, then we have to keep that in mind when we deal with them." And I've noticed that with their own statements about me and their attacks on me since I answered the question that way—it is the only statement I have made—they have never denied the truth of what I said.[1]

———————

[*Alexander Haig*] A major focus of American policy must be the Soviet Union, not because of ideological preoccupation but simply because Moscow is the greatest source of international insecurity today. Let us be plain about it: Soviet promotion of violence as the instrument of change constitutes the greatest danger to world peace.

The differences between the United States and the Soviet Union concern the very principles of international action. We believe in peaceful change, not the status quo. The peoples of the world seek peace, prosperity, and social justice. This is as desirable as it is inevitable. The United States could no more stand against such a quest than we could repudiate our own revolution. We were the first to proclaim that individual liberty, democracy, and the rule of law provided the best framework for the improvement of the human condition. And we have led the attempt since the Second World War to maintain two principles of international action: the peaceful resolution of disputes and the proscription of outside intervention in the affairs of sovereign nations.

In contrast, Soviet policy seeks to exploit aspirations for change in order to create conflict justifying the use of force and even invasion. Moscow continues to support terrorism and war by proxy.

There is an additional dimension to the danger. In regions sensitive to Western interests, in the littorals of critical sea passages, in areas that hardly affect Soviet security, you will find Moscow taking a keen interest in conflict. Thus, Western strategic interests, as well as the hopes for a more just international order, are at stake.

Our objective must be to restore the prospects for peaceful resolution of conflict. We can do this by demonstrating to the Soviet Union that aggressive and violent behavior will threaten Moscow's own interests. We can do this by demonstrating, as we are doing in El Salvador today, that a government bent on making necessary reforms

———————

[1] Among Soviet reactions was this one from a political commentator in *Izvestia:* "There's no point in refuting once more what has long since been thoroughly refuted by life as a completely absurd anti-Soviet cock-and-bull story." (February 1, 1981) See *The Current Digest of the Soviet Press,* Vol. XXXIII, No. 5, March 4, 1981. —Eds.

will not be overthrown by armed intervention supported by Moscow or its surrogates. We can do this by never accepting the Soviet occupation of other countries, such as Afghanistan.

Only the United States has the pivotal strength to convince the Soviets—and their proxies—that violence will not advance their cause. Only the United States has the power to persuade the Soviet leaders that improved relations with us serve Soviet as well as American interests. We have a right, indeed a duty, to insist that the Soviets support a peaceful international order, that they abide by treaties, and that they respect reciprocity. A more constructive Soviet behavior in these areas will surely provide the basis for a more productive East-West dialogue.

2. *Cold War, Cold Comfort* *

By Ronald Steel

The assumptions and consequences of Washington's revived Cold War mentality are critically examined here by the author of the widely acclaimed biography, Walter Lippmann and the American Century *(Boston, 1980). Lippmann himself was an early and cogent critic of original Cold War policies. See his* The Cold War: A Study in U.S. Foreign Policy *(New York, 1947).*

THE Reagan administration's foreign policy is simple and direct. Anti-Sovietism is its name. Every problem in the outside world is viewed through this lens. Racism in South Africa, struggles in the Middle East, revolution in Central America, repression in Argentina—all are seen as props against the background of the great showdown with Soviet communism.

The formula is a potent one. It provides an explanation for our troubles, and suggests a way of resolving them that threatens no special interest groups and upsets no entrenched assumptions. Candidate Reagan expressed it in classic form during the campaign. "Let us not delude ourselves," he said. "The Soviet Union underlies all the unrest that is going on. If they weren't engaged in this game of dominoes, there wouldn't be any hot spots in the world."

* *The New Republic*, Vol. 184, No. 15, April 11, 1981, pp. 15–17.

We would all like to believe it. A world that simple would be a world easier to deal with—a world in which we were always sure who was right and who wrong, who was our foe and who our friend, which responses were necessary and which merely capricious. For a long time we were sure. This does not mean we were necessarily right in being sure, but at least we had few doubts. Then along came Vietnam, and nothing has been quite the same since.

We may well be over our Vietnam syndrome, as has been said, and no longer afraid of using force.[1] But we are not so sure any more of the utility of force and we have come to realize that it can be very expensive to apply. The causes have to be worth the effort, because the effort is a great one, not only for our economy, but for the whole structure and cohesion of our society.

Thus there are two questions we have to ask about anti-Sovietism as a basis for American foreign policy today. One is the old question: is it a relevant response to what is taking place in the world? The second is a new question resulting from the sharp constriction of our circumstances over the decade: can we afford it?

Some may be shocked by the second question, for it implies that we are poor, or that we might be obliged to do less than we should. We are not poor, but we are not so rich as we once were—at least not in relation to many other nations and, more importantly, not in relation to the resources and the productivity on which so much of our prosperity depends. We can do what we must, but we would pay a very high price for doing more than we should. And what we must do is not written on a Rosetta stone that only Ronald Reagan, Alexander Haig, and a few professors playing hooky at the National Security Council can decipher. It is a question of establishing priorities, which means making distinctions between vital needs and idle wishes.

There is nothing new about anti-Sovietism. It has been a staple of American foreign policy, indeed its centerpiece, since the first days of the cold war. It used to be called anti-communism. Now, to take account of the Peking-Moscow squabble, it has been updated, though not necessarily made more precise. It still suffers from most of the old liabilities. It does not distinguish between Soviet policies that are threatening and those merely inconvenient. It defines American interests in terms of what the Soviet Union does rather than in terms of what the United States needs. And in practice, anti-Sovietism as a foreign policy doctrine is vague, emotional, and reactive.

The doctrine is vague, because it lumps together actions such as Moscow's relentless missile build-up with its support of quasi-Marxist

---

[1] See the material on Vietnam, below (Readings 38-41).——Eds.

nationalists in countries like Angola and Ethiopia. The former is a real threat to American security, the latter scarcely even a nuisance. Yet it is Soviet meddling in the third world that obsesses official Washington. Perversely, the only hope for slowing down Soviet missile production—through an arms control accord—is rejected and derided by the very people in this administration whose ostensible task is to achieve such control.

The doctrine is emotional, for it allows a minor ripple to trigger a hysterical response. Witness the supposed "discovery" of the Soviet brigade in Cuba. Although the Russian troops had been there for twenty years, the flap over their rediscovery administered the *coup de grâce* to the limping SALT II treaty. Similarly, information that the rebels in El Salvador received some Soviet weapons was enough to transform a social revolution in that beleaguered country into a cold war confrontation.

The doctrine is reactive, for knee-jerk anti-Sovietism allows Moscow to set the priorities. When the Russians sent troops into Afghanistan to prop up a faltering Marxist regime, a country that had never been of the slightest interest to American policy-makers suddenly assumed critical importance. When Somalia was receiving Soviet largesse and Ethiopia receiving ours, we were assured that Ethiopia was insignificant, while Somalia was one of the key countries of Africa. Now that the United States has switched sides, we are told that Ethiopia, run by Marxists, is really the crucial one.

The major shortcoming of ritualistic anti-Sovietism—its reduction of all the world's ills to a simple equation of us against them—is also part of its appeal. One example is the current effort to redefine terrorism as something that only Communists commit. Thus Alexander Haig has assured us that terrorism in the world—whether it be the hijacking of an airplane or a bomb in a marketplace—is orchestrated by the Soviets. Presumably, although the Secretary of State did not elaborate, they are also responsible for such terrorists as the Red Brigade in Italy, whose "infantile leftism" they have documented, the right-wing death squads in El Salvador, and the police torturers in Guatemala and Argentina. Unfortunately for Secretary Haig, his department, when pressed by reporters, could find no evidence to back up his assertions. This does not mean that the Soviets would be reluctant to support terrorism when it suited their purposes. Other more scrupulous nations have been known to do so. But it does mean that there may be other causes of violence and terrorism, other reasons why Iraqis and Iranians, Arabs and Jews, Pakistanis and Indians are at one another's throats.

Are the current architects of our diplomacy so simple as to believe what they are telling us? Not necessarily. To them there is terrorism, which by definition is Soviet-inspired, and the "regrettable excesses" that our more energetic friends may commit in their pursuit of stabilization and modernization. It is useful to redefine terrorism in order to draw the lines more clearly and rally public support for new policy priorities.

Among those priorities are support for "friendly" dictators regardless of their human rights abuses, military aid to the Salvadoran junta, winking at South Africa's racial programs, rejection of arms control, and, as part of the biggest jump in the nation's military budget in our peacetime history, a greatly expanded fleet and missile arsenal. These policies reflect something quite simple in conception: a return to cold war fundamentalism. It is a policy based on the assumption that if we are tough enough and strong enough we are sure to get our way, because we are certainly pure enough. Thus the new rearmament program—which is, in effect, a massive transfer of wealth from the civilian to the military sector of the economy—is the operating arm of a policy of global military engagement. It requires two things to work: first, acquiescent allies in Europe and Japan to support it by doing their share militarily and adjusting their trade policies accordingly, and, second, a compliant American public to pay for it. A Reagan economic program based on cake for the rich means crumbs for the poor if it is to push through its military expansion program without devastating inflation.

The allies clearly are not buying the administration's rationale. They share neither its assumptions about Soviet behavior nor its prescriptions for how to deal with it. They are dragging their feet, doing only what they must to keep the Americans from becoming angry. The American public supports the policies for the moment because it has been disillusioned by events. It naturally believes in a strong defense, and it wants to believe that this will reverse what it sees as the decline of the past few years. Some national assumptions have been badly buffeted lately. First came the oil shocks that dramatized the nation's vulnerability. Then came the daily humiliations of the hostage drama in Iran. And immediately following the Teheran episode came the Soviet invasion of Afghanistan, raising new anxieties about the ground rules of the cold war.

All these events, occurring in such rapid succession, undermined much of what we have been taught to believe about America's place in the world. Instead of being omnipotent and beloved, we suddenly seemed to be weak and scorned. . . .

That is not an easy adjustment to make. We are tempted to return to the old ways. The virtue of a military buildup is that it seems to offer a quick cure for our troubles. But this is illusory. Usable military power is different from actual hardware. The United States can compete with the Soviet military arsenal, but it cannot, through force of arms, impose a political solution on El Salvador. It can win a military victory in that unhappy country, but this will not in any way affect the size of the Red army or the strength of the Soviet missile arsenal. And there are problems, such as secure access to Persian Gulf oil at a reasonable price, that no amount of American arms can resolve happily.

The kind of military superiority that the United States once enjoyed over the Soviet Union is gone. The Russians, by squeezing their civilians, have the capacity to match us missile for missile. They also have the will to do so. We are playing from our weakest suit by choosing to engage them on that level alone. Our comparative advantage lies not in building weapons, but in the strength of our economy, in our ability to use foreign aid as an arm of our diplomacy and to maintain alliances with those who share our values. A military fix, although tempting, is a delusion.

The attempt to achieve it could also be economically disastrous. This perhaps is the greatest danger of Reagan's arms buildup. It was our enormous economic surplus, as Lester Thurow points out in *Foreign Policy* ["The Moral Equivalent of Defeat," No. 42, Spring, 1981, pp. 114-24.—Eds.], that allowed a succession of postwar American presidents to pursue a policy of global engagement and military activism. That surplus has evaporated, partly as a result of the massive outflow of funds to pay for imported oil, but even more because of a loss of productivity and of competitiveness on world markets.

Anti-Sovietism is not a policy, it is a stance. It promises a cold war victory, but can deliver only military frustration, economic distress, and political disaffection. It is time for those truly concerned about American security to examine the true costs of this policy and to explore alternatives.

Chapter II

THE REAGAN ADMINISTRATION CONFRONTS LATIN AMERICA IN THE THIRD WORLD:

Human Rights, Revolution and the External Totalitarian Menace

Editors' Introduction

THE leading theme of the Reagan administration's foreign policy may be anti-Sovietism, as Ronald Steel showed in Reading 2, but global and military realities have so far ruled out direct confrontation and engagement between the U.S. and the U.S.S.R. The natural terrain for U.S. intervention and attempts to challenge what is perceived as Soviet "expansionism" is the Third World, especially the region historically dominated by the U.S.—Central and South America and the Caribbean. For reasons having in part to do with geography, Washington has chosen El Salvador as the place where, as *New York Times* columnist and former Nixon speech writer William Safire put it, the U.S. can "break the Communist winning streak." (*The New York Times*, February 26, 1981.) A U.S. "victory" against the revolution in El Salvador would help cure the doldrums of the Vietnam Syndrome. The shift from what the Reagan administration sees as the ineffectual and passive policies of the Carter State Department to an aggressive stance is based on attempts to persuade the U.S. public of two dubious assessments: that rebellion inside El Salvador is externally supported and led by the U.S.S.R. and Cuba; and that authoritarian regimes such as the Duarte junta in El Salvador or the former Somoza dictatorship in Nicaragua are palatable in the counter-revolutionary cause. The first assessment is fully explored in Part Four below, especially in the material dealing with the Reagan administration's notorious White Paper on El Salvador. The second is examined in the Readings in this chapter.

3. Dictatorships and Double Standards *

By Jeane Kirkpatrick

Jeane Kirkpatrick was Leavey Professor of Political Science at George-town University and a resident scholar at the American Enterprise Institute when this article was published. Her arguments so impressed Ronald Reagan that he brought her into his Cabinet as U.S. Ambassador to the United Nations. Ambassador Kirkpatrick's human rights views are presented in Reading 50.

THE failure of the Carter administration's foreign policy is now clear to everyone except its architects, and even they must enter-tain private doubts, from time to time, about a policy whose crown-ing achievement has been to lay the groundwork for a transfer of the Panama Canal from the United States to a swaggering Latin dictator of Castroite bent [the late Brig. Gen. Omar Torrijos Herrera—Eds.]. In the thirty-odd months since the inauguration of Jimmy Carter as President there has occurred a dramatic Soviet military buildup, matched by the stagnation of American armed forces, and a dramatic extension of Soviet influence in the Horn of Africa, Afghanistan, Southern Africa, and the Caribbean, matched by a declining Amer-ican position in all these areas. The U.S. has never tried so hard and failed so utterly to make and keep friends in the Third World.

As if this were not bad enough, in the current year [1979] the United States has suffered two other major blows—in Iran and Nic-aragua—of large and strategic significance. In each country, the Carter administration not only failed to prevent the undesired outcome, it actively collaborated in the replacement of moderate autocrats friendly to American interests with less friendly autocrats of extremist persuasion. It is too soon to be certain about what kind of regime will ultimately emerge in either Iran or Nicaragua, but accumulating evi-dence suggests that things are as likely to get worse as to get better in both countries. The Sandinistas in Nicaragua appear to be as skillful in consolidating power as the Ayatollah Khomeini is inept, and lead-ers of both revolutions display an intolerance and arrogance that do not bode well for the peaceful sharing of power or the establishment of constitutional governments, especially since those leaders have made clear that they have no intention of seeking either.

* *Commentary*, Vol. 68, No. 5, November 1979, pp. 34–45.

It is at least possible that the SALT debate may stimulate new scrutiny of the nation's strategic position and defense policy, but there are no signs that anyone is giving serious attention to this nation's role in Iranian and Nicaraguan developments—despite clear warnings that the U.S. is confronted with similar situations and options in El Salvador, Guatemala, Morocco, Zaïre, and elsewhere. Yet no problem of American foreign policy is more urgent than that of formulating a morally and strategically acceptable, and politically realistic, program for dealing with non-democratic governments who are threatened by Soviet-sponsored subversion. In the absence of such a policy, we can expect that the same reflexes that guided Washington in Iran and Nicaragua will be permitted to determine American actions from Korea to Mexico—with the same disastrous effects on the U.S. strategic position. (That the administration has not called its policies in Iran and Nicaragua a failure—and probably does not consider them such—complicates the problem without changing its nature.)

There were, of course, significant differences in the relations between the United States and each of these countries during the past two or three decades. Oil, size, and proximity to the Soviet Union gave Iran greater economic and strategic import than any Central American "republic," and closer relations were cultivated with the Shah, his counselors, and family than with President Somoza, his advisers, and family. Relations with the Shah were probably also enhanced by our approval of his manifest determination to modernize Iran regardless of the effects of modernization on traditional social and cultural patterns (including those which enhanced his own authority and legitimacy). And, of course, the Shah was much better-looking and altogether more dashing than Somoza; his private life was much more romantic, more interesting to the media, popular and otherwise. Therefore, more Americans were more aware of the Shah than of the equally tenacious Somoza.

But even though Iran was rich, blessed with a product the U.S. and its allies needed badly, and led by a handsome king, while Nicaragua was poor and rocked along under a long-tenure president of less striking aspect, there were many similarities between the two countries and our relations with them. Both these small nations were led by men who had not been selected by free elections, who recognized no duty to submit themselves to searching tests of popular acceptability. Both did tolerate limited opposition, including opposition newspapers and political parties, but both were also confronted by radical, violent opponents bent on social and political revolution. Both rulers, therefore, sometimes invoked martial law to arrest, imprison, exile, and occasionally, it was alleged, torture their opponents. Both relied for public order on police forces whose personnel were said to be too harsh, too arbitrary, and too powerful. Each had what the American press termed "private armies," which is to say, armies pledging their allegiance to the ruler rather than the "constitution" or the "nation" or some other impersonal entity.

In short, both Somoza and the Shah were, in central ways, traditional rulers of semi-traditional societies. Although the Shah very badly wanted to create a technologically modern and powerful nation and Somoza tried hard to introduce modern agricultural methods, neither sought to reform his society in the light of any abstract idea of social justice or political virtue. Neither attempted to alter significantly the distribution of goods, status, or power (though the democratization of education and skills that accompanied modernization in Iran did result in some redistribution of money and power there).

Both Somoza and the Shah enjoyed long tenure, large personal fortunes (much of which were no doubt appropriated from general revenues), and good relations with the United States. The Shah and Somoza were not only anti-Communist, they were positively friendly to the U.S., sending their sons and others to be educated in our universities, voting with us in the United Nations, and regularly supporting American interests and positions even when these entailed personal and political cost. The embassies of both governments were active in Washington social life, and were frequented by powerful Americans who ocupied major roles in this nation's diplomatic, military, and political life. And the Shah and Somoza themselves were both welcome in Washington, and had many American friends.

Though each of the rulers was from time to time criticized by American officials for violating civil and human rights, the fact that the people of Iran and Nicaragua only intermittently enjoyed the rights accorded to citizens in the Western democracies did not prevent successive administrations from granting—with the necessary approval of successive Congresses—both military and economic aid. In the case of both Iran and Nicaragua, tangible and intangible tokens of U.S. support continued until the regime became the object of a major attack by forces explicitly hostile to the United States.

But once an attack was launched by opponents bent on destruction, everything changed. The rise of serious, violent opposition in Iran and Nicaragua set in motion a succession of events which bore a suggestive resemblance to one another and a suggestive similarity to our behavior in China before the fall of Chiang Kai-shek, in Cuba before the triumph of Castro, in certain crucial periods of the Vietnamese war, and, more recently, in Angola. In each of these countries, the American effort to impose liberalization and democratization on a government confronted with violent internal opposition not only failed, but actually assisted the coming to power of new regimes in which ordinary people enjoy fewer freedoms and less personal security than under the previous autocracy—regimes, moreover, hostile to American interests and policies.

The pattern is familiar enough: an established autocracy with a record of friendship with the U.S. is attacked by insurgents, some of whose leaders have long ties to the Communist movement, and most of whose arms are of Soviet, Chinese, or Czechoslovak origin. The "Marxist" presence is ignored and/or minimized by American officials and by the elite media on the ground that U.S. support for the dictator gives the rebels little choice but to seek aid "elsewhere." Violence spreads and American officials wonder aloud about the viability of a regime that "lacks the support of its own people." The absence of an opposition party is deplored and civil-rights violations are reviewed. Liberal columnists question the morality of continuing aid to a "rightist dictatorship" and provide assurances concerning the essential moderation of some insurgent leaders who "hope" for some sign that the U.S. will remember its own revolutionary origins. Requests for help from the beleaguered autocrat go unheeded, and the argument is increasingly voiced that ties should be established with rebel leaders "before it is too late." The President, delaying U.S. aid, appoints a special emissary who confirms the deterioration of the government position and its diminished capacity to control the situation and recommends various measures for "strengthening" and "liberalizing" the regime, all of which involve diluting its power.

The emissary's recommendations are presented in the context of a growing clamor for American disengagement on grounds that continued involvement confirms our status as an agent of imperialism, racism, and reaction; is inconsistent with support for human rights; alienates us from the "forces of democracy"; and threatens to put the U.S. once more on the side of history's "losers." This chorus is supplemented daily by interviews with returning missionaries and "reasonable" rebels.

As the situation worsens, the President assures the world that the U.S. desires only that the "people choose their own form of government"; he blocks delivery of all arms to the government and undertakes negotiations to establish a "broadly based" coalition headed by a "moderate" critic of the regime who, once elevated, will move quickly to seek a "political" settlement to the conflict. Should the incumbent autocrat prove resistant to American demands that he step aside, he will be readily overwhelmed by the military strength of his opponents, whose patrons will have continued to provide sophisticated arms and advisers at the same time the U.S. cuts off military sales. Should the incumbent be so demoralized as to agree to yield power, he will be replaced by a "moderate" of American selection. Only after the insurgents have refused the proffered political solution and anarchy has spread throughout the nation will it be noticed that the new head of government has no significant following, no experience at governing, and no talent for leadership. By then, military commanders, no longer bound by loyalty to the chief of state, will depose the faltering "moderate" in favor of a fanatic of their own choosing.

In either case, the U.S. will have been led by its own misunderstanding of the situation to assist actively in deposing an erstwhile friend and ally and installing a government hostile to American interests and policies in the world. At best we will have lost access to friendly territory. At worst the Soviets will have gained a new base. And everywhere our friends will have noted that the U.S. cannot be counted on in times of difficulty and our enemies will have observed that American support provides no security against the forward march of history.

No particular crisis conforms exactly with the sequence of events described above; there are always variations on the theme. In Iran, for example, the Carter administration—and the President himself—offered the ruler support for a longer time, though by December 1978 the President was acknowledging that he did not know if the Shah would survive, adding that the U.S. would not get "directly involved." Neither did the U.S. ever call publicly for the Shah's resignation. However, the President's special emissary, George Ball, "reportedly concluded that the Shah cannot hope to maintain total power and must now bargain with a moderate segment of the opposition . . ." and was "known to have discussed various alternatives that would effectively ease the Shah out of total power" (*Washington Post*, December 15, 1978). There is, furthermore, not much doubt that the U.S. assisted the Shah's departure and helped arrange the succession of Bakhtiar. In Iran, the Carter administration's commitment to nonintervention proved stronger than strategic considerations or national pride. What the rest of the world regarded as a stinging American defeat, the U.S. government saw as a matter to be settled by Iranians. "We personally prefer that the Shah maintain a major role in the government," the President acknowledged, "but that is a decision for the Iranian people to make."

Events in Nicaragua also departed from the scenario presented above both because the Cuban and Soviet roles were clearer and because U.S. officials were more intensively and publicly working against Somoza. After the Somoza regime had defeated the first wave of Sandinista violence, the U.S. ceased aid, imposed sanctions, and took other steps which undermined the status and the credibility of the government in domestic and foreign affairs. Between the murder of ABC correspondent Bill Stewart by a National Guardsman in early June and the Sandinista victory in late July, the U.S. State Department assigned a new ambassador who refused to submit his credentials to Somoza even though Somoza was still chief of state, and called for replacing the government with a "broadly based provisional government that would include representatives of Sandinista guerrillas." Americans were assured by Assistant Secretary of State Viron Vaky that "Nicaraguans and our democratic friends in Latin America have no intention of seeing Nicaragua turned into a second Cuba," even though the State Department knew that the top Sandinista leaders had close personal ties and were in continuing contact with Havana, and, more specifically, that a Cuban secret-police official, Julian López, was frequently present in the Sandinista headquarters and that Cuban military advisers were present in Sandinista ranks.[1]

In a manner uncharacteristic of the Carter administration, which generally seems willing to negotiate anything with anyone anywhere, the U.S. government adopted an oddly uncompromising posture in dealing with Somoza. "No end to the crisis is possible," said Vaky, "that does not start with the departure of Somoza from power and the end of his regime. No negotiation, mediation, or compromise can be achieved any longer with a Somoza government. The solution can only begin with a sharp break from the past." Trying hard, we not only banned all American arms sales to the government of Nicaragua but pressured Israel, Guatemala, and others to do likewise—all in the name of insuring a "democratic" outcome. Finally, as the Sandinista leaders consolidated control over weapons and communications, banned opposition, and took off for Cuba, President Carter warned us against attributing this "evolutionary change' to "Cuban machinations" and assured the world that the U.S. desired only to "let the people of Nicaragua choose their own form of government."

Yet despite all the variations, the Carter administration brought to the crises in Iran and Nicaragua several common assumptions, each of

---

[1] For Vaky's views on Central America after the Sandinista victory in Nicaragua, see his statement before the Subcommittee on Inter-American Affairs of the House Committee on Foreign Affairs at hearings on *Central America at the Crossroads*, September 11, 1979, Washington, D.C.: U.S. Government Printing Office, 1979.—Eds.

which played a major role in hastening the victory of even more repressive dictatorships than had been in place before. These were, first, the belief that there existed at the moment of crisis a democratic alternative to the incumbent government: second, the belief that the continuation of the status quo was not possible; third, the belief that any change, including the establishment of a government headed by self-styled Marxist revolutionaries, was preferable to the present government. Each of these beliefs was (and is) widely shared in the liberal community generally. Not one of them can withstand close scrutiny.

Although most governments in the world are, as they always have been, autocracies of one kind or another, no idea holds greater sway in the mind of educated Americans than the belief that it is possible to democratize governments, anytime, anywhere, under any circumstances. This notion is belied by an enormous body of evidence based on the experience of dozens of countries which have attempted with more or less (usually less) success to move from autocratic to democratic government. Many of the wisest political scientists of this and previous centuries agree that democratic institutions are especially difficult to establish and maintain—because they make heavy demands on all portions of a population and because they depend on complex social, cultural, and economic conditions.

Two or three decades ago, when Marxism enjoyed its greatest prestige among American intellectuals, it was the economic prerequisites of democracy that were emphasized by social scientists. Democracy, they argued, could function only in relatively rich societies with an advanced economy, a substantial middle class, and a literate population, but it could be expected to emerge more or less automatically whenever these conditions prevailed. Today, this picture seems grossly oversimplified. While it surely helps to have an economy strong enough to provide decent levels of well-being for all, and "open" enough to provide mobility and encourage achievement, a pluralistic society and the right kind of political culture—and time— are even more essential.

In his essay on *Representative Government*, John Stuart Mill identified three fundamental conditions which the Carter administration would do well to ponder. These are: "One, that the people should be willing to receive it [representative government]; two, that they should be willing and able to do what is necessary for its preservation; three, that they should be willing and able to fulfill the duties and discharge the functions which it imposes on them."

Fulfilling the duties and discharging the functions of representative government make heavy demands of leaders and citizens, demands for participation and restraint, for consensus and compromise. It is not necessary for all citizens to be avidly interested in politics or well-informed abut public affairs—although far more widespread interest and mobilization are needed than in autocracies. What *is* necessary is that a substantial number of citizens think of themselves as participants in society's decision-making and not simply as subjects bound by its laws. Moreover, leaders of all major sectors of the society must agree to pursue power only by legal means, must eschew (at least in principle) violence, theft, and fraud, and must accept defeat when necessary. They must also be skilled at finding and creating common ground among diverse points of view and interests, and correlatively willing to compromise on all but the most basic values.

In addition to an appropriate political culture, democratic government requires institutions strong enough to channel and contain conflict. Voluntary, non-official institutions are needed to articulate and aggregate diverse interests and opinions present in the society. Otherwise, the formal governmental institutions will not be able to translate popular demands into public policy.

In the relatively few places where they exist, democratic governments have come into being slowly, after extended prior experience with more limited forms of participation during which leaders have reluctantly grown accustomed to tolerating dissent and opposition, opponents have accepted the notion that they may defeat but not destroy incumbents, and people have become aware of government's effects on their lives and of their own possible effects on government. Decades, if not centuries, are normally required for people to acquire the necesary disciplines and habits. In Britain, the road from the Magna Carta to the Act of Settlement, to the great Reform Bills of 1832, 1867, and 1885, took seven centuries to traverse. American history gives no better grounds for believing that democracy comes easily, quickly, or for the asking. A war of independence, an unsuccessful constitution, a civil war, a long process of gradual enfranchisement marked our progress toward constitutional democratic government. The French path was still more difficult. Terror, dictatorship, monarchy, instability, and incompetence followed on the revolution that was to usher in a millennium of brotherhood. Only in the twentieth century did the democratic principle finally gain wide acceptance in France and not until after World War II were the principles of order and democracy, popular sovereignty and authority finally reconciled in institutions strong enough to contain conflicting currents of public opinion.

Although there is no instance of a revolutionary "socialist" or Communist society being democratized, right-wing autocracies do sometimes evolve into democracies—given time, propitious economic, social and political circumstances, talented leaders, and a strong indigenous demand for representative government. Something of the kind is in progress on the Iberian peninsula and the first steps have been taken in Brazil. Something similar could conceivably have also occurred in Iran and Nicaragua if contestation and participation had been more gradually expanded.

But it seems clear that the architects of contemporary American foreign policy have little idea of how to go about encouraging the liberalization of an autocracy. In neither Nicaragua nor Iran did they realize that the only likely result of an effort to replace an incumbent autocrat with one of his moderate critics or a "broad-based coalition" would be to sap the foundations of the existing regime without moving the nation any closer to democracy. Yet this outcome was entirely predictable. Authority in traditional autocracies is transmitted through personal relations: from the ruler to his close associates (relatives, household members, personal friends) and from them to people to whom the associates are related by personal ties resembling their own relation to the ruler. The fabric of authority unravels quickly when the power and status of the man at the top are undermined or eliminated. The longer the autocrat has held power, and the more pervasive his personal influence, the more dependent a nation's institutions will be on him. Without him, the organized life of the society will collapse, like an arch from which the keystone has been removed. The blend of qualities that bound the Iranian army to the Shah or the national guard to Somoza is typical of the relationships—personal, hierarchical, non-transferable—that support a traditional autocracy. The speed with which armies collapse, bureaucracies abdicate, and social structures dissolve once the autocrat is removed frequently surprises American policy-makers and journalists accustomed to public institutions based on universalistic norms rather than particularistic relations.

The failure to understand these relations is one source of the failure of U.S. policy in this and previous administrations. There are others. In Iran and Nicaragua (as previously in Vietnam, Cuba, and China) Washington overestimated the political diversity of the opposition—especially the strength of "moderates" and "democrats" in the opposition movement; underestimated the strength and intransigence of radicals in the movement; and misestimated the nature and extent of American influence on both the government and the opposition.

Confusion concerning the character of the opposition, especially its intransigence and will to power, leads regularly to downplaying the amount of force required to counteract its violence. In neither Iran nor Nicaragua did the U.S. adequately appreciate the government's problem in maintaining order in a society confronted with an ideologically extreme opposition. Yet the presence of such groups was well known. The State Department's 1977 report on human rights described an Iran confronted

> with a small number of extreme rightist and leftist terrorists operating within the country. There is evidence that they have received substantial foreign support and training . . . [and] have been responsible for the murder of Iranian government officials and Americans. . . .

The same report characterized Somoza's opponents in the following terms:

> A guerrilla organization known as the Sandinista National Liberation Front (FSLN) seeks the violent overthrow of the government, and has received limited suport from Cuba. The FSLN carried out an operation in Managua in December 1974, killing four people, taking several officials hostage . . . since then, it continues to challenge civil authority in certain isolated regions.

In 1978, the State Department's report said that Sandinista violence was continuing—after the state of siege had been lifted by the Somoza government.

When U.S. policy-makers and large portions of the liberal press interpret insurgency as evidence of widespread popular discontent and a will to democracy, the scene is set for disaster. For if civil strife reflects a popular demand for democracy, it follows that a "liberalized" government will be more acceptable to "public opinion."

Thus, in the hope of strengthening a government, U.S. policy-makers are led, mistake after mistake, to impose measures almost certain to weaken its authority. Hurried efforts to force complex and unfamiliar political practices on societies lacking the requisite political culture, tradition, and social structures not only fail to produce desired outcomes; if they are undertaken at a time when the traditional regime is under attack, they actually facilitate the job of the insurgents.

Vietnam presumably taught us that the United States could not serve as the world's policeman; it should also have taught us the dangers of trying to be the world's midwife to democracy when the birth is scheduled to take place under conditions of guerrilla war.

If the administration's actions in Iran and Nicaragua reflect the pervasive and mistaken assumption that one can easily locate and impose democratic alternatives to incumbent autocracies, they also reflect the equally pervasive and equally flawed belief that change *per se* in such autocracies is inevitable, desirable, and in the American interest. It is this belief which induces the Carter administration to participate actively in the toppling of non-Communist autocracies while remaining passive in the face of Communist expansion.

At the time the Carter administration came into office it was widely reported that the President had assembled a team who shared a new approach to foreign policy and a new conception of the national interest. The principal elements of this new approach were said to be two: the conviction that the cold war was over, and the conviction that, this being the case, the U.S. should give priority to North-South problems and help less developed nations achieve their own destiny.

More is involved in these changes than originally meets the eye. For, unlikely as it may seem, the foreign policy of the Carter administration is guided by a relatively full-blown philosophy of history which includes, as philosophies of history always do, a theory of social change, or, as it is currently called, a doctrine of modernization. Like most other philosophies of history that have appeared in the West since the 18th century, the Carter administration's doctrine predicts progress (in the form of modernization for all societies) and a happy ending (in the form of a world community of developed, autonomous nations).

The administration's approach to foreign affairs was clearly foreshadowed in [Carter's National Security Adviser] Zbigniew Brzezinski's 1970 book on the U.S. role in the "technetronic era," *Between Two Ages*. In that book, Brzezinski showed that he had the imagination to look beyond the cold war to a brave new world of global politics and interdependence. To deal with that new world a new approach was said to be "evolving," which Brzezinski designated "rational humanism." In the new approach, the "preoccupation" with "national supremacy" would give way to "global" perspectives, and international problems would be viewed as "human issues" rather than as "political confrontations." The traditional intellectual framework for dealing with foreign policy would have to be scrapped:

> Today, the old framework of international politics . . . with their spheres of influence, military alliances between nation states, the fiction of sovereignty, doctrinal conflicts arising from 19th-century crisis—is clearly no longer compatible with reality.[2]

---

[2] Concerning Latin America, Brzezinski observed: "Latin American nationalism, more and more radical as it widens its popular base, will be directed with increasing animosity against the United States unless the United States rapidly shifts its own

Only the "delayed development" of the Soviet Union, "an archaic religious community that experiences modernity existentially but not quite yet normatively," prevented wider realization of the fact that the end of ideology was already here. For the U.S., Brzezinski recommended "a great deal of patience," a more detached attitude toward world revolutionary processes, and a less anxious preoccupation with the Soviet Union. Instead of engaging in ancient diplomatic pastimes, we should make "a broader effort to contain the global tendencies toward chaos," while assisting the processes of change that will move the world toward the "community of developed nations."

The central concern of Brzezinski's book, as of the Carter administration's foreign policy, is with the modernization of the Third World. From the beginning, the administration has manifested a special, intense interest in the problems of the so-called Third World. But instead of viewing international developments in terms of the American national interest, as national interest is historically conceived, the architects of administration policy have viewed them in terms of a contemporary version of the same idea of progress that has traumatized Western imaginations since the Enlightenment.

In its current form, the concept of modernization involves more than industrialization, more than "political development" (whatever that is). It is used instead to designate ". . . the process through which a traditional or pre-technological society passes as it is transformed into a society characterized by machine technology, rational and secular attitudes, and highly differentiated social structures." Condorcet, Comte, Hegel, Marx, and Weber are all present in this view of history as the working out of the idea of modernity.

The crucial elements of the modernization concept have been clearly explicated by Samuel P. Huntington (who, despite a period at the National Security Council, was assuredly not the architect of the administration's policy). The modernization paradigm, Huntington has observed, postulates an ongoing process of change: complex, because it involves all dimensions of human life in society; systemic, because its elements interact in predictable, necessary ways; global, because all societies will, necessarily, pass through the transition from

---

posture. Accordingly, it would be wise for the United States to make an explicit move to abandon the Monroe Doctrine and to concede that in the new global age geographic or hemispheric contiguity no longer need be politically decisive. Nothing could be healthier for Pan-American relations than for the United States to place them on the same level as its relations with the rest of the world, confining itself to emphasis on cultural-political affinities (as it does with Western Europe) and economic-social obligations (as it does with less developed countries)." [Footnote in original.]

traditional to modern; lengthy, because time is required to modernize economic and social organization, character, and culture; phased, because each modernizing society must pass through essentially the same stages; homogenizing, because it tends toward the convergence and interdependence of societies; irreversible, because the direction of change is "given" in the relation of the elements of the process; progressive, in the sense that it is desirable, and in the long run provides significant benefits to the affiliated people.

Although the modernization paradigm has proved a sometimes useful as well as influential tool in social science, it has become the object of searching critiques that have challenged one after another of its central assumptions. Its shortcomings as an analytical tool pale, however, when compared to its inadequacies as a framework for thinking about foreign policy, where its principal effects are to encourage the view that events are manifestations of deep historical forces which cannot be controlled and that the best any government can do is to serve as a "midwife" to history, helping events to move where they are already headed.

This perspective on contemporary events is optimistic in the sense that it foresees continuing human progress; deterministic in the sense that it perceives events as fixed by processes over which persons and policies can have but little influence; moralistic in the sense that it perceives history and U.S. policy as having moral ends; cosmopolitan in the sense that it attempts to view the world not from the perspective of American interests or intentions but from the perspective of the modernizing nation and the "end" of history. It identifies modernization with both revolution and morality, and U.S. policy with all three.

The idea that it is "forces" rather than people which shape events recurs each time an administration spokesman articulates or explains policy. The President, for example, assured us in February of this year:

> The revolution in Iran is a product of deep social, political, religious, and economic factors growing out of the history of Iran itself.

And of Asia he said:

> At this moment there is turmoil or change in various countries from one end of the Indian Ocean to the other; some turmoil as in Indo-China is the product of age-old enmities, inflamed by rivalries for influence by conflicting forces. Stability in some other countries is being shaken by the process of modernization, the search for national significance, or the desire to fulfill legitimate human hopes and human aspirations.

Harold Saunders, Assistant Secretary for Near Eastern and South Asian Affairs, commenting on "instability" in Iran and the Horn of Africa, states:

> We, of course, recognize that fundamental changes are taking place across this area of western Asia and northeastern Africa—economic modernization, social change, a revival of religion, resurgent nationalism, demands for broader popular participation in the political process. These changes are generated by forces within each country.

Or here is Anthony Lake, chief of the State Department's Policy Planning staff, on South Africa:

> Change will come in South Africa. The welfare of the people there, and American interest, will be profoundly affected by the way in which it comes. The question is whether it will be peaceful or not.

Brzezinski makes the point still clearer. Speaking as chief of the National Security council, he has assured us that the struggles for power in Asia and Africa are really only incidents along the route to modernization:

> . . . all the developing countries in the area from northeast Asia to southern Africa continue to search for viable forms of government capable of managing the process of modernization.

No matter that the invasions, coups, civil wars, and political struggles of less violent kinds that one sees all around do not *seem* to be incidents in a global personnel search for someone to manage the modernization process. Neither Brzezinski nor anyone else seems bothered by the fact that the political participants in that arc from northeast Asia to southern Africa do not *know* that they are "searching for viable forms of government capable of managing the process of modernization." The motives and intentions of real persons are no more relevant to the modernization paradigm than they are to the Marxist view of history. Viewed from this level of abstraction, it is the "forces" rather than the people that count.

So what if the "deep historical forces" at work in such diverse places as Iran, the Horn of Africa, southeast Asia, Central America, and the United Nations look a lot like Russians or Cubans? Having moved past what the President calls our "inordinate fear of Communism," identified by him with the cold war, we should, we are told, now be capable of distinguishing Soviet and Cuban "machinations," which any way exist mainly in the minds of cold warriors and others guilty of oversimplifying the world, from evolutionary changes, which seem to be the only kind that actually occur.

What can a U.S. President faced with such complicated, inexorable, impersonal processes *do?* The answer, offered again and again by the President and his top officials, is, not much. Since events are not caused by human decisions, they cannot be stoped or altered by them. Brzezinski, for example, has said: "We recognize that the world is changing under the influence of forces no government can control. . . ." And [Carter's first Secretary of State] Cyrus Vance has cautioned: "The fact is that we can no more stop change than Canute could still the waters."

The Carter administration's essentially deterministic and apolitical view of contemporary events discourages an active American response and encourages passivity. The American inability to influence events in Iran became the President's theme song:

> Those who argue that the U.S. should *or could* intervene directly to thwart [the revolution in Iran] are wrong about the realities of Iran. . . . We have encouraged *to the limited extent of our own ability* the public support for the Bakhtiar government. . . . How long [the Shah] will be out of Iran, we have no way to determine. Further events and his own desires will determine that. . . . It is impossible for anyone to anticipate all future political events. . . . Even if we had been able to anticipate events that were going to take place in Iran or in other countries, obviously our ability to determine those events is very limited [emphasis added in original].

Vance made the same point:

> In Iran our policy throughout the current crisis has been based on the fact that only Iranians can resolve the fundamental political issues which they now confront.

Where once upon a time an American President might have sent Marines to assure the protection of American strategic interests, there is no room for force in this world of progress and self-determination. Force, the President told us at Notre Dame, does not work; that is the lesson he extracted from Vietnam. It offers only "superficial" solutions. Concerning Iran, he said:

> Certainly we have no desire or ability to intrude massive forces into Iran or any other country to determine the outcome of domestic political issues. This is something that we have no intention of ever doing in another country. We've tried this once in Vietnam. It didn't work, as you well know.

There was nothing unique about Iran. In Nicaragua, the climate and language were different but the "historical forces" and the U.S. response were the same. Military intervention was out of the question. Assistant Secretary of State Viron Vaky described as "unthinkable" the "use of U.S. military power to intervene in the internal affairs of another American republic." Vance provided parallel assurances for Africa, asserting that we would not try to match Cuban and Soviet activities there.

What *is* the function of foreign policy under these conditions? It is to understand the processes of change and then, like Marxists, to align ourselves with history, hoping to contribute a bit of stability along the way. And this, administration spokesmen assure us, is precisely what we are doing. The Carter administration has defined the U.S. national interest in the Third World as identical with the putative end of the modernization process. Vance put this with characteristic candor in a recent statement when he explained that U.S. policy vis-à-vis the Third World is "grounded in the conviction that we best serve our interest there by supporting the efforts of developing nations to advance their economic well-being and preserve their political independence." Our "commitment to the promotion of constructive change worldwide" (Brzezinski's words) has been vouchsafed in every conceivable context.

But there is a problem. The conceivable contexts turn out to be mainly those in which non-Communist autocracies are under pressure from revolutionary guerrillas. Since Moscow is the aggressive, expansionist power today, it is more often than not insurgents, encouraged and armed by the Soviet Union, who challenge the status quo. The American commitment to "change" in the abstract ends up by aligning us tacitly with Soviet clients and irresponsible extremists like the Ayatollah Khomeini [in Iran] or, in the end, Yasir Arafat [head of the Palestine Liberation Organization].

So far, assisting "change" has not led the Carter administration to undertake the destabilization of a *Communist* country. The principles of self-determination and nonintervention are thus both selectively applied. We seem to accept the status quo in Communist nations (in the name of "diversity" and national autonomy), but not in nations ruled by "right-wing" dictators or white oligarchies. Concerning China, for example, Brzezinski has observed: "We recognize that the [People's Republic of China] and we have different ideologies and economic and political systems. . . . We harbor neither the hope nor the desire that through extensive contacts with China we can remake that nation into the American image. Indeed, we accept our differences." Of Southeast Asia, the President noted in February:

> Our interest is to promote peace and the withdrawal of outside forces and not to become embroiled in the conflict among Asian nations. And, in

general, our interest is to promote the health and the development of individual societies, not to a pattern cut exactly like ours in the United States but tailored rather to the hopes and the needs and desires of the peoples involved.

But the administration's position shifts sharply when South Africa is discussed. For example, Anthony Lake asserted in late 1978.

. . . We have indicated to South Africa the fact that if it does not make significant progress toward racial equality, its relations with the international community, including the United States, are bound to deteriorate.

Over the years, we have tried through a series of progressive steps to demonstrate that the U.S. cannot and will not be associated with the continued practice of apartheid.

As to Nicaragua, [State Department spokesman] Hodding Carter III said in February 1979:

The unwillingness of the Nicaraguan government to accept the [OAS] group's proposal, the resulting prospects for renewal and polarization, and the human-rights situation in Nicaragua . . . unavoidably affect the kind of relationship we can maintain with that government. . . .

And Carter commented on Latin American autocracies:

My government will not be deterred from protecting human rights, including economic and social rights, in whatever ways we can. We prefer to take actions that are positive, but where nations persist in serious violations of human rights, we will continue to demonstrate that there are costs to the flagrant disregard of international standards.

Something very odd is going on here. How does an administration that desires to let people work out their own destinies get involved in determined efforts at reform in South Africa, Zaïre, Nicaragua, El Salvador, and elsewhere? How can an administration committed to nonintervention in Cambodia and Vietnam announce that it "will not be deterred" from righting wrongs in South Africa? What should be made of an administration that sees the U.S. interest as identical with economic modernization and political independence and yet heedlessly endangers the political independence of Taiwan, a country whose success in economic modernization and egalitarian distribution of wealth is unequaled in Asia? The contrast is as striking as that between the administration's frenzied speed in recognizing the new dictatorship in Nicaragua and its continuing refusal to recognize the elected government of Zimbabwe Rhodesia [the former white minority regime of Ian Smith.—Eds.], or its refusal to maintain any presence in Zimbabwe Rhodesia while staffing a U.S. Information Office in Cuba. Not only are there ideology and a double standard at work here, the ideology neither fits nor explains reality, and the double standard involves the administration in the wholesale contradiction of its own principles.

Inconsistencies are a familiar part of politics in most societies. Usually, however, governments behave hypocritically when their principles conflict with the national interest. What makes the inconsistencies of the Carter administration noteworthy are, first, the administration's moralism—which renders it especially vulnerable to charges of hypocrisy; and, second, the administration's predilection for policies that violate the strategic and economic interests of the United States. The administration's conception of national interest borders on doublethink: it finds friendly powers to be guilty representatives of the status quo and views the triumph of unfriendly groups as beneficial to America's "true interests."

This logic is quite obviously reinforced by the prejudices and preferences of many administration officials. Traditional autocracies are, in general and in their very nature, deeply offensive to modern American sensibilities. The notion that public affairs should be ordered on the basis of kinship, friendship, and other personal relations rather than on the basis of objective "rational" standards violates our conception of justice and efficiency. The preference for stability rather than change is also disturbing to Americans whose whole national experience rests on the principles of change, growth, and progress. The extremes of wealth and poverty characteristic of traditional societies also offend us, the more so since the poor are usually very poor and bound to their squalor by a hereditary allocation of role. Moreover, the relative lack of concern of rich, comfortable rulers for the poverty, ignorance, and disease of "their" people is likely to be interpreted by Americans as moral dereliction pure and simple. The truth is that Americans can hardly bear such societies and such rulers. Confronted with them, our vaunted cultural relativism evaporates and we become as censorious as Cotton Mather confronting sin in New England.

But if the politics of traditional and semi-traditional autocracy is nearly antithetical to our own—at both the symbolic and the operational level—the rhetoric of progressive revolutionaries sounds much better to us; their symbols are much more acceptable. One reason that some modern Americans prefer "socialist" to traditional autocracies is that the former have embraced modernity and have adopted modern modes and perspectives, including an instrumental, manipulative, functional orientation toward most social, cultural, and personal affairs; a profession of universalistic norms; an emphasis on reason, science, education, and progress; a de-emphasis of the sacred; and "rational," bureaucratic organizations. They speak our language.

Because socialism of the Soviet/Chinese/Cuban variety is an ideology rooted in a version of the same values that sparked the Enlightenment and the democratic revolutions of the 18th century; because it is modern and not traditional; because it postulates goals that appeal to Christian as well as to secular values (brotherhood of man, elimination of power as a mode of human relations), it is highly congenial to many Americans at the symbolic level. Marxist revolutionaries speak the language of a hopeful future while traditional autocrats speak the language of an unattractive past. Because left-wing revolutionaries invoke the symbols and values of democracy—emphasizing eglitarianism rather than hierarchy and privilege, liberty rather than order, activity rather than passivity—they are again and again accepted as partisans in the cause of freedom and democracy.

Nowhere is the affinity of liberalism, Christianity, and Marxist socialism more apparent than among liberals who are "duped" time after time into supporting "liberators" who turn out to be totalitarians, and among Left-leaning clerics whose attraction to a secular style of "redemptive community" is stronger than their outrage at the hostility of socialist regimes to religion. In Jimmy Carter—egalitarian, optimist, liberal, Christian—the tendency to be repelled by frankly non-democratic rulers and hierarchical societies is almost as strong as the tendency to be attracted to the idea of popular revolution, liberation, and progress. Carter is, *par excellence*, the kind of liberal most likely to confound revolution with idealism, change with progress, optimism with virtue.

Where concern about "socialist encirclement," Soviet expansion, and traditional conceptions of the national interest inoculated his predecessors against such easy equations, Carter's doctrine of national interest and modernization encourages support for all change that takes place in the name of "the people," regardless of its "superficial" Marxist or anti-American content. Any lingering doubt about whether the U.S. should, in case of conflict, support a "tested friend" such as the Shah or a friendly power such as Zimbabwe Rhodesia against an opponent who despises us is resolved by reference to our "true," our "long-range" interests.

Stephen Rosenfeld of the *Washington Post* described the commitment of the Carter administration to this sort of "progressive liberalism":

The Carter administration came to power, after all, committed precisely to reducing the centrality of strategic competition with Moscow in American foreign policy, and to extending the United States' association with what it was prepared to accept as legitimate wave-of-the-future popular movements around the world—first of all with the victorious movement in Vietnam.

. . . Indochina was supposed to be the state on which Americans could demonstrate their "post-Vietnam" intent to come to terms with the progressive popular element that Kissinger, the villain, had denied.

In other words, the Carter administration, Rosenfeld tells us, came to power resolved not to assess international developments in the light of "cold-war" perspectives but to accept at face value the claim of revolutionary groups to represent "popular" aspirations and "progressive" forces—regardless of the ties of these revolutionaries to the Soviet Union. To this end, overtures were made looking to the "normalization" of relations with Vietnam, Cuba, and the Chinese People's Republic, and steps were taken to cool relations with South Korea, South Africa, Nicaragua, the Philippines, and others. These moves followed naturally from the conviction that the U.S. had, as our enemies said, been on the wrong side of history in supporting the status quo and opposing revolution.

One might have thought that this perspective would have been undermined by events in Southeast Asia since the triumph of "progressive" forces there over the "agents of reaction." To cite Rosenfeld again:

In this administration's time, Vietnam has been transformed, for much of American public opinion, from a country wronged by the U.S. to one revealing a brutal essence of its own.

This has been a quiet but major trauma to the Carter people (as to all liberals), scarring their self-confidence and their claim on public trust alike.

Presumably, however, the barbarity of the "progressive" governments in Cambodia and Vietnam has been less traumatic for the President and his chief advisers than for Rosenfeld, since there is little evidence of changed predispositions at crucial levels of the White House and the State Department. The President continues to behave as before—not like a man who abhors autocrats but like one who abhors only right-wing autocrats.

In fact, high officials in the Carter administration understand better than they seem to the aggressive, expansionist character of contemporary Soviet behavior in Africa, the Middle East, Southeast Asia, the Indian Ocean, Central America, and the Caribbean. But although the Soviet/Cuban role in Grenada, Nicaragua, and El Salvador (plus the transfer of MIG-23's to Cuba) had already prompted resumption of surveillance of Cuba (which in turn confirmed the presence of a Soviet combat brigade), the President's eagerness not to "heat up" the climate of public opinion remains stronger than his commitment to speak the truth to the American people. His statement on Nicaragua clearly reflects these priorities:

> It's a mistake for Americans to assume or to claim that every time an evolutionary change takes place in this hemisphere that somehow it's a result of secret, massive Cuban intervention. The fact in Nicaragua is that the Somoza regime lost the confidence of the people. To bring about an orderly transition there, our effort was to let the people of Nicaragua ultimately make the decision on who would be their leader—what form of government they should have.

This statement, which presumably represents the President's best thinking on the matter, is illuminating. Carter's effort to dismiss concern about military events in this specific country as a manifestation of a national proclivity for seeing "Cuban machinations" under every bed constitutes a shocking effort to falsify reality. There was no question in Nicaragua of "evolutionary change" or of attributing such change to Castro's agents. There was only a question about the appropriate U.S. response to a military struggle in a country whose location gives it strategic importance out of proportion to its size or strength.

But that is not all. The rest of the President's statement graphically illustrates the blinding power of ideology on his interpretation of events. When he says that "the Somoza regime lost the confidence of the people," the President implies that the regime had previously rested on the confidence of "the people," but that the situation had now changed. In fact, the Somoza regime had never rested on popular will (but instead on manipulation, force, and habit), and was not being ousted by it. It was instead succumbing to arms and soldiers. However, the assumption that the armed conflict of Sandinistas and Somocistas was the military equivalent of a national referendum enabled the President to imagine that it could be, and should be, settled by the people of Nicaragua. For this pious sentiment even to seem true the President would have had to be unaware that insurgents were receiving a great many arms from other non-Nicaraguans; and that the U.S. had played a significant role in disarming the Somoza regime.

The President's mistakes and distortions are all fashionable ones. His assumptions are those of people who want badly to be on the progressive side in conflicts between "rightist" autocracy and "leftist" challenges, and to prefer the latter, almost regardless of the probable consequences.

To be sure, neither the President, nor Vance, nor Brzezinski *desires* the proliferation of Soviet-supported regimes. Each has asserted his disapproval of Soviet "interference" in the modernization process. But each, nevertheless, remains willing to "destablize" friendly or neutral autocracies without any assurance that they will not be replaced by reactionary totalitarian theocracies, totalitarian Soviet client states, or worst of all, by murderous fanatics of the Pol Pot variety [in Cambodia].

The foreign policy of the Carter administration fails not for lack of good intentions but for lack of realism about the nature of traditional versus revolutionary autocracies and the relation of each to the American national interest. Only intellectual fashion and the tyranny of Right/Left thinking prevent intelligent men of good will from perceiving the *facts* that traditional authoritarian governments are less repressive than revolutionary autocracies, that they are more susceptible of liberalization and that they are more compatible with U.S. interests. The evidence on all these points is clear enough.

Surely it is now beyond reasonable doubt that the present governments of Vietnam, Cambodia, Laos are much more repressive than those of the despised previous rulers; that the government of the People's Republic of China is more repressive than that of Taiwan, that North Korea is more repressive than South Korea, and so forth. This is the most important lesson of Vietnam and Cambodia. It is not new but it is a gruesome reminder of harsh facts.

From time to time a truly bestial ruler can come to power in either type of autocracy—Idi Amin [Uganda], Papa Doc Duvalier [Haiti], Joseph Stalin, Pol Pot are examples—but neither type regularly produces such moral monsters (though democracy regularly prevents their accession to power). There are, however, *systemic* differences between traditional and revolutionary autocracies that have a predictable effect on their degree of repressiveness. Generally speaking, traditional autocrats tolerate social inequities, brutality, and poverty while revolutionary autocracies create them.

Traditional autocrats leave in place existing allocations of wealth, power, status, and other resources which in most traditional societies favor an affluent few and maintain masses in poverty. But they worship traditional gods and observe traditional taboos. They do not disturb the habitual rhythms of work and leisure, habitual places of residence, habitual patterns of family and personal relations. Because the miseries of traditional life are familiar, they are bearable to ordinary people who, growing up in the society, learn to cope, as children born to untouchables in India acquire the skills and attitudes necessary for survival in the miserable roles they are destined to fill. Such societies create no refugees.

Precisely the opposite is true of revolutionary Communist regimes. They create refugees by the million because they claim jurisdiction over the whole life of the society and make demands for change that so violate internalized values and habits that inhabitants flee by the tens of thousands in the remarkable expectation that their attitudes, values, and goals will "fit" better in a foreign country than in their native land.

The former deputy chairman of Vietnam's National Assembly from 1976 to his defection early in August 1979, Hoang Van Hoan, described recently the impact of Vietnam's ongoing revolution on that country's more than one million Chinese inhabitants:

> They have been expelled from places they have lived in for generations. They have been dispossessed of virtually all possessions—their lands, their houses. They have been driven into areas called new economic zones, but they have not been given any aid.
>
> How can they eke out a living in such conditions reclaiming new land? They gradually die for a number of reasons—diseases, the hard life. They also die of humiliation.

It is not only the Chinese who have suffered in Southeast Asia since the "liberation," and it is not only in Vietnam that the Chinese suffer. By the end of 1978 more than six million refugees had fled countries ruled by Marxist governments. In spite of walls, fences, guns, and sharks, the steady stream of people fleeing revolutionary utopias continues.

There is a damning contrast between the number of refugees created by Marxist regimes and those created by other autocracies: more than a million Cubans have left their homeland since Castro's rise (one refugee for every nine inhabitants) as compared to about 35,000 each from Argentina, Brazil, and Chile. In Africa more than five times as many refugees have fled Guinea and Guinea Bissau as have left Zimbabwe Rhodesia, suggesting that civil war and racial discrimination are easier for most people to bear than Marxist-style liberation.

Moreover, the history of this century provides no grounds for expecting that radical totalitarian regimes will transform themselves. At the moment there is a far greater likelihood of progressive liberalization and democratization in the governments of Brazil, Argentina, and Chile than in the government of Cuba; in Taiwan than in the People's Republic of China; in South Korea than in North Korea; in Zaïre than in Angola; and so forth.

Since many traditional autocracies permit limited contestation and participation, it is not impossible that U.S. policy could effectively encourage this process of liberalization and democratization, provided that the effort is not made at a time when the incumbent government is fighting for its life against violent adversaries, and that proposed reforms are aimed at producing gradual change rather than perfect democracy overnight. To accomplish this, policy-makers are needed who understand how actual democracies have actually come into being. History is a better guide than good intentions.

A realistic policy which aims at protecting our own interest and assisting the capacities for self-determination of less developed nations will need to face the unpleasant fact that, if victorious, violent insurgency headed by Marxist revolutionaries is unlikely to lead to anything but totalitarian tyranny. Armed intellectuals citing Marx and supported by Soviet-bloc arms and advisers will almost surely not turn out to be agrarian reformers, or simple nationalists, or democratic socialists. However incomprehensible it may be to some, Marxist revolutionaries are not contemporary embodiments of the Americans who wrote the Declaration of Independence, and they will not be content with establishing a broad-based coalition in which they have only one voice among many.

It may not always be easy to distinguish between democratic and totalitarian agents of change, but it is also not too difficult. Authentic democratic revolutionaries aim at securing governments based on the consent of the governed and believe that ordinary men are capable of using freedom, knowing their own interest, choosing rulers. They do not, like the current leaders in Nicaragua, assume that it will be necessary to postpone elections for three to five years during which time they can "cure" the false consciousness of almost everyone.

If, moreover, revolutionary leaders describe the United States as the scourge of the 20th century, the enemy of freedom-loving people, the perpetrator of imperialism, racism, colonialism, genocide, war, then they are not authentic democrats or, to put it mildly, friends. Groups which define themselves as enemies should be treated as enemies. The United States is not in fact a racist, colonial power, it does not practice genocide, it does not threaten world peace with expansionist activities. In the last decade especially we have practiced remarkable forbearance everywhere and undertaken the "unilateral restraints on defense spending" recommended by Brzezinski as appropriate for the technetronic era. We have also moved further, faster, in eliminating domestic racism than any multiracial society in the world or in history.

For these reasons and more, a posture of continuous self-abasement and apology vis-à-vis the Third World is neither morally necessary nor politically appropriate. No more is it necessary or appropriate to support vocal enemies of the United States because they invoke the rhetoric of popular liberation. It is not even necessary or appropriate for our leaders to forswear unilaterally the use of military force to counter military force. Liberal idealism need not be identical with masochism, and need not be incompatible with the defense of freedom and the national interest.[3]

4. Totalitarianism vs. Authoritarianism *

By Michael Walzer

Michael Walzer taught at Brandeis, Princeton and Harvard universities before taking his current position as permanent fellow of the Institute for Advanced Studies in Princeton, N.J. Among his many publications are The Revolution of the Saints *(1965);* Obligations *(1970);* Political Action *(1971);* Just and Unjust Wars *(1977); and* Radical Principles *(1980).*

CONSIDER . . . the two major moral/political arguments of the new cold warriors. I'll take them from Jeane Kirkpatrick's *Commentary* article, a particularly good example of contemporary ideology, even if it isn't, or just because it isn't, a particularly good article. The first of these is an argument about political possibility. Communist totalitarianism brings with it a long, dark night. "There is no instance of a revolutionary 'socialist' or Communist society being democratized," writes Kirkpatrick. Our own tyrants, by contrast, are sometimes replaced by democratic regimes—though it is always important for the stability of the new democracy that the replacement take place *very slowly.* Kirkpatrick doesn't discuss what might be called the reverse replacement rate. In fact, I'm afraid, the decline of democracy in the free world is rather more noticeable than its slow advance. In any case, this is a false distinction. Hungary, Czechoslovakia, and Poland probably would be democratic states today were it not for the Red Army. The Red Army is a threat to human freedom, but communism, in these states at least, is an ugly but not a powerful

[3] For a Latin American update on Ambassador Kirkpatrick's views, see her "U.S. Security & Latin America," *Commentary*, Vol. 71, No. 1, January 1981, pp. 29-40.—Eds.

* *The New Republic*, Vol. 185, Nos. 1 and 2, July 4 and 11, 1981, pp. 21-25.

political system. There is nothing in its internal mechanics that rules out a democratic transformation. Assuming that the Russians don't intervene—an unlikely but analytically necessary assumption—the prospects for democracy are probably better, certainly no worse, in much of Eastern Europe than, to cite some of Kirkpatrick's odder examples, in Argentina, Brazil, South Korea, and Zaïre. In all these cases, social structure and political culture are far more important than the current regime in shaping the long-term evolution.

The second argument is about relative brutality. Old-fashioned tyrannies, according to Kirkpatrick, because they don't set out to transform their societies, do much less damage to them. They tolerate existing patterns of misery and injustice, but at least they don't create new ones. And their subjects are accustomed to the old patterns, have long ago adjusted to them and learned how to survive. Hence "such societies create no refugees." This is the "damning contrast" between Communist regimes and "other autocracies." The massive refugee population of the modern world is largely a creation of Communist totalitarianism. It would be nice—not for the refugees but for the ideological peace of mind of the rest of us—if this were true. But it isn't true. The refugees who fled Hungary in 1956 or Afghanistan in 1980 were fleeing the Red Army, not domestic oppression. The million Cubans who have reached our shores since the 1960s probably could be matched by a million Haitians, were the latter given a comparable welcome. And the largest single group of refugees since World War II was produced by Pakistani repression in East Bengal, which was nothing if not old-fashioned. Certainly there are Communist states that fit Kirkpatrick's account. East Germany and Cambodia are different but equally clear-cut examples. But the line she draws is a fabrication.

The contrast between totalitarian and authoritarian regimes is a conceptual contrast, not a practical one. It doesn't conform to, nor does it justify, our actual alliances. It doesn't make Kissinger's Pakistani "tilt" of 1971 smell any better. It doesn't rule out economic (or even military) cooperation with Communist China. One can't pull politics or morality out of a theoretical hat. That sort of thing is always a trick. Theory, *once we have it right*, does nothing more than shape our perceptions, guide our understanding; within the framework it provides, choices still have to be made.

The hardest choice, and the one for the sake of which the new cold war ideology has been worked out, is simply this: an authoritarian regime, old-fashioned, brutal, repressive, allied to the West, is threatened by a revolutionary movement some of whose leaders have totalitarian ambitions and/or Russian connections. What should we do?

The claim of the new cold warriors is that the liberal impulse in all such cases is to support the revolutionaries or at least to desert at the first opportunity the authoritarian regime. And what they want instead is the opposite policy, a steadfast commitment to the regime, because totalitarianism is the greater danger, the irreversible transformation, and so on.

But this is to turn policy into a reflex of ideology (disguised as theory). There just isn't going to be one answer in cases like the one I've described, and to act as if there is one answer—we get it right or wrong, we win or lose—is the beginning of political disaster. Often we can't do anything at all. Or rather, our choice is the same choice that the Russians have faced again and again in Eastern Europe: send in the troops or let the local conflict take its course. But let's assume that there is room, some limited room, for political maneuver (economic aid, military supply, diplomatic pressure, and so on). Then, obviously, the direction of our maneuvers will have to be determined by the shape of the terrain. How much popular support does the regime have? How much capacity for change? Who are the rebels and what is their "cause"? What sorts of alliances have they already made and how stable are those alliances? What are our own strategic interests in the area? That last question is generally taken to mean we should align ourselves with the established regime. In fact, however, if there really are strategic interests, and if we take them seriously, then it would seem to follow that we should line up as early as possible with the side most likely to win, so long as there is a real chance of keeping the winners out of the Russian camp. It is characteristic of the new cold warriors that they would support authoritarian governments both when it is in our interests to do so and also when it isn't—so that one is led to suspect that they just support authoritarian governments. In any case, there probably are such governments that we ought on balance to help. Otherwise, we could hardly have any relations at all with third world states. And there probably are oppositionists and revolutionaries whom we ought on balance to help too.

Rarely, however, in any part of the third world, are there going to be old or new regimes, governments, or movements to which we should be ideologically committed. We don't have to become apologists for the internal policies of our allies. What we owe them at most is critical support. Foreign policy is always a double business: we have to pursue our interests and we have to defend our values. In the long run, we hope that these two efforts come together, but at any given moment there are conflicts and contradictions. Maybe it is in our interest to support, say, the present South Korean regime. But we must also, for the sake of our values, maintain some critical distance from it. And that kind of argument doesn't work only for right-wing regimes. After 1960, it was in our interest that Cuban communism develop in, say, a Yugoslav rather than a Bulgarian direction, and we might have accomplished that, or at least assisted in it, through some sort of economic cooperation. But cooperation would have been no excuse for a failure to criticize Castro's dictatorship, the repression of dissidents, the campaign against homosexuals, and so on.

A policy of this kind assumes that there is no long, dark night, no thousand-year Reich, no totalitarian transformation that is proof against political opposition and social change. That has to be, I think, the working assumption of any sane diplomacy. The new cold warriors exploit what we might think of as the apocalyptic features of the theory of totalitarianism. And in the 20th century it is difficult to avoid some engagement with, some hard contemplation of, apocalypse. In political terms that means that there have been and will be again regimes so evil that the only moral stand one can adopt toward them is absolute opposition. But what policies follow from that moral stand? Surely Stalin's was one such regime, and yet we fought with Stalin against the Nazis. Even evil has its degrees. We must hope—we can reasonably believe—that it also has its duration.

In the third world, at any rate, there is not likely to be much permanence—no sustained development toward modernity and liberty, but also very few stable or solidly established tyrannies. No doubt many of the tyrants will have totalitarian ambitions; the rhetoric of revolution is now the *lingua franca* of the third world. But that only means that there will be many failed totalitarianisms. Whether these failures will be bloodier than the "other autocracies" is a question unlikely to find a yes or no answer. Some of them will and some won't. For our part, we can and should maintain a steady hostility toward every sort of totalitarian ambition. But that is no reason for supporting the "other autocracies" or excusing their bloodiness. We can make the alliances we have to make on both sides of this shadowy line, and we can condemn when we must the internal policies of our allies. I understand, of course, that there are serious diplomatic difficulties involved in any such policy—much discussed and never overcome during the Carter years. But it is a worse policy to refuse altogether to confront those difficulties. The real danger, *the present danger*, of the new cold war ideology is that it will drive us into alliances that our material defense does not require and rule out the outspokenness that the defense of our values does require. And all this for the sake of a misunderstood and badly applied political theory!

But perhaps I overestimate the power of theory (it is a common professional mistake). One might detect among contemporary cold warriors a sneaking sympathy for "traditional autocrats [who] leave in place existing allocations of wealth, power, status, and other re-sources. . . ." On the far left, there is often similar sympathy for revolutionaries who upset those allocations, even if they do so only in order to establish a new tyranny—and this view, too, has its theoreti-cal rationale. But I would propose a different sympathy: for the tortured dissidents, the imprisoned oppositionists, the threatened mi-norities, all the "disappeared" and murdered men and women of all the tyrannies, old and new. And we don't need a political theory to explain why we should keep these people always in the forefront of our consciousness, their names on the tip of our tongues.

5. Reagan's Latin America *

BY TOM J. FARER

Tom J. Farer is Distinguished Professor at Rutgers-Camden Law School and President of the Inter-American Commission on Human Rights of the Organization of American States. Professor Farer's re-election in June 1981 as head of the Commission—he is the first U.S. citizen to hold elected office in the O.A.S.—was unanimous despite an attack on him by the Chilean government for views expressed in the following article. Chile also an-nounced it was suspending cooperation with the Human Rights Commission because of the article. In a written response, Professor Farer pointed out that the facts he cited were consistent with conclusions in a Commission report on Chile.

SOME of President Reagan's advisers believe that Jimmy Carter had a clear policy for dealing with Third World countries, and that it was wrong, above all in Latin America. Probably the most detailed and influential statement of their view is the article "Dic-tatorships and Double Standards." The central problem, according to Professor Kirkpatrick, is "that of formulating a morally and strate-gically acceptable, and politically realistic, program for dealing with

---

* *The New York Review of Books*, Vol. XXVIII, No. 4, March 19, 1981, pp. 10–16. For convenience, some of the author's footnotes have been bracketed into the text by the Editors.

non-democratic governments who are threatened by Soviet-sponsored subversion."

Drawing principally on Iran and Nicaragua, she describes what she takes to be a typical "non-democratic" government and the wrong-headed response to it she had come to expect from the Carter administration.

In such a government, a long-established autocrat is supported by a private army—which owes allegiance to him and his family rather than to some abstract idea of the state. The autocrat tolerates "limited opposition, including opposition newspapers and political parties." But because he is "confronted by radical, violent opponents bent on social and political revolution," he must sometimes invoke martial law to arrest, imprison, exile, "and occasionally, it was alleged" (Kirkpatrick says, referring to the specific cases of Iran and Nicaragua) "torture [his] opponents." The autocrat enriches himself in large part by confusing his own resources with those of the state and makes no attempt "to alter significantly the distribution of goods, status, or power."

In the past, this model autocrat was a good friend of the United States and successive American administrations gave him tangible and intangible support. But then came Jimmy Carter. . . .

Kirkpatrick's remedies follow ineluctably from her diagnosis of Carter's errors. The United States must not undermine friendly authoritarian governments. It may encourage a "process of liberalization and democratization, provided that the effort is not made at a time when the incumbent governemnt is fighting for its life against violent adversaries, and that proposed reforms are aimed at producing gradual change rather than perfect democracy overnight." When Marxists or other enemies of the United States seek violently to overthrow the traditional order, the United States should send aid, not excluding the Marines.

Of this proposal, it may be said, first, that it rests on an almost demented parody of Latin American [and Caribbean] political realities as well as on a grave misperception of Carter's policies and achievements. On the most elementary facts Kirkpatrick is misinformed, for example when she claims that Carter "disarmed" Somoza. Before the last round of the Nicaraguan conflict, Somoza's National Guard bristled with weapons supplied by Argentina and Israel. Passing to more important misconceptions, dictatorial regimes of the Somoza type are far less common today than they were twenty or thirty years ago when Kirkpatrick's views seem to have been formed. A few relics survive: Duvalier, Jr., in Haiti, Stroessner in Paraguay. But in number, population, resources, and strategic importance, such countries are inconsequential compared to the Hemisphere's other nondemocratic, anticommunist governments, including those in Argentina, Bolivia, Brazil, El Salvador, and Uruguay. Nor, despite his success in eliminating all personal rivals, does her model apply to Pinochet's Chile.

In these authoritarian countries, the names at the top can and generally do change without any shifts in the pattern of wealth and political power. Formidable institutions are in control, usually the armed forces, a notable exception being Mexico's dominant political party, [the Institutional Revolutionary Party], and the huge state bureaucracy dependent on it. And these institutions work within a complicated setting of interest groups—including various sectors of the national business community, multinational corporations, the Catholic Church, professionals' guilds, the state bureaucracy, and occasionally (and in most cases marginally) trade unions—all struggling to influence the regime's economic and social policies. It is a political world very different from the one conjured up by Kirkpatrick. [Even outside Latin America, Kirkpatrick's model fits reality poorly. While it covers the little states of the Persian Gulf and Saudi Arabia, and a few African states like Zaïre and the Ivory Coast, it does not apply to such "Free World" allies as Indonesia, Thailand, and South Korea.]

While the eccentricity of Kirkpatrick's account may raise doubts about her competence for public service, what matters more is the effect her account is likely to have on policy makers who confuse it with reality. Any political order sustained by little more than the force of a single autocrat's or family's prestige is bound to be precarious, especially where that prestige is linked to the ruler's bestial behavior or his special relationship with a feared or admired great power. Regarding such cases as the norm, Kirkpatrick not surprisingly demands we form a circle of fire around our protégés as soon as reformers of any kind appear armed in the street. What would she do about those missionaries (nuns?) and other "activists" as she calls them who get in the way of hard-nosed policy? One possible hint appears in an interview Kirkpatrick gave after the election. Commenting on the torture, mutilation, and summary execution of the civilian leaders of El Salvador's left-wing coalition, she said that "people who choose to live by the sword can expect to die by it." [*The New York Times*, December 7, 1980] So apparently any form of association with rebels makes one fair game.

If we turn from Kirkpatrick's model to the real world, we find instead of the old-style caudillos, regimes of a very different character. Roughly half the members of the Organization of American States are recognizable democracies, including, for example, Venezuela,

Colombia, Costa Rica, Peru, the Dominican Republic, and most of the Anglophonic states of the Caribbean. Kirkpatrick has little to say about democracy in such Third World countries other than to doubt its existence when it elects leaders who practice socialism, criticize the United States, and talk with Castro. While castigating Carter for tolerating the Manley regime in Jamaica, she refers to it as a "so-called democracy." One wonders whether the recent transfer of power there has shaken her implied assumption that socialism is totalitarianism aching to be born. For her, the heart of our Third World problem is the regime that is anticommunist, but authoritarian, brutal, poor, corrupt, and hence unloved by the liberals.

One redeeming feature of Kirkpatrick's essay is its demonstration of how a distinction that could be useful, between authoritarian and totalitarian regimes, is being subverted by dogmatists who assign practically all rulers professing capitalism and trying to liquidate leftists to the category of "merely authoritarian" while coincidentally expelling every revolutionary government and movement into the outer darkness of totalitarianim. In this way the distinction has become simply a polemical weapon, useful for attacking Carter's human rights policy and for countering criticism of regimes that brutally crush proponents of reform, liberals, socialists, and Marxists alike.

In order to maintain their Manichaean vision, former liberals like Kirkpatrick must practice a heroic indifference to detail. The revolutionary who haunts their hysterical prose never acquires a face. Neoconservatives ask no questions abut the particulars of time and place and program, about why a man or woman has assumed the awful peril of rebellion; they never ask because, for their crabbed purposes, they have all the necessary answers. Having taken up arms—some of them Cuban or Russian or otherwise tainted—against an anticommunist government, the revolutionary is either a totalitarian communist or a foolish tool, not to mention a "terrorist."

You find an equivalent coarseness of thought in the pages of *Pravda*, where the Soviet counterparts of our intellectual thugs ask not, "Who is Lech Walesa?" but rather, "Whom does Walesa consciously or unconsciously serve?" Since his opponent is a loyal communist government, for *Pravda* the only possible answer is "U.S. Imperialism."

Kirkpatrick herself admits that absolute monsters such as Hitler and Stalin or Pol Pot and Papa Doc Duvalier will occasionally appear at both ends of the imagined political spectrum. What concerns her, however, are the

> *systemic* differences between traditional and revolutionary autocracies that have a predictable effect on their degree of repressiveness. Generally

speaking, traditional autocrats tolerate social inequities, brutality, and poverty while revolutionary autocracies create them.

Traditional autocrats . . . do not disturb the habitual rhythms of work and leisure, habitual places of residence, habitual patterns of family and personal relations. Because the miseries of traditional life are familiar, they are bearable to ordinary people who, growing up in the society, learn to cope, as children born to untouchables in India acquire the skills and attitudes necessary for survival in the miserable roles they are destined to fill.

The other presumed moral advantage of anticommunist autocracies is their capacity for evolution toward more humane societies.

Nothing so well illustrates the stupefying power of dogma than this attribution of permanence to revolutionary regimes and of an always latent fluidity to most conservative ones. In any fair test of durability, the latter make an impressive showing. The Somoza family, for example, lasted forty-five years. By monopolizing so much of the nation's economy, it had, by the time of its overthrow, actually reduced the possibility of democratic evolution.

Military rule in El Salvador, to take another current example, has endured since Franklin Delano Roosevelt's first election. If we use a measure more relevant to human rights and equate the "regime" with a very rigid structure of power and wealth and opportunity, then El Salvador had a stable autocracy from its independence in the early nineteenth century at least until the armed forces coup of 1979. What was characteristic of this period was not "evolution" toward democracy but prevention of that evolution. In Peru, one hundred and fifty years of oligarchic control ended in 1968 not through democratic evolution but by means of reforms imposed by the armed forces.

Authoritarian governments of every ideological hue extend their jurisdiction as far as necessary to achieve their ends. They tolerate autonomous activity outside the formal state structure only when it is harmless or when it is informally but effectively integrated with the regime. In El Salvador before 1979, the military government and a small group of capitalists ("the fourteen families") consciously shared virtually the same interests and acted together. Though the press was nominally free, mass circulation newspapers in San Salvador conformed to the policies of the ruling groups.

"Preserving the existing distribution of wealth and power and poverty" is a deceptive summary of the goals of Kirkpatrick's "traditional autocrats." It is deceptive in that it implies that Latin American nations exist in a state of muscular placidity, as if society were ruled by a group of not necessarily good-natured but decidedly unambitious thugs who have no serious ambition beyond retaining control of their privileges and extorting protection money and are willing to live and let live. When threatened by violent assault, of course they will actively hurt people—the violent malcontents and their sympathizers. But once the problem is liquidated, the "ordinary people" who want only to be left alone will come out of the cellar, where they have been hiding to avoid getting caught in the cross-fire, and docilely resume their "habitual rhythms."

This image is unreal because it misses the dynamic character of contemporary Latin American societies. When the masses are quiet, unambitious rulers can be placid. Today their serenity is constantly disturbed. All the interconnected tendencies of recent years—urbanization, industrialization, rapid population increase, the vast spread of TV and transistor radios, revolutionary ideas about man and society—have unleashed a torrent of demands that may seem all the more terrifying because they cannot be suppressed by a government's administering exemplary punishment from time to time. Feeling a consequent need for sterner and more sweeping measures, rulers claim that national security requires them to impose comprehensive surveillance and more tightly controlled social institutions by increasing the power and reach of public authority.

This political project is "corporatism," fascism's cousin. As the Yale political scientist Alfred Stepan notes in his penetrating study of Peru's corporatist experiment, it has two poles. At the "inclusionary pole," the state offers working-class groups positive inducements to take part in its political and economic plans, as did the first Perón regime in Argentina, Lázaro Cárdenas in pre-war Mexico, and Peru's military government before it turned to the right in 1975. At the "exclusionary pole," the state elite relies heavily on coercion to break up existing working-class organizations and then to institutionalize docility. Chile under Pinochet is a particularly harsh example.

When the second of the two patterns predominates, as in Brazil and Chile following their respective military coups [Brazil in 1964 and Chile in 1973], it follows that universities are purged, political parties dissolved, unions reorganized, dissidents murdered, the Church harassed, all as part of a huge effort first to demobilize the popular classes, and then to direct and strain their demands through new, purified institutions subject to manipulation by the state. In this effort, which has been analyzed with particular brilliance by the Argentine social scientist Guillermo O'Donnell, the ruling groups can be said to be following, consciously or not, the example of empires like that of Rome which for several centuries aggressively expanded its domain in a furius effort to liquidate threats to the status quo before they became unmanageable.

Seeking to preserve their own status quo, uncompromising right-wing governments ape the campaigns of classical revolutionary regimes to remove every source of dissent. They call themselves conservative. They are anticommunist. They will say nice thing about the Free World. And contrary to Kirkpatrick's optimistic speculations, they often take society on a road without any democratic exit.

The defense of right-wing authoritarian regimes finds a receptive, uncritical audience among many Americans because deeply ingrained ideological commitments affect their moral sensitivity. Anyone familiar with conditions in Haiti, for example, knows that its desperately hungry people would emigrate en masse if only a country able to provide life's basic needs would open its doors. Although poverty and the nature of the Duvalier regime are linked, since that autocracy is noncommunist the U.S. government presumes that its refugees who reach our shores merely flee economic "conditions" and must therefore be turned back. On the othr hand, practically all Cubans who arrive here are presumed to be fleeing political persecution rather than economic privation.

Another case of selective perception: If a revolutionary state commands people to move from one section of a country to another, we naturally condemn this ugly act as violating the right to travel freely and choose one's place of residence. But if the state enforces an absentee landowner's decision to expel sharecroppers, who have tilled the land for generations, and if the landowner's choice was a rational response to market forces, even if those forces were themselves determined by political decisions about subsidies or the tariff on imported farm equipment, many economists will applaud it. Farming will be more efficient, free marketeers will say, and sharecroppers will eventually find employment in more productive and hence better-paying activities. Or at least, it is claimed, they would if only markets could be manipulated to function in accordance with theory.

The account of the Third World provided by Kirkpatrick and those who think like her obscures the realities of life under authoritarian governments—not only the torture and murder of political dissidents but also the more subtle yet often more comprehensively destructive acts carried out through the operation and manipulation of economic forces in societies with vast gaps between the power and education and wealth of relatively few people and the rest of the population, a pattern of inequality often inherited from a precapitalist era. In countries like Brazil and Guatemala, these differences and the statist tradition that goes with them multiply the community-shattering impact of capitalism by placing the state at the service of a relatively few powerful people.

Acting through the state, the few can require proof of land tenure which illiterate peasants cannot produce. They can manipulate the exchange rate to encourage high technology imports at the expense of high employment. They can prohibit strikes and hold wage increases below the rate of inflation. They can subsidize large-scale agriculture and monopolize irrigation, while withholding subsidies for basic consumption goods. They can and do intervene in a thousand ways which have the predictable effect of uprooting whole communities because neither they nor the state apparatus is a neutral arbiter guided by some abstract calculus of national interest. One certainly need not be a Maxist to see this. And one needs only a minimum of candor to admit it.

Quietly and anonymously, economic and social forces unleashed or at least aided by the state can eliminate entire cultures. Sylvia Hewlett notes in her recent study of Brazil that there remained during the 1950s "a major concentration of indigenous tribes (numbering approximatley 200,000 people) in the Amazon and central regions. . . ." [*The Cruel Dilemmas of Development: Twentieth Century Brazil* (New York, 1979), p. 171] As a consequence of the decision to open up these regions through highway building, colonization schemes, and other means, the indigenous population is disappearing. Some Indians will survive disoriented, adrift on the edge of an alien world. As for their "habitual patterns of family and personal relations," soon the world will forget that they ever existed.

Honest scholarship would have to ask what is the difference between a revolutionary state that decides to eliminate a group with bayonets and one that proceeds to do so by indirection. Both claim that they are promoting modernization and advancing national interests as defined by those who rule. Yet one case rightly horrifies us and will command the attention of Walter Cronkite while the other passes almost unnoticed.

Conservatives are properly impressed by Brazil's rapid expansion and the deepening of its industrial base during the era of intense political repression—1968-1973. They tend to be silent about its record in producing equity or welfare. A recent World Bank study using 1977 figures estimates that 65 percent of the Brazilian population age fifteen and above is functionally illiterate; the figure runs close to 90 percent in rural areas. ["Brazil: Human Resources Special Report," World Bank Staff Working Paper (Washington, D.C., 1979), pp. 28-31] Roughly 20 percent of the children in Brazil are in a state of second or third degree malnutrition (body weight 25 percent or more below normal).

According to figures cited by Hewlett, between 1960 and 1973 the rate of infant mortality in São Paulo (the richest part of Brazil) increased 45 percent to a high of ninety-seven deaths per thousand live births.

[This might have something to do with the fact that in the ten years following the coup of 1964, the percentage of national income obtained by the wealthiest 10 percent of the population increased from 39 to 50. Sri Lanka's per capita income is roughly one-eighth of Brazil's, or about the same as that of a town in the rural northeast of Brazil; its infant mortality figure is about half of São Paulo. Life expectancy in Sri Lanka is sixty-eight. See tables in James P. Grant's *Disparity Reduction Rates in Social Indicators*, Overseas Development Council, Monograph No. 11, 1978.] Life expectancy for the middle and upper classes of São Paulo is estimated to be around sixty-seven. The poor in parts of the rural northeast still have a life expectancy of only about forty years. Such misery is no doubt "familiar," as Kirkpatrick claims, but unlike our new ambassador to the U.N., even a minister in the Brazilian government wonders if it is bearable. In a recent interview with *Veja*, Brazil's equivalent of *Newsweek*, the present Minister of Industry and Commerce, João Camilo Penna, said:

> The country possesses today a social stratum with high managerial capacity that has, however, a great debt with 40 million humble Brazilians. A debt that, if it is not paid, will result in these humble people being turned into humiliated people. And after humiliated people, I don't know.

Preoccupied with such games as distinguishing between the "authoritarian" and the "totalitarian," many people concerned with U.S. diplomacy have failed to notice changes in Latin American institutions that have been unfolding in the shadows cast by state and private terrorism. Perhaps the most important of these is the emergence of national human rights movements. Under a variety of names, often supported by the Catholic Church, these movements have united hereditary political enemies in alliances reminiscent of wartime France. In countries where the armed forces agree to return to their barracks, these Latin analogies to the Resistance could emerge as stable, center-to-left political coalitions able to carry out orderly programs of economic and social reform. In most of the Western hemisphere today, moreover—unlike postwar Western Europe—the orthodox Moscow-oriented party is only a fragment of the left, in many countries a trivial one. [Moreover, unlike some leftist groups, the communist party during the past two decades with few exceptions—e.g., recently in El Salvador—has generally sought popular front alliances and opposed armed revolution. For that reason, particularly during the 1960s, romantic followers of Che Guevara despised the orthodox communists. In the El Salvador case, most of the likely participants in a conventional popular front, including the social democrats, had already decided to back an armed struggle for social change.]

The experience of modern authoritarian government has enhanced the prospects for such coalitions. Frustrated in the 1960s by the obduracy of vested interests, their imagination fired by illusions about the Cuban revolution, susceptible to a rigidly Marxist view of norms and political institutions, reformers in such countries as Brazil, Colombia, and Chile tended to see democratic politics only as the means of preserving privilege. They became correspondingly insensitive to the violence lying beneath the accumulated restraints and tolerance of relatively decent social orders.

They have since learned how ferociously competent modern security forces can be and how private leftist terrorism can evoke deep antipathy throughout societies with liberal if not always strictly democratic traditions; the result in such countries as Argentina, Uruguay, and Brazil has been increased support of unrestrained counterterrorism. However, moderates and conservatives who have seen their children ground up in the state's security machine also have had a lesson in the difficulty of stopping violence once it rushes into the streets.

The failure of Cuba's economic model is another factor in the education of the left. Fidel Castro himself has helped to disseminate the bad news and has drawn one of the appropriate conclusions. In conversations with Alfonso Robelo, leader of the political opposition to the present Nicaraguan government, and with Sandinista leaders, Castro emphasized the importance of preserving a significant private business sector. Some Central and South American leftists may still be reluctant to admit it, but they cannot indefinitely evade the fact that a commitment to a private sector is also a commitment to some species of political pluralism.

Advocates of democratic reform face enormous difficulties. In many Latin American countries a demographic explosion is taking place while the economy relies on a capital-intensive technology that was developed in the labor-scarce states of Europe and North America—a combination that usually creates very high levels of unemployment. Also imported from the developed states are consumer appetites that stimulate the greed of the well-to-do. Because international capital is hard to obtain, politicians and businessmen feel they must compete for it by suppressing every sign of social disorder; and modern technology provides an apparatus for official terror beyond the dreams of nineteenth-century rulers. Western stagflation meanwhile threatens export markets and consequently the ability to finance growth of any kind.

The rush to authoritarian governments in the Sixties and early Seventies heightened academic appreciation of these and related obstacles, and encouraged a pessimistic determinism about projects for social and political reform. But the failure of countries like Chile and Uruguay to reproduce the Brazilian economic "miracle" by combining assaults on the working class with an open door to international capital has helped to undermine confidence in the stability of that formula for social order. It received another blow recently when Uruguayan voters rejected a constitution designed by the armed forces to perpetuate their rule. The democratic impulse has not yielded to competing claims to legitimacy.

The great question is whether reform coalitions can increase equity and welfare without sacrificing the long-term growth necessary for peaceful relations between classes. If they can, they should satisfy the demands of the Latin American military officers who have seized power in order to halt class warfare and the consequent disintegration of all traditional institutions, including the armed forces themselves. Plausible blueprints are available. In the case of Brazil, for instance, a recent confidential study shows how moderate changes in government policy designed substantially to reduce inequality could also do much to relieve the shortages of energy and foreign exchange that threaten the country's future. A more equitable distribution of income would coincidentally benefit domestically controlled private businesses because they enjoy a comparative advantage over multinational corporations in producing basic consumer goods.

Most of Latin America is now open to renewed projects for democratic social reform, or could soon become so. Carter helped to shape this more promising situation by insisting that the way a regime treats its own people has to affect the quality of its relations with the United States. Having initially disarmed himself by forswearing intervention in trade or private capital as a means of defending human rights, he could, however, offer few incentives and he used few convincing threats. By 1977, only a derisory amount of bilateral economic aid was available to reward good behavior.

In a few cases Carter could and did block or delay aid to authoritarian states such as Argentina from international financial institutions; but various, partially self-imposed, constraints made this a rarely used and only marginally threatening weapon. In cautioning authoritarian governments against repression, Carter drew mainly on the accumulated prestige of the United States among Latin American military establishments and the upper classes. His considerable achievements, including fair elections in the Dominican Republic, are partly owing to the weight of American influence, but primarily to the gathering force of human rights as an ideal that cuts across deep divisions of class and ideology in Latin America. That force powerfully multiplied the effect of Carter's efforts.

Simply by acting to demonstrate some continuity in Washington's support for human rights, Ronald Reagan could easily match Carter's achievement. He needs to act quickly. His victory has particularly encouraged the predators in those few remaining social jungles where an alliance of corrupted soldiers, industrialists, and landowners would rather fight to the last worker, peasant, politician, and priest than accept reform.

While campaigning for the presidency, Mr. Reagan allowed certain ideologues who were vindictive toward all critics of traditional capitalist order to speak in his name. Responsible Republicans such as Congressman Jack Kemp should urge the president to reject association of American power with conservatism that relies on vicious repression. They should act because it is the right thing to do; and because it is in the national interest that Latin Americans succeed in establishing capitalism with a human face.

PART TWO

SOCIAL FORCES AND IDEOLOGIES IN THE MAKING OF CONTEMPORARY EL SALVADOR

EDITORS' INTRODUCTION

Coffee was king [in early twentieth century El Salvador]; it earned the country's foreign exchange, paid for its imports, provided revenue for central and local government, financed the construction of roads, parks and railways, gave employment—permanent or seasonal—to a large part of the population and made the fortunes of a few.

—David Browning, *El Salvador* (1971)

IN his classic discussion of oligarchy the ancient Greek philosopher Aristotle defined this form of government as a corruption of aristocracy, where presumably the noble and virtuous rule. An oligarchy exists, "when men of property have the government in their hands." [1] In the broad sense of rule by the wealthy and powerful, most governments are to some extent oligarchies, whatever other formal designation may be applied to them. Although they fit into the Aristotelean definition, the clusters of plantation owners, industrialists, and high military officers that make up the traditional oligarchies of Latin America are a special case. Their historical genealogies may be traced back to the *Conquistadores* of the early sixteenth century and the colonial elites, whose special privileges under Spanish and Portuguese royal power far exceeded anything comparable in the British colonial settlements to the north.[2]

Post-colonial political oligarchies in the Central American region that is the focus of this book evolved characteristic political and social patterns during the eighteenth and nineteenth centuries. These included intense rivalries between factions of the oligarchies; periodic *coups d'état* (*golpes de estado*, in Spanish), which were not revolutions but rather palace rebellions; habitual intervention of countries in the affairs of their neighbors; and political changes that involved little more than circulation of power, prerogatives, and offices among the relatively small elite. The conflicts tended to be disputes *within*

---

[1] Aristotle, *Politics*, Sections 1279–1281.
[2] Clarence H. Haring, *The Spanish Empire in America* (New York, 1963), esp., pp. 27–28.

the oligarchy over who would enjoy the lucrative privilege of exploiting the peasant masses.[3]

Both earlier and in the twentieth century, the military was an integral part of the oligarchies of Central America, and participated in the circulation of elites that comprised political life in these countries. High military positions were—and are—frequently open only to favored sons of the oligarchs, or serve as stepping stones into the oligarchies. The military's function was to keep "order" in the interests of the economic and political elite. The lower ranks of the army were usually filled with peasant conscripts, who, of course, had no say on how military power was used, and many of whom welcomed the regular pay and freedom from agricultural toil as a relief from destitution and direct exploitation.[4] The army served to keep a lid on popular discontent endemic to a system that functioned well only from the point of view of the dominant oligarchies and then only until the early 1960's.

By the time John F. Kennedy became President of the United States, an enormous population rise, fluctuating markets for Latin American agricultural staples, and political pressures were combining to produce unprecedented levels of popular discontent in the region. The Cuban revolution had suggested one possible reaction to this discontent, and one that not only generated panic among the oligarchies, but also stimulated Cold War fears among U.S. policymakers as well. The Kennedy administration launched the Alliance for Progress as a U.S.-aided reform program aimed at diverting burgeoning popular discontent into moderate channels. But this modern reform was too little and too late; [5] by the end of the decade sustained indigenous guerrilla movements had spread through all the countries of Central America, except the lone democracy, Costa Rica.

The local oligarchies used their military forces to put up a fierce

---

[3] See the patronizing treatment of Central American "palace revolts" in Dana G. Munro, The Five Republics of Central America (New York, 1918), Chap. IX, and the far more sophisticated interpretation in José Nun, "A Latin American Phenomenon: The Middle Class Military Coup," in Latin America: Reform or Revolution, James Petras and Maurice Zeitlin, eds. (New York, 1968), pp. 145–85.

[4] For an analysis of trends in the Latin military, see Edwin Lieuwen, Arms and Politics in Latin America (New York, 1967); and Robert V. Elam, "Appeal to Arms: The Army and Politics in El Salvador, 1931–1964" (Ph.D thesis, University of New Mexico, 1968). The Editors also benefited from a conversation on this topic with Professor John A. Womack, Jr., of Harvard University.

[5] Among the many obituaries for the Alianza Para el Progreso, one of the most poignant is "The Alliance that Lost its Way," by Eduardo Frei Montalva (leader of the Chilean Christian Democracy), reprinted in Irving Louis Horowitz, Josué de Castro and John Gerassi, eds., Latin American Radicalism (New York, 1969), pp. 457–68.

campaign of terror against the insurgents. The U.S. government, always more favorable to established, authoritarian regimes of the right than to left-wing insurgents,[6] gave military aid to the oligarchies, but was recently unable to prevent a popular resistance movement from overthrowing the almost half-century-old Nicaraguan dictatorship imposed by the Somoza family. The already embattled oligarchies across the border in El Salvador and Honduras and in nearby Guatemala may well be facing a similar fate and the U.S. government, which seems to have committed itself to them, may well be drawn into yet another lost cause.

6. El Salvador:
A Political Chronology *

By CISPES

Mid-1800s. The commercial lands which had been used by peasants to grow food for their own consumption are expropriated by government decree and consolidated into large farms to grow coffee. "Fourteen Families," the core of the emerging El Salvador oligarchy, control the export crops, in particular coffee.

1930. The Salvadoran Communist Party (PCS) is formed, uniting leaders of many of the local unions of the Regional Federation of Salvadoran Workers (FRTS).

1930. May Day, 80,000 workers and peasants march into San Salvador demanding minimum wage for farm workers and relief centers for the unemployed.

1931. Arturo Araújo is elected president, but is deposed by the military led by Vice President Gen. Martínez. The oligarchy gives the mandate to the military to rule El Salvador.

1932. The military government refuses to allow the seating of PCS candidates, who win in municipal and legislative elections. Economic conditions are grave. The PCS responds with a call for uprisings simultaneously in the cities, countryside and military garrisons.

---

[6] Although this was the *de facto* policy long before Ronald Reagan arrived in the White House, he and his advisers have made this point an ideological keystone of their administration.

* Compiled by Committee in Solidarity with the People of El Salvador [CISPES]. See below, Bibliography and Resources, for data on CISPES. The Editors have updated the chronology from March, 1981.

Three days before the uprising, Augustín Farâbundo Martí and other leaders are arrested. Because of a communications breakdown, Salvadoran peasants and farm workers nevertheless march into the cities as originally planned. Virtually unarmed, the rebels cannot defend themselves against the military. As a result, 4,000 are killed and the uprising crushed.

As a lesson, the army begins what comes to be known as the "*Matanza*," the massacre. Within the first few weeks the army and paramilitary forces kill over 30,000 people. Peasant leaders are hung in the town square. By the time the *Matanza* is over, 4% of the population is killed, the PCS liquidated, the FRTS annihilated and the Indian population forced to abandon their native dress, language and cultural activities.

1931-44. Martínez rules for 13 years, his policies preventing industrialization.

1944. Martínez is forced from power but the military continues to rule.

Late 1940s. This is a period of major economic transformation. A new coalition is formed of the military technocrats and a tiny industrial bourgeoisie, with part of the coffee oligarchy. Martínez's anti-industrial laws are abolished. U.S. manufacturing investments begin.

1950. Col. Oscar Osorio becomes president in fraudulent elections. Continued repression is viewed as a necessary complement to reforms, which are intended to induce economic modernization, rationalize an otherwise archaic society and produce a modest facade of democracy.

1950s. The Revolutionary Party of Democratic Unity (PRUD) is formed as the official party of the coalition of the military and the bourgeoisie who want modernization. Its policies lead to the growth of the Salvadoran economy and the development of small middle and working classes in the cities.

1961. The Central American Common Market is formed with support from U.S. Providing a "free trade zone" in El Salvador, Guatemala, Honduras, Nicaragua and Costa Rica, the U.S. views the common market as providing the necessary political infrastructure for the investment of U.S. capital.

1962. The PRUD party is by this point thoroughly discredited because of continued election frauds, the failure to improve living conditions and uninterrupted repression. The same ruling military oligarchy coalition reconstitutes the party as the Party of National Conciliation (PCN) and Col. Rivera comes to power. The PCN rules for the next 17 years.

1962-67. Rivera is the first to have truly contested elections and allowed opposition parties for the first time since 1934. Three main opposition parties quickly emerge. The Christian Democratic Party (PDC), supported by European Christian Democracy and by local professionals, quickly becomes the largest opposition party. The National Revolutionary Movement (MNR) is a small party, comprised of professionals and intellectuals. The National Democratic Union (UDN) emerges, which includes the PCS, outlawed in 1932.

1969. War breaks out between Honduras and El Salvador, precipitated by Honduras in an effort to expropriate the lands of peasants who had migrated from El Salvador after losing their land to the coffee and cotton plantations. The Central American Common Market collapses. The Christian Democrats, the MNR and the UDN form a coalition called the National Opposition Union (UNO).

1970-72. The manipulation by the military of the elections of 1970 and the blatant fraud in the 1972 elections announce to many sectors that meaningful reform via elections will not work.

1970-75. Popular armed elements emerge. The popular Liberation Forces (FPL) develops from a split within the PCS. The FPL argues for both armed action and mass organizing. The People's Revolutionary Army (ERP) develops from a split in the left wing of the Christian Democratic Party and primarily focuses on armed struggle. The National Resistance (RN), like the FPL, urges both military action and mass organizing.

1975-80. Thousands of people, from the worker, peasant, teacher, student, and church sectors come together in the popular organizations, using civil disobedience and mass protests as their tactic. The popular organizations are linked to the popular armed movements.

1977-79. The PCN selects Gen. Carlos Romero to replace Col. Molina in the 1977 "elections." Romero represents the far right, repression-without-reform faction. Under Gen. Romero there is a major escalation of government terror.

June-July, 1979. Archbishop Oscar Romero (no relation to Gen. Romero) becomes an outspoken critic of the military's rule and economic injustice. The excesses of Gen. Romero's regime earn the condemnation of Amnesty International and other human rights organizations. Finally, the government's repression becomes an intolerable embarrassment to the Carter administration and the victory of the Sandinistas in nearby Nicaragua makes the U.S. fearful of backing an unpopular dictator.

Oct. 15, 1979. The first "revolutionary junta" is formed. A U.S.-backed bloodless coup overthrows Gen. Romero and sets up the Revolutionary Governing Junta (committee) of two military and three civilians from the center and moderate left. A truce with the popular organizations is worked out. Many members of the UNO coalition join the government in various ministerial and subministerial positions. A proclamation of Oct. 15 is issued which calls for nationalization of foreign trade in coffee and sugar; establishment of an investigatory commission on political prisoners and the disappeared; beginning a land-reform program; mobilization of international support.

By December it becomes clear that none of the measures will be carried out.

Jan. 3, 1980. The civilian members of the junta, virtually all the civilian members of the cabinet and most civilian subministers resign over the continued repression of the government and paramilitary forces.

Jan. 6, 1980. Archbishop Romero calls on the people to back the popular organizations and "preserve the liberation process."

Jan. 9, 1980. A second governing junta is constituted, again with two military and three civilian members.

Jan. 11, 1980. The popular organizations begin to unify. The People's Revolutionary Bloc (BPR), the United Front for Popular Action (FAPU), the Democratic Nationalist Union (UDN), the Feb. 28th Peoples Leagues (LP-28) and the People's Liberation Movement (MPL) come together to form the Revolutionary Coordinating Committee of the Masses (CRM).

Jan. 22, 1980. 200,000 march in San Salvador to celebrate the popular unity.

Feb. 17, 1980. Bishop Romero denounces the "unscrupulous military" and calls on Christian Democrats to stop serving the junta as a "cover for repression." In a letter to President Carter, Romero demands the U.S. stop military, economic and diplomatic intervention.

March 3, 1980. The second junta falls and a third is created. Civilian members resign from the second junta to protest continued repression.

March 6, 1980. The new junta announces a land-reform program under the direction of the U.S. State Department and the American Institute for Free Labor Development, an affiliate of the AFL-CIO which has known links with the CIA. At the same time, a state of siege is imposed as peasants are attacked by the military and paramilitary forces.

March 23, 1980. Bishop Romero denounces the agrarian reform as "reforms bathed in blood" and calls on the military to disobey their commanders.

March 24, 1980. Bishop Romero is assassinated by right-wing forces while celebrating mass.

April 2, 1980. U.S. approves $5.7 million in military aid to El Salvador.

April 18, 1980. Thousands attend ceremony to celebrate the creation of the Democratic Revolutionary Front (FDR), a broad coalition of the CRM, the social democratic party, Christian Democrats fed up with the junta, 80% of the trade unions, church people, professionals, students, small business people and the National and Catholic universities. It is the largest political movement in El Salvador's history.

May 14, 1980. 600 peasants fleeing rural repression massacred at the Sumpul River by Salvadoran and Honduran troops.

June 24, 1980. Three-day general strike is 90% successful. Army occupies National University, killing 50.

Aug. 12, 1980. Three-day general strike a partial success. Government bombs sections of San Salvador, killing 200.

September, 1980. U.S. sends $20 million economic aid to El Salvador to make a total of $90 million for 1980.

Oct. 4, 1980. Army begins military offensive in Morazán region, creating 24,000 refugees and 3,000 dead.

November, 1980. The Farabundo Martí Front for the National Liberation is formed as the political-military arm of the FDR. It brings together the FPL, the ERP, the RN, as well as the PCS and the newly formed Central American Revolutionary Workers Party (PRTC).

Nov. 28, 1980. Six leaders of the FDR assassinated by Security Forces and paramilitary agents.

Dec. 3, 1980. Four U.S. churchwomen assassinated by the National Guard.

Dec. 4, 1980. Carter administration suspends military and economic aid to El Salvador.

Dec. 6, 1980. Bishop Rivera y Damas denounces U.S. military aid for facilitating "repression against the people and persecution of the church."

Dec. 13, 1980. Third junta dissolves. Fourth junta forms with José Napoleón Duarte as President. U.S. reinstates economic aid.

Dec. 15, 1980. U.N. General Assembly passes a resolution condemning the repression in El Salvador, with 55 countries abstaining.

Dec. 16, 1980. U.S. government loans $20 million to El Salvador government.

Dec. 18, 1980. U.S. government loans a further $45.5 million, bringing the total aid for 1980 to $150 million.

Dec. 26–27, 1980. FMLN, the political-military arm of the FDR, attacks four major towns in the northern province of Chalatenango, where the Salvadoran government maintains police and military installations.

Jan. 5, 1981. AFL-CIO representatives Michael Hammer and Mark Pearlman, who had been working in El Salvador as advisers on the land-reform program, and José Viera, the president of the Salvadoran Institute for Agrarian Transformation, are murdered by 2 right-wing hit men.

Jan. 11, 1981. A general offensive of the FMLN begins.

Jan. 13, 1981. The FDR calls for a general strike.

Jan. 14, 1981. The U.S. administration resumes fiscal year 1981 military assistance to El Salvador. That aid—$5 million in Foreign Military Sales credits and $420,000 in Training Funds—had been held up on Dec. 5, 1980 after the murder of four U.S. churchwomen. In addition, the U.S. sends six advisers to El Salvador.

Jan. 15, 1981. About half the shops in San Salvador are closed, in addition to the walkout of 20,000 government workers.

Jan. 17, 1981. U.S. administration invokes special executive powers to send an emergency package of $5 million in lethal military assistance to El Salvador.

Jan. 18, 1981. The U.S. approves an additional $5 million in military aid, bringing the total for the first three weeks of 1981 to $10 million. The latest aid package includes three military advisory teams.

Feb. 7, 1981. The FDR calls for "a dialogue with the U.S. government." "We want to find a way to end the violence," an FDR spokesman explains.

Feb. 11, 1981. The Reagan administration drops U.S. insistence on an investigation into the death of the four U.S. churchwomen as a condition for giving economic and military aid to El Salvador.

Feb. 23, 1981. The State Department releases a major "White Paper" purporting to show that what is occurring in El Salvador is indirect armed aggression by the Soviet Union, Cuba, North Vietnam and other communist-bloc governments. Mexican Foreign Minister José Velasco calls the document an attempt by the U.S. "to transfer its confrontation with the Soviet Union to Latin America."

March 7, 1981. State Department spokesman James R. Cheek denies the authenticity of a "dissent paper" from within the government that takes issue with administration policy.

March, 1981. Secretary of State Alexander Haig denies on several occasions that the United States would look favorably upon a coup by the rightist oligarchy. The comments come in response to statements by rightist leader Roberto D'Aubuisson in El Salvador.

March, 1981. The Salvadoran junta names an electoral committee to pave the way for "free elections" in 1982. Duarte wants a "dialogue" but no negotiations with the Democratic Revolutionary Front. He invites opposition figures back to take part in electoral process but admits he cannot assure their safety should they return.

April and May, 1981. The U.S. Congress passes strictures on U.S. aid to El Salvador which require President Reagan to certify that the Salvadoran government is dedicated to assuring human rights and prepared to negotiate.

May 3, 1981. 100,000 Americans rally at the Pentagon in opposition to U.S. involvement in El Salvador.

June, 1981. Efforts at pursuing mediation in the Salvadoran conflict by the Socialist International (separate missions by Hans Wischniewski of the West German Social Democratic Party and Ed Broadbent of the Canadian New Democratic Party) end in failure. The Christian Democratic/military junta refuses to negotiate.

June, 1981. The Salvadoran Association of Jurists declines to participate in preparations for 1982 elections because of the continuing terror and state of siege.

July, 1981. Duarte calls conservative businessmen trying to roll back limited land reform and nationalization of banks "the biggest threat" to the junta. "The private sector," says Duarte, "is in its final offensive."

July 2, 1981. Newly-elected French Socialist President François Mitterrand expresses support for the Salvadoran rebellion. "It is a question of people refusing to submit to misery and humiliation," he states. Two days later, the French Socialist Party promises an FDR delegation "all possible support" in the struggle.

July 17, 1981. The Reagan administration declares itself committed to a "political solution" in El Salvador, by which it means support for the 1982 proposed elections rather than, as European and Latin American allies have urged, negotiations with the FDR.

Aug. 28, 1981. A joint French and Mexican declaration giving official recognition to the Salvadoran opposition as a representative political force.

7. Class Struggle and Civil War in El Salvador *

BY HARALD JUNG

There are few histories in English that cover the important period in Salvadoran political development between the massacre of 1932 and the

---

* From *New Left Review* [London], No. 122, July–August, 1980 *fraudulent presidential balloting of 1972. In this analysis by Harald Jung, the complicated political scene in El Salvador is traced back to the social and economic developments of the last five decades.*

THE military coup in El Salvador of October 15, 1979, provoked a new and remarkable twist in the bloody social conflicts which have wracked this Central American republic. The former dictator, General Carlos Humberto Romero, was replaced by a junta which proclaimed the need for sweeping reforms and which initially attracted the support of Christian Democrats, Social Democrats and Communists. The most important groups of the armed revolutionary left maintained an attitude of watchful hostility towards the reformist junta, and in the days following the coup there were clashes in several working class districts around the capital between the army and the leftist guerrillas. It quickly became clear that the new government could not carry through its program of reforms in most parts of the country and was unable either to suppress rightist terrorism directed at the popular forces, or even to control its own military and security apparatus. In December the Social Democrats and Communists withdrew support from the junta and in subsequent months some of the Christian Democrats have followed suit. On March 24 Archbishop Oscar Romero was assassinated; on the previous day he had made an impassioned appeal for an end to military repression and had declared that soldiers were not obliged to obey orders that were contrary to their conscience. Between January and June over two thousand people were killed as a result of official or paramilitary violence, while in May the Salvadoran high command declared that two northern provinces, Morazán and Chalatenango, were "military emergency zones." In January and mid-April the oppositional guerrilla forces moved to form a wider united front and to integrate some of those who had formerly supported the reformist Government set up in October 1979. The mounting popular opposition to military repression in El Salvador has often been compared to the last stages of the struggle against Somoza in Nicaragua. Yet, as we will see, El Salvador's particular socio-economic and political development has been different from that of Nicaragua and does not lay the basis for the same type of polarizations. In El Salvador the rightist para-military groups can command some sectional support while the military-sponsored government continues to proclaim the need for reform and to receive the support of some Christian Democrats and the United States.

El Salvador remains as ever an agricultural country. In 1974 agriculture made up 26 percent of the GNP, and in 1977 it provided around four-fifths of revenues from exports. In 1975 more than 60 percent of the population were classed as agricultural. The rural sector is thus of fundamental importance for all political developments.

The division in land utilization between cattle-raising haciendas and villages cultivating maize, which dated from the colonial epoch, was overridden by the introduction of coffee planting. Between 1880 and 1912, the common lands of the villages in the hilly volcanic regions were for the most part sold to urban middle- and upper-class families at giveaway prices, a small portion alone being distributed among the villagers. Since the coffee tree needs five years growth before its first harvest, its cultivation is only possible for persons with a certain amount of capital, and hardly at all for small farmers, for whom the land has to provide their basic foodstuffs. Right from the beginning, therefore, coffee was concentrated pre-eminently in the hands of a small and relatively rich coffee bourgeoisie owning large estates.

At first, these big coffee planters maintained the traditional relations of production that existed on the haciendas. The workers (*colonos*) received a plot of land on which to cultivate food crops in return for their work for the landowner. Since in the coffee-growing regions, however, the land left to the *colonos* could be more profitably used for coffee cultivation, the *colono* system was already replaced by wage labor in the 1920s. The workers no longer received any land for their own use, but only a primitive hut on the estate. During the 1940s and 1950s, with the extension of coffee cultivation (annual receipts from coffee exports rose by a factor of ten), the number of landless rural laborers also rose in proportion to the traditional *colonos*. In the 1950s, modern technology took root in coffee cultivation and made possible a reduction of the permanently employed labor force. In the 1960s, the era of the Alliance for Progress, social legislation and a guaranteed minimum wage was introduced for the permanent employees, so as to forestall the radicalization of the growing (illegal) trade-union organization in the countryside. The coffee bourgeoisie subsequently counteracted the tendencies of the workers to organize, as well as the minimum wage, by seeking to reduce to a minimum the number of permanent employees, replacing labor by capital, so that they only needed to employ a larger number of workers for the short periods of harvesting. A mobile rural proletariat of seasonal workers now grew up, with the chance of finding employment on the coffee estates only between November and March.

This process of replacing permanent employees by seasonal workers, which in coffee cultivation took place only slowly on account of the relatively narrow limits of mechanization imposed by natural conditions, was repeated far more violently in cotton cultivation. The rapidly rising demand for cotton on the world market in the early 1950s opened up the lower lying valleys and coastal areas to agricultural production for export. The land used for cotton was generally leased by the big landlords to capitalist farmers. Fifty-two percent of the cotton fields, at the beginning of the 1970s, were leased in this way, with 83 percent being operated by middle and large enterprises. The *colonos* of the haciendas, who had no legal title to the land that they tilled, had to make way. Since cotton cultivation required still less labor than cattle-raising, and experienced an enormous intensification in the course of the 1950s (the yield per hectare doubling from 1950 to 1960), only a small proportion of the former *colonos* found work in cotton growing, and generally only then during the months of harvest. From *colonos*, they became landless peasants and seasonal workers.

Coffee and cotton remain El Salvador's principal export products. In the late 1970s, coffee comprised between 80 and 90 percent of export revenue, and cotton between 10 and 15 percent. The growth of a mobile rural proletariat, employed only on a seasonal basis, can thus be seen as characteristic for virtually the entire agricultural export sector. At the same time, the mechanization of the agricultural export economy led to a reduction in the number of workers employed in agriculture from 310,097 in 1961 to 267,079 in 1975. The old *colono* system now exists on only a few obsolete haciendas, although in the late 1960s, a middle strata of peasants managed to develop and become quite significant on the basis of sugar cultivation.

The expansion of the agricultural export sector also had its effects on the peasant subsistence economy and the small peasants. In El Salvador 10 hectares is generally taken as the minimum amount of land required to support an average peasant family. In 1971, only 19,951 (5.2 percent) out of 384,540 families engaged in agriculture possessed 10 hectares or more, 15.6 percent cultivated between 2 and 10 hectares, and 245,015 (63.7 percent) less than 1 hectare. Of the peasants with less than 1 hectare, only 24 percent actually owned the land that they tilled, as did only 31 percent of the peasants with between 1 and 2 hectares. The great mass of small peasants are thus directly affected by changes in the conditions of farm leases.

Traditionally, the big landowners leased out portions of their land to small peasants on a sharecropping basis. This pre-capitalist rent in kind was gradually replaced from the 1950s onwards by a variable money rent, with the expansion of the export economy and the emergence of capitalist farmers. The small peasants could not pay the rising land prices and rents, and had to move out.

The rural banking sector controlled by the agricultural bourgeoisie also compelled many peasants to give up their holdings. Between 1961 and 1975 export-oriented undertakings received between 80 and 90 percent of agricultural credits; 87 percent of all these credits, in 1971, went to farms with more than 10 hectares, and only 1 percent to farms with less than 1 hectare. Ninety-five percent of the land belonging to farms with less than 2 hectares was used in 1971 for the production of basic necessities. In the context of an export-oriented agricultural policy, it seemed inopportune to promote this. Many small peasants were therefore forced before harvest time either to borrow from local moneylenders at exorbitant interest rates, or else to sell their crops in advance at cut price, simply so as to feed their families. They thus got into a chronic cycle of unending debt, and had sooner or later to sell their land.

The process of expropriation and expulsion of small peasants, side by side with a simultaneous reduction in employment in the expanding export cultivations, were aggravated in their social consequences because of the limited amount of land available in El Salvador for agriculture, and an annual population growth of 3.1 percent. In 1975, the total population stood at 4.1 million, a density of 192 per square kilometer. A steadily growing number of independent peasants were thus pressed together on a shrinking area. From 1950 to 1961 the number of farms with less than 10 hectares rose in the cotton-growing regions by 72 percent, while the average size of these farms fell by 54 percent. From 1961 to 1975, the number of independent peasants, together with their dependents, rose from 176,051 to 339,601. From 1961 to 1971, the number of peasant families with less than 10 hectares grew by 126,839, out of which the number of families with under 2 hectares grew by 37,194 and the number of completely landless peasant families by 81,657. The number of peasant families with more than 10 hectares grew by only 354.

The big export businesses became ever more concentrated in a few hands. In 1971, 0.5 per cent of all agricultural enterprises (those with more than 200 hectares) farmed some 34 percent of the agricultural area, while 52 percent of the peasants (those with less than 2 hectares) farmed only 3.7 percent. Since one family often owns several large agricultural holdings, the real extent of concentration is still higher. In 1971, six families alone possessed as much land as 80 percent of the rural population together.

This situation can be summed up as follows:

1. The agricultural export sector is in the hands of a small number of families.

2. Over the last three decades, permanent workers in the agricultural export cultivations have been increasingly replaced by migrant workers employed only seasonally.

3. The expansion of the export sector is reducing the agricultural land that remains for the small peasants. At the same time, the number of jobs in export cultivations is on the decline, so that a growing agricultural population has to feed itself as peasants off a shrunken area of land. For three decades the size of these peasant farms has been declining, and 95 percent of them do not have sufficient land to guarantee their own subsistence. These small peasants have to compete with the landless seasonal workers for jobs on the big exporting estates.

4. Some 64 percent of rural families are seasonal and migrant workers, with no land or less than 1 hectare. Their number is growing rapidly, particularly the number of completely landless families, even though the number of jobs for wage workers in agriculture is declining. This means a constant rise in underemployment and unemployment in the countryside.

Socio-Economic Development in the Towns

The industrial development that has taken place since 1930 and particularly in the 1960s proved unable to absorb the labor power set free in the agricultural sector. Due to the low purchasing power of the mass of the population, and the preference for luxury import goods on the part of those with most money to spend, the local market could only develop a weak demand for locally produced consumption goods. Manufacturing industry, therefore, is not just the further development of traditional handicrafts, but predominantly a capital-intensive export industry concentrated in the hands of a few big bourgeois families. Often the same families accumulated wealth in the agricultural export sector, financed the industrialization boom of the 1960s and subsequently themselves became industrial capitalists. At the present time, the entire economy of El Salvador is dominated by some fourteen families, all involved in agriculture, finance and industry, even if their specializations are somewhat different.

The development of a capital-intensive export industry only created a small number of new industrial jobs. Between 1961 and 1971 the manufacturing sector grew by 24 percent, while the number of people employed in this sector grew by only 6 percent. The number of employees in manufacturing as a proportion of the economically active population fell from around 13 percent in 1961 to some 10 percent in 1971 and 1975. The number of workers in manufacturing industry grew by only 2,500 between 1961 and 1971. The number of wage earners in the sectors of mining, manufacturing, construction and transport, storage and communication (i.e., those that could be described as the classical industrial proletariat) remained virtually constant throughout the 1960s, and only began to increase after 1971, rising by 32,000 to a total of 152,000 in 1975.

In the wake of the industrialization of 1961–1975, the total number of wage earners not employed in agriculture grew by about one-third, from 246,000 to 361,000. The total of self-employed in the non-agricultural sectors, however, almost tripled in the same period, from 68,000 to 193,000. This expresses on the one hand the sharp growth of an independent middle class, on the other a process of marginalization. Out of these 193,000 independently active, 131,000 were involved in commerce and 11,000 in the service sector. Both these categories in statistics for developing countries generally conceal a vast number of shoeshiners, lottery-ticket sellers, street traders, prostitutes, washerwomen, etc. The number of self-employed in commerce grew from 47,000 in 1971 to 131,000 in 1975, but it can hardly be assumed that in these four years El Salvador, with an increase of 122,000 in the total number of economically active, counted 84,000 successful new business people among these. In 1975, 126,000 urban wage earners were employed in the service sector. This total also conceals untold thousands of marginalized people, most of whom have fled into the cities from underemployment and unemployment in the countryside. The capital-intensive export industry could not provide sufficient jobs for these migrants, and compelled them to lead a marginalized existence in the ever growing slum districts in and around San Salvador.

To sum up: Industrialization produced an industrial proletariat that comprises 42 percent of all urban wage earners and 27 percent of all these economically active in the urban sector. Compared with other developing countries, the industrial proletariat is thus relatively well developed in the urban sector. At the same time, the middle class of self-employed and people active in professional services and commerce has expanded. Most of all, however, there has been an explosion in the number of petty retailers and street traders, now running into the tens of thousands. These traders should be classed as marginalized people without adequate income. The surplus of petty traders reduce one another's sales and profit potentials. The number of those marginalized elements who perform personal services and odd jobs should also be estimated in tens of thousands. Among others, this group includes the more than 40 percent of all urban wage earners who in 1974 were receiving less than the legal minimum wage of 28.70 *colones* (about £5) per week. But the economic position of the industrial workers has also deteriorated in the 1970s. While the number of these workers has risen, the index of real industrial wages has fallen by 1975 back to the level of 1965, after rising briefly until 1970-71.

The Political Implications of Social Stratification

The political developments in El Salvador must be viewed against this socio-economic background. The expansion of the agricultural export sector did not mean a simple proletarianization of the peasants, a process that would have smoothly transformed the agricultural population into a revolutionary subject. This interpretation, of a kind often met with in the works of left-wing writers, may well be correct in the long run. In a shorter timescale, however—and in El Salvador this has been under way for at least 40 years—the transformation that follows in the wake of the expansion of the agricultural export sector gives rise to a whole range of different groups of peasants and agricultural wage workers, with very different immediate interests based on differing relations of economic dependence. These different immediate interests of small peasants, seasonal workers, worker-peasants, small farmers, permanent plantation workers, etc., time and again serve to impede and destroy the political unification of the agricultural population, even though all these elements are completely subject to a common exploitation by the agricultural oligarchy. This is all the more true for an agricultural population which has to compete for the daily necessities of life on an inadequate land surface and in a hopelessly overfilled labor market. And this competition does not merely determine whether life is more or less comfortable, it also determines the very life or death (from starvation) of individual family members. Political conduct, "good" or "bad," can lead to a peasant having his conditions of existence taken away, it can decide which out of three or four seasonal workers gets the one job, whether a permanently employed agricultural worker continues in his privileged position, etc.

Similar factors destroying the solidarity of the exploited masses also exist in the towns. The wage struggles of the industrial proletariat, to which the urban trade unions confined their activity during the 1960s, can scarcely manage to win the solidarity of those who rarely receive a wage. The masses of marginalized elements, as an industrial reserve army, pose a constant latent threat to unskilled workers. For any worker who is fired, there are ten unemployed who are ready to take his or her place. These marginalized masses are in constant competition for the few irregular jobs in the street markets, in personal services, petty crime, etc. The petty bourgeoisie and the urban middle strata similarly have their own particular interests. "Society is transformed into a conglomerate of people fighting for their survival, without considering or reflecting on who are their true enemies," in the words of a group of Salvadoran social scientists, who characterize their country's society as "disintegrated and organized along alienated lines of battle."

Given an existence of this kind, whether individual and sectoral particular interests end up preventing or dissolving the process of political solidarity and unification of the exploited population is decisively dependent on the extent to which the rulers manage to reinforce these particular interests politically. This is all the more so in that those social sectors that might potentially be united have only a relatively short history, lacking a tradition of struggle that dates back even one generation, such as might be able to harmonize differing immediate interests of particular social groups in the interest of a long-run goal.

Political Development up to the 1970s

The El Salvador military regime understood very early the possibilities of this situation for a policy of "divide and rule." Already in January 1932, only a month after seizing power, the military rulers received an important lesson.

In the 1920s groups of working-class activists had risen among the urban artisan population, defining themselves as Communists in the wake of the Russian Revolution. Between 1928 and 1931 coffee prices and the wages of coffee workers fell by more than 50 percent. Against this background, the Communist and revolutionary trade unions in the west of El Salvador succeeded in organizing some 80,000 workers in the coffee plantations and leading major strikes and demonstrations. The relatively free presidential elections of 1930 saw these working-class activists supporting the coffee planter Arturo Araújo, who presented himself as a champion of reform. On assuming office, however, Araújo found himself unable to carry out his promised reforms, owing to the precarious economic situation. The generals accused the President of incompetence, overthrowing him at the end of 1931 and appointing General Martínez as President. In January 1932 Martínez permitted local elections to be held with the participation of the Communists. After the Communists had won the vote in certain coffee-producing districts in the west of the country, the generals refused to allow them to take office. The Communists called for an uprising. On the night of 22nd–23rd January, agricultural workers armed with machetes attacked and occupied public buildings in the western districts. The revolt "was concentrated in the western coffee-growing areas, where coffee had already spread to cover most of the ground in the areas of cultivable altitude, and the rural population was already almost completely dependent on seasonal wage labor on the coffee plantations; there was no space left for them to plant subsistence crops. This process had not gone so far in the eastern coffee-producing zone where there was no revolt." The uprising came to grief due to the division between the pure wage workers and the *colonos* and worker-peasants. The generals butchered between twenty and thirty thousand workers.

Martínez found a *modus vivendi* with the Salvadoran bourgeoisie. The military kept the office of President and the politically important ministries, while the key positions in economic policy were filled by representatives of the bourgeoisie, and in part completely withdrawn from state control. All matters of management and regulation that bore on the cultivation and marketing of coffee were dealt with not by the ministry of agriculture, but by associations and organizations of the coffee bourgeoisie itself. This applied also to the Central Reserve Bank and the Banco Hipótecario, the latter controlling credit to the rural sector. This division of functions between the military and the bourgeoisie continued right through to the 1970s, and emerged intact from all government crises and coups. Political differences within this bourgeois-military alliance, between the reform-oriented forces and those that were exclusively repressive, cut through the bourgeoisie and the military alike.

During the Second World War the Salvadoran economy experienced a recovery which gave an impetus to the democratic forces among the urban workers and artisans, who revolted in 1944 against the extremely repressive regime of the time. These received active support from the students, and even from sections of the bourgeoisie and the military. Even though Martínez was able to suppress the rebellion, the U.S. ambassador in El Salvador declared him "redundant," and he resigned. Following a democratic interlude in summer 1944, the purely repressive faction of the army pushed its way to power again, until it was overthrown in its turn in December 1948 by a new military coup led by Oscar Osorio.

Osorio and his sucessor Lemus (after 1956) aimed to establish a second pillar for the system alongside the bourgeois-military alliance, by reinforcing the division between workers, peasants and the marginalized population. Their policy was to split these sectors along three lines in the following fashion:

1. While the formation of trade unions still remained illegal in the countryside, and the agricultural export economy could expand without government regulation, in the towns a policy of industrialization was pursued, giving the growing industrial working class a certain privilege vis-à-vis the mass of the population. These workers were granted a relative freedom of trade-union organization, a minimum wage legislation and system of social welfare, as well as a housing program.

2. While the agricultural workers and the small peasants practicing a subsistence economy were prey to the expansion of export cultivation, with no protection from the state, the military sought to create or maintain a stratum of middle peasants, involved in family-based commodity production, by way of state credits and the control of basic grain prices.

3. While moderate demands for reform as well as wage demands were granted to the urban trade unions, revolutionary forces, whether within or outside of the trade unions, were mercilessly persecuted, imprisoned and murdered.

Despite this policy, by 1959–60 the militant left in the towns had so gained in strength that one section of the military and the bourgeoisie saw their only opportunity to stave off crisis in far-reaching reforms. In 1960 they overthrew Lemus, formed a transitional government together with socialist representatives of the working class, and prepared to hold free elections in which the militant left was also permitted to take part. This sharp turn to the left led to a new military coup in 1961 under Julio Rivera. Since the support for the transitional government lay principally in the towns, the mass of the agricultural population being still unorganized and to a large extent uninvolved, any resistance was condemned in advance to failure. For a second time, the divisions between the popular sectors played into the hands of the military in a crisis situation.

Julio Rivera and his successor Fidel Sánchez Rivera (after 1967) understood these lessons well. They refined the divisions and strengthened them organizationally. In the towns a new middle stratum had grown up in the wake of industrialization. The generals permitted this stratum to organize political parties. In the universities the regime permitted the left a certain freedom of debate. The urban working class was allowed to organize trade unions for the purpose of wage demands, while working-class militants, and groups that aimed at any social transformation, were still persecuted and even murdered. In the countryside, trade-union organization continued to be forbidden. At the same time, however, 1965 was set as the date for social and minimum-wage legislation for the permanently employed rural workers, so that these were given a certain privilege over the mass of seasonal workers.

The regime then began to organize the groups and individuals whom it had thus privileged. In the 1950s, already, the ruling circles and their party, the Partido de Conciliación Nacional (PCN) sought to build up trade unions among the urban working class that were friendly towards the regime. They gradually succeeded in establishing the Confederación General de Sindicatos (GGS), which at the beginning of the 1960s had more than 15,000 members, twice as many as the left-wing independent unions. In 1957–58 most of the latter had combined to form the Confederación General de Trabajadores Salvadorenos (CGTS). By a combination of concessions to the industrial working class on the one hand, and brutal suppression of left-wing unionists on the other, the regime forced these independent unions from the mid 1960s onwards to confine their activity to economic demands. This abandonment of political demands and struggles found expression in the replacement of the CGTS by the Federación Unitaria Sindical de El Salvador (FUSS).

In the countryside, any attempt at autonomous organization was brutally suppressed. At the same time, however, the military regime attempted to win certain sections of impoverished peasants behind it. In the early 1960s it began to build up a paramilitary anti-revolutionary organization in the countryside called the Organización Democrática Nacionalista (ORDEN). By 1964–65 ORDEN had already assumed a firm structure. It won its members by helping them to escape the worst poverty. Small peasants who joined the organization could be granted favorable credit terms, while seasonal workers could hope for permanent employment. Privileged members or sympathizers of ORDEN would be engaged for public works in the rural districts. In some cases hospital beds or school places were provided for ORDEN members and their families. For many small peasants, ORDEN provided the only escape from poverty. In return, the ORDEN members supervised the villages in which they lived, reported attempts at subversion, watched over the rest of the agricultural population, and sometimes actually liquidated those who were rebellious. By the early 1970s, ORDEN had covered every village and town with a dense network of informers and collaborators. While the number of armed and military organized members of ORDEN never rose above 10,000, it is estimated to have had up to sixty or a hundred thousand loose or occasional collaborators. If family members are added, we can say that at least one- to two-tenths of the entire rural population were linked up with ORDEN in one way or another. ORDEN directly supported the Guardia Nacional and the president. The generals thus understood how to extract political benefit for their regime from the very poverty of the agricultural population.

The Development of Resistance

The industrialization and political "liberalization" in the towns was accompanied by the development of urban opposition parties and groups. Whereas the bourgeoisie traditionally occupied the key posts in the governing party (PCN) together with the military, during the 1960s a political tendency with the slogan of democratization gained strength even within the fourteen great families of El Salvador. This faction was led by the De Sola family and their Miraflor group of companies, who became consistent opponents of the military regime in the course of the 1970s.

The development of new urban middle strata—either petty bourgeoisie or highly skilled professionals—gave the Partido Demócrata-Cristiano (PDC) its social base. The PDC, formed in 1960, stood for a policy of reform, in which positions of the Chilean Christian-Democrats mingled with social democratic elements. The party demanded freedom of organization for agricultural workers and an economic policy that would accelerate national development by the full use of labor power, rather than the employment of modern machines that had to be paid for by foreign debts. The PDC attracted a steadily growing support in the towns, and in the countryside it organized the first groups of rural workers and peasants out of which the revolutionary people's organizations of the mid 1970s were to emerge.

An older party of liberal opposition, the Partido Acción Renovadora (PAR), also took a turn to the left in the mid 1960s, and adopted left social democrat positions. It called for a fundamental agrarian reform, a far-reaching program of labor procurement by the government, a national cooperative for the marketing and storage of agricultural products, progressive income tax, and a social policy in the interest of the underprivileged sectors.

Once the 1967 elections had shown that the reforming social-democrat positions had found a strong base among the urban working class, the PAR was banned by the military regime. In place of the PAR, there appeared a party of social democrat intellectuals, the Movimiento Nacional Revolucionario (MNR), founded in 1964-65, and the Unión Democrática Nacionalista (UDN), founded in 1968-69, which incorporated former politicians from the left wing of the PAR, and was also strongly influenced by the illegal Partido Comunista Salvadoreño (PCS).

The PCS had increasingly oriented itself after the defeated insurrection of 1932 to trade-union work in the towns, and in the 1960s it confined even this trade-union work to economic demands. Both the Communist-dominated Confederación Unificada de Trabajadores Salvadoreños (CUTS), with some 26,000 members, and the other major urban trade-union grouping, Fesinconstrans, with about 28,000, had stood almost exclusively for economic demands up to the beginning of the 1970s. On the political level, the PCS agitated chiefly for democratic reforms. In the universities it played an important role in organizing Marxist discussion circles, out of which the first beginnings of a guerrilla struggle developed in the course of the 1970s.

It can broadly be said that up to the end of the 1960s the agricultural population was either not organized at all, or was organized in the interest of the regime, while in the towns the middle strata and the working class overwhelmingly followed Christian Democrat and Social Democrat orientations, while the trade unions confined themselves to economic demands. Only in the early 1970s did a broad-based process of radicalization commence, for which the following factors were responsible.

1. The year 1969 saw a war between El Salvador and Honduras, attributable essentially to an ever-growing indebtedness of Honduras towards El Salvador and to the illegal immigration of tens of thousands to Honduras. After the war the border between the two countries was closed, and Salvadorans driven off the land could no longer move across to the relatively thinly settled Honduras. The number of marginalized and completely landless people rose in the early 1970s by leaps and bounds.

2. The number of industrial workers also underwent a steep rise in the first half of the 1970s. At the same time the real wage level constantly fell. The purely economic policy of the trade unions, which had still been successful in the 1960s, had come up against its limits.

3. The PDC, MNR and UDN had combined for the presidential elections of 1972 into the Unión Nacional de Oposición (UNO), under the leadership of the Christian Democrat Napoleón Duarte. It was only through blatant electoral fraud that the PCN managed to secure the victory of its presidential candidate. A constitutionalist faction in the army made a coup against the illegal government and installed Duarte as president. After a few days, however, Duarte was overthrown by the reactionary majority of the armed forces under

Colonel Molina. Molina became president. Duarte was imprisoned and exiled, along with many other politicians from the urban opposition parties. These reform oriented parties were thus thrown into uncompromising opposition to the regime.

4. The regime stepped up its repression against even the reformist left. Numerous intellectuals and trade unionists were imprisoned and expelled from the country. ORDEN and the terrorist organizations of the radical right began a policy of systematic persecution and assassination of trade unionists, peasant leaders and intellectuals. Persecution of the urban and reformist organizations also led to their radicalization and to attempts to bring the reformist forces, whose perspectives had come up against their economic and political limits, together with the revolutionary groups.

In June 1974, the peasant league Federación Católica de Campesinos Salvadoreños (FECCAS), set up in the 1960s by the Christian Democrats and the Catholic church, combined together with the left trade-union organization FUSS, the teachers' union ANDES, and other trade-union organizations, into the Frente de Acción Popular Unifacada (FAPU). Representatives of the reform-oriented political parties took part in FAPU as observers. FAPU viewed the Molinas regime as a fascist military dictatorship. In its strategic perspective, the mass organizations of the left, and the revolutionary sectors of workers, peasants, intellectuals and the church, should join together with the democratic and reformist forces into a broad political front (Frente Político Amplio) against the regime. By combining parliamentary and extra-parliamentary struggle, this front should struggle in the first instance against the rising cost of living, and for minimal democratic liberties.

The question of an alliance with the reformist forces, however, led to a split in the FAPU. The peasant league FECCAS, increasingly radicalized in a Marxist direction, split away from the FAPU in 1975. This move was followed by other mass organizations of the left. In the same year, FECCAS joined forces with the left-wing rural workers' Unión de Trabajadores del Campo (UTC) and certain urban trade unions and students' and teachers' organizations, to form the Bloque Popular Revolucionario (BRP). Since FECCAS and UTC, each with 6,000 members, were by far the strongest individual organizations of the militant left, the Bloque was not only the dominant opposition force in the agricultural sector, but the largest revolutionary organization in El Salvador in general. By 1978 the Bloque was estimated to have around 30,000 members.

The Bloque concentrated its activity on mobilizing and organizing the workers and peasants, and aimed to establish a revolutionary people's government (Gobierno Popular Revolucionario) on the basis of a workers' and peasants' alliance under proletarian leadership ("*alianza obrero-campesina con hegemonia proletaria*"). FAPU, on the other hand, remained more open to an alliance with the reformist parties and worked together with them on various committees. But FAPU, too, worked in the long run for a "revolutionary people's government of workers and peasants."

In parallel with these mass organizations, the early 1970s saw the development of a guerrilla struggle. The oldest guerrilla group, the Fuerzas Populares de Liberación (FPL) was formed in 1970 from the radical wing of the Communist party and Marxist discussion circles in the universities. The FPL saw its activity as defense and protection against ORDEN and other repressive forces directed against the peasants' and workers' organizations. From 1967–77, the FPL was able to recruit a large number of workers as the repression against the trade unions was intensified.

The Ejército Revolucionario del Pueblo (ERP) was formed in 1972. When one of its leaders, the historian and writer Roque Dalton García, criticized the military activism of the ERP and called for the subordination of armed struggle to political struggle, he was liquidated in 1975 by the militaristic faction of the ERP. This led to a split in the ERP and the foundation of the Fuerzas Armadas de Resistencia Nacional (FARN). The FARN kidnapped several representatives of multinational firms in El Salvador, as well as members of the country's fourteen families, holding them for ransom, and obtaining more than 40 million dollars between 1975 and 1979. Even if the connections between the popular organizations and the guerrilla groups are not visible, it is clear that a part of this sum found its way to the popular organizations.

The Intensification of the Situation
from the Mid 1970s

In the mid 1970s, the situation facing the military regime was as follows:

1. Against the background of an economic development locked in crisis, there was a rapid growth in the number of discontented workers, of landless and unemployed agriculturalists, and, in the slum quarters, of the marginalized population.

2. Revolutionary mass organizations had arisen alongside the mass organizations of the government. And while the lower strata of the population were still divided among themselves, now those that were hostile to the government were also organized.

3. The urban parties and trade unions that in the 1960s had been moderate and oriented to reform were now radicalized.

4. The state's monopoly of violence had been broken. If the security forces of the military and the reactionary bourgeoisie fired on the workers and peasants, then the guerrilla groups also fired on the military and the bourgeoisie.

5. The bourgeoisie was itself split into a reactionary wing and a wing with a democratic orientation. There were even constitutionalist groupings within the military itself, and these had proved strong enough in 1972 to make a coup against the electoral fraud.

In 1975–76 the Molina government sought to defuse this critical situation by a cautious agrarian reform. The rural oligarchy and the association of private businessmen, ANEP, raised a storm against even the first timid reform project; 59,000 hectares in the eastern cotton-growing region was to be distributed to 12,000 peasant families, and the big landowners were to receive the full market price. The proprietors affected organized themselves in the Eastern Region Farmers' Front (FARO), which soon spread right across the country and, together with ANEP, mobilized almost the entire private sector against the reform. This led to a government crisis, with the opponents of reform and the extreme right wing of the PCN and the military under General Romero emerging as victor. This right wing, together with ANEP and FARO, organized the radical right terrorist groups Falange and UGB, who proceeded with murder, torture and terror against both revolutionary and reformist forces in the trade unions, parties, popular organizations and church. By electoral fraud, this right wing under Romero managed to seize the presidency as well in 1977.

Only a few days after Romero's "electoral victory" on 28 December 1977, the military massacred demonstrators in San Salvador. In memory of this massacre, a third left organization, formed in 1978, took the name Liga Popular 28 de Febrero (LP-28). Under Romero, ORDEN and the UGB stepped up their terror. For many reformists, there was no choice left but exile (even many members of the De Sola family left the country), or adhesion to the revolutionary underground. The revolutionaries defended themselves. While the reformist parties and organizations were robbed of their leaders and condemned to inactivity, a particular polarization took place in the rural sector. Every small town and even every village saw a split between the supporters of ORDEN (generally small peasants) and those of the Bloque and the FAPU (mostly rural laborers). ORDEN and the military persecuted every individual suspected of subversion, and 1977 saw bloody attacks upon sectors of the agricultural population. The popular organizations and guerrilla groups resisted bravely.

In the rural districts, the beginnings of a civil war developed in the most literal sense of the term, growing still more intense after November 1977, when the "law in defense and guarantee of public order" came into force. It was not just the armed forces that fought against the agricultural population in these regions, but the armed forces together with one section of the rural population who fought against the other section.

In San Salvador, members of the popular organizations occupied foreign embassies and churches, to draw attention to the massacres in the rural districts and compel the release of political prisoners. While the majority of the Catholic clergy supported the moderate opposition forces, a minority, under the leadership of the archbishop of San Salvador, Oscar Romero, in certain cases actually supported the demands of the popular organizations. In both universities, following various massacres of students by the military from 1975 onwards, the guerrilla groups found a pool for recruitment upon which they could draw almost without limit.

At the same time, falling prices for coffee in the world market and a bad harvest in 1978 owing to climatic conditions, as well as a high rate of inflation, led to declining real wages for rural workers and a consequent rise in their combativity. By the late summer of 1978, the domestic political situation in El Salvador had developed into a permanent violent conflict between the extreme right (and its supporters among the agricultural population) and the popular organizations and guerrilla groups of the left. From September 1978 onwards, the U.S., under the direct influence of the popular insurrection in neighboring Nicaragua, sought once again to bring into play the moderate opposition forces and to compel the Romero government to democratic concessions. By now even the Salvadoran private sector, and its ANEP organization, were pressing Romero to make such concessions after resistance by FARN and continuing violent clashes had led to a hectic flight of capital (some 300 million dollars in 1978). The majority of foreign business people had left the country. The Japanese business community, for example, declined from 2,400 to 200 individuals.

At the beginning of March 1979, Romero gave in, repealed the public order law and was immediately faced with strike action by sections of the urban working class, now dominated not by the moderate unions but by the revolutionary popular organizations. It was significant that these strikes included political action in solidarity with the demands of other striking workers.

The workers in the La Constancia and La Tropical bottling plants, a majority of whom were organized in the unions of the Bloque, and a minority in those of the FAPU, went on strike in support of thirty concrete economic and social demands. The army intervened. On 10 March violent clashes took place between demonstrators and the armed forces, with at least seven demonstrators being killed. During the following days, 24 other factories came out on strike in solidarity with the workers of La Constancia and La Tropical. On 19 March the power workers' union, its 1,500 members belonging to FAPU, called a 23-hour sympathy strike, crippling industry and commerce. The power workers locked themselves in the power stations and threatened to blow these up if the military intervened. The armed forces and bosses admitted defeat. Twenty of the thirty demands of the bottling plant workers were conceded.

The right wing made a brutal reply. By the end of April, ORDEN had murdered more than fifty members of the Bloque in the countryside and in the slums. Also in March and April, more than 130 people vanished without trace. At the same time, the Carter administration stepped up its attempt to put together a bloc of the center that could launch a democratic initiative. This bloc was to consist of the Christian Democrats, the De Sola family and a group of parliamentarians including the President of the National Assembly, Leonardo Echevarría. In February, Echevarría had already met Carter for a "working breakfast." The extreme right, for its part, lined up behind the Hill family (one of the fourteen families), and Colonel Eduardo Iraheta, and opted for a decisive violent destruction of the left. General Romero's decline now began.

At the beginning of May the Bloque occupied the embassies of Costa Rica and France, as well as the San Salvador cathedral, demanding the release of five of its leading members. A demonstration in front of the cathedral was fired on by the army. More than 20 demonstrators were killed on the steps of the church (some sources say 40). Archbishop Oscar Romero supported the demands of the Bloque. The Christian Democrat leader, Colonel Ernesto Claramount, living in exile in Costa Rica, called for a coup by the constitutionalist sectors of the army. General Romero, following diplomatic pressure from the U.S., declared himself ready for a "national dialogue" with the moderate opposition parties. The popular organizations, however, were to be excluded from this dialogue. On 22 May the military fired on a demonstration by the Bloque, killing 14 people. Altogether during that month, 188 people died in clashes of this kind.

While these clashes and the guerrilla war in the countryside continued throughout the summer, the U.S. succeeded in wresting from General Romero the concession that the moderate opposition politicians (Christian Democrats) could return from exile, while seeking to build up Napoleón Duarte as the leading figure of the moderate opposition. These attempts were also supported by Archbishop Oscar Romero, who increasingly distanced himself from the Bloque for its use of violence. The "national dialogue" failed to take place, as General Romero did not accept the preconditions placed by the Christian Democrats and the MNR, demanding the disbanding of ORDEN and the UGB.

The Coup and the New Junta

The victory of the Sandinistas in Nicaragua was seen by the popular organizations in El Salvador as proof that a dictatorship really could be overthrown by a determined population. In September the unrest in both town and country rapidly intensified, workers supporting the Bloque and the FAPU occupying four factories in San Salvador, and the popular organizations declared 1980 the year of liberation.

The increasing polarization and the failure of attempts at a "national dialogue" left the moderate opposition forces only the solution that the Christian Democrat leaders had already called for in May. On 15 October 1979 a section of the army made a coup, overthrew Romero, disarmed all the officers who had held ministerial posts in Romero's government, dismissed the armed forces' ten generals and prematurely retired many higher and middle-ranking officers. The new junta and cabinet was an alliance between conservatives and left Christian Democrats and Social Democrat forces from the urban sector, intent on "radical reforms" within the capitalist system. Not only were the extreme right excluded, so too were the popular organizations and those forces set on abolishing the capitalist system itself.

FAPU was represented by Jaime Abdul Gutiérrez (a junta member), conservative, from a pro-U.S. faction in the army, which has allowed the overtly fascist elements in the military, implicated in numerous crimes against the population, to go about unpunished. The Defense Minister, Colonel José García, belonged to this same faction. Colonel Adolfo Arnoldo Majano (a junta member) represented a group of young constitutionalist officers, who were suppressed in the army, but gained strength following the coup of 1972 and were held not to have "compromised with imperialism." Mario Andino (a junta member), head of the local Phelps Dodge subsidiary, represented that faction of the fourteen big bourgeois families led by the De Solas, who stood for a democratic initiative and agrarian reform, but could do nothing against the reactionary agrarian oligarchy.

The new agriculture minister also belonged to this reform-oriented faction of the fourteen families. He was already minister of agriculture under Molina, subsequently resigning when his land reform projects were rejected. Román Mayorga Quirós (a junta member), rector of the Catholic university UCA, represents a policy oriented towards Catholic social doctrine, pragmatically set on concrete measures to improve the situation of the lower strata of the population. The education minister and the minister for planning also belong to this political tendency. Guillermo Ungo (a junta member) is head of the social-democratic MNR, while the finance minister and the justice minister were both also close to the right wing of that party. The Christian Democrats provided the foreign minister and the minister-president. The economic ministry was given to a bourgeois technocrat; the ministry of labor to a leading member of the Communist Party.

This composition makes clear that the new government essentially aimed at an effective economy with a strong social component. The junta proclaimed its intention to guarantee freedom of political and trade-union organization without ideological discrimination, as well as freedom of speech, press and assembly. In the junta's program, the prevailing economic and social structures were said to post obstacles to the country's development. Above all, a basic agrarian reform and a reform of the financial system were promised. On the other hand, the program guaranteed private property in its "social function."

Despite this declaration of intent, the junta immediately proclaimed a state of emergency and banned meetings of more than three people. Security forces raided four of the occupied factories and arrested more than 70 workers. The popular organizations accordingly viewed the junta as simply a new form of the familiar Salvadoran military dictatorship, and called for a new popular uprising. This insurrection, however, failed to materialize. By the end of October, several clashes had taken place between demonstrators and security forces, in which more than 100 demonstrators were shot. The junta declared that both the arrest of workers and the murder of demonstrators were the acts of groups in the security forces that were not under its control. In the second week of November, 60 members of the National Guard were discharged, 12 being brought before the courts. After the Bloque had occupied the economic and labor ministries for some two weeks, the junta agreed in principle to the Bloque's demands for higher wages, lower basic food prices, a freeze on bus fares, freedom for political prisoners, the dissolution of ORDEN and a settlement to several labor disputes.

After subsequent dialogues between the popular organizations and the junta, arranged via the Sandinistas, the popular organizations confined their agitation to concrete demands. The Bloque's spokesperson, Juan Chacón, declared: "This is the first Salvadoran government that recognizes the justice of our demands."

The Collapse of the Junta and the Turn Towards Civil War

The bourgeois-military junta and its cabinet were in fact a combination of forces whose social base lay only in a minority of the Salvadoran population. To the left, there stood the revolutionary popular organizations with their strong support among the rural workers, sections of the small peasants, industrial workers, marginal population, students and the lower ranks of the clergy. To the extent that the transformation of the rural economy, as depicted above, expelled ever larger sections of the rural population even from the transitional forms between independent work and wage labor, turning them into pure agricultural wage laborers, the socio-economic basis of the split in the agricultural population disappeared and the revolutionary left tended to gain growing influence in the countryside. To the right of the junta, there were the members of ORDEN (even if this organization was formally disbanded), which still had considerable influence among the small peasants and marginal population, and among those who saw themselves faced with the loss of a relative privilege in poverty by the junta's reform policy; groups whose social base (the socio-economic fragmentation of the agricultural population) was becoming ever more narrow—a fact that only intensified their violent readiness for self-defense. Also on the extreme right were to be found the great majority of the bourgeoisie, of the fourteen great families and of the senior military commanders. In the middle stood the government, supported by the reform-oriented urban middle strata, by a small minority of the bourgeoisie proper, by sections of the industrial working class and the army, and the majority of the higher clergy. And this government of the center was itself split into numerous factions, which Lilian Jiménez of the Communist Party saw as stretching from Communist through fascistoid officers, and which can be divided into two major blocs: on the one hand the bloc of the bourgeoisie and military, for whom the intended reforms were only an extreme measure for de-escalating the domestic political situation, and who therefore sought to restrict the reforms to those necessary for this end; on the other hand the young constitutionalist officers, the intellectuals and the politicians of the traditional urban opposition parties, for whom these reforms were only the first step in a series of far-reaching structural measures. This internally divided government was forced by the pressure of the revolutionary popular organizations, as well as by its own supporters among the urban population, to a reform policy that had to be pursued against a right wing prepared to oppose it by all possible means.

Faced with this situation, the government's internal unity inevitably collapsed, with the two blocs pulling increasingly apart. From last November [i.e., of 1979], all proposed reforms were wrecked in the same way. The junta declared a reform measure. The business associations prevented its practical execution and frequently found support for this in the right-wing bloc within the government. This right-wing bloc was led by the defense minister José Guillermo García and included the junta members Colonel Jaime Abdul Gutiérrez and Mario Andino. Workers under the leadership of the popular organizations then sought to compel the reform by mass struggle. The extreme right-wing fraction of the armed forces and police brutally repressed the workers, either with support from the right-wing bloc within the government, or in flagrant contravention of the junta's instructions. By the end of 1979, 350 people had been killed by the armed forces since the junta took power. The conflict that led to the collapse of the government also proceeded in the same way. The left demanded wage increases for the coffee workers. In the first half of December, the junta accepted this demand and decreed an increase. The coffee planters ignored the decree. Agricultural workers went on strike and occupied the plantations. Sections of the armed forces evicted the workers with the most brutal violence—not on government orders, but with cover from the right wing in the junta and cabinet. Forty workers were murdered on one farm alone, "El Refugio." In this way, the junta and cabinet lost more and more power to the commanders of the armed forces and the right-wing bloc.

At the end of December nine civilian ministers demanded that the junta take a clear position against the terror campaign abetted by the extreme right wing in the military. They also demanded the resignation of the defense minister and Mario Andino. They demanded, too, that the leadership of the armed forces accept democratization—otherwise they would themselves resign. In the beginning of January [of 1980] the left-wing civilian junta members Róman Mayorga Quirós and Guillermo Ungo stepped down, leaving the big bourgeois Mario Andino as the only remaining civilian. The entire cabinet resigned as well, with the sole exception of the defense minister. The right-wing bloc had won the day, and any reformist solution to El Salvador's problems was now impossible. The officers could only find a right-wing fraction of the Christian Democrats to collaborate with them in a new government.

The year 1980, proclaimed by the popular organizations as the "year of liberation," began with the preparation of civil war. The popular organizations and guerrilla groups on the one hand, ORDEN and the business associations on the other, stepped up their efforts to arm their supporters. The traditional parties of the urban opposition and the trade unions overwhelmingly came down on the side of the popular organizations. The clandestine Communist party made known its agreement with the FLP and FARN guerrillas. The three popular organizations and the UDN established coordinating organs at the local and national levels with the aim of achieving the unity of the left. This revolutionary bloc has been working since the middle of January to establish a "Unidad Popular" that would encompass the more progressive sections of the army (loosely organized around the young constitutionalist officers) as well as the traditional urban opposition parties, groups and trade unions. By the end of the month, the university intellectuals of UCA, the MNR and sections of the Catholic clergy under the leadership of Archibishop Romero declared themselves ready to support this Unidad Popular. A further section of the clergy, under the leadership of Bishop Pedro Aparicio, declared a crusade against communism. Rank-and-file priests and monks, for their part, joined the revolutionary organizations by the hundreds.

A deep split also developed within the armed forces. A crucial role in the coup of 15 October 1979 had been played by the "Juventud Militar" group of young constitutionalist officers. This movement can be seen as the successor to the reform-oriented wing of the armed forces of the late 1940s, 1950s and 1960s. In 1968–69 Colonel Adolfo Majano had established a training program in the military academy designed to familiarize competent officers with socio-political problems, so as to form a military cadre able to deploy instruments of social and economic policy, as well as weapons, in dealing with their country's problems. The socio-economic situation rapidly brought home to the officers who experienced this program that El Salvador's problems could only be mastered by radical structural changes. Juventud Militar thus envisaged not only political democratization, in accordance with the Salvadoran constitution, but also the nationalization of foreign trade and the banks, and agrarian reform to promote national economic development.

With this ideological development, Juventud Militar gradually eroded the prevailing consensus between the extreme right wing of the military and the moderate reform wing. Even though these two factions had taken turns in overthrowing one another over the previous four decades, neither had ever sought the other's total elimination. Juventud Militar, however, was repressed as far as possible under the Molina and Romero governments. It sought in turn, after the coup of 15 October 1979, to neutralize the right-wing senior officers by setting up soldiers' councils designed to invigilate recalcitrant commanders. It seems that this experiment backfired in several military zones and strengthened the hand of the Defense Minister, José García, who emerged as the most powerful member of the junta. In early March the Government announced sweeping measures nationalizing the banks and effecting an agrarian reform. The assassination of Archbishop Oscar Romero appears to have been a calculated rightist provocation, aimed at exacerbating tension as well as eliminating an influential opponent. In early May Majano attempted to arrest one of the commanders of the paramilitary forces linked to García, Roberto D'Aubuisson. This attempt met strong resistance within the military hierarchy. García dismissed Majano from his post and appointed Jaime Abdul Gutiérrez as sole Army commander. This marked the eclipse of the "pro-constitutionalist" faction and the imposition of ultra-rightist hegemony within the junta. The U.S. Ambassador, Robert White, was said to have played a "mediating role" in these events.[1]

Meanwhile the military and para-military forces passed ahead with their version of the agrarian reform. This entailed not only renewed offensives in the countryside but also a division of some large estates in the interests of the leaders and supporters of ORDEN. In this way the rightists have found a way to exploit the reform program for their own ends, sacrificing the interests only of weaker, or more liberal-minded, land owners. The junta continues to represent a section of the Christian Democrats and to enjoy the support, or toleration, of the bulk of the bourgeoisie. So long as there is no open split in the armed forces the position of the Salvadoran junta remains much stronger than that of Somoza's regime in 1978-9 since the latter had, by this time, lost any significant social base.

8. *The Politics of Salvadoran Christian Democracy* *

By Stephen Webre

From the days of John F. Kennedy's "Alliance for Progress" Christian Democratic parties in Latin America were viewed as representatives of mod-

---

[1] For former Ambassador White's views on the current situation in El Salvador, see Readings 42 and 52.—Eds.

* From *José Napoleón Duarte and the Christian Democratic Party in Salvadoran Politics 1960-1972*, Louisiana State University Press, 1979.

eration and reform—an alternative to Castroism as well as the vulgar feudal orders of a Stroessner in Paraguay or a Trujillo in the Dominican Republic. Reactionaries and supporters of military dictatorship taunted the Christian Democrats as "watermelon men"—"green on the outside, but Red on the inside" for their notions about land reform and returning the colonels to their barracks. For the U.S., however, the Christian Democrats represented a force that would ameliorate the myriad political, economic and social ills and reduce the Latin left to irrelevance without affecting U.S. strategic interests and multinational profits.

The Salvadoran Christian Democratic Party—the party of junta president Napoleón Duarte—is described in the following excerpt from Stephen Webre's book.

Stephen Webre has been a Doherty Fellow researching local administration and the defense of corporate privilege in 17th century Guatemala. He received his M.A. degree from Newcomb College, Tulane University. The book from which the following piece is excerpted was originally Webre's M.A. thesis.

THE period of democratic experimentation in El Salvador in the 1960s coincided with a time of apparent electoral stability in many Latin American countries and thus served to confirm the beliefs of those who argued that the process of political development was linear and cumulative and would inevitably lead to a golden era of civil supremacy and parliamentary democracy. Somehow the collapse in 1964 of the boisterous Brazilian democracy went unappreciated amidst the general optimism. Few people would have guessed that the authoritarianism of the Brazilian colonels and not such enthusiastically welcomed democratic regimes as that of Rómulo Betancourt in Venezuela would come to characterize Latin America in the 1970s or that even such countries of long democratic tradition as Chile and Uruguay would ultimately produce repressive regimes.

What non-Communist progressives sought in Latin America in the years immediately following the Cuban revolution was a safe reformist alternative to the threat of a proliferation of Castroist revolutions in the area. The most substantial tradition for such a movement was that provided by the Peruvian APRA and such other "social democratic" parties as Acción Democrática in Venezuela and Liberación Nacional in Costa Rica. Although these movements enjoyed impeccable democratic credentials forged in the struggle against dictatorship that passed for revolutionary activity in most of Latin America before the triumph of Fidel Castro, they had over the years grown staid and conservative. Another possible model, although one peculiar to a single country, was the Mexican PRI.

A third alternative, which must have seemed to come virtually from nowhere in the late 1950s and early 1960s, was Christian Democracy. The expansion of this movement was remarkable. By 1964, the year of the first Christian Democratic victories in El Salvador, there were similar parties in sixteen of the twenty Latin American republics. Only Honduras, Paraguay, Haiti, and Cuba lacked them. For the most part, Christian Democracy in Latin America was a relatively recent phenomenon. Although the oldest parties, those of Uruguay and Chile, were of much earlier origin, most of the parties were founded in the period following World War II. Their leaders were inspired by the role European Christian Democratic parties had played in the postwar recovery of West Germany, Italy, and France.

The early 1960s were important years for Christian Democracy in all of Latin America. In 1963, the Peruvian Christian Democrats joined the government in coalition with Fernando Belaúnde Terry's Acción Popular and, by the end of the year, elected one of their own leaders mayor of Lima. In Venezuela, Rafael Caldera's Social Christian COPEI placed second in the 1963 presidential race and was the only party that actually gained in voter support over the previous elections. By far the most successful of all the Latin American Christian Democratic parties in 1964, however, was the Chilean PDC. In the municipal elections in 1963 the Christian Democrats had suddenly replaced the Radicals as Chile's leading political party. Then in 1964 Eduardo Frei Montalva's triumph in the presidential race made Chile the first Latin American republic to come under a modern Christian Democratic administration.

Many observers hailed Frei's victory as the coming of a new era in Latin America—an era in which social injustice would fall beneath the onslaught of humane and Christian government operating in an open atmosphere of democracy and liberty. To reformers, progressives, even revolutionaries who found communism distasteful, Christian Democracy seemed to offer an excellent alternative. Frei's defeat of a Communist-backed coalition led by Salvador Allende Gossens offered encouragement to those who feared that all of Latin America was in imminent danger of Communist takeover. The Communists themselves recognized the potential significance of this setback. Although Radio Havana attributed the Frei victory to fraud, intimidation, and bribery, Cuban Prime Minister Fidel Castro candidly admitted that "sometimes our opponents surpass us in ability."

By the end of the decade, it would become abundantly clear that Christian Democracy was no more a panacea or a wave of the future than had been the APRA movement or even the guerrilla socialism practiced by Castro in Cuba. In particular, observers tended to overlook the importance of the fact that Frei owed his victory to a coalition with Chile's intransigent right. Still, in 1964 when Frei's triumph was fresh, all was euphoria and optimism.

Latin American Christian Democrats state with pride that theirs is an ideological movement, a claim significant in a region where political parties have seldom been more than vehicles for personal ambition, with little goal other than the conquest and enjoyment of high political office. From the beginning, the leaders of the Salvadoran PDC emphasized this major difference between their party and the crowd of ephemeral, personalist parties that continued to characterize Salvadoran politics. Their party, they declared upon announcing its formation, would be "permanent [and] purely ideological in character, . . . something new in our country."

The most important single source of inspiration for the Christian Democratic movement has been the social doctrine of the Roman Catholic church, especially as set forth in Pope Leo XIII's encyclical *Rerum Novarum* (1891). Leo attacked both Marxist socialism and classical liberalism. He admitted the similarity between many socialist tenets and the teachings of the Gospel, but he condemned the notions of economic materialism and determinism as denials of the spiritual nature of man. He defended private property as a natural right but cautioned that it must be held and used in a socially just manner. He upheld the rights of labor against capitalist exploitation and called for state intervention on behalf of workers. He urged trade unionization, collective bargaining, experiments in agricultural cooperatives, cooperation among the classes (whose natural enmity he denied), and the preservation and strengthening of such traditional social institutions as church and family. In short, his was a call for Christians to work together to build a better society based upon traditional spiritual values and founded in the teachings of the Catholic church. Forty years later, Pope Pius XI echoed Leo's ideas in his *Quadraggesimo Anno* (1931), a condemnation of laissez-faire liberalism and defense of proletarian organization. More recently, two encyclicals of Pope John XXIII, *Mater et Magistra* and *Pacem in Terris*, have provided further reinforcement for the Social Christian position as has the important *Populorum Progessio* (1967) of Paul VI.

The Christian Democratic party of El Salvador emerged from a series of meetings dedicated to the study of the writings of these men and others. The men who participated in these discussions were mostly lawyers who had studied political theory at the National University. They were also Catholics attracted by the spiritual foundation of Christian Democracy. Roberto Lara Velado, Abraham Rodríguez, and such younger men as the student leaders Héctor

Dada Hirezi, José Ovidio Hernández, and Carlos Herrera Rebollo, were all familiar with the works of Maritain, Caldera, and Frei. On the other hand, some were not so well read. Party leader Napoleón Duarte, an engineer by training and profession, freely admits the deficiency of his own ideological preparation. In the early days of the movement, he devoted his time and talent almost exclusively to the mechanical aspects of party organization, leaving theory to the lawyers and humanists.

Not surprisingly, the Catholic background of Christian Democracy at times caused the movement to be identified in the public mind with the church itself. In Latin America, where passivism and obscurantism rather than progressivism traditionally characterized the social attitude of the ecclesiastical establishment, this was potentially a source of great misunderstanding and embarrassment. The radical and Marxist Left often criticized the Christian Democrats for their supposed "clericalism." The truth was, however, that, despite the religious inspiration and symbolism evident in the movement, there were no formal and very few informal ties between it and the church. In fact, in most cases neither the parties nor the church was willing to accept or encourage any such cooperation. Christian Democracy is not a religion. It is a social and political movement concerned with worldly rather than heavenly kingdoms. The founders of the Salvadoran party made their position as clear as possible when they declared that the PDC "categorically denies that it is in any way directed by the Catholic Church or any other religious body, believing that politics and religion should not be mixed."

While the Left has attacked the Christian Democrats for their "clericalism," the Catholic Right has generally disowned them for their progressivism. There are some issues upon which the PDC and conservative churchmen and laity have found agreement, such as support for religious education and opposition to birth control, but there are many others on which they have remained antagonists.

In addition to the accusation of clericalism, another charge frequently leveled at the Christian Democrats was that they were an international party. They denied this, but Christian Democracy was in fact an international movement and the individual parties always stressed their ties with one another. Since 1947 there has been a hemispherewide confederation of Social Christian parties, the Christian Democratic Organization of America (Organización Demócrata Cristiana de América, ODCA), which, while it cannot compel adherence to its policies, does exercise a great deal of influence over its member organizations.

In the eyes of nationalists both right and left, the international character of the Christian Democratic movement was only slightly more suspect than its emphasis upon a foreign policy of international cooperation. The Salvadoran PDC was as concerned with national autonomy and rights as any nationalist group, but—with the notable exception of its wholehearted support of the government's position in the 1969 war with Honduras—it generally translated this concern into a call for cooperation, regional integration, and international social justice, instead of an irrational isolationism. Of particular interest to El Salvador's Christian Democrats was the strengthening of the Latin position in the Organization of American States, the defense of the rights of smaller countries in the United Nations and of producer nations in world markets, and the economic integration of Central America.

The PDC, in fact, favored an international order from which imperialism and colonialism of all types were absent. To critics who charged that Christian Democrats took their orders from Rome, Caracas, or Santiago de Chile, Roberto Lara Velado replied not only that this was not true but also that, even if it were, these were hardly sinister imperial powers on a level with Washington, Moscow, or Peking, from whom the official party and the Marxists derived their inspiration. Christian Democracy, Lara Velado explained, differed from the two major alternatives in that it was not an imperial ideology. According to him, liberalism and communism both required the subordination of smaller states to larger ones in order to function properly. Thus, while the liberal and Communist systems achieved their highest expression in the world's three great imperial states—the United States, Russia, and China—Christian Democracy was more suited to the small national or territorial state that wished only to safeguard its own rights and autonomy.

The Salvadoran PDC repeatedly condemned colonialism and was as critical of the Soviet version as of the North American, citing Cuba as a victim of both forms. The party's first national convention in San Salvador in 1961 condemned the Cuban revolution as a betrayal of the Cuban people's struggle for liberation and warned of the threat it posed of Soviet domination in the Caribbean. Equally conscious of a threat from the North, the Christian Democrat minority in the Salvadoran Legislative Assembly successfully urged the passage in 1965 of a resolution condemning the United States military intervention in the Dominican Republic. On the issue of economic penetration, Lara Velado opposed the establishment of a local branch of the First National City Bank of New York, as "another spearhead of foreign imperialism," and Abraham Rodríguez, in his 1967 presidential campaign, condemned the Rivera government's policy of floating large foreign loans for public works projects, then using the money to buy foreign materials and hire imported workers and technicians. In 1969, José Napoleón Duarte, then serving as mayor of San Salvador, shocked a gathering of Central American municipal officials in Vera Cruz, Mexico, by condemning United States policy in Latin America as designed to "maintain the Iberoamerican countries in a condition of direct dependence upon the international political decisions most beneficial to the United States, both at the hemispheric and world levels. Thus [the North Americans] preach to us of democracy while everywhere they support dictatorships."

Continentwide, Christian Democrats resist location within the simplistic typology of Right-versus-Left. A Nicaraguan Social Christian leader has made perhaps the most precise statement of this problem:

> If by left we understand the struggle for social justice, the great battle for the social and economic redemption of the people, the incorporation of workers and peasants into the mainstream of culture and civilization, then undoubtedly we are leftist. If, however, by left is understood historical materialism, communist totalitarianism, and the suppression of liberty, then in no way are we leftists. If by right is understood the conservation of the spritual values of civilization, the historical legacy of humanity, and the dignity and liberty of man, then there can be no doubt that we are rightists. But if by right we understand the conservation of an economic order based on the exploitation of man by man, on social injustice, we energetically refuse the name of rightists.

Adhering to Catholic teaching, Christian Democrats rejected the belief in the ultimate perfectability of man and the determinism therefore inherent in laissez-faire liberalism and Marxist socialism. But the movement itself drew fire from critics for the "determinism" supposedly implicit in its own belief in the inevitability of revolution in Latin America. Christian Democrats believed that the inequities in Latin American society must eventually lead to violence if they were not corrected. Since they did not believe that most of these inequities could be remedied short of drastic structural change, they called in reality for a "revolution" of their own, a peaceful, Christian revolution to prevent a violent, materialist one.

The word "revolution" often appeared in the polemics of the Salvadoran party. A revolution, the party declared in 1966, was unavoidable. But, spokesmen hastened to add, the Christian Democratic revolution would not be violent or destructive of national institutions. Rather it would be a scientifically and technically planned process designed to effect, within the limits of liberty and national reality, a peaceful and rapid change in political, economic, and social structures. In his political memoirs, Napoleón Duarte rejects the Marxian notion that the clash of thesis and antithesis must necessarily lead to a constructive synthesis. It is just as likely to lead to the reinforcement of the thesis or to an orgy of wasteful violence. Change is necessary, Duarte is in effect saying, but it cannot be undertaken lightly or without careful preparation. He likens the revolution contemplated by the Christian Democrats to a controlled chain reaction produced in a nuclear reactor.

The Christian Democratic call for "revolution in liberty" aroused suspicion among observers of all political persuasions. One Uruguayan leftist saw it as an attempt on the part of the Catholic bourgeoisie to "short-circuit" the aspirations of the workers by bringing about minor social change, preserving capitalism, and restoring the temporal authority of the church. In El Salvador, a right-wing clerical polemicist who often faulted the Salvadoran PDC for the thoughts and actions of its Chilean counterpart accused the Christian Democrats of adopting Marxist theory and giving the concept of revolution priority over that of liberty. The notion of the inevitability of such a revolution he condemned as Hegelian and, therefore, presumably determinist, Marxist, and heretical. Finally, he charged that Christian Democrats prefaced democracy with the word "Christian" for the same reason Communists used "people's"—to deceive the masses.

The Christian Democrats had quite definite ideas about the kind of world they hoped to build as a result of their "revolution." The new regime would above all be one of democracy and social justice. From the beginning the Salvadoran party declared these popular aspirations to be its overriding goals. The PDC used the word democracy in the classic political sense—open elections, respect for the dignity of the individual, the guarantee of human and constitutional rights, and an end to persecution and imposition. By social justice the Christian Democrats meant the just payment of labor, the economic and cultural redemption of the peasantry, and a more equitable distribution of property and the fruits of production. Party leaders here placed the greatest stress on the right of the individual Salvadoran to gain a decent living from his work. Above and beyond any moral basis for this position, both Duarte and Lara Velado argued that a more just diffusion of Salvadoran wealth would be beneficial to the nation as a whole, as the increased number of consumers would serve as a stimulus to industrial growth and the widened propertied class would contribute to political stability.

The minimum acceptable standard of living in El Salvador, as defined by party leaders at a round table discussion in 1962, would be one in which every citizen would be guaranteed: (1) a nutritious and filling diet; (2) sanitary, comfortable housing; (3) adequate shoes and clothing; (4) access to medicine and health care; (5) the basic skills of literacy and sufficient vocational preparation to contribute in a productive fashion to the economy; (6) protection in his or her old age.

The key to social justice, according to the PDC, was structural reform designed to remove the obstacles the old order posed to the economic development of the country. It first set forth its plans to accomplish this on a national level in the presidential campaign of 1966–1967. In their platform of that year, the Christian Democrats declared their primary goal to be full employment at dignified wage levels. Since El Salvador had a large corps of unemployed or underemployed citizens, the necessity of a high rate of economic growth was obvious—especially since the rapid increase in population meant that more than 30,000 new workers joined the labor force each year. As more than 60 percent of the existing labor force was already competing for a limited amount of work in the agricultural sector, the PDC hoped to incorporate the increment into nonagricultural pursuits by fostering industrial development and national productivity in general. How this prodigious feat was to be accomplished never was clear, but party leaders constantly invoked the sacred precepts of economic planning and state direction as the answer to the nation's ills.

While they called for industrialization, the Christian Democrats placed virtually equal emphasis upon increasing productivity in the agricultural sphere. They urged a program to increase crop yields, but warned against the ruthless exploitation of the nation's soil resources without attention to the problem of conservation—a particularly important consideration in a country as small as El Salvador. The agricultural problem had a troublesome social aspect as well. Something must be done to insure a decent living for the vast numbers of landless or nearly landless peasants who lived by selling their labor to the large operators. The demand for itinerant farm workers was seasonal. The PDC estimated in 1967 that the average laboring *campesino* worked only 120 days out of the year and guessed the productive income lost each year due to this situation to be more than 80 million colones. The government could employ some of these workers on housing and transportation infrastructure projects, the party declared, but the only lasting solution would be some sort of alteration of the prevailing pattern of land use and ownership.

The Christian Democrats' moderate proposals received little criticism from the left in El Salvador, largely because the government was a more prominent target. Certain facets of the PDC program, however, scandalized traditional liberals on the right who chose to regard the party's approach to the problems of urban and rural labor as an attack upon private property. Very early, party leaders made it clear that they did not consider labor to be a commodity subject to the caprice of the law of supply and demand. When the editorial staff of *El Diario de Hoy* uncritically attacked this position as Marxism, Roberto Lara Velado replied that workers were as much investors as were stockholders and, as such, deserved a share of the company's profits as well as a guarantee of a decent living. He went on to distinguish the Christian Democratic position, based upon the human dignity of the individual worker, from the alternative positions of liberalism and communism. Whereas in a liberal system the means of production remained in the hands of private capital and in a Communist system in the hands of the state, Lara Velado argued, in an ideal Christian Democratic community production would be a free and dignified collaboration between capital and labor. The concept of free collaboration of capital and labor along with the related concept of "communitarian" ownership of the means of production were popular themes in abstract discussions, but party ideologues rarely approached the question of practical implementation.

Although conservatives, usually arguing weakly from the Chilean experience, charged that Christian Democrats favored the destruction of private property as an institution, the position of the Salvadoran PDC on this issue was essentially conservative. In an early declaration the party maintained its belief that property was a natural right justified in that it constituted a fair reward for work and provided for the satisfaction of the individual's present and future material needs. The Christian Democrats, however, also believed that social justice required property-holding to be broadly diffused throughout society. To effect this, they urged just compensation for labor and easily accessible credit to encourage savings and consumption on the part of wage-earners. They also demanded state protection for small proprietors in agriculture, industry, and commerce. The stated economic and social aim of the PDC was the growth of a large, comfortable middle class. Such a class, it believed, would provide the backbone for a stable economy and a durable democracy. As party leaders declared on many occasions, the solution of El Salvador's social problems did not lie in pulling down the oligarchy, but in elevating the oppressed.

Of special concern to Christian Democrats in general and of the Salvadoran party in particular was the position in society of the family and, closely related to this, the position of women. The PDC saw the family as the basic unit of society and repeatedly expressed a determination to strengthen it. According to the party, the family was the primary nucleus of socialization, education, moral formation, and economic activity, and a strong family could provide the vanguard in every struggle from that against hunger to that against juvenile delinquency.

A major obstacle to the achievement of family strength and stability in El Salvador has been the large number (about 50 percent) of households formed from "free unions" instead of legal marriages. This has particular implications for the position of women in society. In the lower classes where the entire family must function as a productive unit in order to stay ahead of starvation, the needs of the family have forced the Salvadoran woman to serve as breadwinner as well as mother. Working-class men, repeatedly bested in the uphill struggle to maintain a hovel full of hungry children, often leave home in search of work, or simply out of frustration. Many never return, abandoning their families entirely. In the city of San Salvador, the vast majority of the market vendors are women, many of whom must provide for families without any assistance from men. In recognition of this situation, the PDC called early for legislation to protect the economic rights of wives and mothers and to require fathers and husbands to meet their domestic responsibilities. Only with her economic interests thus protected, the party declared in its Mother's Day message for 1961, could the Salvadoran woman be free "to accomplish her grand mission as queen of the home and educator of her children."

PDC concern for women's rights and interests was not completely altruistic, of course. Since 1945, women have become increasingly important as voters and political leaders in Latin America. Politicians, Christian Democrats not the least among them, have been quick to recognize this. Women have been particularly receptive to the message of Christian Democracy because of its religious inspiration and because of its emphasis upon social stability and family security.

From a broad examination of party pronouncements on various issues it soon becomes apparent that, although the rhetoric of the PDC may at times have been radical or even revolutionary, the ends and means it actually proposed in El Salvador were generally moderate and at times socially conservative. The PDC's interest in political reform and espousal of traditional Western democratic values are reminiscent of the program of the moderate rightist "Old Guard" PAR which it displaced in 1964 as the dominant opposition party. The movement's scriptural inspiration and its emphasis upon Christian morality appealed particularly to traditionalist sentiment in society as did its claim to be an ideology compatible with El Salvador's Hispanic heritage. The PDC's call for regional (that is, Hispanic) solidarity to be accompanied by the rejection of "alien" ideologies, such as communism and liberalism, represented an attachment to the fundamentals of Salvadoran culture and society. Similarly conservative was the party's desire to maintain an ordered society along established lines through the strengthening of traditional social institutions, such as the family and the church.

The economic programs of the Christian Democratic party may appear at first examination to have been more radical than its social goals. But one should remember that the economic changes the party proposed were designed specifically to achieve the restoration of its vision of an ideal social order. Party theorists were thoroughly committed to the concept of private property which they did not believe to be mutually exclusive with social justice. While they did recognize the need for more broadly distributed property-holding (and, therefore, a large middle class) in order to achieve social justice and political stability, they spoke more of diffusion than of redistribution. The goal was to create new wealth through industrial growth and increased productivity in general and to insure its fair distribution in society, rather than to divide up existing property. In the one area of Salvadoran economic life where this course was clearly impossible, that of land ownership, Christian Democrats agreed, however reluctantly, to the necessity of expropriation and redistribution. But, even here, the PDC opposed precipitous action. The process of redistribution must be keyed to the development of markets, roads, and technical education, in order to guarantee that the peasants would be able to exploit their new holdings in the most efficient manner. Above all, the Christian Democrats insisted that the expropriated landowners be compensated for their lost property.

Salvadoran Christian Democracy was in many ways an ideology well suited to the middle-class lawyers and other professionals who founded and led the party. While it adopted a moral orientation toward the question of social justice, it did not question the concept of class advantage itself. It retained private property as the foundation of economic life and assumed individual inequities in its distribution, condemning such inequities only when they were so gross as to threaten social order and development. It sought the support and cooperation of disadvantaged members of society in order to promote changes that it believed would contribute to the orderly expansion of a propertied middle class, and saw the growth of such a class as the best guarantee of political democracy and a tranquil social order. To manage social tensions from below, the PDC urged the organization of the masses into associations (syndicates, cooperatives, neighborhood organizations) similar to those interest and professional guilds (*gremios*) the elites had always employed to articulate and defend their class positions. The party also advocated measures designed to ease access to the middle class from below and welfarist programs designed to ameliorate the lot of those who inevitably would remain at the bottom. The Christian Democrats hoped through education not only to promote social stability but to inculcate the masses with middle-class values. Thus the PDC stressed wholesomeness and respectability in family life and campaigned against nonmarital unions, irresponsible fathers, alcoholism, and other such socially dissolutive practices as gambling and prostitution.

In spite of the protestations and denials of Christian Democratic leaders, not only in El Salvador but all over Latin America, it is hard to avoid the judgment of one North American scholar that Christian Democratic social theory is "essentially traditional, Catholic corporatism." Christian Democracy is not forward-looking; it is backward-looking: back past the dehumanizing rise of liberalism and nationalism, past the centralizing age of political absolutism, past the secularizing world of the Renaissance, back to the medieval ideal of unity and order, to a world where all Christendom was theoretically a community and where the moral laws that guided man's spiritual and personal life supposedly guided his political and economic activities as well. The applicability of this charming vision to modern industrial society is, of course, highly questionable.

Prescribing against the possibility of social violence from below was a simple matter when compared to the necessity to manage elite attitudes. The PDC's vision of an ideal society, while moderate, required significant concessions on the part of an established oligarchy that had developed an elaborate moral vision of its own to justify the existing order. While the goal of a revolution accomplished solely through Christian suasion and moral education is an attractive one to those who abhor bloodshed, one must be skeptical about its chances for success in any society, much less one such as El Salvador's where the privileged have routinely demonstrated their willingness to employ any means whatsoever to preserve intact their advantages by stifling all but the most innocuous attempts at change. One must particularly doubt the wisdom of advocating the diffusion of power and decision-making responsibility in a region where a major difficulty for governments (whatever their form) has always been that they have generally not been powerful enough to enforce compliance with policies other than those most favorable to established interests.

PART THREE

EL SALVADOR: ASPECTS OF THE PRESENT CRISIS

EDITORS' INTRODUCTION

WHILE the previous Readings and Introductions of this book have dealt with the ways in which the current crisis in Central America have been conceptualized in the U.S. (the notion, for example, of the omnipresent "Soviet threat"), and with the historical backgrounds, we turn now to the actual components of that crisis—the revolutionary organizations, the widespread terror, the process of land reform in El Salvador and the role of the Church. In war, as Herodotus noted, truth is the first casualty. The Salvadoran civil war has generated its share of myths and misconceptions. Here we present materials from a variety of perspectives from which readers can distinguish fact from fiction, rhetorical statements from actual social forces.

The present ruling junta in El Salvador tries to portray itself as a moderate middle way between the extremes of the right and left. Its leader and chief spokesman, the Christian Democrat, José Napoleón Duarte, claims to represent an authentic centrist force contending against tyrants on either side. As such, Duarte and his junta have won the backing of the U.S. government and substantial military aid from Washington. Yet, many are skeptical of this view of Duarte; they suggest that his role may be that of a front man, utilized by the Salvadoran oligarchy and its military allies to insure the continual flow of support and arms from the U.S.

Similarly, the process of land reform serves as the centerpiece of the attempt to portray the junta as a legitimate government with the interests of the Salvadoran peasantry at heart. But behind the glowing reports of agrarian progress lurks a more complex and even sinister reality: a program in which the public relations announcements far outstrip any change in land tenure in the Salvadoran countryside. In the pages that follow, the land reform program is debated among specialists, including some of its actual designers and administrators. These contending treatments are a basis for any genuinely informed opinion on this tangled subject.

The Salvadoran opposition to the junta, and to its programs, is set forth in this part of the book in materials hitherto mostly accessible to specialists on Central America: the actual platforms and statements of the oppositional groups drawn from fugitive pamphlets and monitored radio broadcasts. The organization, positions, personnel and commitments of the Democratic Revolutionary Front (FDR) and of the Farabundo Martí Liberation Front are presented in detail. Their January, 1981, offensive failed in its announced aim of bringing down the junta, yet it also resulted in an open, continuous rebel presence in the mountainous regions adjoining Honduras, and in the ability of the guerrillas to mount assaults against government strongholds in El Salvador's cities, such as the attack on the southern seaport, La Unión, in June, 1981. The rebels have also carried on an intensive campaign to win support from world public opinion, and thus far have received endorsement from many of the democratic nations of Latin America, from much of western Europe, from a joint French-Mexican declaration, and from the Socialist International, which has tried (unsuccessfully so far) to bring about a negotiated solution to the conflict.

Material is also presented on the terror now being conducted in El Salvador, which most observers concede emanates primarily from the oligarchs and groups favorable to the political right. Almost the only issue left to debate is the extent to which the Salvadoran junta itself is responsible for the outrages. The U.S. government's position is a variation of the "rogue cop" theory: that the terror is the lamentable work of military/security forces "out of control," and thus not the direct responsibility of the junta. On the other side is much grisly evidence that killings and torture are carried out within the command structure of the current Salvadoran regime and that these tactics are part of the larger strategy of the U.S.-backed junta to crush the left, and to prevent "another Vietnam" in El Salvador. (A later part of this book will explore the extent to which Washington authorities, striving in their way to avoid "another Vietnam," are making some of the same mistakes which drew the U.S. into the costly and tragic Indochina conflict in the 1950s and 1960s).

Finally, in our account of the basic social forces at work in El Salvador, we must deal with the Roman Catholic church. This pivotal institution holds the allegiance of broad strata of the population, and embodies hopes for a better tomorrow. In transition between its former role as supporter of the established order, and its new mission as sanctifier of a righteous liberation struggle against oppressive rule, the Salvadoran church is a microcosm of the larger conflict in Central America.

Chapter I

THE *Frente* IN THE CIVIL WAR

Editors' Introduction

THE U.S. State Department argues that the guerrillas of El Salvador lack popular support. It claims their previous ability to exploit legitimate grievances against past regimes has been undermined by the reforms of the Duarte government. They are, in short, little more than a small band of Marxist terrorists, externally armed, advised and organized, "interested only in obtaining power through brute force." [1]

Considerable evidence exists in this volume to refute this simplistic notion that El Salvador is nothing more than a Soviet grab for power in this hemisphere.

Journalists and members of Congress have visited guerrilla and refugee camps and found a growing harmony between guerrilla and peasant—so much so that the junta has increasingly adopted the Vietnam solution of separating the guerrilla fish from the friendly peasant ocean in which they swim by draining the ocean. [2] The vast numbers "drained"—some 200,000, by one account, are refugees—is testimony to a different reality from that seen by the U.S. State Department.

Not only has Duarte's land reform been a failure, but the evidence mounts that the guerrillas have strengthened their position significantly since the failure of their "final offensive" in January, 1981, and may now control as much as 20-25 percent of the land area of El

---

[1] John A. Bushnell, Acting Assistant Secretary for Inter-American Affairs, before the Subcommittee for Inter-American Affairs of the House Foreign Affairs Committee, March 5, 1981, reprinted in the *Department of State Bulletin*, April, 1981, p. 41.

[2] See T. D. Allman, "Rising to Rebellion," *Harpers*, March, 1981; Raymond Bonner, "The Agony of El Salvador," *The New York Times Magazine*, February 22, 1981; Alex Drehsler, "The Rebels of El Salvador," *The Boston Globe*, March 8, 1981.

Salvador (mostly in the north along the Honduras boundary and in the southeast).[3]

Moreover, the Democratic Revolutionary Front (FDR), a coalition of, among others, labor unions, professional associations, peasant organizations, and church groups, has in its leadership a large number of Christian Democrats, Social Democrats and other non-Marxists, many of whom were until recently officials of the junta, including its president, Guillermo Ungo.

But legitimate questions can be raised about the degree of power held by FDR moderates. Will they, when and if victory comes, be shunted off by radical Marxists in the Farabundo Martí National Liberation Front (FMLN)? The latter, after all, have the moral credentials—they did the fighting and the dying. More important, they will have the guns and *de facto* military control.

Experiences as varied as Vietnam and Zimbabwe (formerly Rhodesia) provide contrasting precedents. Buddhists and other non-Communist members of South Vietnam's National Liberation Front were in the final analysis window dressing to be discarded after victory. On the other hand, Marxist Robert Mugabe of Zimbabwe, perhaps recognizing a different set of economic imperatives, has been unexpectedly moderate in power.

Even the case of a sucessful revolution in neighboring Nicaragua offers little in the way of what to expect in El Salvador. Nicaragua was less an example of a peasant war than that of a popular, multiclass uprising against an entrenched dictator.[4] Factory owners joined with their workers in the general strike linked to the final offensive

---

[3] See NACLA *Report on the Americas,* "Central America: No Road Back," Vol. XV, No. 3, May–June, 1981, pp. 11–14.

[4] In this respect, Nicaragua can be compared to Cuba, where a multiclass struggle took place against Fulgencio Batista. One key difference between the two revolutions is the role played by the church. In Cuba, the peasants were less influenced by the church, which was tied to the middle and upper classes and soon became part of the counterrevolution. By contrast, the Nicaraguan church supported the revolution, even to the point of condoning armed struggle. Its priests and nuns have been mainstays of the revolution and a vital part of its leadership, although the hierarchy has become less sympathetic to the Sandinista government because of the latter's commitment to a genuine social revolution.

If Cuba ended up being a Communist state and a steadfast ally of the Soviet Union, it remains an intriguing historical question of whether it had to turn out that way. Had there been no embargo, no Bay of Pigs invasion, no unremitting U.S. hostility the first years of the revolution, could Cuba have had a neutralist Communist regime, like Yugoslavia, or even an exciting experiment in democratic socialism? Nicaragua offers the United States a unique opportunity to avoid the past. Or repeat it! See Reading 46 below.

against Anastasio Somoza in June, 1979.[5] Also the extreme left in Nicaragua was never as influential as its counterpart in El Salvador. Lastly, the "final disposition" of the Nicaraguan revolution is yet to be determined.[6]

We are led to the conclusion that no one can offer advance assurance that the revolution in El Salvador will not end up a left-wing dictatorship. Bloody civil wars often do in countries lacking democratic traditions, examples being China, Vietnam and Cuba. On the other hand, Spain, Greece and the Philippines show that when the right triumphs, years of authoritarian rule and coup-ridden regimes are the results.

But matters could be different in Central America if the United States gives the FDR and, in Nicaragua, the Sandinista government a degree of breathing room. Revolutionaries in both countries are undoubtedly aware that twenty years of revolutionary rule in Cuba have amply demonstrated the enormous difficulties that arise when a Western-oriented economy in Latin America is totally severed from the United States. It is in the clear interest of whatever coalition comes to power in El Salvador—even the most left-wing—to maintain economic relations with the United States. But will the United States be willing to maintain economic relations with a revolutionary El Salvador?

U.S. magnanimity has thus far been nowhere visible in postwar Vietnam. Nor has Washington ever suggested détente should include Cuba. Rapprochement with China only exists because the latter promises to be a useful card against the Soviet Union. The example of Chile, where the CIA played a covert role in overthrowing the Allende government, even indicates an unwillingness on the part of the United States to accept duly elected governments which try to build socialism peacefully and democratically.

To a great extent, therefore, the ability of the Salvadoran revolutionaries to carry out their commitment to structural change democratically and without terror, depends on the willingness of the United States to permit a "socialist" state to exist in Central America.

If, instead, the United States escalates and prolongs the civil war by an extravagant military commitment to the junta, the power and influence of Marxist guerrillas in the FMLN will be strengthened at the expense of moderate civilians in the Democratic Revolutionary

---

[5] NACLA, op. cit., p. 11.
[6] See Readings 45 and 46.

Front.[7] Washington will have helped bring about precisely what it sought to avoid.

9. The Salvadoran Left *

By Latin America Regional Report

The Latin American Regional Report *is one of eight newsletters published by Latin American Newsletters Ltd., London, England. Approximately two months after the following article was published, in October, 1980, the various guerrilla organizations completed their consolidation by forming the Farabundo Martí National Liberation Front (FMLN).*

SINCE April [1980] the left, both moderate and revolutionary, has been united in the Frente Democrático Revolucionario (FDR), a coalition of more than 20 popular organizations, political parties and labor federations, as well as the main Salvadoran guerrilla groups.

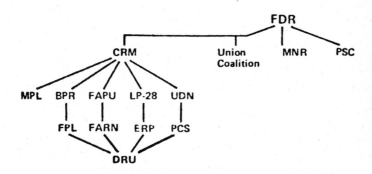

The Bloque Popular Revolucionario (BPR), probably the largest organization in the coalition, claims a membership of more than 80,-

---

[7] Elsewhere, in the epilogue to this book, Carlos Fuentes writes that by helping the military in El Salvador, the United States is helping to create Communism. However, by propping up a discredited military junta, the State Department wins even if it loses since the Communism created after such a devastating civil war is likely to be so repressive that it can only serve as a negative model for others. Only a consummate cynic would think it was planned this way.

* From *Latin American Regional Report*, Mexico and Central America, August 15, 1980.

000. The strength of the BPR, which was formed in 1975, is its base among the peasantry. It also includes groups of teachers, students, trade unionists and slum dwellers. Its armed wing, the Fuerzas Populares de Liberación (FPL), is the largest Salvadoran guerrilla group and was formed in 1970.

The next largest popular organization, the Frente de Acción Popular Unificada (FAPU), has its strongest base in the urban working class. It was formed in 1974 and its labor membership includes the power workers' union, which is capable of bringing the nation's economic activity to a rapid halt.

FAPU has links with radical sectors of the military; its armed wing, the Fuerzas Armadas de Resistencia Nacional (FARN), has been pushing for an insurrection sooner rather than later, and believes it could have some support within the armed forces. The BPR and FPL are more cautious; they have said that the opposition first needs to build up diplomatic support abroad.

The most adventurist of the revolutionary groups is the Ligas Populares 28 de febrero (LP-28), which seems to be mainly student based. Its armed wing, the Ejército Revolucionario del Pueblo (ERP), refused until recently to join the other guerrillas in a joint military command. Its differences have largely been with the FARN, which split from the ERP after the latter murdered the revolutionary poet, Roque Dalton, in a dispute over strategy in 1975. The ERP and LP-28 led an abortive attempt at insurrection shortly after last October's military coup [1979].

Since 1968 the Unión Democrática Nacional (UDN) has operated as the legal front for the illegal Communist Party, PCS. From last October to the New Year cabinet crisis it supported the military/civilian government, and party members held some important posts, including the labor ministry. The PCS functions as the UDN's armed wing.

In January [1980] the BPR, FAPU, LP-28 and UDN set up the Coordinadora Revolucionaria de Masas (CRM), which now also includes a smaller popular organization, the Movimiento Popular de Liberación (MPL). In May, the four guerrilla groups formed a joint military command, the Dirección Revolucionaria Unificada (DRU).

Of the political parties in the FDR, the Movimiento Revolucionario (MNR) is a small social democratic organization whose leader, Guillermo Ungo, resigned from the ruling junta in the New Year cabinet crisis. The Partido Social Cristiana (PSC) was formed following a left-wing split from the Christian Democrats in April. PSC leaders such as Héctor Dada and Rubén Zamora held key government posts before they resigned in protest against the military's repression and failure to carry out reform.

The FDR also includes a coalition of six leading labor unions, with a total of some 100,000 members. The FDR's secretary general, Enrique Alvarez, is one of a number of political independents active in the organization. Alvarez, a former agriculture minister, hails from the Salvadoran landed oligarchy. For the Church, the late Archbishop Oscar Romero declared shortly before his death that the FDR should be called on to form a government. His successor, Arturo Rivera y Damas, has been less clear, though the publications of the archbishop's office staunchly support the FDR.

The combined guerrilla groups are estimated to number 15,000 well-trained men and women under arms. Even the official press has been forced to take note of actions involving units of up to 500 guerrillas (common in the case of the FPL). The guerrillas may have as many as 80,000 in reserve. Arms are the main problem: they are mostly light—FAL rifles and Israeli light machine guns, plus hand guns—and considerably inferior to those of the military.

10. Who Makes Up the Opposition in El Salvador? *

BY REPRESENTATIVES GERRY E. STUDDS,
BARBARA ANN MIKULSKI AND ROBERT EDGAR

The following statement was presented to the Foreign Operations Subcommittee, House of Representatives, February 25, 1981. It was based on a trip to Central America, January 9-19, 1981.

Gerry E. Studds (D/Mass.) studied at Yale University and served in the State Department before being elected to Congress in 1972. Bob Edgar (D/Penna.) studied at Drew University and was former Protestant chaplain at Drexel University. He was first elected to Congress in 1974. Barbara Ann Mikulski (D/Maryland) studied at Mt. Saint Agnes College and at the University of Maryland School of Social Work. Before her election to Congress in 1976 she was City Councilwoman in Baltimore.

T HERE are five basic categories of people in opposition to the government in El Salvador. 1. Social Democrats, 2. dissident

---

* From the Congressional Record, February 26, 1981, pp. E756–E757.

Christian Democrats, 3. many independent professionals, bureaucrats, students and technicians, 4. many of those involved in the Church, and 5. fifth and largest, the popular organizations which represent not only the guerrillas but thousands of unarmed campesinos and the poor as well. . . .

Consider . . . some of those now in opposition to the "centrist" government of El Salvador:

Guillermo Ungo: Member of the first junta, strongly supported at the time by the United States. He resigned on January 3, 1980, arguing that "the Revolutionary Government junta has only minimal, and essentially formal, power. It lacks the capacity to lead the process of democratization and social change." Ungo, a Social Democrat, is now the leading Member of the Revolutionary Democratic Front.

Ramón Mayorga: A University Rector, who also served in the first revolutionary junta. He resigned along with Ungo, and is currently teaching in Mexico.

Colonel Adolfo Majano: A member of both the first and second juntas, Majano is the youngest and most charismatic of the democratic military leaders who had begun to emerge in El Salvador. His ouster by the military shortly after the nuns were killed in December was aimed at solidifying right-wing control over the military at the time they were under attack in the United States and elsewhere. Majano was arrested last week in El Salvador, for the crime of being in opposition to the government.

Héctor Dada Hirezi: Minister of Foreign Relations in the first junta, then a member of the second junta. Resigned on March 3, 1980, saying: "While it is true that the obstacles along the road have been enormous, it is equally true that the Junta is incapable of acting against those whom I perceive to be the principal opponents of the process, and it is clearer with each passing day that those persons are encysted in the very structure of the government. The democratic government to be developed is traveling a road towards total perversion."

Dada, formerly a Christian Democrat, is now working in Mexico.

Rubén Zamora: Minister to the Presidency in the first junta, Zamora was also a leading member of the Political Commission of the Christian Democratic Party. He resigned along with Héctor Dada, and is now serving as a member of the Political-Diplomatic Commission of the Revolutionary Democratic Front.

Roberto Lara Velado: A founder of the Christian Democratic Party, and Secretary-General of the party for 10 years. Velado was appointed by the first junta to the task of examining charges of repression by the military. After several months of frustrated attempts to have his recommendations for investigations taken seriously, he resigned.

Alberto Arene: A Member of the Political Commission of the Christian Democratic Party during the first and second juntas. An economist, he resigned from the government in March, 1980, and is now representing the Revolutionary Democratic Front in Rome.

Francisco Díaz: Formerly Executive Secretary of the Christian Democratic Party, he resigned from his post in March, 1980, and now represents the Revolutionary Democratic Front in Quito.

Héctor Silva: Former Executive Secretary for the Christian Democratic Party in the eastern zone of El Salvador, he also resigned last March and is now working on behalf of the Revolutionary Democratic Front.

Jorge Villacorta: Served as Sub-Secretary of Agriculture during the first and second juntas, and was one of the most prominent planners of the Agrarian reform program. He resigned in late March because of the violence of the military. He now lives in Costa Rica, with a $10,000 price on his head.

Julietta De Colinderes: Former Secretary for Women's Affairs within the Christian Democratic Party. Resigned in March, 1980, and is now working in Mexico for the Revolutionary Democratic Front.

Oscar Menjivar: Sub-secretary of Economics in the first junta, and Secretary in the second junta. Also a former member of the Executive Committee of the Christian Democratic Party. Resigned in March, 1980, now living in Managua.

Areonette de Zamora: Member of the Christian Democratic Party, and served on the Municipal Council in San Salvador. Resigned shortly after her husband, Marion Zamora, also a Christian Democratic official, was assassinated. She now works in Mexico for the external commission of the Revolutionary Democratic Front.

Eduardo Colindres: Served as Minister of Education in the second junta, and was Secretary for Doctrine within the Christian Democratic Party. He resigned late last March along with Villacorta.

Finally, one should note the words of Salvador Samayoa, Minister of Education and Agriculture Minister Enrique Alvárez Cordova, at the time of their resignation from the first junta in January, 1980:

"Real power is exercised by the head of the Ministry of Defense and Public Safety . . . transcending the authority of the governing Junta and against the democratic aspirations of our people. . . ."

The opposition in El Salvador is currently a very diverse group, but we in the United States have the capacity to unite them, to bring together Marxists and non-Marxists; guerrillas and those who abhor the use of violence; the religious and the non-believers; the educated and the poor; the Christian Democrats and the socialists. Yes, we have the power to unite them in opposition to ourselves, or to any policy which provides arms to those who use such weapons to make economic and social progress in El Salvador impossible.

11. The Guerrilla Army *

By Radio Liberation and an FMLN Commander

The Farabundo Martí National Liberation Front (FMLN) seems to be modeled on the guerrilla armies of China, Cuba and Vietnam. Part of their success can be attributed to an ability to induce large numbers of the enemies' armies to defect. The first piece which follows (part A) makes clear that the FMLN is making a similar effort. Successful guerrilla armies do more than fight. By concerning themselves with the health, education and social needs of the peasants, guerrillas win their sympathy and support (part B).

THE fighting people are building a new army. In our fatherland there is suffering but there are also heroic sacrifices that are building a new society, erected on the ruins of the old oppressive structures. It is a fact that the fascist army is collapsing at the same time that the people's army is growing.

The people's army is completely different from the gorilla [sic] army. Besides its growth, in our army's ranks there is friendship and brotherhood. There are no arbitrary and cruel chiefs in it. All its members see each other as brothers without distinctions in seniority, social position or ranks. What unites us is the resolute decision to fight and our eyes are always set on the great objective of achieving a bright future of peace and freedom for our fatherland.

In his message to his comrades in arms who are still in the despicable army of the fascists, Lt. Col. Ricardo Bruno Navarrete has described the joy he felt at the warm reception he received when he joined our army. Lt. Emilio Mena Sandoval and Lt. Marcelo Cruz, along with the compañero commanders of the FMLN [Farabundo

---

* From Radio Liberation, January 17, 1981, reproduced in the Foreign Broadcast Information Service, Daily Reports, January 19, 1981, and from *Barricada*, Managua, June 1, 1981, reprinted in the Foreign Broadcast Information Service, Daily Reports, June 5, 1981.

Martí National Liberation Front], have been at the head of the battles of our forces in Santa Ana where they are getting ready for new offensives. They remain in the frontline despite the fact that the liar junta has tried to misinform the people by saying that they are in Guatemala. The troops, which joined the Farabundo Martí National Liberation Front along with the lieutenants, continue alongside our brother fighters in the common struggle.

Another thing that distinguishes the new army from the fascist army is the high morale of its fighters which has led them to acts of great heroism. Our army is not an army of mercenaries because it is an army with ideals of justice and freedom. The FMLN fighters struggle and face death with heroism for the noble and just cause of the people. It is led by our political-military leadership, forged in the daily struggle, filled with privations and sacrifices which has armed it with a courage of steel, revolutionary conscience and a spirit of sacrifice, characteristics that the fascist officers of the gorilla army do not have and will never have because they are a handful of corrupt and murderous traitors.

In the new army of the liberated fatherland there is room for the troops and officers of the enemy's army who join the ranks of the people. The democratic revolutionary government will create a new type of army made up of the popular revolutionary army and the honest and patriotic individuals in the ranks of the troops and officers of the current army. The incorporation of officers Mena Sandoval, Cruz and Navarrete has already made a reality the proposal contained in the platform of the Democratic Revolutionary Government.

Long live the Democratic Revolutionary Government! Long live the new popular revolutionary army! Long live the incorporation of the honest officers, noncommissioned officers and soldiers in the ranks of the FMLN!

B. FMLN Commander Rigoberto Hernández (June 1, 1981)

The concerns and needs of the community are constant. Children, women, old people and fighters need food. People must learn to read and write, and they require medical attention and an armed defense. It is here that the FMLN power comes into play. The FMLN plans the mechanisms for the planting of staples, mainly corn and beans. Coordination is established with the few revolutionary doctors stationed in the military area so that they can attend to the people's health. Coordination mechanisms are established with the militias and they distribute the tasks of building defenses against air and artillery attacks, construction of communications trenches and so forth.

The organization also guarantees the safety and maintenance of the troops who are constantly fighting inside and outside the region.

In order to promote production, fighters have a schedule in which each unit participates in planting and cultivating staple grains. This is coordinated by the FMLN directorate.

They Teach Reading and Writing. A literacy campaign is being promoted by teachers and clergywomen at the battlefront. Every morning and afternoon children and adults attend makeshift classrooms or sit under trees where they are taught to read and write in a manner adapted to the specific conditions in which Salvadoran workers live. When the junta's army attacks, pencils and notebooks are immediately exchanged for rifles, shotguns, antipersonnel bombs or any other manufactured or homemade weapon.

The FMLN power in rural areas, scattered throughout the country, is the structural base for a new people's power on Salvadoran territory, a power parallel to the one supported by the armed forces of the junta to keep power in the hands of a local oligarchy which, allied to the United States, has maintained this system over 50 years. It is slowly but surely crumbling.

12. The "Final Offensive" *

BY COMMANDER SALVADOR CAYETANO CARPIO

After a number of communiqués from the Farabundo Martí National Liberation Front (FMLN) to the people of El Salvador to prepare themselves for the task ahead, a "final offensive" against "the Christian Democrat-military dictatorship" was launched in January, 1981, with the statement reprinted below—General Order No. 1—read by Commander Salvador Cayetano Carpio over Radio Liberation. As part of its plan, the FMLN called for a general strike on Tuesday, January 13: "Compañero worker, peasant, public employee, businessman, student, market vendor and people in general—Join the strike and participate in the construction of a

---

* From a text signed by the general command of the Unified Revolutionary Directorate of the Farabundo Martí National Liberation Front, January 10, 1981. It was broadcast over (clandestine) Radio Liberation on January 11, 1981, and apears in the Foreign Broadcast Information Service, Daily Reports, January 12, 1981.

more just society; join the general strike and cooperate with the fighters of the FMLN in a strong movement that will crush the tyranny that has subdued our people for 50 years" (Radio Liberation, January 13, 1981, published in the Foreign Broadcast Information Service, Daily Reports, January 14, 1981).

While there are conflicting accounts about the degree of success of the strike—an American financial source acknowledges 26 factories struck and 20,000 workers out (Journal of Commerce, January 15, 1981)—*it is clear that the general strike, like the "final offensive" itself, fell short of its objective. Even though the FMLN was to report over Radio Liberation (January 29) that "the big combative phase that falls within the framework of the revolutionary general offensive is being successfully fulfilled by the regular guerrilla and militia units of our revolutionary people's army," (Foreign Broadcast Information Service, Daily Reports, January 30, 1981), the offensive proved to be premature, especially in San Salvador, and a setback for the FMLN. (For an excellent analysis of the strike and final offensive, See* Central America: No Road Back, NACLA Report on the Americas, Vol. XV, No. 3, May–June, 1981.)

The junta could claim a short-lived victory. By spring, shifting back to more familiar guerrilla tactics, the FMLN had established eight separate military fronts and extended its de facto *control over much of the terrain north of the Pan American Highway—the part adjoining the Honduras border—in Chalatenango and Morazán provinces, as well as elsewhere in the southeast.*

THE Unified Revolutionary Directorate [DRU] of the FMLN, which has assumed the general command of all the revolutionary armed forces of the five organizations which make up the FMLN, addresses all the heroic people of El Salvador, workers and peasants, revolutionary men and women, democrats and patriots:

The time has come to begin the decisive military and insurrectional battles for the seizure of power by the people and for the establishment of the democratic revolutionary government.

Decades of suffering and more than 50 years of military dictatorship are about to be eradicated forever by the thrust of popular combat. At this historic moment, which is crucial to the destiny of the Salvadoran and Central American peoples, the DRU of the FMLN, which is the general command, calls on all the people, the workers, peasants, students, teachers, employees, democratic sectors, progressive soldiers and officers, religious sectors, everyone, men and women, the combatants of the regular and guerrilla revolutionary units, the militias of the revolution and the combative masses to immediately begin the military actions and the popular insurrection to achieve the triumph of the revolution.

We call on all the people to rise up as a single man, with all means of combat, under the orders of their immediate chiefs, in all war fronts and throughout the national territory to courageously fight until the definite defeat of the regime of oppression and genocide of the local oligarchy and imperialism. All to the battle!

We issue a call to all the progressive and patriotic soldiers and officers to join the ranks of the people. It is the time for them to identify themselves with their brother workers, to turn their weapons against the cruel and bloody chiefs of the high command and the commanders of the counterrevolutionary army.

The time for the revolution has arrived. The time for liberation has come. The definite victory is in the hands of this heroic and courageous people who for so many years have shed their blood to obtain the right to be free, to enjoy democracy, real independence, social progress, sovereignty and self-determination.

At this historic moment, when all the people are rising up to achieve their freedom, we can confirm with emotion that the Salvadoran people are not alone. All our Central American and Latin American brothers are with us. All the peoples of the world are with us. Onward heroic Salvadoran people! To total combat until final victory is achieved! To the shattering military battles! To the popular insurrections! To prepare the general strike! To victory! United to fight until the final victory! Revolution or death, we shall win!

13. Platform of the Revolutionary Democratic Government *

On February 27, 1980, the coordinating committee of the Salvadoran revolutionary organizations (CRM) made public its programmatic platform reproduced below. Calling for such economic measures as nationalized banking, foreign trade and electricity distribution, and a deepening agrarian reform, along with such social measures as low-cost housing, a national health system and a literacy campaign—all within a framework designed to benefit

---

* From *Barricada*, March 4, 5, 1980, published in Managua. The translation is by Intercontinental Press.

small- and medium-sized private businesses, owners of real estate and land-owners—the writers of the platform see the revolution they espouse as "popular, democratic and antioligarchic" and the only path to "true and effective national independence."

A few months later, a Revolutionary Manifesto of May 1980 (see the U.S. Department of State release, June 17, 1980) was issued by the Unified Revolutionary Directorate (DRU). The formation of DRU was a significant step towards the unity a successful guerrilla struggle requires. The various guerrilla groups still remained separate entities but now had "a single leadership, a single military command and single command unit." (Later, in October, they were to merge into the Farabundo Martí National Liberation Front.) This manifesto—more inspirational in tone—echoed the programmatic platform without its detail. According to the ideological lens it now wears, the Reagan State Department characterized this manifesto as follows: "In May 1980, the leftist opposition to the government formed the Unified Revolutionary Directorate (DRU), which in its manifesto is dedicated to the establishment of a Marxist, totalitarian government in El Salvador" (U.S. Department of State Bulletin, March, 1981, p. 10).

THE economic and social structures of our country—which have served to guarantee the disproportionate enrichment of an oligarchic minority and the exploitation of our people by Yankee imperialism—are in deep and insoluble crisis.

The military dictatorship is also in crisis, and with it the entire legal and ideological order that the oligarchic interests and the U.S. imperialists have defended and continue to defend, oppressing the Salvadoran people for half a century. Victims of their own contradictions, the dominant classes have failed due to the decisive and heroic action of the people's movement. It has been impossible to stave off this failure, even with more and more brazen intervention of the United States in support of such efforts against the people.

Unswerving commitment to the interests and aspirations of the Salvadoran people by the revolutionary organizations has led to the deepening and strengthening of their roots among the vast toiling majority and the middle sectors. Being so rooted in the people, the revolutionary movement is now indestructible. It constitutes the only alternative for the Salvadoran people, who can be neither stopped nor diverted from their struggle to gain a Free Homeland in which their vital desires will be made real.

The economic and political crisis of the dominant classes on the one hand, and on the other the forward impulse of the decisive political force in our country, the people's movement, have given rise to a revolutionary process and to conditions in which the people can assume power.

The revolutionary transformation of our society—submitted up to now to injustice, betrayal, and pillage—is today a near and possible reality. Only in this way will our people gain and insure the democratic rights and freedoms that have been denied to them. Only the revolution will resolve the agrarian problem and generate for the masses of peasants and agricultural wage workers material and spiritual conditions of life favorable to the immense majority of our population who are today marginalized and submerged in poverty and cultural backwardness. It will be the revolution that will gain true political independence for our country, giving the Salvadoran people the right to freely determine their destiny and attain true economic independence.

This revolution is therefore popular, democratic, and antioligarchic, and seeks to conquer true and effective national independence. Only the revolutionary victory will halt the criminal repression and make it possible for the people to enjoy the peace that today they lack, a solid peace based on freedom, social justice, and national independence.

The revolution that is on the march is not, nor can it be, the work of a group of conspirators. To the contrary, it is the fruit of the struggle of the entire people—of the workers, the peasants, the middle layers in general, and all sectors and individuals that are honestly democratic and patriotic.

The most conscious and organized ranks of the Salvadoran people, now multitudinous, are fighting in a more and more broad and united way. The worker and peasant alliance—through its combativity, level of consciousness, daring, organization, and spirit of sacrifice for the sake of the people's triumph—has proven to be the most solid basis for guaranteeing the firmness and consistency of the entire liberation movement. Expressing the unity of the entire people, this movement unites the revolutionary forces and the democratic forces—the two great torrents generated by the long struggle carried out by the Salvadoran people.

The decisive task of the revolution on which completion of all its objectives depends is the conquest of power and the installation of a *revolutionary democratic government*, which at the head of the people will launch the construction of a new society.

Task and Objectives of the Revolution. The tasks and objectives of the revolution in El Salvador are the following:

1. To overthrow the reactionary military dictatorship of the oli-

garchy and Yankee imperialism, imposed and sustained against the will of the Salvadoran people for fifty years; to destroy its criminal political-military machine; and to establish a *revolutionary democratic government*, founded on the unity of the revolutionary and democratic forces in the People's Army and the Salvadoran people.

2. To put an end to the overall political, economic and social power of the great lords of land and capital.

3. To liquidate once and for all the economic, political, and military dependence of our country on Yankee imperialism.

4. To assure democratic rights and freedoms for the entire people— particularly for the working masses, who are the ones who have least enjoyed such freedoms.

5. To transfer to the people, through nationalizations and the creation of collective and socialized enterprises: the fundamental means of production and distribution that are now hoarded by the oligarchy and the U.S. monopolies, the land held in the power of the big landlords, the enterprises that produce and distribute electricity and other monopolized services, foreign trade, banking, and large transportation enterprises. None of this will affect small or medium-sized private businesses, which will be given all kinds of stimulus and support in the various branches of the national economy.

6. To raise the cultural and material living standards of the population.

7. To create a new army for our country, one that will arise fundamentally on the basis of the People's Army to be built in the course of the revolutionary process. Those healthy, patriotic, and worthy elements that belong to the current army can also be incorporated.

8. To encourage all forms of organization of the people, at all levels and in all sectors, thus guaranteeing their active, creative, and democratic involvement in the revolutionary process and securing the closest identification between the people and their government.

9. To orient the foreign policy and international relations of our country around the principles of independence and self-determination, solidarity, peaceful coexistence, equal rights, and mutual respect between states.

10. Through all these measures, to assure our country peace, freedom, the well-being of our people, and future social progress.

The Democratic Revolutionary Government—Its Composition and Platform of Social, Structural and Political Changes. The revolutionary democratic government will be made up of representatives of the revolutionary and people's movement, as well as of the democratic parties, organizations, sectors, and individuals who are willing to participate in the carrying out of this programmatic platform.

This government will rest on a broad political and social base, formed above all by the working class, the peasantry, and the advanced middle layers. Intimately united to the latter forces will be all the social sectors that are willing to carry out this platform—small and medium-sized industrialists, merchants, artisans, and farmers (small and medium-sized coffee planters and those involved in other areas of agriculture or cattle raising). Also involved will be honest professionals, the progressive clergy, democratic parties such as the MNR (Movimiento Nacionalista Revolucionaria—Revolutionary Nationalistic Movement), advanced sectors of the Christian Democracy, worthy and honest officers of the army who are willing to serve the interests of the people, and any other sectors, groups, or individuals that uphold broad democracy for the popular masses, independent development, and people's liberation.

All these forces are now coming together to make up a revolutionary and democratic alliance in which the political and/or religious beliefs of all are respected. The organized form to be taken by this voluntary alliance at the service of the Salvadoran people will be the result of consultations among all those who make it up.

Immediate Political Measures. 1. A halt to all forms of repression against the people and release of all political prisoners.

2. Clarification of the situation of those captured and disappeared since 1972; punishment of those responsible (be they military or civilian) for crimes against the people.

3. Disarming and permanent dissolution of the repressive bodies—ANSESAL, ORDEN, National Guard, National Police, Treasury Police, and Customs Police, along with their respective "Special Sections;" of the Gotera "Counterinsurgency School" and the so-called Armed Forces Engineering Training Center in Zacatecoluca; of the cantonal and suburban military patrols; of the oligarchy's private paramilitary bands; and of all other kinds of real or nominal organizations dedicated to criminal action or slander against the people and their organizations. The current misnamed security bodies will be replaced by a civilian police force.

4. Dissolution of the existing state powers (executive, legislative, and judicial); abrogation of the Political Constitution and of all decrees that have modified or added to it.

The *revolutionary democratic government* will decree a constitutional law and will organize the state and its activities with the aim of guaranteeing the rights and freedoms of the people and of achieving the other objectives and tasks of the revolution. In doing so, the *revolutionary democratic government* will adhere to the United Nations' "Universal Declaration of Human Rights."

The constitutional law referred to above will remain in force while the Salvadoran people prepare a new political constitution that faithfully reflects their interests.

5. Municipal government will be restructured so as to be an organ of broad participation by the masses in managing the state, so as to be a real organ of the new people's power.

6. The *revolutionary democratic government* will carry out an intense effort of liberating education, of cultural exposition and organization among the broadest masses, in order to promote their conscious incorporation into the development, strengthening and defense of the revolutionary process.

7. The People's Army will be strengthened and developed. It will include the soldiers, noncommissioned officers, officers, and chiefs of the current army who conduct themselves honestly, reject foreign intervention against the revolutionary process, and support the liberation struggle of our people.

The new army will be the true armed wing of the people. It will be at their service and absolutely faithful to their interests and their revolution. The armed forces will be truly patriotic, the defenders of national sovereignty and self-determination, and committed partisans of peaceful coexistence among peoples.

8. Our country will withdraw from CONDECA (Central American Defense Council), from TIAR (Rio de Janeiro Inter-American Defense Treaty), and from any other military or police organizations that might be the instruments of interventionism.

9. The revolutionary democratic government will establish diplomatic and trade relations with other countries without discrimination on the basis of differing social systems, on the basis of equal rights, coexistence, and respect for self-determination. Special attention will be paid to the development of friendly relations with the other countries of Central America (including Panama and Belize), with the aim of strengthening peace and upholding the principle of nonintervention. Close fraternal relations with Nicaragua will especially be sought, as the expression of the community of ideals and interests between our revolution and the Sandinista revolution.

Our country will become a member of the Movement of Nonaligned Countries and will develop a steadfast policy toward the defense of world peace and in favor of détente.

Structural Changes. The revolutionary democratic government will:

1. Nationalize the entire banking and financial system. This measure will not affect the deposits and other interests of the public.

2. Nationalize foreign trade.

3. Nationalize the system of electricity distribution, along with the enterprises for its production that are in private hands.

4. Nationalize the refining of petroleum.

5. Carry out the expropriation, in accord with the national interest, of the monopolistic enterprises in industry, trade, and services.

6. Carry out a deep-going agrarian reform, which will put the land that is now in the hands of the big landlords at the disposal of the broad masses who work it. This will be done according to an effective plan to benefit the great majority of poor and middle peasants and agricultural wage workers and to promote the development of agriculture and cattle raising.

The agrarian reform will not affect small and medium landholders, who will receive stimuli and support for continual improvements in production on their plots.

7. Carry out an urban reform to benefit the great majority, without affecting small and medium owners of real estate.

8. Thoroughly transform the tax system, so that tax payments no longer fall upon the workers. Indirect taxes on widely consumed goods will be reduced. This will be possible not only through reform of the tax system, but also because the state will receive substantial income from the activity of the nationalized sector of the economy.

9. Establish effective mechanisms for credit, economic aid, and technical assistance for small and medium-sized private businesses in all branches of the country's economy.

10. Establish a system for effective planning of the national economy, which will make it possible to encourage balanced development.

Social measures. The revolutionary democratic government will direct its efforts in the social arena toward the following objectives:

1. Create sufficient sources of jobs so as to eliminate unemployment in the briefest possible time.

2. Bring into effect a just wage policy, based on:

a. Regulation of wages, taking into account the cost of living.

b. An energetic policy of control and reduction of the prices charged for basic goods and services.

c. A substantial increase in social services for the popular masses (social security, education, recreation, health care, etc.).

3. Put into action a massive plan for construction of low cost housing.

4. Create a Unified National Health System, which will guarantee efficient medical service to the entire population (urban and rural). Preventative care will be the principal aim.

5. Carry out a literacy campaign that will put an end to the social defect of illiteracy in the shortest possible time.

6. Develop the national educational system so as to assure primary education to the entire population of school age and substantially broaden secondary and university education. Quality and scientific-technical diversification will be increased at all levels, and free education will be progressively introduced.

7. Promote cultural activity on a broad scale, effectively supporting and stimulating national artists and writers, recovering and developing the cultural heritage of the nation, and incorporating into the cultural assets of the broad popular masses the best of universal culture.

It is the unanimous opinion of the popular and democratic forces that only through realization of the measures contained in this platform can the deep-going structural and political crisis of our country be resolved in favor of the Salvadoran people.

Only the oligarchy, U.S. imperialism, and those who serve their antipatriotic interests are opposed to and are conspiring against these changes. Since October 15, 1979, various parties and sectors have vainly attempted to use the government to carry out a large part of the measures we propose without first overthrowing the old reactionary and repressive power and without installing a truly revolutionary and popular power. This experience has confirmed with full clarity that only the united revolutionary movement in alliance with all the democratic forces can carry out such a work of transformation.

The moment is approaching for this historic and liberating victory, for which the Salvadoran people have struggled and heroically shed so much of their blood. Nothing and no one will be able to prevent it.

For the unity of the revolutionary and democratic forces!

Toward the conquest of the revolutionary democratic government!

Chapter II

TERROR AND CIVIL WAR

Editors' Introduction

THE Reagan Administration has chosen to focus on what it calls international terrorism rather than on human rights. Terrorism, though, is not so easily defined.

Were the wartime bombings of London or Dresden, not to mention the atom-bombings of Hiroshima and Nagasaki, simply the legitimate exercise of military force or were they instead (or also) examples of organized terror? The matter is made more complicated with the increased appearance of "irregular war" in which there is great difficulty distinguishing the combatants from those neutral or uninvolved. Still, as Harry Rositzke, a long time CIA operative, persuasively argues, we should in principle distinguish between acts of terror which have no realistic political purpose—random hijackings, bombings, Italian Red Brigades-style murders—from wars for national liberation.[1]

No government is ideologically pacifist. "Terror," in the form of guerrilla warfare, is employed by Afghan insurgents against Soviet and Soviet-supported troops. How do we distinguish between the "good" terrorism we support and the "bad" terrorism of guerrillas we condemn? Like the concept of "just war," legitimacy depends on the moral values of those making the distinctions and their evaluations of the context.

The investigation which followed the murder of the four American churchwomen, as well as data in other Readings that follow, give one a feel for the El Salvador context. It was learned the women had been buried in a common grave near the roadside ditch they had been found in. Local authorities were following the standard procedures

---

[1] *The New York Times*, July 20, 1981.

set for them by the security forces. The Justice of the Peace told Ambassador White that two or three informal burials of unidentified bodies occurred every week. The stench of death is commonplace in El Salvador.

In defense of the junta, and its "centrist" president, José Napoleón Duarte, the U.S. State Department has denounced terror in El Salvador which it generally attributes to leftist guerrillas, though upon occasion to rightist extremists.[2] There is little evidence, though, that Washington has made much effort to stop the rightist terrorism it has condemned though it has sent massive military assistance to the junta to contain or destroy leftist "terrorism."

The weight of evidence is that the vast preponderance of terror, and death, should not be attributed to the left but to the government. Nothing guerrillas do during the course of their struggle, as one lesson of Vietnam shows, can match the devastation of a regime equipped with the latest in modern weaponry, even one using only helicopters. Those shipping armaments to El Salvador must bear an increasing responsibility for the terror raining down on Salvadorans. Government terror has also uprooted vast numbers and made them refugees (many residing miserably in Honduras).

Moreover, as emphatically stated by a former captain in the Salvadoran army, "It is a grievous error to believe that the forces of the extreme right operate independent of the [government] security forces."

Governmental violence in El Salvador should occasion little surprise since we are referring to a successor regime of one that slaughtered tens of thousands of peasants in the thirties. In recent years the butchery, rape and mutilation it is responsible for has earned it special notice in a region increasingly populated by brutal regimes.

None of the above is meant to deny that terrorism is not also used as an instrument of policy by leftist guerrillas, or that innocents are not on occasion, or even more frequently, killed; nor even that the brutalizing effect of a long war may not lead to harsh reprisals, in the event of victory (though by no means does it follow inexorably, a case in point being Zimbabwe).

Nonetheless, from the guerrilla perspective, it would be moral esca-

---

[2] The deaths of what turned out to be twenty-three civilians (and which originally appeared to be the work of a "death squad") prompted a Press Statement of April 9, 1981, which condemned the violence of far right and far left. This expression of support for a moderate center beset by extremist forces proved to be exceptionally inapt and ill-fated: that very day the Salvadoran armed forces explained why they had killed the twenty-three "terrorists." See the Foreign Broadcast Information Services, Daily Reports, April 9, 1981.

pism to equate the terror of a military regime in defense of an entrenched oligarchy with that used by revolutionaries seeking to overthrow it. Since the Salvadoran junta has already been widely and strongly condemned for its extensive violations of human rights, the continued struggle to overthrow it is apt to draw the increased sympathy of people the world over. The nature of this struggle and of the terror being employed in El Salvador is explored in these Reading's.

14. Salvador's Plight Tears a Famous Family Apart *

BY WARREN HOGE

José Antonio Morales Ehrlich is second to President José Napoleón Duarte in the current Salvadoran junta. Two Morales sons are guerrillas. A moving account of this family riven by civil war is provided by Warren Hoge, New York Times Bureau Chief in Brazil. The editors have incorporated into the story the open letter, referred to by Hoge, written by the son, José Antonio Morales Carbonell, to his father. At a later point there is a summary of a conversation held with the senior Morales by members of the U.S. House of Representatives Barbara Mikulski, Robert Edgar and Gerry E. Studds during their January, 1981, fact-finding trip to Central America.

THE extent to which El Salvador is a country at war with itself is reflected in the experiences of the Morales family, one of the best known in the capital city.

The father, José Antonio Morales Ehrlich, was the Mayor of San Salvador and is now one of the four members of the junta that rules the nation. Two of his sons have joined the guerrillas fighting to topple the Government.

The rift in the family is deep and hurtful. . . .

That has not kept [the subject] from being a much discussed item. Young Antonio saw to that by writing an open letter to his father. . . .

---

* From *The New York Times*, June 4, 1981. Text of the letter from NACLA Report, July-August, 1980. The conversation with José Antonio Morales Carbonell is from *Central America, 1981*, Report to the Committee on Foreign Affairs, U.S. House of Representatives, March, 1981.

Dear Father,

On May 30, 1979, I had to leave the country with a group of com-
pañeros to visit the embassies of France, Venezuela and Costa Rica, to
demand freedom for our captured leaders. . . . Today, on my return after a
long trip through various countries of Europe, I want to tell you that the
entire world is exasperated. From every corner you hear Basta Ya!
—Enough!—to the repression against the Salvadoran people.

It is inconceivable that after so few months in government, your seemingly good intentions . . . have been converted into such enormous compromises and complicities with the number-one enemy of humanity:
Yankee Imperialism.

Compromises that seem to know no limits!

Compromises that have taken more lives than the last years of the
military tyranny!

I remember that some time ago you told me . . . that the enormous
crisis of imperialism in our country, caused by the uncontainable rise of
the revolutionary movement, had to be used to present a more favorable
alternative to U.S. interests and, at the same time, to carry out genuine
changes in our country. . . .

But in the end, what are those promised changes?

The famed Agrarian Reform?

Or the permanent state of siege . . . ?

The famed nationalization of banks and foreign trade?

Or the growing and shameless intervention of Yankee Imperialism, that
sends personnel trained in counter-insurgency techniques and other spe-
cialties; that sends a permanent and constant stream of arms and war
supplies to strengthen the puppet armies and the para-military bands of
assassins. . . .

It is really dishonorable to be in your situation, and still try to hide from
the world the reality of violence and repression that our people suffer
daily, crudely attributing it to the supposed provocations of the revolutionary organizations.

I am certain that you yourself don't believe that!

You should follow the example of the other Christian Democrats that
decided to stop supporting the repressive regime, to stop serving as a
"progressive" cover, in exchange for a few crumbs of power and to stop
cynically attributing these desertions to merely "sentimental" motives.

At this point there are no longer intermediary positions, things are totally clear: one is either on the side of the oppressed, or on the side of the
oppressors. To stay on their side makes you responsible as well for the
crimes committed against the people—crimes committed by your very
colleagues.

The least you can do at this moment is to be loyal to the principles you taught me.

Do it for your family, your children. . . .

Do it for the thousands of workers and peasants and for all our people who suffer hunger, misery, exploitation and oppression.

Do it for a minimum sense of human compassion, that I cannot believe you have lost.

It is lamentable to me that you find yourself in this situation, but I remember that you taught me to be clear, a clarity that obliges me to tell you . . . that I am ready to give the last drop of my blood for the liberation of our people; I have faith in the power and creativity of the people's forces and I am convinced that the only way to defeat the enemy is with arms in hand, destroying completely the repressive apparatus and creating a more just society, free of misery and exploitation. . . .

Your son,

> *José Antonio Morales Carbonell*
> *El Salvador, April 19, 1980*

[Hoge's account resumes.] Mr. Morales has not seen his 21-year-old son Carlos Ernesto in more than a year. There are persistent rumors that the boy's head was left on the father's doorstep and others that the father identified his son's mutilated body from among the corpses that appear by the side of outlying roads each morning. Mr. Morales, however, said that he believed Carlos Ernesto was still alive and that he had information he was somewhere outside the country.

Twenty-two-year-old Antonio was arrested a year ago and is in a jail for political prisoners in Santa Tecla, five miles from here [San Salvador]. Antonio and his father resemble each other and are similarly genial, but the settings in which they were interviewed attest to the separate paths they have chosen.

Mr. Morales spends his days in the presidential palace in a chandeliered office with beige taffeta curtains, champagne-colored carpeting and period furniture. An enormous oil painting depicting the country's liberator on his deathbed prompts him to quip to visitors that he hopes it does not portend the future of the junta.

His son occupies the upper berth of a bunk bed in the old high-ceilinged prison. Revolutionary slogans are daubed in red on the walls of the dark corridors of the building. . . .

As a sociology major at the Catholic University, he became a leader of student organizations and further identified with the political dissidence of peasant and worker groups.

"I used to argue with him personally," the father said. "Like me, he wanted change, but I believed in democracy and he supported the

Marxists. I told him Marxism was obsolete, that our model was better."

"You know," said a friend, "it would not have been hard to have become radicalized in José Antonio's house. He's very outspoken, and he was always denouncing the military and the oligarchy." The son artfully touched on the point in his letter. "The least you could do at this point," he wrote, "is to act in a way that is faithful to the principles you taught me."

Father and son see each other on public visiting days when, under motorcycle escort, Mr. Morales makes the trip out from the capital in his armored van.

Do they talk politics? "It's very difficult because our positions are so very different," said the son. "We really arrive at nothing so we prefer to talk about the family."

Four other Morales children are in school in Costa Rica. The family spent two years of exile there after Mr. Morales raised charges of fraud in the 1977 elections in which he ran for Vice President. Antonio said the other children had no "political definition." He produced a picture of his sister from a shirt pocket. . . .

The present family crisis struck in May 1979 when Mr. Morales, still in exile, was watching televised accounts of the occupation by Salvadoran leftist groups of the French Embassy here. One of those who filed out of the mission after the Government agreed to permit the occupiers to leave the country was his son Antonio.

Antonio was to travel during the next 10 months in unidentified European countries before returning under cover to El Salvador in April 1980. He was arrested by the National Police last June 13 in a housing project near the National University. . . .

When his parents confronted him in the office of the National Guard commander, he asked them about Carlos Ernesto and learned that his brother had joined the armed revolution also. "That made me really happy," he recalled. "It demonstrated that as much as they kill and capture us, there will still be others ready to take our places. . . ."

Morales [speaking to the members of the U.S. House of Representatives] believes that neither a pure capitalist nor a pure Marxist approach will succeed in El Salvador. He wants to see a political and social democracy put in place, through economic and agrarian reforms, coupled with elections planned for 1982 and 1983. These plans hinge on the government's ability to bring peace to the country.

Morales explained that the reform strategy was based on the need to oust the oligarchy which has historically dominated farming, marketing, and banking systems within El Salvador. The government's approach was to begin by seizing the land and turning it over to the campesinos who have historically worked these lands. The next step was to nationalize the exporting and banking sectors, in order to guarantee a market for the country's goods and to see that credit would be available for nonoligarchial agricultural endeavors. "We desired," says Morales Ehrlich, "that these three pillars be placed at the service of the people."

He said that the agricultural reforms were proceeding quite satisfactorily, despite the violence, and cited the record-high production of basic grains.

With respect to security matters, Morales Ehrlich said that the government was seeking to isolate the armed extremes, but that they were willing to include all others, even some of those not in opposition, within a democratic regime. He said that the extreme right wing was now very weak, and that they no longer have the ability to successfully launch a right-wing coup.

The left, on the other hand, has lost popularity because of its refusal to cooperate with the reforms, because of its continued use of violence, and because it has sought to damage the economy of the country. All of those steps, argues Morales Ehrlich, are strategic errors, unpopular with the people in both the cities and the countryside.

For all intents and purposes, says Morales Ehrlich, the left is 100 percent Marxist. The other opposition groups, such as the Social Democrats, are so lacking in public support that their entire movement could fit into a "microbus."

Morales Ehrlich is optimistic about the future because he thinks that the power of both extremes has been reduced, and that the split in the military has been resolved by the ouster of Colonel Majano. He says that the military is a partner in the reform process, despite its occasional mistakes from a human rights point of view. He says that changes have been made in an effort to exert greater control over the military, but that those could not be made public for three reasons:

(1) Any military official publicly denounced for committing atrocities would be killed by the left;

(2) It is not proper for one partner in government to condemn the actions of another partner; and

(3) Anything which publicly embarrasses the military provides a benefit to the Marxists.

Therefore, instead of putting military outlaws on trial, the worst of them have been assigned to desk jobs or given scholarships to study abroad.

Morales Ehrlich argues that the increasing desperation of both the extreme left and the extreme right will cause both of them to continue to decline in popularity, thereby strengthening the government and producing a period of peace and security for the country.

Morales Ehrlich then discussed, quite poignantly, the fact that his two sons are guerrillas currently fighting to overthrow the government of which he is a part. He attributes this to his own exile, which began in 1977, and which he says deprived his sons of proper guidance. They fell under the influence of priests, university professors and Cubans who turned them into committed Marxists. They have since proven immune to his arguments and have chosen to follow a separate path.

Moving on to geopolitics, Morales Ehrlich concluded by arguing that the hand of Russia is plain in the actions of the Salvadoran left. He says that this is a fact which would not be obscured or ignored through some sort of romantic commitment to human rights.

He claims that the apparent success of the agrarian reform is threatening to Nicaragua—whose own land reform has been a disaster. The key difference, says Morales Ehrlich, is that the Salvadoran campesinos are allowed to own land, while Nicaragua has simply substituted Sandinista control for that of Somoza.

He believes that Cuba is deeply involved in aiding the Salvadoran left but that it is sometimes difficult to prove. All the information received by the Salvadoran Government concerning the involvement of outside countries in the violence is provided to them by the U.S. Embassy.

Morales Ehrlich said that he expected the violence to die down beginning in March, and that conditions would gradually improve during the remainder of the year. The birth pains of the new Salvadoran democracy, he said, were almost at an end.[1]

---

[1] What these pains might be were suggested by Robert A. Pastor, who coordinated Latin American and Caribbean affairs on the National Security Council staff in the Carter White House: the right (by which he means the Salvadoran oligarchy and conservatives from Guatemala, Argentina and the United States) "believes the communist cancer has reached an advanced state in El Salvador, and radical surgery—meaning perhaps 200,000 deaths—is necessary to excise the malignancy." ("Three Perspectives on El Salvador," *SAIS Review,* Summer 1981, Number 2).— Eds.

15. The Frente's Opposition: The Security Forces of El Salvador *

BY CYNTHIA ARNSON

Cynthia Arnson is an associate of the Institute for Policy Studies, Washington D.C., under whose auspices this research was conducted. Elsewhere (Reading 34), she has analyzed the U.S. role in beefing up the Salvadoran military forces.

THE official government security forces consist of the Army, the Navy, and the Air Force; all are under the direction of the Minister for Defense and Public Security. Three para-military units—the National Guard, the National Police, and the Treasury Police—are also under the direction of the Defense Ministry and are usually commanded by Army officers. An additional unit, the Customs Police, is under the jurisdiction of the Department of the Treasury. The Territorial Service, made up of Army reservists, numbers about 75,000. Its membership overlaps with that of ORDEN (Organización Democrática Nacionalista), a para-military unit under the Ministry of Defense and by custom headed by the President of the Republic.

The Army. With 9,000 men and five infantry regiments, the Army is the largest official state security organization. Its Chief of General Staff commands all other armed forces units. Besides providing for "external defense," the Army ". . . is charged with assisting in the maintenance of public order and participating in civic action." The Territorial Service is directly under Army jurisdiction.

The Navy. Formed in 1952 out of the Coast Guard, the Salvadoran Navy of 140 men has coastal patrol and search and rescue responsibilities. With only four small patrol boats, the Navy has little combat capability.

The Air Force. Consisting of 200 men, the Air Force was designed to support ground troops through aerial surveillance, airdrop, resupply, and transport.

The National Guard. Created in 1912 by Spanish officers, the Na-

---

* From the Institute for Policy Studies, Resource Publication, March 1980. Updated figures from an interview, U.S. Department of State, July 15, 1981. The army and security forces have been substantially expanded in recent months. The figures cited represent the most accurate estimates available.

tional Guard functions as a militarized police force, with detachments in most rural towns and villages. With approximately 3,000 men, it is organized into five commands with regional headquarters throughout the country. The National Guard, essential in maintaining political control in rural areas, has normally been under the direction of an Army major.

The National Police. Numbering about 2,800 men, the National Police is responsible for "law and order" in urban areas and for criminal investigations throughout the country. It works in close collaboration with the National Guard and the military. The Investigative Division of the National Police constitutes the country's intelligence unit, and investigates political as well as criminal cases.

The Treasury Police. With about 1,500 men, the Treasury Police serves as a support force for the National Guard and the National Police. It also has responsibility for customs duties. In this capacity, it is aided by the Customs Police, numbering about 530, with border control and narcotics control duties.

Para-military forces are as follows:

ORDEN (Organización Democrática Nacionalista). Founded in 1968 by General José Alberto Medrano ". . . to make a barrier to the attempts of the communists to provoke subversion in the countryside," ORDEN is a civilian para-military organization of 50,000–100,000 which enjoyed full government support. Its members were authorized to carry firearms and often worked in collaboration with government security forces, in addition to engaging in violent and repressive measures of their own. ORDEN was formally prohibited by Decree Law 12 of the first civilian-military junta that overthrew General Romero. General Medrano has called for its reconsitution, however, as the National Democratic Front.

White Warrior's Union (Unión Guerrillera Blanca—UGB). The UGB is a right-wing terror squad which threatened in 1977 to execute all Jesuit priests in the country for being "communists." The UGB is believed to have links to the Eastern Region Farmer's Front (Frente de Agricultores de la Región Oriental—FARO), a landowners' organization instrumental in blocking the implementation of the Agrarian Reform Act of 1976.

Anti-Communist Armed Forces of Liberation—War of Elimination (Fuerzas Armadas de Liberación Anticomunista—Guerra de Eliminación—FALANGE). FALANGE is a right-wing death squad consisting of active, retired, or off-duty members of the security forces.

Organization for the Liberation from Communism (Organización para la Liberación del Comunismo—OLC). Created after the overthrow of Romero, the OLC stated in a February communiqué that ". . . the Communists and their followers are our country's worst enemies. Our entire war is aimed at them and we are willing to offer our lives in the course of this war."

16. Communiqué from a "Death Squad" *

BY THE MAXIMILIANO HERNÁNDEZ MARTÍNEZ SQUAD

Proudly claiming credit for the November 27, 1980, abduction and assassination of six civilian leaders of the Democratic Revolutionary Front (FDR), the Maximiliano Hernández Martínez Squad takes as its name that of the general responsible for the massacre of some 30,000 peasants in 1932.

The six included Enrique Alvarez Córdoba, president of the FDR, and Juan Chacon, secretary general of the People's Revolutionary Bloc. The "death squad" abducted the FDR leaders from a press conference which was being held in an archbishopric legal assistance office in a San Salvador seminary. The Democratic Revolutionary Front and the archbishopric legal assistance office attributed the murders to the government's security forces but the governing junta denied any complicity and officially denounced the slayings.

While the bodies lay within the metropolitan cathedral of San Salvador, a powerful bomb exploded at its main door and set the church on fire. A church bombing should occasion little surprise when groups like the Maximiliano Hernández Martínez Squad have publicly warned that "priests who favor the Marxist terrorist bands" will be killed "if they continue with their sermons which are poisoning the minds of Salvadoran youths" (La Prensa Gráfica, November 28, 1980, reprinted in the Foreign Broadcast Information Service, Daily Reports, December 1, 1980).

THE "Maximiliano Hernández Martínez Squad," which claimed credit for the abduction and assassination (of the six leaders of the Revolutionary Democratic Front), has issued a message in which it "calls on the national conscience not to be intimidated by false

---

* From El Diario de Hoy, San Salvador, December 1, 1980, reprinted by the Foreign Broadcast Information Service, Daily Reports, December 3, 1980.

prophets who say nothing when communists destroy businesses, burn coffee sheds, kill peasants, and cruelly assassinate military personnel, security agents and soldiers, but react profusely when communists are executed."

The "squad" notes that the leaders of the Catholic Church "said nothing when South African Ambassador Dunn was killed, when progressive industrialists were kidnapped or when peasants were massacred in San Pedro Perulapan and San Esteban Catarina, where the communists had imposed their will by force. In those cases, there was no clamor for respect for human rights, nor was there any [cry of] injustice. In those cases, no defenders were forthcoming for those humble sons of the people. Now that six criminals, who led the mobs, have been executed by the people, however, the church leaders come out in defense of human rights. That is hypocrisy," the communiqué states.

Lastly, the "squad" urges the church hierarchy, U.S. diplomats and military leaders not to allow themselves to be deceived and instead urges them to react in the proper manner to this event which is nothing special since it is an action which is being taken to demand justice in the face of ineffective laws.

17. A Tragic Nuns' Tale *

BY THE SPECIAL PRESIDENTIAL MISSION TO EL SALVADOR

In early December, 1980, the world was shocked to learn of the brutal slaying of three American nuns and an American lay church worker in El Salvador. Coming only days after the assassination of the six civilian leaders of the Democratic Revolutionary Front (see Reading 16), the Carter Administration responded to this outrage by suspending military aid on December 5. A special U.S. mission was then sent to El Salvador, consisting of William D. Rogers, former Under Secretary of State for Economic Affairs and Assistant Secretary of State under President Ford, and Assistant Secretary of State William G. Bowdler (accompanied by Luigi R. Einaudi of the Department of State's Bureau of Inter-American Affairs). Their report is reprinted below.

Charges that would not be laid to rest that the junta was involved in a

---

* U.S. Department of State press release, December 12, 1980.

coverup, if not outright complicity,[1] forced the Duarte regime in early May to detain six members of the Salvadoran National Guard as suspects. Amid unconfirmed reports that the men have been released from jail to enjoy "provisional freedom," Acting Archbishop Rivera sharply criticized the junta in early August, 1981, for laxity in its investigation.

SISTER Ita Ford was an American citizen and a member of the Maryknoll order. She had been requested by the Apostolic Administrator of San Salvador to go to the refugee settlement in Chalatenango in July, 1980. She worked under the supervision of Father Efrain López distributing food, clothing and medicine to the poor and the dispossessed and lived in a modest parish house. Sister Maura Clarke joined Sister Ita in Chalatenango in August of 1980.

Chalatenango is an area particularly marked by competing violence between the left and right. During the latter part of November, it is reported that a sign appeared over the door of the Chalatenango parish house stating that all who lived there were Communists and anyone who entered would be killed. Neither Sister Ita, Sister Maura nor local clergy gave the sign any special attention.

All the Maryknolls of the Central American region meet in assembly every year. Sister Ita Ford and Sister Maura Clarke, together with Sister Madeline Dorsey and Sister Teresa Alexander, two other Maryknoll sisters who work in the Diocese of Santa Ana (and whom we interviewed), left El Salvador by plane on November 26 to go to the annual meeting, held in Managua, Nicaragua.

The four Maryknolls could not obtain reservations on the same plane back to El Salvador. Accordingly, Sisters Madeline and Teresa returned on a TACA flight arriving at the El Salvador International Airport at about 4:30 p.m., Tuesday, December 2. There they were met by two other American citizens, Ursuline Sister Dorothy Kazel and Jean Donovan, a lay volunteer, both of whom were engaged in similar parish work in the city of La Libertad. Sister Dorothy and Jean Donovan drove Sister Madeline and Sister Teresa to La Libertad, then returned to meet Sisters Ita and Maura at the airport. Sisters Madeline and Teresa understood the four intended to sleep at the parish house in La Libertad, and that Sisters Ita and Maura planned to drive to Chalatenango the following day.

---

[1] In a story by John Dinges put out by Pacific News Service and quoted by Alexander Cockburn (*Village Voice*, July 15-21, 1981), it is indicated that the killing may have been planned at high levels rather than being the product of trigger-happy military killers out of control.

Sister Ita and Sister Maura arrived at the El Salvador International Airport from Managua on a COPA flight at approximately 6:30 p.m. the evening of December 2. Sister Dorothy Kazel and Jean Donovan arrived in their white 1978 Toyota van at approximately the same time to pick them up.

The airport was filled with foreigners arriving to attend the funeral the next day of the leaders of the leftist Democratic Revolutionary Front (FDR) kidnapped and murdered on November 27. The level of tension was high throughout El Salvador. Security forces patrolled the airport and its access roads.

The four Americans met and, while waiting for their baggage, chatted with a group of Canadian churchmen. The Canadians left the airport first, at approximately 7:00 p.m.

We have not identified anyone who saw the four American churchwomen alive after the Canadian group left them at the airport baggage pickup station.

The next morning, Wednesday, December 3, between 10:00 and 11:00 a.m., Father Schindler of the La Libertad parish called the U.S. Consul in El Salvador and said that Sister Dorothy and Jean Donovan had not appeared at a meeting they were to attend, and that he could not locate them. The Consul immediately called Col. López Nuila, Chief of the National Police, and told him of the disappearance. Col. López Nuila asked if the nuns were wearing habits. He was advised they were not. The Colonel promised to institute a nationwide search. A few hours later the Ambassador arranged to have the Minister of Defense advised. The Minister promised to do everything in his power to find them.

Father Schindler evidently spent the rest of Wednesday, December 3, searching for the missing women. (We were unable to talk with him in El Salvador; he was in the U.S. for the funerals.) At about 8:00 p.m. that night, he found their Toyota van on a road about ten miles northwest of the airport, in the direction of the City of San Salvador. The license plates had been removed and the van was burned so badly it had to be identified by the engine number.

That same evening, December 3, the Canadian group telephoned and asked to see Ambassador White the next morning. The Ambassador and the Consul met with them at the Hotel Camino Real at about 8:30 a.m. on Thursday, December 4. The Canadians told them that they had seen the four American churchwomen at the airport on the evening of December 2. They also told him that, while driving away shortly before the likely departure of the four Americans, they had been stopped by a small group of uniformed men at a checkpoint on the outskirts of the airport. The Canadians were made to exit one of their two vehicles and minutely searched at gunpoint. A U.S. Embassy chauffeur, who was at the airport on official business that same evening, said that he saw two National Guard patrol cars and a jeep checking vehicles at random as they left the airport.

The Canadians said they believed themselves in danger. Since there is no Canadian Embassy in El Salvador, they asked for U.S. Embassy protection on their return trip to the airport. The Ambassador agreed to take them personally in his car.

On the way, the group stopped to examine the burned van.

When he arrived at the airport, at about 9:30 a.m., on Thursday, December 4, the Ambassador was advised by radio that the Embassy had been called by the Vicar of the Diocese of San Vicente. The Vicar had been told that the bodies of the "American nuns" were buried near Santiago Nonualco, a remote village some 15 miles northeast of the airport, and about 20 miles from where the van had been found northwest of the airport.

The Ambassador and the Consul drove there immediately; the trip into what is a rugged and mountainous part of the country took some time. After several inquiries, a local villager directed them to the grave, which he called that of the "American women," beside a back road some way out of Santiago Nonualco. When they arrived at the site, at about 1:30 in the afternoon, Father Paul Schindler was already there. He too had received word from the parish priest. Reporters from San Salvador and foreign media representatives began to arrive. Some villagers started to open the grave. No authorities were present when they began. About 3:00 p.m., the secretary of the Justice of the Peace, who performs the functions of a county coroner, arrived from Santiago Nonualco. He gave permission for the bodies, already uncovered, to be removed from the grave. Shortly thereafter the Justice of the Peace, Juan Santos Ceron, appeared.

All four women had been shot in the head. The face of one had been destroyed. The underwear of three was found separately. Bloody bandanas were also found in the grave.

From the information gathered by the Ambassador, the Consul and clergy from the crowd around the gravesite, and in the preliminary police reports provided us subsequently, it appears that local villagers heard a vehicle and shots late in the night of December 2. At dawn the next day, December 3, a villager discovered four bodies along the roadside. An hour or two later, the owner of the field where the bodies were found drove to inform local authorities. Two National Guardsmen and three Civil Guards appeared and ordered the villagers to dig a common grave a few feet from where they had been found. The Justice of the Peace and his secretary arrived at 9:30, certified the bodies as those of "unknowns," and authorized burial. By midday, the grave was filled over.

According to the accounts given the Ambassador and others on December 4, one victim had been found nude below the waist; out of respect, a villager had replaced her jeans before burial. The villagers took the bodies to be those of "blond foreigners" and subsequently informed church authorities.

After the disinterment, the Ambassador and Consul drove the Justice of the Peace and his secretary to San Salvador. In the course of the drive, the Justice of the Peace said that about 8:30 a.m. the previous day, December 3, the Commander of the Militia of Canton San Francisco Hacienda had notified him that there were four dead women on the road near Hacienda San Francisco. The Justice of the Peace and his secretary had then cooperated in the burial, following procedures they said had become standard at the direction of the security forces. They told the Ambassador that two or three such informal burials of unidentified bodies occurred every week.

As of this writing, no complete autopsy or other physical analysis has been performed that would enable investigators to determine the precise nature of the violence done to the four women.

According to the brief report on the cause of death prepared at the direction of the Justice of the Peace before the informal burial, one of the victims had been shot through the back of the head with a weapon that left exit wounds that destroyed her face; the other three had entry wounds, one in the temple, the others in the back of the head, but apparently no exit wounds. Those present at the disinterment, however, had the impression that the wounds were more extensive, that several had been caused by high-caliber bullets, and that the bodies were also bruised.

After the bodies reached San Salvador, Junta Member Colonel Gutiérrez responded immediately to Ambassador White's request to send forensic surgeons to do a formal autopsy. However, although the forensic surgeons arrived within an hour, they refused to perform the autopsy. The reason given was that no surgical masks were available. Only a routine medical examination was performed.

We add that the Sisters' van was found at a location some 20 miles away from where the bodies were found in the opposite direction from the airport. The burning of the van at this location suggests an attempt to deceive or mislead anyone searching for the women.

Such, in broad outline, are the facts that have come to light thus far: the women were last seen by the Canadians at the airport about

7:00 p.m. December 2. Their bodies were found shortly after 5:00 a.m. the next day by villagers in a remote area about 15 miles away. We have no direct proof of their whereabouts in the intervening period.

18. Have You No Sense of Decency, Sir? *

By Anthony Lewis

In the following piece, Anthony Lewis expresses disgust at Secretary of State Haig for his insensitivity and levity towards the murder of the church workers described in the previous reading. Lewis is a regular columnist for the Op-Ed page of the New York Times.

E VERY so often in our open society a public figure inadvertently displays his true character in a way that, once understood, can never be forgotten. It happened to Senator Joseph McCarthy when, cornered, he tried to distract the Army-McCarthy hearings by slandering a young lawyer. It happened the other day to Alexander Haig.

The flurry over the Secretary of State's power in the Reagan Administration is not what I have in mind, significant as it has been. That affair turned on the not very amazing discovery that Haig is an ambitious man. Someone in the White House finally noticed that he had a lean and hungry look.

The personally more revealing moment came a few days earlier [March 18, 1981], when Haig spoke about the killing of three Catholic nuns and a lay worker in El Salvador last December. His words did not get much notice at the time. They deserve attention.

The Secretary of State was testifying before the House Foreign Affairs Committee. He said this:

"I'd like to suggest to you that some of the investigations would lead one to believe that perhaps the vehicle that the nuns were riding in may have tried to run a roadblock, or may accidentally have been perceived to have been doing so, and there'd been an exchange of fire and then perhaps those who inflicted the casualties sought to cover it up. And this could have been at a very low level of both competence

---

* From *The New York Times*, March 29, 1981.

and motivation in the context of the issue itself. But the facts on this are not clear enough for anyone to draw a definitive conclusion."

The next day newspapers reported Haig suggesting that the four American churchwomen may have tried to run a roadblock and been killed in an exchange of fire with security forces. That same day Haig appeared before the Senate Foreign Relations Committee, and Senator Claiborne Pell of Rhode Island asked him about his comment.

"I'm glad you raised it, Senator," Haig replied, "because I read some of the press reportings, which were of course not what I said."

He explained that an autopsy on one women showed the death bullet to have gone through glass first. That meant, he suggested, that one soldier might have fired through a car window, and then others panicked.

"I laid that out as a, one of the prominent theories as to what happened; and I hope that it does not get distorted or perverted emotionally and incorrectly."

Senator Pell asked whether he was suggesting the possibility that "the nuns may have run through a roadblock." With a tone of amazement in his voice, Haig said:

"You mean that they tried to violate . . .? Not at all, no, not at all. My heavens! The dear nuns who raised me in my parochial schooling would forever isolate me from their affections and respect."

Pell asked about the phrase "exchange of fire" used by Haig. "Did you mean that the nuns were firing at the people, or what did 'an exchange of fire' mean?"

Haig chuckled. Then, with an air of levity he continued:

"I haven't met any pistol-packing nuns in my day, Senator. What I meant was that if one fellow starts shooting, then the next thing you know they all panic."

That was Haig's testimony. What does it have to do with the facts?

From what is known and has been published, the four women were picked up on the way from the airport to their house late in the afternoon. They were killed many hours later, in a different place. They were shot in the head at close range. None of those facts is consistent with a mix-up at a roadblock.

Haig's "prominent" theory has in fact never been taken seriously in the investigation of the killings, according to people involved in that investigation. An early report that glass fragments had been found in one of the bodies was later called erroneous.

The theory sounds, indeed, as if it could have been based on something floated by the Salvadoran right to obstruct a real investigation. From the start the effort to find the killers has run into obstacles in El Salvador. For two weeks U.S. diplomats could not even get local doctors to perform autopsies; the doctors were afraid of finding something that pointed to the security forces. The F.B.I. has waited two months now for Salvadoran officials to send some promised fingerprints.

Whatever the effect of Haig's comments in El Salvador, they say a good deal about their author. An American Secretary of State, talking about the vicious killing of four American women, suggested that they were responsible in some measure for their fate. The next day, challenged, he tried to slither away, joking and expressing amazement and blaming the press.

Some who heard Haig felt outrage, but no member of Congress expressed it. No one followed the example of Joseph N. Welch, counsel in the Army-McCarthy hearings, and said: "Have you no sense of decency, sir, at long last? Have you no sense of decency?"

19. The Death Squads Do Not Operate Independent of the Security Forces *

By Captain Ricardo Alejandro Fiallos

Ricardo Alejandro Fiallos was a Captain in the Salvadoran army. In December, 1980, he was forced to flee El Salvador after having received anonymous death threats for criticizing the military's lack of professionalism and its role in perpetuating atrocities against the civilian population.

I SPEAK to you this morning as an officer in exile of the Salvadoran Army. Despite the risks which this type of public testimony holds for members of my family who still remain in El Salvador, I feel that it is critical that members of the Congress as well as the people of the United States understand the role played by the high military command as well as the directors of the security forces in El Salvador and the nature of their involvement in the violence which continues to afflict my country.

It is important to understand that the base of power in El Salvador does not lie in the hands of the President of the Junta, José Napoleón Duarte, nor with the other civilian members of the Junta. Rather, it

---

* From testimony before the Subcommittee on Foreign Operations of the House Appropriations Committee, April 29, 1981.

is the high command of the armed forces and, more specifically, Colonels José Guillermo García and Jaime Abdul Gutiérrez, along with the directors of the security forces, who wield the real power in El Salvador. An example of this is evidenced by the fact that despite two official requests from President Duarte to the Minister of Defense, Colonel García, to remove Colonel Francisco Moran as the head of the Treasury Police, due to the involvement of this branch of the security forces in the brutal assassination of various mayors, most of whom were Christian Democrats, Moran still retains his position.

It is a grievous error to believe that the forces of the extreme right, or the so-called "death squads," operate independent of the security forces. The simple truth of the matter is that "Los Escuadrones de la Muerte" are made up of members of the security forces and acts of terrorism credited to these squads such as political assassinations, kidnappings, and indiscriminate murder are, in fact, planned by high-ranking military officers and carried out by members of the security forces. I do not make this statement lightly, but with full knowledge of the role which the high military command and the directors of the security forces have played in the murder of countless numbers of innocent people in my country.

During the period in which I worked as a doctor in the military hospital, I treated numerous members of the security forces. In inquiring as to the cause of their injuries, which is a normal medical procedure in the hospital, various individuals told me as well as other doctors that they had been injured in the act of "eliminating" civilians.

Let me make it clear that not all of the armed forces in El Salvador are implicated in the types of crimes which I have mentioned. The principal problem lies in the high military command and in the directors of the security forces, not in the ranks of the army, and it is these individuals who, without a doubt, constitute the gravest threat to the future of El Salvador. Until the officials of the high military command are replaced and the security forces completely restructured and brought under strict control, there will be no end to the violence which is destroying my country, and no possibility of establishing a democratic government.

Finally, due to the fact that the center of power in El Salvador lies in the high military command and the directors of the security forces, any military assistance or training which the United States provides to the current government is perceived by the people of El Salvador as support for the forces of repression which are destroying the country.

Unless the United States government ceases its support for the current regime and attempts to encourage an end to the state of siege and a political settlement which, by definition, must include the opposition forces, there will be no peace in my country.

20. My Lai In El Salvador: The Sumpul River Massacre *

BY A PRESBYTERY OF HONDURAS

As Warren Hoge writes, in The New York Times, *June 8, 1981, "reports of deliberate killings of noncombatants during El Salvador's civil war" are difficult to confirm. "Many times no one has been left to tell what happened." Tragically, it can be reliably reported that a mass killing took place at the Lempa River on the Honduras border on March 17, 1981. Eyewitnesses include Rev. Earl Gallagher, a Brooklyn-born Capuchin priest working in Honduras, and Yvonne Dilling, a refugee worker from Fort Wayne. With low-flying Salvadoran helicopter pilots firing down on refugees trying to cross the Lempa into Honduras, and with a Salvadoran gunship and Salvadoran soldiers raining down rockets, automatic-weapons fire and grenades, children clung to Father Gallagher's beard as he swam them to safety while Ms. Dilling tied infants to herself with her bra straps to carry them over the river. Over 200 are believed to be dead or missing.*

Father Gallagher had also visited the site of an earlier and even larger massacre on the Sumpul River—also on the Honduras border—the day after it took place. "There were so many vultures picking at the bodies," he recalled, "that it looked like a black carpet." Included below is a brief account of the earlier massacre in which perhaps 600 died. The event has been compared to the My Lai atrocity in Vietnam.[1]

THE most evident example of harassment and cruelty happened last May 14. The day before, several trucks and vehicles of the Honduran Army arrived filled with soldiers. Without stopping, they went 14 kilometers further down, to near the Sumpul River, the

---

* From testimony entered into the Congressional Record, September 24, 1980, by Senator Edward Kennedy, pp. S13375–S13379.
  [1] In 1968, an American military company, headed by Lt. William Calley, entered the Vietnamese village of My Lai and without provocation gunned down 347 civilians, most of them women and children, some infants.

border between Honduras and El Salvador, near the Honduran towns of Santa Lucia and San José. The megaphones directed to Salvadoran territory shouted out the prohibition against crossing the border.

On the opposite side, at around 7 a.m., in the Salvadoran village La Arada and its surrounding area, the massacre began. A minimum of two helicopters, the Salvadoran National Guard, soldiers and the paramilitary organization ORDEN opened fire on the defenseless people. Women tortured before the finishing shot, infants thrown into the air for target practice, were some of the scenes of the criminal slaughter. The Salvadorans who crossed the river were returned by the Honduran soldiers to the area of the massacre. In mid-afternoon the genocide ended, leaving a minimum number of 600 corpses.

Days before, according to the Honduran press, in the city of Ocotepeque, bordering Guatemala and El Salvador, there was a secret meeting of high military commanders of the three countries. The news was officially denied shortly afterwards.

A minimum of 600 unburied bodies were the prey of dogs and vultures for several days. Others were lost in the waters of the river. A Honduran fisherman found five small bodies of children in his fishtrap. The Sumpul River was contaminated from the village of Santa Lucia.

21. *Conversations with Salvadoran Refugees* *

By Representatives Gerry E. Studds,
Barbara Ann Mikulski, and Robert Edgar

During their fact-finding trip to Central America, Representatives Barbara Mikulski, Robert Edgar and Gerry E. Studds conducted interviews with Salvadoran refugees who managed to make it into Honduras.

THOSE interviewed describe what appears to be a systematic campaign conducted by the security forces of El Salvador to deny any rural base for guerrilla operations in the north. By terroriz-

---

* From *Central America, 1981*, Report to the Committee on Foreign Affairs, U.S. House of Representatives, March, 1981.

ing and depopulating villages in the region, they have sought to isolate the guerrillas and create problems of logistics and food supply.

This strategy [reminiscent of what was previously tried in Vietnam] was recently summarized by one military commander, who told the *Boston Globe*:

> The subversives like to say that they are the fish and the people are the ocean. What we have done in the north is to dry up the ocean so we can catch the fish easily.

The Salvadoran method of "drying up the ocean" involves, according to those who have fled from its violence, a combination of murder, torture, rape, the burning of crops in order to create starvation conditions, and a program of general terrorism and harassment.

This violence has produced a steady stream of refugees across the border into neighboring Honduras, where the U.N. estimates more than 25,000 refugees are living on the charity of international relief agencies and the hospitality of Honduran peasants who are desperately poor themselves.

The following is an outline of the statements made by refugees to the Mikulski party; as summarized on the scene by the translator accompanying the group:

Interview—Woman No. 1. This woman fled in November 1980: She was 9 months pregnant.

The Army was setting up guns, heavy cannon, artillery on the hills around their village, bombing the villages and forcing the people away. As soon as the child was born, she could hear shots in the distance, and they were killing a woman from her village. She quickly tied herself together and took the child and ran up into the mountains. No one helped her in the birth. Her husband was the only person with her and the children.

They fled their village; they went to another valley. The Army had burned their homes, the clothes of the people and had burned the crops.

They continued hiding in the mountainsides. If people were caught in the village, they would kill them. Women and children alike. She said that with pregnant women, they would cut open the stomachs and take the babies out. She said she was very afraid because she had seen the result of what a guard had done to a friend of hers. She had been pregnant and they took the child out after they cut open her stomach. And where she lived they did not leave one house standing. They burned all of them.

Ms. Mikulski. Did the soldiers use American helicopters?

Answer. She doesn't know where they came from, but the airplanes came. There was a plane flying overhead and people were nervous because they didn't know what it was about, and they remembered what the planes were like in Salvador. She said they would flee and they would give their children cold tortillas, and a little bit of sugar so they would not cry because they were afraid that if they cried, the Army would find them and if they found them, they would kill all of them.

Interview—*Woman No. 2.* She says that she would like to tell us the following: That many of her family were killed. About 7 months ago, they killed one of her family and the child was an infant and is now in a hospital in a nearby town close to death. The army threw the baby in the river when they found them, and they took them into the woods and later they were found. She personally saw children around the age of 8 being raped, and then they would take their bayonets and make mincemeat of them. With their guns they would shoot at their faces.

She said, "Even going to the mountainside, you weren't safe, for the military has huge machines, and set up mortars on the mountain and shoot at the villagers."

Question. These were army troops or guards?

Answer. Troops. Army.

Question. Did the left ever do these things?

Answer. No. No, they haven't done any of those kinds of things . . . but the army would cut people up and put soap and coffee in their stomachs as a mocking. They would slit the stomach of a pregnant woman and take the child out, as if they were taking eggs out of an iguana. That is what I saw. That is what I have to say.

Interview—*Man No. 2.* Two of his neighbors belong to the paramilitary organization, ORDEN. He knows personally of several assassinations that they committed. And he was afraid that if they went to the town where the commandant was, they would also be murdered in the same way.

He is saying that the Government of El Salvador is saying that the United States is helping them. He has fear that this aid will be used against the people across the border of El Salvador. Once they keep on pushing people out, they are going to come across the border and use that same armament in this country.

Ms. Mikulski. Is it the helicopters?

Answer. Yes, it is the helicopters. They are up in the air and they shoot at us. And we are completely defenseless. We have our ax and machetes to clean the earth with and to cultivate the land, and that is all we have against the helicopters.

Ms. Mikulski. Has the left done anything against him?

Answer. No, they don't kill children. We don't complain about them at all.

Interview—Woman No. 5. In her town, the army took off three boys from a bus and took them to a little canyon and killed them. She saw them when they took them off the bus and then they covered them with dirt and stones and sticks. A 13, a 16 year old, another one 20. And the families after 3 days found them and buried them by the river. And once she saw them kill six women.

First they killed two women and then they burned their bodies with firewood. She said, one thing she saw was a dog carrying a new born infant in its mouth. The child was dead because it had been taken from the mother's womb after the guard slit open her stomach.

Ms. Mikulski. How were the other two women killed?

Answer. First, they hung them and then they machinegunned them and then they threw them down to the ground. When we arrived the dogs were eating them and the birds were eating them. They didn't have any clothes on. They had decapitated one of the women. They found the head somewhere else. Another woman's arm was sliced off. We saw the killings from a hillside and then when we came back down we saw what had happened. While we were with the bodies we heard another series of gunshots and we fled again.

Ms. Mikulski. Why does she think the soldiers did that to the women?

Answer. Because they were looking for anyone they could find in that area of the country, they were killing everybody. They were looking for people to kill—that's what they were doing.

No, it's the military that is doing this. Only the military. The popular organization isn't doing any of this.

22. Repression in El Salvador*

By AMNESTY INTERNATIONAL, U.S.A.

Amnesty International is a London-based, private human rights organization, with U.S. offices in New York and Washington. It was founded in 1966 and received the Nobel Peace Prize in 1977.

THE present submission highlights human rights abuses in El Salvador since October 1979 when a civilian-military government

---

* From testimony before the Subcommittee on Inter-American Affairs of the Committee on Foreign Affairs of the U.S. House of Representatives, March 1981.

came to power, ousting the former regime of General Romero. The new civilian-military junta publicly committed itself to "promote and encourage the true exercise of human rights" and to act on the recommendations put forth by the Inter-American Commission on Human Rights of the Organization of American States, as approved at its Eighth General Assembly in 1978.

Today, more than one year after the government took office, some 8,000 Salvadorans are estimated to have died as a result of political violence; government forces have been reportedly implicated in at least 6,000 of these deaths.

Repression at the hands of the government security forces and paramilitary groups has continued to escalate in recent months. Characteristic of these abuses are summary executions, arbitrary detentions, disappearances and torture by conventional security forces as well as paramilitary groups such as ORDEN. (ORDEN, now renamed Frente Democrático Nacionalista, is still under army command although the government of El Salvador promulgated a decree declaring that the paramilitary group would be disbanded. No provision was made, however, for the confiscation of ORDEN armament and ORDEN forces have continued to work in coordination with the conventional security forces). Among the targets of repression are peasants, youth, human rights activists, trade unionists, academics, journalists and clergy.

While these abuses have occurred against a background of civil warfare between government forces and guerrilla organizations (themselves guilty of serious abuses), evidence reaching Amnesty International indicates that the majority of victims of torture and death at the hands of the security forces have not generally been proven to have any direct involvement in armed insurrection. Most of the deaths have taken place after the victims had been seized from their homes or work places and were defenseless.

During 1980, the government of El Salvador repeatedly claimed that independent "anti-communist" death squads beyond official control were responsible for these abductions and murders. This assertion, however, directly contradicts evidence compiled by Amnesty International from hundreds of individual cases attributing responsibility for serious violations of human rights to regular security forces. It would appear that by consistently attributing the detentions, tortures and assassinations of alleged members of the opposition to groups beyond official control, the government of El Salvador is seeking a means of evading responsibility for the actions of its own security forces.

Repression Against Specially Targeted Sectors of Salvadoran Society. The following selection of cases, which Amnesty International believes to be representative of recent human rights violations in El Salvador, includes incidents of political violence since January, 1980. These cases reveal a selective pattern of repression targeted against specific sectors of the population. The victims of these extra-legal measures are characterized by their association, or alleged association, with peasant, labor or religious organizations, with the trade union movement, with professional associations or with political parties or other organizations that do not actively support the present government.

Academics. The teaching sector has been one of numerous targets of repression under the present government in El Salvador. During 1980, persecution of academics intensified sharply. From January to October 1980, at least 90 teachers were murdered by security forces in El Salvador in a pattern of selective repression aimed at eliminating the leadership of the National Association of Salvadoran Educators (Asociacíon Nacional de Educadores de El Salvador: ANDES), the national teachers' union, which is a member of the *Bloque Popular Revolucionario* (a broad coalition of unions which includes peasants, teachers, students and shantytown dwellers), one of the largest political opposition groups in the country. In the same period, at least 19 primary and secondary schools (both public and church) have been raided by security forces. On July 26, 1980, the army carried out a military occupation of the National University, resulting in the deaths of 22 students. As a result of such persecution, many teachers have gone into exile and 85% of the schools in the eastern departments of La Unión, San Miguel, and Usulutan have been forced to close their doors.

Journalists. A number of both Salvadoran and foreign journalists have been killed or expelled during the past year. On July 12, 1980, Jaime Suárez Quemain and César Navarro, editor and photographer of the Salvadoran opposition newspaper *La Crónica,* were found dead with signs of torture. On August 8, 1980, Ignacio Rodriguez, a correspondent for the Mexican magazine *El Proceso,* was shot dead. John Sullivan, a U.S. national and free-lance journalist, was abducted on December 2, 1980. On January 15, 1981, nine staff members of the Salvadoran newspaper *El Independiente* were abducted; the paper was subsequently forced to close down.

Internal Refugees. Among the people in El Salvador who have been killed or disappeared since the beginning of 1980 have been thousands of peasants in rural regions who have fled areas of armed conflict.

Amnesty International has received numerous reports of repression against such internal refugees. Reports received in October 1980 indicate that police and military forces in the Department of Morazán were removing internal refugees from the camps and then summarily executing them. These reports indicated that the areas had been closed to both Salvadoran and foreign journalists, and to local human rights organizations because of abuses committed by the security forces in counter-insurgency operations. This isolation of internal refugees from independent international observers increases fears for the safety of thousands of internal refugees now being sheltered in the centers.

Amnesty International has asserted that a campaign of murder and abduction has been launched against peasants in El Salvador. The announcement of the agrarian reform program was coupled with the arrival of troops (operating in open coordination with the paramilitary group ORDEN), ostensibly to carry out agrarian reform programs. These operations have resulted in the abduction and murder of hundreds of men, women, and children, the razing of villages and the destruction of crops in the Departments of Suchitoto, Morazán, Cuscatlán, and Chalatenango. In another incident on May 14, 1980, an estimated 600 peasants were reportedly massacred by Salvadoran troops along the Honduras/El Salvador border, as they attempted to escape National Guard operations and reach safety in Honduras.

Similar attacks have occurred on repeated occasions in the past. Sources within El Salvador indicate that of the 8,000 Salvadorans estimated to have died in political violence during 1980, 3,300 were peasants.

Human Rights Monitors. Those who monitor human rights abuses have also been the targets of assassinations, bombings, detention and torture.

The El Salvador Human Rights Commission (CDHES), an independent human rights monitoring group, provides assistance to victims of human rights abuse and publicizes their cases. The CDHES has been subjected to frequent harassment. The Commission is one of the few institutions in El Salvador independent of political opposition groups that has spoken out strongly in condemnation of the torture, arbitrary detentions and summary executions that have been carried out on a massive scale since January, 1980. The Commission offices have been destroyed by bombings three times this year, and several members of their staff have been assassinated. Victor Medrano, the information and administration secretary of the CDHES, was abducted by armed plainclothesmen in San Salvador on January 25, 1981. Victor Medrano was subsequently released on February 11, 1981 following international protest on his behalf. Two other members of the Commission have been killed over the past year. Maria Magdalena Enriquez, the Press Secretary of the CDHES, was seized on October 3, 1980 by National Police officers in the presence of numerous witnesses. Her body was found two days later in a shallow grave. On October 25, 1980, Ramon Valladares Perez, administrator of the Commission, was shot dead while driving a car in the capital. As in hundreds of similar cases, authorities refused to acknowledge these detentions and have denied responsibility for the fate of the victims. Latest reports indicate that repression against the Commission has forced closure of their offices in El Salvador and many of its remaining staff have been forced to leave the country.

The Church in El Salvador has publicly and repeatedly been threatened with violence by anonymous, pro-government groups. . . .

Today, the eyes of the international community are cast on El Salvador, a tiny country beset by soaring violence and government-sponsored repression. A country whose government continues to violate the international standards of government conduct set forth in the American Convention on Human Rights to which it is a party. A government which has not complied with the Inter-American Commission on Human Rights recommendations approved in 1978 on the occasion of the Eighth General Assembly of the Organization of American States. A government which has been cited for its human rights violations by the United Nations General Assembly in its December 15, 1980 vote, calling "upon governments to refrain from the supply of arms and other military assistance in the current circumstances." A government which has shown itself unwilling to stop the brutal repression of its people. These are the central features of El Salvador's political landscape against which U.S. policy towards El Salvador should be reviewed.

Chapter III

PEASANTS AND OLIGARCHS IN THE AGRARIAN REFORM

Editors' Introduction

NOT only in El Salvador, but throughout the nonindustrial world, land shortages and rising population growth have provided the matrix for social struggle and demands for land reform.[1] The situation in El Salvador, the most densely populated area in Latin America, is particularly critical, and is intricately involved with the political problems of that tiny country.

The land reform program initiated by the current Salvadoran regime in March of 1980 has been at the center of controversy, both in El Salvador and among defenders and opponents of the junta abroad. Defenders of the current junta, and its reform-advocating President, José Napoleón Duarte, frequently cite the agrarian reform program as evidence of the good intentions of the Salvadoran government. In the U.S. one of the most vehement supporters of the Duarte government, and its reformist policies, is the executive branch of the American Federation of Labor/Congress of Industrial Organizations, the mainstream of organized labor. For example, a spokesman of the AFL/CIO foreign policy bureau, the American Institute for Free Labor Development, William C. Doherty, Jr., finds the Salvadoran agrarian reform to be a sign of the essential moderation and good will of the Duarte regime, and dismisses criticism as the carping of extremist groups.[2]

---

[1] See Paul R. Ehrlich, Anne H. Ehrlich and John P. Holdren, *Ecoscience: Population, Resources, Environment* (San Francisco, 1977), Chap. 7; Emma Rothschild, "Food Politics," *Foreign Affairs* (January, 1976).

[2] See Doherty's article, "U.S. Labor's Role in El Salvador," *Free Trade Union News*, Vol. 36, No. 2, February 1981. Not all U.S. trade unionists are supporters of the Duarte regime and of Washington's role in El Salvador. Many local affiliates of the AFL/CIO have taken openly critical positions. In February, 1981, for example,

However, some of the readings in this section present a more pessimistic picture of the agrarian reform, placing the program more firmly in the tragic politics of El Salvador than do Duarte's uncritical defenders. Particularly pertinent is the testimony of the administrator of the junta's earliest efforts at land reform, Leonel Gómez, who concludes that after the first year, the program had become a failure, and functioned mainly to bolster the reformist image of the oligarchic regime in El Salvador.

Many press reports suggest the validity of Gómez's interpretation, and that of other critics of El Salvador's agrarian program. A report in the *Wall Street Journal* pointed out that land reform "is crippled by delays and by the fears of many peasants, who say they have seen their friends dragged off and shot by uniformed men." The *Journal* cited an agrarian reform institute official, who "attended to a group of peasants who had abandoned their farms after 12 of their leaders were lined up and shot." That official told the reporter he counted 200 killings alone tied to land reform, "only three or four of which were committed by the left. The widespread belief among peasants is that the military is responsible for most of the killing."[3] A more recent dispatch from El Salvador by *New York Times* correspondent Raymond Bonner reports sharp limitation on the program of land distribution by the government, exempting cotton areas from the program, for example. (For Bonner's article, see Reading 28, below).

Thus, the argument that land reform in El Salvador can be evaluated apart from the violence that is engulfing the country, offered by agrarian consultant Roy Prosterman, who had helped design the agrarian reform for the U.S.-supported governments in Vietnam, should be subjected to the closest scrutiny. "Land reform," writes Irving Howe in *Dissent*, "would/could make a major difference only if it were accompanied by physical security for political dissidents and recalcitrant peasants were able to create their own free and autonomous institutions."[4] In this struggle, sometimes muted, sometimes violent, is to be found the real meaning of land reform in El Salvador.

---

some 50 trade union leaders in the New York area formed a "Labor Committee in Support of Democracy and Human Rights in El Salvador," based on the following principles: support of self-determination for El Salvador; condemnation of U.S. military intervention; and affirmation of basic democratic rights for the people of El Salvador. For the labor group's address, see below, Bibliography and Resources.

[3] Steve Frazier, "Military Coup Feared in El Salvador," *The Wall Street Journal,* Dec. 9, 1980.

[4] Howe, "Looking into El Salvador," *Dissent* (Summer, 1981), pp. 285–88.

23. The Need for Agrarian Reform *

By Laurence R. Simon and James C. Stephens, Jr.

OXFAM-America is a nonprofit agency that funds self-help development and offers humanitarian assistance in the Third World. It makes grants to people in some of the poorest parts of the world who are seeking to develop their own food supply and other resources. It also promotes relief and development assistance for developing nations. It currently is assisting the Nicaraguan people in reconstruction programs with grants for medical services and agricultural projects. OXFAM began in England in 1942 as the "Oxford Committee for Famine Relief," and there are now OXFAMs in five countries, which share a network of 50 field directors. Laurence Simon is Director of Education and Issue Analysis. James C. Stephens, Jr., is a member of the Department of History, University of Chicago.

THE lack of extensive agrarian reform seriously impedes the future economic growth of El Salvador. Since 1881, when the nascent planter oligarchy abolished communal forms of land tenure, evicting thousands of Indian and Mestizo villagers from the fertile central highlands to plant coffee, El Salvador's agrarian reality has been characterized by a growing dichotomy between large landed estates devoted to commercial export crops and small subsistence plots of basic food crops, with as much as 65 percent of the population landless.

In 1971, half of El Salvador's 271,000 farm units consisted of less than one hectare of very poor soil; ninety percent were smaller than five hectares. (Nine hectares are the minimum necessary to provide subsistence for a family of six.) Less than one percent of the units, farms of more than 500 hectares, controlled more than 15 percent of the land. A study by Melvin Burke reveals that six Salvadoran families held more land than 133,000 small farmers.

Each year, hundreds of thousands of peasant families migrate seasonally from small plots to commercial plantations, unable to subsist on their own units. This pattern of agricultural life reflects the predominant pattern of land use.

Land Use Patterns. Agriculture accounts for over twenty-five per-

---

* Excerpted from: *El Salvador Land Reform: 1980-1981–Impact Audit* (OXFAM-America).

cent of El Salvador's GNP, more than any single sector of the economy, and agricultural activities absorb 50 percent of the economically active population. Agricultural exports represent ninety percent of the value of exports outside Central America. Of the country's 2,098,-000 hectares, one third is not in production, leaving 1,580,000 for farming. Much of that land, however, is either unsuitable for intensive agriculture or currently utilized as pasture. The 1974 Agricultural Zonification Study of the OAS, gives the following breakdown of El Salvador's land resources:

(1) 18.3 percent of El Salvador's land is suited for intensive crops, mechanization, and irrigation—classes I, II, and III.

(2) 6.1 percent is classified as medium quality soils suitable for limited cultivation but subject to erosion—class IV.

(3) 18.3 percent is not suitable for intensive cultivation; it is subject to serious erosion—class VI. It is, however, suitable for perennial and tree crops.

(4) 56.7 percent is classified as V, VI, and VII. Depending on the specific class, it needs either drainage, terracing, or other land improvements.

In El Salvador, it is common practice for small farmers and peasants to devote the greatest proportion of their land to annual crops such as corn, beans, and sorghum. On microplots smaller than one hectare over 95 percent of land is devoted to cultivation of basic grains; less than 1 percent of land lies fallow. Conversely, on land of 100 hectares and larger over 50 percent lies fallow and less than 20 percent is planted with basic grains.

Land use follows the same patterns for permanent crops, of which coffee, the backbone of the economy, comprises over 90 percent of the value. Only 9 percent of permanent crops are grown on farms larger than 500 hectares, but over 63 percent are grown on farms of 5-200 hectares.

(1) More of El Salvador's land resources were used for extensive cattle grazing than for the production of food crops.

(2) Only 10 percent of El Salvador's land was planted with permanent crops.

(3) Despite rapid population growth and increased demand for basic grains, the amount of pasture land remained unchanged.

(4) During a period of sharply increasing unemployment more labor un-intensive export crops were planted at the same time that more labor-saving machinery was utilized.

Land use patterns are critically related to agricultural growth and increased employment. Agrarian reform should move to redress the imbalance between the large estate, the latifundia, and the minifundia.

Land Tenure Arrangements. There have been three major developments during the past 20 years:

(1) The rapid expansion of the landless rural laborers.

(2) The rapid growth of rental arrangements.

(3) The marked decline in permanent resident laborers, *colonos.*

According to a 1976 United Nations Study, *Realidad Campesina y Desarrollo Nacional*, the number of landless (that is those without access to land either by renting, sharecropping, or ownership) mushroomed from 12 percent to 40 percent between 1960 and 1975 because of reductions in the number of permanent resident laborers and temporary landed laborers, the displacement of laborers by labor-saving machinery on export crop plantations, and a reduction in the tide of rural-to-urban migrants. Informed sources believe that the landless rural laborer constitutes as much as 60 percent of the rural population today. The significance of this figure cannot be overstated. *As will be documented in this report, the majority of the rural population—landless and poorest—are excluded from any potential benefits under the present land reform.*

The second important development has been the expansion of tenancy arrangements. Between 1950 and 1971 the number of rented landholdings has increased more than 100 percent, from 33,000 to 76,000. In 1971, of 271,000 agricultural units, 28 percent were rented on the basis of varied forms of payment. Perhaps the most striking aspect of the rental situation in El Salvador is the diminutive size of land parcels. More than 98 percent of renting occurs on parcels smaller than 5 hectares—considerably below the land minimum required for subsistence. And more than 60 percent of all land holdings were operated by some form of rental or lease arrangement in 1971.

The increase in rented parcels reflects an expansion of wage labor on plantations, the monetization of the rural economy, the conversion of *colono* lands to rental arrangements in the wake of a 1965 minimum wage law, and, finally, the division of several large properties into rental units. It is evident that the size and number of rental plots is one of El Salvador's urgent agrarian problems.

There has been a sharp decline in the number of *colonos*, permanent resident laborers who normally were given access to a small plot of land in return for part of their crop and labor. As more plantations increase the use of labor-saving machinery and employ landless temporary laborers, the number of *colonos* and *colonaje* arrangements has rapidly diminished. From a high of 55,000 in 1961 the number of landholdings with *colono* arrangements fell to 17,000 by 1971. As [Alastair] White observes,

> . . . planters now found that it paid to reduce the number of *colonos* to around the number needed at slackest times of the year, relying on labor hired for specific tasks, and usually for one or two days only. . . .

Income Distribution. A direct corollary of the concentration of land holdings, patterns of land use, and increase in landlessness is the acutely skewed distribution of income. Over two-thirds of the population receive less than one-third of disposable income. On the other side, less than 2 percent of the population possesses one-third of the income. Less than 6.5 percent of the coffee growers control over 78 percent of income derived from profits.

According to the Congressional mandate which required U.S. AID to establish an income limit for rural poor, 83.5 percent of the rural population receives less than $225 per capita. Sixty percent of El Salvador's rural families earn less than the minimum $528.00 (1976 prices) needed to buy subsistence food products.

The source of income is highly correlated to size of landholding. The larger the landholding the greater the proportion of income derived from agricultural activities and vice versa. While *campesinos* with less than one hectare earn 80 percent of income in off-farm wages, farmers with 10 to 50 hectares earn over 80 percent of income from agriculture. The skewed distribution of income in El Salvador has severely hindered the growth of domestic markets and the economic modernization of El Salvador. It is one of the issues that agrarian reform must address.

Underutilization of Labor. The combination of minifundia and sharp seasonal fluctuations in the demand for labor on commercial farms produces a chronic underutilization of labor. PRELAC of the International Labor Organization reports that El Salvador has the highest degree of labor underutilization in Latin America. More than 50 percent of the rural labor force is unemployed more than two-thirds of the year. From 1950 to 1970, rural unemployment figures have oscillated between 45 and 50 percent, indicating that only 35 percent of the population is active during the whole year.

Summary. The yardstick for agrarian reform in El Salvador must be the extent to which it addresses the issues of land concentration, inefficient use of land, growing landlessness, skewed income distribution, and chronic underutilization of labor.

24. The False Promise— and Real Violence— of Land Reform in El Salvador *

By Peter Shiras

Peter Shiras is now a Washington, D.C.-based writer, and was a former consultant to the Inter-American Development Bank.

AT the heart of [the] disputes about El Salvador lies its land reform program. On some points, no dispute exists. Certainly, the land reform has stirred opposition from wealthy Salvadoran landlords and hard-line sectors of the military. No one disputes that their opposition has been violent. All six of the Americans killed in El Salvador were murdered by these right wing opponents of the land reform; two of them, Michael P. Hammer and Mark David Pearlman, were advisers to the Salvadoran government on land reform and were killed along with Rudolfo Viera, the Salvadoran official in charge of land reform. Viera's deputy, Leonel Gómez, has gone into exile to save his own life. Hammer blamed the right for 80 percent of the bloodshed in a *Washington Post* interview one week before his death. At the same time, everyone agrees that the land reform has failed to satisfy the left in El Salvador. The Democratic Revolutionary Front (FDR) makes clear its intention of overthrowing the current junta in San Salvador. Certain other facts can not be disputed: more than 10,000 Salvadorans were killed in 1980 alone.

After those facts are entered, we have political disputes and interpretations, particularly in the U.S. The Carter State Department and much of the U.S. media contend that the San Salvador junta represents moderation and a courageous attempt to steer a middle course between the revolutionary, totalitarian left and the extreme right. The Reagan transition team announced that it considered Carter's policies in El Salvador excessively reform-minded. Mexico, Canada, Nicaragua and most of the social democratic parties of Western Europe (including the Austrian and West German governing parties) have endorsed the Salvadoran rebels, the Democratic Revolutionary Front (FDR). A very broad coalition of Americans, the U.S. Commit-

---

* From *Food Monitor*, Jan.–Feb. 1981; no. 20.

tee in Solidarity with the People of El Salvador, took a full page ad in the February 3 *New York Times,* calling for a cutoff of American military assistance and stating support for the Democratic Revolutionary Front (FDR).

What has the land reform in El Salvador accomplished? What were its motives? Why has it failed to achieve even a modicum of peace and social justice?

Land Reform in Practice: Phase I. The land reform initially decreed on March 6, 1980 was divided into two phases: Phase I affects all properties over 500 hectares (one hectare equals 2.47 acres), which according to the original announcement number 376 and cover approximately 16 percent of the country's agricultural land. Phase II was to affect all properties between 100 or 150 (depending on the quality of the soil) and 500 hectares, covering 1,739 properties, approximately 340,000 hectares or 23 percent of the agricultural land area. The government began to implement Phase I immediately, but Phase II has been indefinitely postponed.

A number of factors seriously compromised the impact of the initial phase of the land reform. According to the 1971 census, 69 percent of the land in farms over 500 hectares is either used for pasture or it is not cultivated at all. Furthermore, only 9 percent of the nation's coffee land is affected by Phase I since most of the coffee farms are less than 500 hectares in size. Coffee is El Salvador's major export crop and represents the backbone of the oligarchy's power.

Landlords also found ways of subverting the Phase I reforms, legally and illegally, with and without government help. Some landlords liquidated their assets by driving tractors and machinery to Guatemala, slaughtering their cattle and even removing barbed wire fences from pasture land. The government was slow to react, and did not prohibit removal of assets until two months after Phase I was announced.

Some owners have been content with the generous compensation that the government offers, 25 percent in cash and 75 percent in bonds. Some landlords with farms less than 500 hectares in size are taking advantage of the favorable terms offered by the government and are selling their properties. As many as one-third of the farms which the government claims to have expropriated fall into this category of voluntary sales. Many in this group have large, secure interests in other sectors such as industry and agricultural processing and have left El Salvador for the safer havens of Guatemala City and Miami.

For those owners who remain, however, all hope is not lost. Through a Committee of Devolution, as many as 45 estates have been returned to their former owners by the government. Although some of these properties were returned because they were improperly registered as over 500 hectares, many others are sweetheart deals that have long been commonplace between the military and the wealthy families in El Salvador.

Widespread violence has characterized the reform process, and fear has been perhaps, the most important factor limiting participation in Phase I reforms. This point will be covered in more detail in the discussion of Phase III, but it is also relevant in analyzing the failure of the reform to reach the poorest of the poor. The large population of temporary workers—estimated to constitute anywhere from one-third to 60 percent of the agricultural labor force—has been intimidated by the very military forces supposedly providing peasants with protection. Members of the local paramilitary organizations and government collaborators count heavily among the beneficiaries of Phase I.

The Illusion of Reform. In a press conference in San Salvador on May 14, 1980, Colonel Abdul Gutiérrez announced that there would be no more reforms carried out beyond Phase I and Decree 207. This announcement, which received no media coverage in the United States, cut the agrarian reform announced on March 6 in half. Phase II would have affected much larger proportions of El Salvador's three major crops: coffee, cotton and sugarcane. Over four times as much coffee land, for example, would have been expropriated under Phase II.

Phase II would have cut deeply into the power of the oligarchy. Despite all the limitations, large landholders and hard-line military officers had strongly opposed Phase I reforms. The government needs the continued support of the Phase II landlords to hold power, so it is less than surprising that the more radical redistribution has been postponed.

Just how much was accomplished without the Phase II implementation? The initial report in *The New York Times* (March 7) stated that "El Salvador's military/civilian junta expropriated 60 percent of the country's best farmland. . . ." In fact, all the potential land available under Phase I and II amounts to only 39 percent of the nation's total agricultural land, not to speak of its best land. On March 8, Alan Riding reported in the *Times* that 300,000 hectares were to be expropriated under Phase I and then on March 10 reduced his figure to "224,000 hectares, approximately 25 percent of the cultivable land here." In fact, according to the 1971 agricultural census, 224,000 hectares is only 16 percent of El Salvador's agricultural land. To cite one more example, according to Carter Administration spokesman William G. Bowdler, again reported in *The New York Times*, the reforms involve two-thirds of the country's best agricultural land. Actually, over half of the 16 percent eligible for expropriation is pasture, woods or other unutilized land, not prime agricultural land. Less than 5 percent of total agricultural land under intensive cultivation is subject to expropriation under Phase I and II.

Decree 207: Land to the Tiller. In the agrarian reform program prepared by the first junta in October, Phase III consisted of a plan to promote collectivization of small farms and the formation of cooperatives in order to increase the efficiency of small, scattered plots of land characteristic of the minifundia system in much of Central and South America. Over 70 percent of all farms in El Salvador are under two hectares in size and, according to a U.S. AID study, "The small farmer in El Salvador is essentially without access to agricultural credit." The difficulty in getting credit and other services to some 200,000 small farms is immense. The Ministry of Agriculture planned to introduce some forms of collectivization to overcome these problems.

On April 29, the third junta announced that Phase III of the reform (upgraded to Phase II now since the original Phase II was not to be implemented) would consist not in any effort to collectivize farms, but rather in an institutionalization of the minifundia system by converting all present tenants into the owners of the plots they were farming, no matter how small they might be. The former owner would be compensated, but the junta stressed that the law, Decree 207, would "immediately convert 150,000 families into small owners." As one AID official put it, "There is no one more conservative than a small farmer. We're going to be breeding capitalists like rabbits."

But even AID realized the problems. In an August 8 memo, AID said:

> Phase III is closely identified in El Salvador with the U.S. government and the American Institute for Free Labor Development (AIFLD). Phase III presents the most confusing aspect of the reform program, and it could prove especially troublesome for the U.S. because it was decreed without advance discussion except in very limited government circles, and, we are told, it is considered by key Salvadoran officials as a misguided and U.S.-imposed initiative.

Its proponents billed the programs as "self-executing," but to quote from the same U.S. AID memo, experts from the Land Tenure Center state:

> The creation of an impossibly complex land registry snarl as perhaps 200,000 or more parcels suddenly need definition, registry, and mortgage management is a real possibility. Similarly, credit, input delivery, and espe-

cially marketing services must be created for the beneficiaries who formerly, in many cases, depended on their patronos for such services.

Actual implementation of Decree 207 has hardly proceeded. Many tenants are reluctant to claim their land under the law and the government lacks the capability or desire to carry out the law. Many tenants rent land from relatives or others who are practically as poor as they are and thus are not inclined to dispossess their neighbors. On the other hand, owners of larger tracts are generally hostile. The same memo states that landlords have forced tenants to renounce their claim to the land or, if they refuse, they are simply evicted from the property, increasing the problem of landlessness. Fear of reprisals by landlords has kept others from participating in the programs. Without access to credit and without any political power in San Salvador, the peasant tenant or owner will remain as indebted and powerless as ever. . . .

In El Salvador, as in Vietnam, the U.S. finds itself supporting a regime that lacks popular support and is fighting a largely rural-based guerrilla movement that enjoys the wide support of the peasantry. In El Salvador, as in Vietnam, the U.S. response has been a coordinated program of rural pacification and counter-insurgency, with land reform playing a critical role.

Conceptually, according to Robert Komer, the first head of the pacification optional program in Vietnam, the program had two goals:

(1) Sustained protection of the rural population from the insurgents, which also helps to deprive the insurgency of its rural popular base; and,

(2) Generating rural support for the Saigon regime via programs meeting rural needs and cementing the rural areas politically and administratively to the center.

In the Vietnam case, the "protection of the rural population" was carried out by the so-called Phoenix program, under which some 30,000 Vietnamese peasants were killed for being alleged Viet Cong guerrillas or their sympathizers. Land reform constituted the core of the second aspect of the strategy, "generating rural support for the Saigon regime." A key aspect of the whole process of rural pacification is the combination of civil and military operations under one unified management. The military counter-insurgency and the civilian land reform were part and parcel of a united strategy whose sole purpose was to defeat the enemy, both politically and militarily. Land reform was the carrot; counter-insurgency was the stick.

The substance of El Salvador's Land-to-the-Tiller program is practically the same as its Vietnamese forerunner. Not only are the general guidelines of the two programs identical, but even the form of landlord compensation, in both cash and bonds, and the emphasis put on landlord compensation are the same in both instances. Even the claims made for the two reforms sound alike. A 1970 *New York Times* editorial referred to Vietnam's land reform as "probably the most ambitious and progressive non-Communist land reform of the twentieth century." William Bowdler, Carter's Assistant Secretary of State for Inter-American Affairs, describes El Salvador's land reform as "one of the most significant such efforts in the hemisphere," while the reform's shadow author, Roy Prosterman, describes it as "the most sweeping agrarian reform in the history of Latin America." The transplanting of the Vietnam program to El Salvador is undoubtedly the work of Dr. Prosterman.

Prosterman, a law professor at the University of Washington in Seattle, has long been a proponent of the use of land reform to combat rural insurgency movements, a position he set forth in a 1972 article in *Foreign Policy*. Prosterman's involvement in Vietnam began with an article he published in the *Cornell Law Review* in 1967 entitled, "Land Reform in South Vietnam: A Proposal for Turning the Tables on the Viet Cong." This article outlined his Land-to-the-Tiller program and was eventually presented in draft form to President Thieu. It was not until the political and military shock of the Tet offensive in January 1968 that both Washington and Saigon recognized the need for land reform and the stepped-up program of pacification described by Robert Komer. In an unpublished manuscript, Prosterman refers to a House Foreign Operations and Government Information Subcommittee report released in March 1968 that states, "Land reform is an essential element of the pacification program and the resolution of the present conflict may well hinge on the success of pacification."

Prosterman has taken a leave of absence from his teaching duties at the University of Washington and is acting as unpaid adviser to the government of El Salvador. He is also a consultant to the American Institute for Free Labor Development (AIFLD), an AFL-CIO sponsored organization whose ties to the CIA have been extensively detailed in the documentary, "On Company Business," shown on public television. At least one AFL-CIO Central Labor Council has called for the disassociation of the AFL-CIO from AIFLD for its Salvador connections.

John Bushnell, former Deputy Assistant Secretary of State for Inter-American Affairs, presented an accurate assessment of U.S. intentions in El Salvador in his testimony on March 25 before the House

Subcommittee on Foreign Operations: "I would like to stress that contrary to widespread misperception, our security assistance proposals are neither unrelated nor contradictory to our support for reform in El Salvador. Land redistribution would not be possible were it not for the protection and security provided by the Salvadoran military for the new owners and the civilian technicians and managers helping them."

Consider the type of "protection and security" offered to the civilian population: A technician with the government's Institute for Agrarian Reform (ISTA) tells this story: "The troops came and told the workers the land was theirs now. They could elect their own leaders and run the co-ops. The peasants couldn't believe their ears, but they held elections that very night. The next morning the troops came back and I watched as they shot every one of the elected leaders."

Similarly, in June, the following event was reported by *The Washington Post:* A squad of more than 20 men in National Guard uniforms with complete battle dress and an armored car drove to a government agricultural cooperative with a list of cooperative leaders considered to be subversive. Twelve of the leaders—the local directors who are supposed to carry out government-related reforms—were killed and the 160 families living there fled in terror.

In response to this massacre, the Unión Comunal Salvadoreño (UCS), a government-recognized peasant union organized by AIFLD in the 1960's, issued a communiqué by eight of its thirteen departments condemning such violence, stating their lack of support for the land reform and concluding that they found themselves facing a situation in which the very campesino who had finally taken hold of the land was being eliminated.

On May 6, 900 employees of the Ministry of Agriculture went on strike for forty-eight hours to protest the violence carried out against peasants and technicians alike and they demanded to know why Decree 207 had been instituted in contradiction to original plans and why Phase I lands were being returned to their prior owners. To counter claims that the violence is being carried out by the left, a group of 174 Christian Democratic mayors issued a statement stating, "We know that the attacks do not come from the extreme left, and we are officials of the present government." Refugees who have fled their homes in the countryside report the use of tactics reminiscent of the Vietnam era. These include the burning of crops and houses, search and destroy missions, and the use of helicopter gunships to "pacify" zones suspected of harboring guerrilla organizations. An October 24 *New York Times* article states, "Guerrilla spokesmen said that United States military advisers were taking part in the offensive, which has involved the use of incendiary bombs and napalm against rural hamlets."

In El Salvador today, a reign of terror exists that can only be compared to Vietnam in its brutality and intensity.

25. El Salvador's Land Reform— The Real Facts and the True Alternatives *

By Roy L. Prosterman

Roy L. Prosterman, as the previous article indicated, is considered the major author of the section of El Salvador's land-reform program known as "Land to the Tiller." (Prosterman was behind a similar program in Vietnam.) A law professor at the University of Washington in Seattle, Prosterman went on leave from his job to function as an adviser to the Unión Comunal Salvadoreña (UCS) in El Salvador and as a consultant to the American Institute for Free Labor Development.

I DEPLORE the violence being committed by the right wing of El Salvador's security forces, and believe it must be ended. I oppose the sending of U.S. military advisers, and believe that clear conditions must be placed on economic aid. But I believe that nothing is accomplished—for the people of El Salvador, or for the half-billion people on our planet who still struggle to wrest a living from land that is not their own—by denying the reality or the importance of El Salvador's land-reform program, or by denying support to that program. More than 10,000 peasants gathered in San Salvador on April 9, 1981, in the biggest popular manifestation in fifteen months, to demand that *their* land reform be carried through to its full completion. Those are the voices that must be heard, and those are the demands that must be supported with our aid. Not the voice of the remote, convoluted reasoning which would see the land reform undone—and which would make common ideological cause with the most extreme elements of the U.S. and Salvadoran right to achieve that end.

Since March 6, 1980, Salvador's land reform has expropriated ap-

---

* From Food Monitor, July-August 1981; no. 22.

proximately 700,000 acres out of that country's 1,600,000 acres of cropland—44 percent of the total—and transferred it to over 210,000 out of the 300,000 nonlandowning agricultural families, reducing the number of tenants and landless laborers from 37 percent of the country's total population to 11 percent. As in any massive program of social and economic transformation rapidly carried out, vital steps remain for completion of the process. To forestall any attempts at reversal, formal titles need to be issued to both co-ops and individual ex-tenants perpetuating their rights, and the modest compensation to ex-landlords needs to be paid. In addition, a remaining phase of the reform, which would add another 110,000 acres of cultivated land (this is net of "reserve area" rights, comprising some 160,000 cultivated acres in this size category) and benefit most of the remaining landless, needs to be resuscitated.

The chief contentions that have been offered by some against the land reform have about them an odd air of Alice-in-Wonderland, of reality-denial, so wide of the mark are they:

(1) It is asserted, for example, that the farms given the 150,000 families of former tenants are too small, and that "9 hectares" (22 acres) is a minimum farm for adequate subsistence in El Salvador—but to provide all of El Salvador's agricultural families a farm of this size would require twice the land area of the entire country, and about six times the present total of El Salvador's cropland (tenants alone would require twice the total cropland).

(2) Some seem to suggest this problem would be solved with collectivization. Even apart from the fact that El Salvador's tenants, like tenants everywhere, strongly object to being collectivized, this loses sight of the fact that collectivization doesn't create new land. The only conceivable justification for forced collectivization would be *if* the same amount of land produced more under that mode of organization—and all available experience is that collectivized land produces less per acre, not more. (Cuba imports 75 percent of its food—importing as of the late 1970's 1.8 million metric tons of cereal per year, while producing about 550,000 metric tons, as reflected for example in the 1978 FAO Production and Trade Yearbooks—while its cane productivity is the lowest per acre of any major producer. Russia depends on 3 percent of its land held in "private plots" outside the collectives for 24 percent of the value of its total agricultural production.)

(3) Again, it is said that tenants "rotate" extensively, and won't receive the land left fallow. Apart from its dubious reading of the law, this contention is just plain wrong: the 1971 Census indicates a maximum of 10 percent of the area of the small holdings left fallow (that

is for owner-operators, and for tenants it is clearly less), and the leading authority on El Salvador's agriculture states flatly, "The present pressure of population makes any form of migratory agriculture, with periods to allow the soil to recuperate, impossible" (Browning, *El Salvador: Landscape and Society*, p. 301).

(4) Itinerant landless laborers, who are neither tenants nor permanent agricultural workers, are alleged to be excluded, and then further alleged, by one critic, to constitute "312,000" families. The contention is preposterous. Articles 21 and 19 of the law very clearly include them as beneficiaries, and their maximum possible number can be calculated as follows: 480,000 (the total number of rural families), minus 270,000 (the number of such families already on holdings previously either owned or tenanted), minus non-agricultural families and permanent-labor families. The number of itinerant laborers is around 100,000, and close to half of them are already beneficiaries settled on the big estates taken in the first step of the reform.

(5) Or, the reform is alleged to be insignificant because the now-delayed second phase would have affected medium-size plantations with "60%" of the coffee. In fact, those plantations have 30% of the coffee, according to the Census. The big estates already taken are estimated to have 22 percent of the coffee (along with 28 percent of the cotton and 50 percent of the cane). The related contention that "over four times as much" coffee land would be taken under the delayed phase as has already been expropriated under "Phase I" is thus clearly erroneous. Are these same critics willing to denigrate the Nicaraguan land reform because it only took 15 percent of the coffee? And whatever happened to the idea of "food first"?—the Salvadoran reform, thus far consisting of "Phase I" plus land-to-the-tenants ("Phase III"), has transferred *most* of the corn and bean land.

(6) Finally, reliance is placed on selective quotations from a single Agency for International Development anthropologist, who spent a brief period in El Salvador back in May of 1980, when the reform had barely gotten underway, and whose criticisms have been repudiated by the rest of his agency. Listen to what AID had to say in July, 1980:

A *priori*, it was patently clear that ISTA [the Salvadoran agrarian reform agency] did not have the management, human and physical resources to carry out Phase I. Yet, the intervention was executed, campesinos were organized, and a relatively normal level of production maintained. ISTA rose to the task surprisingly well with staff and vehicles which were later released when the crisis passed. Remarkable institutional elasticity was demonstrated, not only by ISTA but by most of the public sector agricultural institutions.

In fact, in late March of 1981, briefings with 35 field supervisors and the leadership of the largest peasant union—the Unión Comunal Salvadoreña (UCS), which supports the reform and turned out 10,000 people on April 9—indicated that the reform process thus far has been "80 percent" successful in the beneficiaries' eyes. (It is UCS, not, as Mr. Shiras suggests, the government of El Salvador, for which I have been "acting as unpaid adviser," in cooperation with the AFL-CIO sponsored American Institute for Free Labor Development.) This doesn't mean that more isn't needed or that backsliding is not a danger: it *does* mean, I think, that we should concentrate on the real needs to strengthen and complete the reform, rather than playing into the hands of right-wing critics of the process.

Clearly the reality of El Salvador's land reform is accepted among people who have excellent reputations for objectivity and for strong criticism of the government's failures to control violence by its security forces. Archbishop James A. Hickey, testifying on March 5, 1981 before the Barnes subcommittee in the House on behalf of the U.S. Catholic Conference (the agency which represents the U.S. Catholic bishops on public-policy issues), gave as his main reason for opposing military aid that it would increase the danger of a rightist coup, which, "in my judgment, would in turn provoke reversal of the land reforms and an increased repression of the people that could result in a civil war of immense proportions." He added that "the absolutely necessary reforms" require "continuing amounts of United States economic assistance," and that, "in distinction from its position on military aid, the USCC does not oppose economic aid, it encourages it." In a colloquy with members of the subcommittee, Archbishop Hickey affirmed that the characteristics of the land reform were essentially as I have detailed them above. San Salvador's acting Archbishop Rivera y Damas, the close friend and mentor of slain Archbishop Romero, in an interview with the National Catholic Reporter News Service (carried, for example, in the *Catholic Standard* on March 19, 1981), stated, "Look, the call to revolution by the Frente [the Revolutionary Democratic Front—the umbrella political group which includes the armed revolutionary groups, the small Social Democratic party, and others] did not get the popular support they thought it would. That is evident. It makes one see that the majority of the population does not share the Frente's point of view. What is the reality? I would say that many accept the civilian-military junta as the lesser evil. But one also has to take into account that the junta has also achieved substantial reforms, especially in the area of agrarian reform." When the Frente's "final offensive" and call for a "general uprising" failed so badly in January, 1981, Alan Riding wrote in *The New York Times* (Feb. 8, 1981), "They apparently miscalculated the impact on peasants of land reforms decreed by the Junta in March. There was no popular uprising." On March 15 and 16, 1981, the *Times* did long investigatory pieces on the land-reform program, highly favorable in their conclusions.

Indeed, Archbishop Romero himself gave an interview two days before his assassination, which was published in the *Manchester Guardian Weekly* of April 6, 1980. At that point, the phase of the reform that takes large estates had been enacted, and the Archbishop said, "The agrarian reform is, by all means, a good thing. It has taken away all the landholdings larger than 1,200 acres, and they are to be given to the people. In itself, this is good." He then spoke of the state of siege, "supposedly to keep the right from interfering with the reform," but under which, "in areas not affected by the reform, the military is quite active, the people are being repressed."

The Archbishop, unlike some of the recent critics of the reform, was completely honest: the reform and the repression were, and remain, independent, coexisting realities, the one very good, the other very bad. It is no more logical to deny the reality of the reform because of the repression than to deny the reality of the repression because there has been reform.

Peter Shiras' article in the Jan./Feb. issue of this magazine, "The False Promise—and Real Violence—of Land Reform," is one of those which essentially attacks the purpose rather than the reality of the reform. Very little is said by Mr. Shiras to directly negate the facts about the reform. Rather, the heart of his argument appears to be that, in South Vietnam, "The military counterinsurgency and the civilian land reform were part and parcel of a united strategy whose sole purpose was to defeat the enemy, both politically and militarily." Since he finds the Salvadoran land reform similar, at least with respect to the portion giving land to 150,000 tenant families, he seemingly concludes that El Salvador's land reform thereby loses all independent significance, and must be disregarded.

Mr. Shiras' argument is flawed in its history, since so far from being part of our government's "united strategy" in South Vietnam, the U.S. and the Agency for International Development had to be dragged, kicking and screaming, to a position of support for a major land reform—which did not come until the 1970's, in the twilight of U.S. involvement. I played a role in this process, which was followed closely in the media (see, for example, Elizabeth Pond, "Viet Land Reform Gathers Speed," *The Christian Science Monitor*, June 18, 1969, p. 1, and editorial, *The New York Times*, April 9, 1970). Finally, peasant grievances were dealt with, as 900,000 tenant families became owners (they still are: the new government is unwilling to face the agricultural or political consequences of collectivizing them). Vietcong recruitment skidded from 7,000 a month to 1,000 a month while land reform was being carried out, but there were clearly a wide range of problems—from the whole divisions coming down from the North, to the corruption and military nepotism in the South—that the land reform could not deal with.

In his discussion of land reform in Vietnam, Mr. Shiras further refers to a 1968 House subcommittee report which terms land reform an essential element of "pacification." He does so, however, without noting that in 1968 the term "pacification" had not yet taken on the Orwellian meaning it was to assume in the later stages of the Vietnam conflict, but rather connoted an effort to *reduce* violence through a process of effectively addressing fundamental social and economic grievances.

My actual views have been expressed with sufficient clarity, I think, in a series of articles and interviews stretching back to 1966, in contrast to what Mr. Shiras' piece contrives to suggest of my views. They are that land reform and repression, in South Vietnam as in El Salvador, so far from being "part and parcel of a united strategy," in fact operate at total cross-purposes. A "reign of terror" or a "Phoenix program," such as Mr. Shiras alludes to, is wholly *inconsistent* with both the agricultural and political purposes of land reform: the agricultural impact of such violence is strongly adverse, since it interferes with planting and harvesting and marketing, and its political impact is the exact reverse of land reform's—adding to the peasant's grievances, rather than subtracting from them.

I want to be very clear that I do not condone or justify, in any way, the violence by the Salvadoran government's security forces (in Vietnam, far from being for the violence, my position was that of *Negotiation Now*, calling for an immediate, standstill cease-fire in connection with the reform program). The indiscriminate violence being committed by Salvador's security forces must be ended, and I was saying so, in El Salvador and here, months before the death of the nuns and of my friends working with the land-reform program finally galvanized the public into awareness of the situation.

Ultimately, Mr. Shiras' view is flawed in its logic, since seemingly any reform whose purpose is "political"—that is, to deal with grievances within the system, so that revolution will, to that extent, be unnecessary—is to be considered a non-fact. Does Mr. Shiras propose that El Salvador's land-reform laws be repealed, that the 700,000 cultivated acres (and 300,000 uncultivated acres) thus far expropriated should be returned to the former landlords, and the 210,000 beneficiary families informed that their rights have been summarily terminated?

One reason why attacks on the land reform of this genre are being launched, I think, is that there is a good deal of self-delusion about two other basic facts of the Salvadoran situation. Mr. Shiras' piece is apparently premised on the notion that: (1) violence against the Salvadoran people by government forces is at the highest level it could possibly be (suggested in his comment that "a reign of terror exists that can only be compared to Vietnam in its brutality and intensity"), and (2) the Salvadoran people broadly support, and want to be governed by, the Frente (suggested in his comment that the Junta "is fighting a largely rural-based guerrilla movement that enjoys the wide support of the peasantry").

However, both of these premises are false.

First, the present violence, horrendous though it is, is a long way from the worst that could happen. Over 10,000 died in 1980, as Mr. Shiras notes. But in 1932, in a matter of months, El Salvador's security forces put down a peasant rebellion with a loss of somewhere between 7,000 and 30,000 lives. This occurred at a time when the population was only 1.5 million. A proportionate death toll, in today's El Salvador of 4.8 million, would be as high as 96,000. (Mr. Shiras collaborated with Philip Wheaton on the EPICA report titled "Agrarian Reform in El Salvador: A Program of Rural Pacification," which uses a figure of 30,000 for the deaths in 1932 [p. 2].) [1] A death toll proportionate to what was experienced in the Mexican revolution, or Spanish Civil War, over a period of several years, could be as high as 250,000. Based on both its own experience and the civil war experiences of other countries (all without "benefit" of contemporaneous U.S. military aid to the government), El Salvador's people are still very far indeed from experiencing the worst violence they might experience.

Secondly, the Frente does not, by all present evidence, command anything close to majority support. A coalition of the left that could bring 100,000—mostly peasants demonstrating because of their grievances—into the streets of San Salvador in January, 1980 could bring only 2,000 out on May 1, after the reform was promulgated. (On April 9, 1981, 10,000 peasants were gathered by the Unión Comunal Salvadoreña, not by the Frente, to *support* the land reform rather than oppose it.) The Frente's three calls for "general strikes" in mid-1980 were successively greater fiascos, as was the so-called "final offen-

---

[1] Ecumenical Program for Inter-American Communication and Action. For EPICA's address, see Bibliography and Resources, below.—Eds.

sive" and call for a "general uprising" in January, 1981. Rivera y Damas' recent comments, and Alan Riding's, are quoted above.

With the two premises, of maximum present violence and Frente popularity rejected as inaccurate, the calculations regarding the minimal risks and potential benefits of a cutoff of all U.S. aid implicit in Mr. Shiras' article—and explicit in the position of the "Committee in Solidarity with the People of El Salvador" (CISPES), which he cites approvingly, and which expressly supports the Frente and makes ending U.S. support for the land reform its first priority—are stood on their head.

In fact, a withdrawal of U.S. economic support from the present government would in all likelihood trigger a coup of the right, not a victory of the left. The unfettered right would launch a 1932-style *real* "reign of terror," and would simultaneously attempt to reverse and dismantle the reforms. The impact of such repression and attempted reversal would be to dramatically increase the numbers of those in armed opposition to the government—and a civil conflict would commence between two well-matched and utterly polarized extremes, each probably drawing on support from outside (the far-right forces almost certainly from Guatemala and quite likely from Argentina). The ultimate result—after incalculable death, hunger, and suffering—might be a government of the Frente, or of an extreme Pol Pot faction on the left, or of ex-Major D'Aubuisson or the "death squads" on the extreme right. No one can claim the ability to predict the result of such a conflict.

In other words, if *this* land reform is lightly and cavalierly denied support, and destroyed, it is likely to be a very long road—and an enormous amount of suffering—before any *other* land reform comes to take its place.

Those who really care about El Salvador's peasants will, I think, join me in urging that economic aid to the land reform be continued, but that it be *conditioned* on completion during 1981 of the bulk of the titling process, for both ex-tenants and co-ops on large estates, and on the ending of security-force violence directed against the peasants, with clear orders to the field, backed up by whatever disciplinary sanctions are necessary to enforce those orders.

In a situation such as El Salvador's, where many lives are at stake, there are particularly important obligations, in any discussion of what U.S. policy should be, to be careful in getting the facts right, to be clear on what actions one wishes the U.S. to take based on these facts, and to be scrupulously honest about the likely consequences of those actions for the people of El Salvador. If the U.S. had a magic wand that it could wave, ending all the killing and transforming the Sal-

vadoran government instantly into a Swedish-style democracy, the
case for waving it would be very strong. Unfortunately, there is no
course of action available that can lead to such an unambiguous,
rapid, and benevolent outcome. There are some courses of action,
however—especially if the land reform is made a whipping-boy for
frustrations over entirely different policies—that can create outcomes
of an order of magnitude worse than what El Salvador is experiencing
now.

26. El Salvador's Land Reform:
A Real Promise, but a Final Failure *

BY LEONEL GÓMEZ

*Leonel Gómez was formerly the chief adviser to Rodolfo Viera, the head
of ISTA, El Salvador's institute for land reform. After Viera's assassination
by military death squads, Gómez went into exile, and now lives and writes in
the United States.*

I CAN find much that I agree with in Peter Shiras's article and in
the OXFAM report on land reform in El Salvador, which comes
to similar conclusions. But I think there are some significant errors in
both matters of detail and in the broad view of what is going on in El
Salvador.

As bad a picture as both Shiras and the authors of the OXFAM
report paint, the real situation in El Salvador is actually much worse.
Shiras argues that the land reform provides a license for the military
in El Salvador to kill peasants. Peasants are indeed being killed, and
the blame rests squarely on the military. But the sad truth is that the
army has never asked for a license nor looked for an excuse to kill
campesinos.

The land reform was not developed by the army. In fact, it was
initiated by legitimate reformers who hoped to change Salvadoran
society. These reformers sought to include the *campesino*—to give
him status, dignity and respect. Alas, most of these reformers have
been forced out of the program's administering agency, ISTA, since

---

* From *Food Monitor,* July–Aug. 1981; no. 22.

its inception. My own associate and supervisor, Rodolfo Viera, was assassinated by right-wing death squads because he valiantly exposed corruption in the program. Those who fight for the *campesinos* do so at risk to their own lives.

Shiras writes that under Phase I of the land reform, "only nine percent of the coffee lands is affected since most of the coffee farms are less than 500 hectares in size." The second point is correct. But in reality, Phase I had a much greater effect on the Salvadoran oligarchy than Shiras indicates. Thirty-seven percent of the cotton lands were redistributed, as were 34 percent of the coffee-growing lands; the balance of redistributed land was in sugar cane, corn and cattle-grazing acreage. Cotton and coffee are both major export crops and both form the backbone of the Salvadoran oligarchy. In addition, the original agrarian reform was accompanied by the nationalization of the banks and of the coffee-exporting trade.

Shiras, moreover, is mistaken when he terms the compensation offered for Phase I of the reform generous. The government offered owners 25 percent in cash and 75 percent in bonds, but Shiras fails to point out that the bonds would mature in thirty years! Moreover, the amount of compensation was based on 1976 tax returns filed by the landowners, and their statements underestimated the value of the land in the interest of tax avoidance.

While administering the land-reform program with Viera, we found no evidence to support the allegation that landowners drove tractors and machinery across the border to Guatemala. Shiras is correct to note that owners did slaughter cattle and remove barbed wire fences. As for the return of confiscated land to former owners, most of that resulted from sheer confusion. Deeds were not always clear, and ISTA was not always certain what land it was entitled to redistribute and what land fell outside Phase I. Some of the forty-five returned estates were less than 500 hectares in size, and were not eligible for Phase I redistribution. In only one of those forty-five cases was I fairly certain that corruption was involved. The Venicia e Prussia estate outside of San Salvador consisted of 1,500 hectares and its market value was approximately $8 million. Yet this estate was returned to its former owners by the new Sub-Secretary of Agriculture, Lt. Colonel Galileo Torres. That transfer was clearly illegal. Agrarian judges are supposed to be appointed and have the only power to decide on cases of devolution of land to former owners. But in reality, Colonel Torres became the only man in El Salvador who held in his hands the power to return land to former owners—a power he quickly put to use. In the case of the Venicia e Prussia estate, I suspect that an exchange of money between Torres and the landowners was his primary motive for so acting. We administrators at ISTA sought to have the land returned to the *campesinos*. President Duarte eventually conceded that we were correct, but the land has still not been returned, and the President of the co-op at this estate was murdered.

That incident clearly reflects the deep problems we have with the current government. There are other examples of which people are not aware. A twelve-day strike took place in May of 1980. What was unique was that the strike was conducted by ISTA workers responsible for production, and engineers and technicians. Their strike was against the junta, because the government was not providing the Phase I co-ops with necessary fertilizer and seed. A delay of another fifteen days would have cost up to 25 percent of the crop yields. The strike was a success, and the government delivered the fertilizer and seeds. Despite the civil war, 1980 produced a fairly successful harvest. Only the ISTA lands that previously were under military administration were incapable of producing a successful yield—a fact which demonstrates the corruption of the military.

The murders of *campesinos* by the military, the violence and the terror practiced by ORDEN have to be the central issues of any discussion about El Salvador. What role does land reform play in that violence? To argue that land reform serves as a pretext for the murder of peasants by the army is to give the army an excuse they do not need. To argue in that fashion is to misunderstand and underestimate the brutality of the army. Nor does the claim that the reform was intended to flush out the peasant leaders for killing stand up to scrutiny.

Phase I lands were the lands of the wealthiest of the wealthy. Those who worked there were steadily employed. They were trusted and hence relatively conservative *campesinos*. Moreover, the violence connected with the land reform began not with the onset of the reform—but four months later. When the army came back to the co-ops seeking money for protection, for gasoline, and for out and out bribes—and when *campesinos* refused to meet their demands—then the army began its reign of terror on the co-ops.

Shiras is correct to note that the land reform failed to reach the poorest of the poor. And while I think that El Salvador's situation is very different from Vietnam's, Shiras's criticism of AIFLD and of Roy Prosterman does not disturb me. Our land-reform program gave them an opportunity to build up points for the next U.S. AID grant. Decree 207 and the "Land to the Tiller" section gets us into a complicated area of discussion. The OXFAM report errs when it states that the tenant farmers move around a great deal. There is simply no idle land, and extreme competition exists for what land does exist.

None of the tenants under Decree 207 were forced to accept land; they were only free to claim it. One hundred fifty thousand families are estimated to have been renters. They were the people to be affected by Decree 207. Yet—after one whole year—only two hundred have received any title to the land which is supposedly theirs to till. Not one of the ISTA leadership ever favored placing Decree 207 before Phase II. We simply did not view it as workable.

Near the end of his article, Shiras quotes from Jorge Villacorta's statement of resignation as Sub-Secretary of Agriculture. Jorge attacked the state of violence and the repression. His views are very important. Agrarian reform must involve more than the transfer of land. It must be a process, a relationship between people—not just a statute. It must reflect a spirit of change and a commitment to new priorities—a commitment to dignity and respect for the *campesinos* and a clear willingness, even eagerness, to give power to the powerless. That spirit existed at one point in El Salvador's land reform, but it exists no longer. It has been replaced by the interest of the military rulers whose sole concern is for increased U.S. military and economic aid, for increased power, and an increased ability to rule, to kill and to corrupt. U.S. aid has helped the military—and, as a result, ISTA is quickly falling into the military's control.

27. El Salvador's Land Reform: The Relationship of Reform to Repression *

By Peter Shiras

WITHOUT entering into a point-by-point rebuttal of Mr. Prosterman's objections to my article, let me instead comment briefly on the over-all thrust of his remarks. Mr. Prosterman, like both the Carter and Reagan administrations and the junta in El Salvador, would have us believe that the land-reform process in El Salvador is essentially good while the military repression is bad. Therefore we should support the reform (and the reformers), while opposing (or at least not actively supporting) the repression and the repressors.

---

* From *Food Monitor*, July–Aug. 1981; no. 22.

This argument is totally unrealistic for two reasons. First of all, while I agree with Mr. Gómez that initially there were genuine reformers participating in the government and there was a genuine commitment by these people to land reform, at the present time all of these reformers are either dead or exiled. Any leadership for reform, both at a national level and at the local level, has been systematically eliminated by the government and its military and paramilitary security apparatus. Thus, there are no reforms to support.

Secondly, there is no question but that the military high command controls the government (including President Duarte) in El Salvador, and any U.S. aid, economic or military, strengthens the hand of that military government. The land-reform program cannot be divorced from the political context in which it takes place just as U.S. economic aid cannot be neatly separated from military aid—both are tools to prop up a government directly responsible for the deaths of over 12,000 of its own citizens last year. No matter what guise U.S. aid takes, the result will be to prolong in power this brutally repressive Salvadoran government.

El Salvador desperately needs a comprehensive land-reform program to redress the grievous inequities in the rural agrarian structure, but first it needs a government genuinely committed to reform so that a mockery is not made of the term land reform.

28. Salvador Land Program Aids Few*

By RAYMOND BONNER

The author of the Reading that follows is a relative newcomer to journalism. After taking a law degree at Stanford University, Raymond Bonner practiced public-interest law with Ralph Nader. He also served on the board of directors of Consumers Union, and headed up a unit on white-collar crime in the office of the San Francisco district attorney. Joining The New York Times as a regular correspondent in 1981, Bonner covered developments in El Salvador and Central America in June and July of that year.

IT has been nearly a year and a half since the Government of El Salvador inaugurated one of the most sweeping land redistribu-

---

* From *The New York Times*, August 3, 1981.

tion programs ever attempted in Latin America. But here on this 1,500-acre farm, which has been converted to a peasant-run cooperative, the milking stalls are empty.

The last of the 900 dairy and beef cattle were sold in the weeks before the government expropriated the farm and turned it over to the peasants who had been working here. That was in March 1980. Since then, the cooperative has been unable to obtain bank financing to start a new herd. The banks it dealt with were taken over by the government at the same time as the land-redistribution program was decreed.

There was widespread hope that the program, which involves the creation of such cooperative ventures, would not only reduce the power of the right-wing oligarchs in El Salvador, but also help win the allegiance of the peasants from the leftist guerrillas who are at war with the government. But the program has so far drawn only mixed reviews from Salvadorans and United States officials.

El Salvador, which has five million people and is about the size of Massachusetts, is the most densely populated nation in Latin America. According to the Salvadoran agency responsible for administering the program, less than 15 percent of the country's farmland is now owned by cooperatives. Put another way, only 386,010 people, less than 10 percent of the population, have benefited from the conversion into cooperatives of 282 privately owned cotton, coffee, sugar cane, cattle and other kinds of farms during the first phase of the program.

Asked whether the program had been a success so far, a conservative Salvadoran businessman replied, "Economically no, politically, yes." He was expressing the general view here among private businessmen as well as Salvadoran and United States Government officials.

Peter Askin, the director of the office here of the United States Agency for International Development, which has been working closely with the government in planning and carrying out the program, said, "It has not been a total economic success.

"But," he added, "up to this point it has been a political success. I'm firm on that. There does seem to be a direct correlation between the agrarian reforms and the peasants not having become more radicalized."

The United States Congress has authorized $62,558,000 for the program, according to the aid agency. "One of these days, Congress is going to ask what we have gotten for that investment," Mr. Askin said.

Languid men, machetes dangling from the waistbands of their work-soiled pants, propped themselves against a broken tractor at the farm here. The farm was formerly owned by the Regalado brothers, members of one of the country's wealthiest families, but, according to the peasants, they had never lived there. Asked how their lives now compared with their lives in those days, the peasants answered, "The same." Then, as now, they earn the equivalent of $36 every two weeks.

"But we have faith," the cooperative's president said, standing in a small office where a picture of one of the former owners still hangs crooked on the blue-green wall above wooden shutters that swing open onto a vista of palm trees and the lush green slopes of a volcano. "There will be profits in the future," he said. "The land is rich."

Under the first phase of the land-redistribution program, all farms larger than 1,235 acres were ordered expropriated, with compensation, and turned over to the peasants who had been working them. The second phase calls for the similar conversion of rural estates larger than 247 acres. And the third stage, which is usually referred to as the "land-to-the-tiller law," provides that peasants who were working as tenant farmers will become the owners of the smaller plots, all tiny, many on seemingly vertical hillsides. The last stage has not yet begun.

A few miles from here, at the 1,675-acre San Rafael el Provenir cooperative, only three pieces of farm machinery are parked under the corrugated tin roof of the machinery shed. The machinery is rented, not owned. Five small tractors, two rice combines, four trucks and 1,200 cattle were sold by the former owners two weeks before the farm became a peasant cooperative.

A tall green chalkboard is propped against the wall of the administration building. In neat columns are listed the income, expenses and profits that the cooperative expects from the cultivation of rice, corn, beans, coffee and sugar cane. A profit of 111,892 colones, or $44,756, is projected for this year. But there is a notation that the cooperative will have to pay the government 320,000 colones, or $128,000, to be used to recompense the former owners. So there will be a net loss.

According to Mr. Askin, several cooperatives have shown a profit, some have broken even, but most are in the red. An employee in El Salvador's Institute of Agrarian Transformation said that only about 10 of 282 cooperatives had paid their bank loans in full. Some of the defaults, which Mr. Askin described as "sizable," may have to be written off as start-up costs, he said.

The question, Mr. Askin said, is, "what price is the country going to pay for the political benefits?"

According to Mr. Askin, coffee production has declined 10 to 30 percent since the private owners lost their farms, and there has been a decrease of 30 to 40 percent in the cotton acreage. In recent years, these crops have brought in about 70 percent of the country's export earnings.

But, Mr. Askin said, there will be an increase this year in the production of basic grains such as corn, rice and sorghum.

If the cooperatives are to be economically successful, Mr. Askin said, they must be viewed as business enterprises and less as social and political experiments. In addition to technical agricultural assistance and easier access to financial credits, he said, the cooperatives most need "business acumen." They need business, bookkeeping and accounting advisers, he said.

Title to the properties is held by the Institute for Agrarian Transformation, not the cooperatives, and the institute decides how each cooperative's income will be allocated—whether, for example, it is distributed as profits, used for capital improvements or transferred to other, financially ailing, cooperatives.

Even the most ardent supporters of the agrarian changes agree that the institute has been inefficient and corrupt.

El Salvador's armed forces helped carry out the first phase of the land redistribution, occupying the largest estates so that former owners would not interfere with the government takeover. United States and Salvadoran government officials have pointed to this as evidence that the army is no longer serving the landed oligarchy as it did for generations.

But the institute and church leaders have charged that the National Guard and Treasury Police, which operate primarily in rural areas, have killed institute workers and peasant leaders.

And according to an institute worker, more than 40 percent of the peasant cooperatives are paying tribute to the army, an average of $120 a month for each of the six to eight soldiers who "guard" the ranches, he said.

Another major criticism of the first phase is that only a limited number of peasants have been permitted to participate. According to the Agency for International Development, 38,000 families are cooperative members. The number could be twice that, Mr. Askin said.

Meanwhile, few of the former owners have received the compensation, in bonds and cash, that the law provides. Because the government lacks the money to pay the previous owners, one business leader suggested recently that the farms should be returned to them.

A United States government official said here recently that the program's chances of success would be enhanced considerably if the former owners were paid. "It would get them off the government's back," he said.

The Minister of the Economy has proposed that they be allowed to use their government-issued bonds to buy industries and companies owned by a government investment corporation. This way, the minister said, the former owners would become industrialists. Mr. Askin agrees with the proposal because "the country must industrialize."

"The quality and amount of land cannot support a population this size, let alone double, which it might be by the year 2000," Mr. Askin said.

More than 85 percent of the coffee, 75 percent of the cotton and 60 percent of the sugar cane is still grown on farms controlled by a relatively few people. According to an employee of the Institute of Agrarian Transformation, many of these lands are owned by the same people who lost their larger estates in the Phase I conversion.

The United States Ambassador, Deane R. Hinton, said recently that the second phase of the program would not be carried out.

The third phase, the land-to-the-tiller law, has been evaluated by United States and Salvadoran leaders almost exclusively in political terms. The prototype for the law was developed in Vietnam by Roy L. Prosterman, a professor at the University of Washington Law School, who was instrumental in the adoption here of a similar program.

"The left fears land reform," Mr. Prosterman told a group of apprehensive Salvadoran businessmen last year. "It deprives them of their most valuable weapon in implementing revolution because they can no longer appeal to the landless."

Since its announcement in early 1980, the land-to-the-tiller law has been harshly criticized primarily because for more than a year no titles were issued to an estimated 125,000 peasant beneficiaries. Now, according to the Agency for International Development, about 500 titles have been issued, usually in ceremonies presided over by a member of El Salvador's governing junta.

A large landowner, who supports the concept of land redistribution, criticizes the land-to-the-tiller law on agricultural principles. The new peasant owners of the tiny plots, she says, will necessarily continue to plant rice, beans and corn for consumption by their families. Thus, she says, there will be no crop rotation and the soil will quickly be depleted.

A Marxist professor here argues that the goal of land reform should not be the creation of landowners but a more equitable distribution of wealth, which for El Salvador's peasants means food.

This, he says, is not achieved by giving a peasant title to a piece of land, which is often too small and of such poor soil that it cannot even grow enough food for an average-size family. Instead, he says, the peasants should be organized into some form of cooperatives, which are agriculturally and economically more efficient.

A Jesuit priest recently criticized the entire land redistribution program because it was hastily put into effect without any significant contribution by the peasants. "It was imposed by the junta," he said, "without ever asking the peasants what they wanted."

Asked if a less-than-perfect program was not better than no land redistribution, he said. "No, it would have been better not to have done anything."

Chapter IV

THE CHURCH AND LIBERATION THEOLOGY

Editors' Introduction

EVERY religious viewpoint has to grapple with the problem of theodicy, the reconciliation of divine justice with the palpable reality of evil and suffering on earth. Most often this is accomplished by assuring people that God's infinite wisdom and mercy will eventually prevail, even if life looks grim in the present, and injustice and exploitation run rampant. The problem of theodicy is raised in José María Argueda's moving novel of contemporary Latin America, *Todas las Sangres (All the Blood,* Buenos Aires, 1964), which includes among its characters a priest who tries to assure his parishioners that they must bear misfortunes because God is everywhere—with all people and all classes. But a peasant, a humble tiller of the soil, questions the priest closely on what appears like a rationale for manmade injustice. "Was God in the heart of those who broke the body of the innocent teacher Bellido?" the peasant inquires. "Is God in the bodies of the engineers who are killing [the river] 'La Esmeralda'? In the official who took the cornfields away from their owners . . . ?"

Questions like these have been intensified within the Roman Catholic churches of Latin America during the last two decades. Some churchmen persist in the traditional mold—upholding the established order, blessing the oligarchs and urging the masses to be long-suffering and to avoid militant struggle. But increasingly, brave parish priests, and even an occasional bishop or archbishop, have stepped forward to speak out against injustice and oppression. Aligning themselves with the oppressed groups, these progressive churchmen risk the displeasure of the privileged elites, who often send gunmen to "liquidate" radical priests. Apparently such a martyrdom came to the outspoken Archbishop Oscar Arnulfo Romero, head of the Roman

Catholic church in El Salvador until his assassination in the early spring of 1980. As a martyr, Romero might prove to be no less a threat to the Salvadoran oligarchs than he was in real life.

In addition to animating the Latin American clergy,[1] and attracting missionaries from such places as the United States to assist in the struggles for social justice,[2] the outburst of radical religious commitment has also taken the form of a new doctrinal outlook, the so-called "Liberation Theology." The tenets of this theology stress the church's primary mission to minister to the poor and downtrodden rather than to serve the wealthy and powerful. Priests and lay "Delegates of the Word" in El Salvador and elsewhere have fanned out into the countryside as well as the urban centers, bringing the message that the people's poverty is not willed by God but is the result of historical patterns of oppression that cannot be overcome without popular insurrection.[3] Thus, priests and believing Catholic men and women have become revolutionaries in El Salvador. It is a situation which is repeating itself throughout Central and South America, and it suggests that a far more complex process of social change is underway there than many U.S. officials, who tend to reduce matters to "the Soviet threat," are able to perceive.

29. The Cross and the Sword in Latin America *

By ALAN RIDING

Alan Riding is Mexico City bureau chief for The New York Times. *His dispatches from El Salvador were among the earliest to appear in the U.S.*

---

[1] Perhaps the most dramatic example of a revolutionary priest was Camilo Torres of Colombia, who in his own words "took off my cassock to be more truly a priest." Believing that "the Catholic who is not a revolutionary is living in mortal sin," Father Torres took to the mountains, where four months later he was killed in battle, February 15, 1966. See John Gerassi, ed., *Revolutionary Priest: The Complete Writings and Messages of Camilo Torres* (New York: Vintage, 1971), pp. 28–31.

[2] Priests and nuns from the Maryknoll Order, some of whom, like Archbishop Romero, have found martyrdom in Central America (see Reading 17), are among this group.

[3] An important, recent work is Gustavo Gutiérrez, *A Theology of Liberation* (New York, 1977).

* From *The New York Review of Books*, May 28, 1981.

press. He continued to file stories from El Salvador until rightist death threats forced his departure in late 1980.

AFTER the 1959 Cuban revolution, guerrilla groups appeared across Latin America, their ranks crowded with urban middle-class student radicals anxious to emulate Fidel Castro. But, as Ernesto Che Guevara learned to his cost; they had neither support nor organization among the peasants, workers, and slum-dwellers in whose name they were acting. And, gradually, they were wiped out— in Venezuela, Peru, Bolivia, Brazil, Uruguay, Guatemala, the Dominican Republic, and, finally, Argentina.

In Central America, however, a new generation of guerrilla groups emerged in the late 1970s, this time made up largely of Indian and *mestizo* peasants and factory workers. And when repression came on a scale exceeding even the horrors of Argentina, the guerrilla movements survived; in Nicaragua, they seized power in July 1979; and in El Salvador and Guatemala, they are still at war with brutal military regimes.

What happened, then, to make the armed struggle seem alive in Central America today when it proved so hopeless in South America a decade or so ago? Poverty is certainly not the answer, because Bolivia, for example, is decidedly more backward than El Salvador. Repression as a catalyst for rebellion is also an unlikely explanation since official terror did, in fact, eliminate the guerrillas in Guatemala in the late 1960s. Nor, despite the Reagan administration's insistent assurance, is Cuban involvement a major factor since, disillusioned by the failure of its effort to "export" revolution to the continent, even Havana was caught off guard by the surge of popular unrest in Central America.

Rather, the key lies in the changing role of the Roman Catholic Church. It is not the only reason—the Carter administration's human rights policy undoubtedly helped to destabilize the region's near-feudal political structures; the dimensions of the tiny Central American republics also create a "politics of scale" in which the ingredients for revolution can reach the combustion point more easily—but the most important single variable is the church.

In the early 1960s, the Roman Catholic Church, still sharing the fears of communism of the ruling élite, had yet to address the root causes of poverty. But by the late 1970s, important parts of the church were not only busily promoting political organization among the poor masses, but they were also increasingly identified with radical groups. In Central America, at least, activist priests served as a bridge between the guerrillas and the poor and helped make armed struggle legitimate, while Christian revolutionaries took up arms and helped to temper the Marxist dogmatism of the rebel groups. The church changed, but so did the left.

It is not difficult to argue that the metamorphosis of the Church is the most significant political development in Latin America since the Cuban revolution. And it is made easier by the fact that so little else has changed. The economic structures of the continent are still designed to bring growth for the few rather than development for the many. Political freedom is even scarcer than two decades ago, as corrupt and repressive military regimes proclaim themselves to be the predestined saviors of "Christian civilization." And, as the Reagan administration has set out to demonstrate, the inability of the United States to understand the complex social and political dynamics of the region as anything but "communist agitation," remains pure and intact.

A good place at which to begin the education of the new administration on Latin America would be Penny Lernoux's fine book about the church in Latin America, *Cry of the People.* The publishers have probably lost Ms. Lernoux a few readers by describing the book as recounting "United States involvement in the rise of fascism, torture, and murder and the persecution of the Catholic Church in Latin America," because, in reality, her book is not a standard radical tract on the evils of "Yankee imperialism" south of the border. Rather, it tells a story of far greater importance: how the centuries-old alliance of Sword and Cross in Latin America is suddenly falling apart.

The significance of this can only be truly recognized by taking account of the church's historical role in the continent, starting with the religious justification that the missionaries provided for the Spanish conquest of the mainland early in the sixteenth century. Throughout the colonial era, in fact, the church stood close to political power. And, as a wealthy landowner in its own right, it also exercised enormous economic influence. There were some notable defenders of the Indians among the clergy, not least Bartolomé de las Casas in Mexico, but on the whole the Church was identified with a colonial system—and with such niceties as the Inquisition—that kept the Indians in a state of serfdom. Even after independence from Spain in the early nineteenth century, little changed. And, while the church lost much of its real estate in the liberal reforms that swept the continent between 1850 and 1880, its vast influence over the people soon replenished its political strength.

Only in this century did the church suffer two serious reverses—

when it backed the losing side in both the Mexican and the Cuban revolutions. Yet, despite the fierce anticlericalism that led to the persecution of Catholic priests and the brutal suppression of the *Cristero* rebellion in Mexico in the 1920s and 1930s, the Catholic hierarchy is still a powerful conservative force in Mexico today. In Cuba, the communist regime has come to recognize that persecution is the surest way of preserving religious fervor but those who are openly Catholic are still subject to considerable pressure and encounter difficulty in their careers.

Elsewhere in Latin America, the church remained wholly in league with the ruling economic and political elites. In Argentina, for example, well-to-do families would ensure that at least one son joined the army and another entered the church. In rural areas, local priests controlled the peasantry more effectively than any band of landowners' *pistoleros*. In the cities, the clergy was dedicated largely to educating the children of the rich, passing on social and political values often unchanged for centuries. The Catholic hierarchies, on the other hand, played politics at the highest level, willing to bless— literally—the most distasteful of regimes on the one condition that their power was recognized and respected. Leading bishops, in fact, often seemed as comfortable rubbing shoulders at social gatherings with presidents, generals, and landowners as they did at the altar.

The Cuban revolution, however, sent shock waves through the religious as well as political structures of the continent. Politically, the church's response was not unlike that of the United States: Washington rushed to prepare the continent's armies to combat "communist subversion" while also promoting reforms through the Alliance for Progress, and the church stepped up its anti-communist rhetoric but also helped to found Christian Democratic parties formally committed to social reform.[1]

But there were also serious institutional motives for alarm: the churches of the continent were growing emptier by the year, while the shortage of young men willing to take up orders was forcing bishops to "import" more and more priests from Ireland, Spain, and the United States. Further, with the church seemingly out of touch with contemporary realities, growing numbers of priests and nuns were renouncing their vows. The church was in fact facing a challenge to its survival as both a religious and political institution.

The first important signs of change came from Rome. Pope John XXIII issued his revolutionary encyclicals *Mater et Magistra* in 1961 and *Pacem in Terris* in 1963 which emphasized the right to educa-

---

[1] See Reading 8, above.—Eds.

tion, a decent standard of living, and political participation. The second Vatican Council, which ended in 1965, then established the equality of laity, priests, and bishops and indirectly stimulated the emergence of the so-called "Church of the Poor," comprising grass-roots Christian communities. Finally, Pope Paul VI's encyclical *Populorum Progressio*, dealing with the economic, social, and political rights of mankind, set the mood for the second Latin-American Episcopal Conference in Medellín, Colombia, in 1968.

"Medellín produced the Magna Carta of today's persecuted, socially committed Church, and as such rates as one of the major political events of the century," Ms. Lernoux notes. "It shattered the centuries-old alliance of Church, military and the rich elites." Pope Paul himself traveled to Colombia for the meeting, telling a crowd in Bogotá: "We wish to personify the Christ of a poor and hungry people." In their final document, the bishops of the continent developed this theme, denouncing "institutionalized violence" and the "international imperialism of money," and committing themselves to the "option of the poor."

In reality, with the exception of a few bishops, such as northeast Brazil's Dom Helder Cámara, most prelates were not yet identified with the struggle of the poor and oppressed. But there were many younger priests, frequently Spanish-born or European-educated, who were waiting for the theological green light that Medellín gave their social and political activities: suddenly they could wield the words of the pope and their bishops as powerful revolutionary weapons. And, from this group, which included Peru's Gustavo Gutiérrez, Brazil's Leonardo Boff, and El Salvador's Catalan-born Jon Sobrino, emerged the so-called Theology of Liberation. In fact, when many bishops recognized that the political implications of the Medellín documents were far more radical than they intended, they seemed anxious to reverse themselves, and the battle between conservatives and "progressives" inside the Latin American church began.

The principal factor of radicalization, though, was no more theological than the fierce repression unleashed by the military regimes that were seizing power across South America at the time. The year 1968, for example, was the year of Medellín, but it was also the year that Brazil's ruling generals turned nasty. Brazil's bishops, still digesting the Church's new social philosophy, were suddenly forced to defend a number of Dominican priests who were arrested—with the usual trappings of torture—for involvement with leftist guerrillas. Circumstances, then, more than initiative led Brazil's Catholic hierarchy into its first serious confrontations with the military regime. And, having jumped to the aid of radical priests, the bishops had little choice but to speak out against abuse of radical members of the laity. With the local press censored and opposition politics banned, the church was alone, its voice amplified by the surrounding silence.

The case of Brazil is particularly important, not only because liberal bishops are now in a majority in the world's most populous Catholic nation, but also because it has become the laboratory for the Church of the Poor. The human rights advocacy of the Brazilian Catholic Church has inevitably attracted most attention. São Paulo's valiant Cardinal Paulo Evaristo Arns has dared to challenge publicly the fiercest of hard-line generals, holding defiant funeral masses for political prisoners tortured to death, even endorsing strikes from the pulpit. . . .

In Central America, however, the growth of church radicalism was different. Throughout the 1960s, the tiny republics of the isthmus remained political backwaters. The guerrilla movement in Guatemala brought political violence, but no popular mobilization, while El Salvador, Nicaragua, and Honduras were all ruled by the traditional triumvirate of oligarchy-army-church.

The problem facing restless sectors of the church, then, was not how to defend government critics from repression, but how to awaken poor peasants and workers from the apathy, resignation, and religious fatalism of centuries. In doing so, however, many priests themselves became more radical. They saw that their mobilization of the poor only brought on repression. And, as peaceful methods of protest and pressure became suicidal, they could not dispute the logic of taking up arms. Only a few priests actually joined the guerrillas, but the number who sympathized with *la revolución* grew rapidly. The impact on rural populations above all was dramatic: suddenly priests were telling peasants that the armed struggle was also a Christian cause.

In the Indian villages of the Guatemalan highlands, where the visiting *padre* is traditionally the only trusted white man, priests first became involved in promoting a cooperative movement in the mid-1970s. When this became the target of landowners worried that the peasants might stop migrating at harvest-time to the coastal cotton and sugar plantations, a more radical peasant movement emerged. The priests by then had recognized the natural leaders of the Indian communities and served as a bridge between them and the new Committee for Peasant Unity, which was in turn linked to the guerrillas. Soon afterward, for the first time, Guatemala's Indians began joining the guerrillas.

The activities of the church in El Salvador are better known because of the outspoken denunciations, and subsequent murder, of

Archbishop Oscar Arnulfo Romero in 1980. Yet, the less visible work of ordinary priests among the poor was, at least in the long run, more significant politically. Starting in the early 1970s, more and more priests and nuns began trying to stir the country's deeply impoverished peasantry, first by forming *comunidades de base* from which lay preachers—known locally as Delegates of the Word—emerged as community leaders, then by encouraging the landless peasants to campaign for an agrarian reform. One group of Jesuits, for example, took over the parish of Aguilares, twenty-five miles north of San Salvador, and helped to organize the first strike ever in a local sugar mill. They also prompted the local peasants to join the Christian Federation of Salvadoran Peasants—or FECCAS—which by the end of the decade was providing the main rural support for the Popular Forces of Liberation, one of El Salvador's five armed groups.

By 1976, the military government was alarmed at the growing impact of the radical priests and the "hostile" pastoral letters of the aging archbishop, Monsignor Luis Chávez y González. The government therefore put pressure on the Vatican to retire Bishop Chávez and was delighted when the conservative bishop of San Miguel, Monsignor Romero, was named in his place. The activist priests, on the other hand, were depressed by the appointment. In his book, *Archbishop Romero: Martyr of Salvador*, Father Plácido Erdozaín recalled his image of the prelate shortly before the change in February 1977: "Churchy, lover of rules and clerical discipline, friend of liturgical laws, he was convinced that 'the most important thing is prayer and personal conversion.' " A number of foreign priests even thought of going to some other country "where we would be able to do pastoral work among and with the people—the people's church."

Inexperienced politically and insecure theologically, however, Romero proved willing to listen to the radical priests who sought his ear. Further, after he took over, the new archbishop was forced to take public stands, denouncing first a massacre that followed protests against an electoral fraud on February 28, 1977, and then the murder, on March 12, of Father Rutilio Grande, one of the Jesuits working in Aguilares. In May, another priest was murdered, and in June Aguilares was attacked by the army, which set up barracks in the local church. By mid-1977, relations between church and state were worse than ever. Archbishop Romero refused to attend the inauguration of the new president, General Carlos Humberto Romero (no relation), while all the Jesuits in El Salvador were threatened with assassination if they did not leave the country.

Like so many Latin American bishops before him, then, Romero moved from defending his own clergy to defending the poor and oppressed in general. And, with all the opposition intimidated into silence, he was soon the only critic to be heard. Through the priests that surrounded him, he also met the leaders of the emerging militant peasant and labor groups and, in his sermons, he began to echo some of their positions. Then, in November 1978, a priest, Ernesto Barrera, was killed in combat alongside guerrillas of the Popular Forces of Liberation. The archbishop was shocked and confused, Erdozaín recalled, but was also forced to address the question of revolutionary violence for the first time. It was an important turning point in Romero's political conversion. He decided, for example, to attend Barrera's funeral and later said:

> When a dictatorship seriously violates human rights and attacks the common good of the nation, when it becomes unbearable and closes all channels of dialogue, of understanding, of rationality, when this happens, the church speaks of the legitimate right of insurrectional violence.

The archbishop always insisted that he was not a politician and should therefore not be asked for political solutions to El Salvador's crisis. But, as the most popular public figure in the country, he was unavoidably drawn into politics. When young army officers ousted General Romero in October 1979, for example, several liberals consulted the archbishop before joining the junta; the new regime's only credibility came through a request by the archbishop that it be given time to prove its good will. And when all liberals in the government resigned ten weeks later, after a promised program of reforms had been blocked by the army, they again sought the prelate's approval for their move. Members of the Christian Democrat party, who to this day share government with the army, then replaced them in the junta. Soon afterward, Romero spoke words that still apply today:

> The real power is in the hands of the most repressive sector of the armed forces. If the junta members do not wish to be accomplices in these abuses of power and outright criminal behavior, they should publicly announce the names of those responsible and apply the necessary sanctions, for their hands are red with blood.

By early 1980, the archbishop felt he would soon die. "If they kill me, I will rise again in the Salvadoran people," he told a Mexican journalist. "I'm not boasting or saying this out of pride, but rather as humbly as I can." In his sermon on March 23rd, Romero addressed the country's soldiers: "No soldier is obliged to obey an order contrary to the law of God. It is time that you come to your senses and obey your conscience rather than follow sinful commands." The Army High Command saw this as a call to mutiny and was enraged. The following evening, as he celebrated mass in the small chapel of the cancer hospital where he lived, Romero was struck in the heart by a single bullet fired by a sniper standing at the door of the building.

Even before his death, though, there were serious tensions within the Salvadoran church. In the country's six-member Episcopal Conference, Romero was in a minority, supported only by Bishop Arturo Rivera y Damas of Santiago de María and sharply criticized by the rest for being "manipulated" by "communist" priests and, worse, by the Jesuits. Further, one month before his murder, Romero returned home depressed from a visit to Rome where Pope John Paul II had expressed his open disapproval of the church's deep political involvement in El Salvador.

When the Vatican appointed Bishop Rivera y Damas as Apostolic Delegate and Acting Archbishop, then, he was instructed to work for the unity of the church. He had the reputation of being progressive, but he adopted a more centrist position, criticizing each extreme with equal fervor. The activist clergy, by now thoroughly identified with the guerrilla movement, were dismayed and bitter. Yet, more political and less emotional than his predecessor, Rivera insisted that violence no longer offered an answer. Instead, he urged the U.S. to suspend military aid to the junta and called for a negotiated solution to the conflict.

In El Salvador, though, as elsewhere in Latin America, the Catholic Church remains deeply divided. Conservatives dominate the hierarchies in Argentina, Colombia, and Mexico as they do the Secretariat—through the manipulative Archbishop Alfonso López Trujillo of Medellín—of the Latin American Episcopal Conference. Even in Nicaragua, where the church endorsed the 1979 insurrection against the Somoza regime and, for the first time, seemed to be on the side of revolutionaries, most bishops are now hostile to the Sandinist government and are aligned with its conservative business and political critics.

But a new popular church is nevertheless emerging on the continent, in some countries supported by the bishops, in others strongly opposed. For example, the priests and nuns who helped organize the urban slums of Nicaragua for the uprising against the Somozas are still working among the poor and still support the revolution. And, despite pressure from Rome, three priests have refused to resign as Cabinet ministers in the Nicaraguan government. Elsewhere, from Paraguay to the Dominican Republic, the *comunidades de base* are growing steadily. *The Challenge of Basic Christian Communities,* which brings together papers presented to a seminar in Brazil last year by the region's top liberation theologists, confirms the dynamic strength of the movement. Among the authors are Gustavo Gutiérrez, Leonardo Boff, Jon Sobrino, Miguel Concha, and Juan Hernández Pico.

Had these essays been prepared by the State Department, they would be stamped "Top Secret" because they reveal the profound social and political changes taking place among the Latin American Catholic masses. But in practice, while annoyed and upset by the anti-Americanism of some Latin American bishops, the U.S. has failed to recognize the structural changes being wrought by the Catholic Church. Until just a few weeks before his death, for example, Archbishop Romero was being dismissed by the U.S. Embassy in San Salvador as just "another agitator" rather than being recognized as the symbol of a national mood.

The Reagan administration's response to the leftist challenge in El Salvador, however, is the climactic proof of Washington's inability— or unwillingness—to understand the region: a complex problem is explained away as the result of Soviet bloc arms shipments, while U.S. military aid and advisers take the place of a sophisticated political response. U.S. policy is in fact an amazing tribute to Fidel Castro: it imagines, quite erroneously, that Cuba could orchestrate from afar the kind of revolutions that are erupting from the very bowels of Central America. In reality, these movements are being stirred by more powerful forces—the human instincts of hunger and faith. But U.S. policy toward Latin America has no room for such subtleties.

30. Oscar Romero:
Archbishop of the Poor *

BY PATRICK LACEFIELD

These excerpts are from an interview with Archbishop Oscar Arnulfo Romero in August, 1979—two months before the coup which overthrew the military dictatorship of General Carlos Humberto Romero and ushered in the first junta. Interviewed near the chapel where he would be gunned down while celebrating mass on March 24, 1980, the Archbishop expressed hope that peaceful channels for social change in El Salvador were still real possi-

---

* From *Fellowship Magazine*, November, 1979.

bilities. *Only later, after the first junta—to which he gave tacit support—failed would he put the church firmly behind the center-left opposition to the junta. This brought martyrdom to this most gentle, modest and strong-willed of men. Archbishop Romero was interviewed by Patrick Lacefield, one of the editors of this volume.*

P**ATRICK LACEFIELD:** The principles of liberation, of liberation theology that emerged from Medellín and Puebla, have drawn a sort of battleline between the church and the government in many countries.[1] How does the church in El Salvador apply these principles to the objective realities it encounters?

Monsignor Romero: This is a Latin American problem. There are two trends in the Latin American church. One is the conservative school which we tried to push a little in Medellín and Puebla and, of course, the other is the progressive. There are two trends in the church here also, but I do not particularly like to call these trends conservative and progressive because this implies a division within the church.

I do not wish to say that there is a division but rather that there is pluralism. The progressive trend promotes the liberation themes of Medellín and Puebla. The former Archbishop, Monsignor Chávez, initiated the application of the principles of the Second Vatican Council and Medellín. When I was appointed Archbishop three years ago, I only continued with the trend already initiated.

The circumstances in these last three years have been very hard and therefore our program has been more visible. There is much persecution of the church because the church is standing against repression and injustice, in accordance with the principles of Medellín and Puebla. The archdiocese of El Salvador becomes more and more aware every day that this is the correct and true interpretation. What happened at Puebla ratified the authenticity of these liberation principles. We can concentrate on these words emerging from Puebla: preferential treatment for the poor. It can be made concrete.

Q. Can you speak of the recent persecution of the church? I know that there was a priest, Padre Palaiso, killed in June.

A. These are the facts. There was the assassination of Padre Palaiso, and the expulsion of Padre Astor Luis, a Salvadoran whom the government will not allow to return from Colombia. When we attempt to investigate, to find the reasons for this, we are only told: "superior orders." There is also a Belgian priest, a Father Juan

---

[1] See Reading 29.—Eds.

D'Planck, whom the government will not allow into the country. He visits Belgian priests working in Latin America.

The government has continued a campaign of misinformation about church activities, our communities and priests. There is support for campaigns denouncing me through the media, with radio programs and paid advertisements in the newspapers. I might also mention our inability to use the communications media because they are all under the control of the capitalists and the government, the oligarchy. The only exceptions are the archdiocese radio station (which broadcasts the Archbishop's Sunday homilies throughout the country) and our weekly paper *Orientación*.

There has been government interference with the frequency of the radio station. A recent declaration of the Human Rights Commission of the Organization of American States clearly says that there has been systematic persecution of the church in El Salvador.

Q. For many people, particularly in the countryside, the church is the only means of opposition communication, especially now since *La Crónica* is gone [the only opposition daily, whose offices were destroyed by the right-wing terror group, the White Warriors Union, in late June]. Is this not true?

A. It is not the "opposition" really, because the church is not a political party. Rather it is the Gospel's voice, denouncing injustice and oppression. With the return of Dr. Morales Ehrlich [the Christian Democratic vice-presidential candidate in the 1977 elections] from exile, he is becoming a voice of the opposition in the political field and this is hopeful. There is also a new press service, API—Independent Press Agency—that will take up much of the news that *La Crónica* printed.

Q. Are you optimistic or pessimistic about progress toward democracy and human rights in El Salvador? How will such progress come about—by elections, government reforms, or armed rebellion?

A. I am optimistic from the point of view of Christian hope. This is the hope I try to communicate to the people, because I am certain there is a God who is close to our problems and He will not let us down. But in addition to this, from a human point of view, I believe there are peaceful solutions. I believe in the ability of our people if only they are given an opportunity to participate. Here is where the difficulty lies. As long as there is repression and any discordant voice, any left voice against the government—whether a political party or a popular group—is repressed, there will be a problem. Elections alone are not the answer. If elections are a *part* of the process of freedom for the people, then I do believe in them. Because of this, it is imperative that these repressive actions by the government be stopped.

Q. And what of "The Dialogue" by General Carlos Humberto Romero following the massacre of demonstrators in May that the government and some opposition elements sit down to discuss national affairs?

A. There is no credibility for "The Dialogue." It is a forum, not a dialogue. A dialogue implies the presence of, and a toleration for, dissenting voices. In order for these voices to be heard, it is necessary to have a climate where repression is not feared. It is absurd that a national dialogue is called during a state of siege [a mild form of martial law], and that during this state of siege more acts of violence have been committed by the extreme right, and also—in revenge—by the extreme left. There is no appropriate climate for a dialogue at present.

Q. What were your feelings in May when government troops massacred peaceful demonstrators on the steps of your church, the Metropolitan Cathedral? What were your thoughts and what did you feel in your heart?

A. I expressed as always the rejection of such a crime, such violence. But as a Christian I am moved to call for conversion, for sinners to repent. I expressed my solidarity with the families of those killed and my solidarity with the just claims of the people. I pointed out the causes of these outrages, particularly social injustice and the lack of participation by Salvadorans in the goods of the society and the political process. As long as these profound conflicts exist, violence will continue and I regret that new crimes will be committed.

Q. In many Latin American countries, most notably and recently Nicaragua, Christians—even priests—have taken up arms in the struggle for liberation. Do you feel this runs counter to the Gospel tradition of love for all of mankind, the imperative for reconciliation and the belief in the inherent worth of all human beings?

A. Regrettably, it is an historical fact that many freedoms have to be won by bloodshed. Christian ethics admits of violence for a just cause. There are even constitutions that admit the right of the people to rebel; the church also admits this right. When there is a tyrannical situation, insufferable to the people, and it has not been possible to change the system by pacific means, then violence is justified on the condition that the evil of the rebellion does not become worse than the evil of the status quo.

In principle, Christians prefer peace. I believe that the power of nonviolence is much stronger than violence because it carries the power of love and the conviction that we are all brothers. This fraternal inspiration resolves unjust situations much better. The principles of the church are predicated on the conversion of mankind. However, as Pope Paul VI said, the Christian knows how to struggle and how to fight, but prefers peace. We too prefer peace but preach the legitimacy of the just war.

Q. You have been nominated for the Nobel Peace Prize by 132 members of the British Parliament and sixteen U.S. Congressmen. The church in El Salvador may be in the most difficult situation in the world and I know that you have received numerous death threats. What sustains you in your work, your commitment and your dedication?

A. Regarding the Nobel Peace Prize, I am deeply grateful for the nomination and have expressed my gratitude to the British Parliament, to the U.S. Congressmen, and all those who have indicated solidarity with this nomination. The nomination signifies to me very great moral and international support for our struggle. I am almost certain I will not receive the prize because there are so many political and diplomatic concerns that are not within my grasp. But the nomination itself is prize enough for me. I would accept it not for myself, but as an award to the cause of human rights.

What sustains me in the struggle is my love for my God, my desire to be faithful to the Gospels, and my love for the Salvadoran people—particularly the poor. I could not say whether the church in El Salvador is experiencing the most difficult times in the world today but churches all over the world—particularly in the United States—have given us beautiful testimonies of their solidarity.

Q. Can you talk very briefly about your background before you became archbishop?

A. I was born in a small town in the department of San Miguel [in eastern El Salvador] into a lower middle-class family. My father was the telegraph operator in town. I attended seminary in San Miguel, San Salvador and Rome and spent most of my life as a parish priest in San Miguel. I suppose I could have been called a conservative. However, I followed the principles of the Second Vatican Council with considerable interest. I noticed the changes that the Vatican was asking of us.

Later I came to San Salvador and served as secretary of the Bishops' Conference and in those years lived a very private life, anonymous you might say. Then I was appointed auxiliary bishop in the town of Santiago de Maria where I became very close to the problems of the campesinos, and then the bloody repression began. This was 1975.

Then, in 1977, I was appointed archbishop. The circumstances were difficult. Priests were being exiled and, a month after I assumed office, Padre Rutilio Grande was assassinated. This gave me the impetus to put into practice the principles of Vatican II and Medellín which call for solidarity with the suffering masses and the poor and encourage priests to live independent of the powers that be. My predecessor had initiated this work and I continued on with it.

It was precisely those young priests involved in experiments of "conscientization" with the peasants and urban shantytown dwellers who feared that I was a conservative and would put an end to the process. However, circumstances made me very understanding of the plight of the church, and we have worked very well together.

Q. Is there any message that you would like me to take back to the Christian community in the United States?

A. I have expressed my appreciation to the U.S. religious community before and welcome this opportunity to reiterate that appreciation. I have received many expressions of solidarity from bishops, priests, religious communities and individual Christians, not only in the Catholic community but from all denominations. To all of them: I thank you for this fraternal feeling.

Some have been so kind as to say that we are an example of faithful followers of the Gospels. I would beg that they pray for this to be true because this praise is most encouraging. We will try to live up to their opinions of us.

31. The Church in Salvador: Which Side Are You On?

BY ARCHBISHOP RIVERA Y DAMAS AND RADIO VENCEREMOS

The excerpts that follow graphically illustrate the battle for the hearts and minds—and the souls—of Salvadoran Christians. Acting Archbishop Rivera y Damas lends critical support to the ruling junta and levels an evenhanded broadside at both the left and the right for the ongoing violence. Radio Venceremos, the voice of the Democratic Revolutionary Front and the Farabundo Marti Liberation Front, invokes the words and deeds of Rivera y Damas' predecessor, Oscar Arnulfo Romero, who moved toward open support for the rebellion just prior to his assassination by rightist elements in March of 1980. (See previous Reading.)

Rivera y Damas Appeals for Peace in Sunday Sermon *

THE apostolic administrator of San Salvador today announced the reopening of two of the church's news media and issued an emotional appeal to the parties to the conflict to achieve peace in El Salvador.

In his Sunday sermon at the San Salvador Cathedral, Msgr. Arturo Rivera y Damas said the church "wants to contribute to alleviating and shortening the Salvadoran conflict, and that is why I ask for respect for the majority of the people who don't want violence and who do want a return to normal.

"There is a left that is struggling for power and wants to impose its ideology. There is a right that quietly but very effectively wants to recover power and reestablish its ideology," Rivera y Damas said.

"But there is also a government junta and an army that want to implement their ideology. While these parties fight," the monsignor added, "the people are suffering and shedding their blood."

"According to a conservative estimate, more than 6,000 Salvadorans have died so far this year as a result of political violence," Rivera y Damas said. Nevertheless, the legal aid office of the archbishopric, which is an institution at the service of the poor and is financed by the archbishopric, said last week that in the first four months of 1981, 7,780 people had died in political violence in El Salvador.

Msgr. Rivera y Damas today withdrew from the legal aid office its function to be a spokesman for the archbishopric in certain legal issues of displaced people or refugees that it usually deals with. He announced that the only official spokesman will be Msgr. Freddy Delgado, information secretary.

The apostolic administrator of San Salvador, who replaced the assassinated Msgr. Oscar Arnulfo Romero, also referred to the forthcoming reopening of two news media of the Catholic Church, the weekly *Orientación* and Radio YSAX, which have been victims of right-wing repression.

Rivera y Damas recalled the cases of *Diario Latino, La Crónica, El Independiente, Orientación*, Radio YSAX and Radio Cadena Cen-

---

* Text from the Spanish from Panama City, Panama ACAN News Service, May 31, 1981 (Foreign Broadcast Information Service, May 31, 1981).

tral, whose workers, newsmen or owners suffer intimidation, imprisonment or exile. Nevertheless, the apostolic administrator said, it is a positive step by the government to lift the ban on the radio news network "although the stations still cannot give national news and can only provide international news."

At the end of the sermon he asked the right wing and the left wing to stop the kidnappings "since these actions increase the country's moral, political, social, religious and economic chaos."

Radio Venceremos Criticizes Acting Archbishop *

We were considerably amazed to read in the local newspapers recently the statements made by the acting archbishop of San Salvador, Arturo Rivera y Damas, concerning violence in our country.

We realize that one of the main concerns of the church during these troubled historical times is precisely the grievous bloodletting our people are enduring. We also remember that when Monsignor Rivera assumed office as acting archbishop of San Salvador he said he would follow the path charted by our unforgettable Monsignor Oscar Arnulfo Romero.

When we speak of this charted path we refer to something very clear: Monsignor Romero's line leaves no room for ambiguity. It is a clear and precise fact that he adopted a coherent attitude about the role that the church is supposed to play in situations like the one our people are currently facing.

Definitely, the regime has made no concessions whatsoever as far as its policy of extermination is concerned. On the contrary, we can state most assuredly and with full backing from the people that government repression has grown a thousandfold. Monsignor Rivera y Damas also said that, in his opinion, our forces are trying to prevent the population from regaining their confidence and from looking for ways to return to a normal situation.

We want to believe that these assertions were made out of naivete and not out of malice, because the exact opposite is happening and this fact is known by vast democratic and progressive sectors throughout the world. Any distortion of fact in this connection is absolutely preposterous. It is precisely our vanguard, the Farabundo Martí National Liberation Front, which, listening to the chorus of voices clamoring for a political solution to the conflict and in a bid to spare our

---

* Excerpted from the Spanish from Radio Venceremos on May 31, 1981. (Foreign Broadcast Information Service, June 2, 1981.)

already martyred people further bloodshed, has agreed to and made specific proposals to find a political solution to the crisis.

It is a fact that Monsignor Rivera y Damas' statements are a shift away from a neutral position and are so biased and dangerous that they can only result in backing, and to a certain extent covering up the criminal actions which the paramilitary groups, the security corps and the army carry out daily against our people. We are certain that this type of attitude in no way helps establish the appropriate climate to find a political solution to the present crisis and at the same time ruins the church's chances of really playing a role in the mediation process.

32. The Sign of Resurrection in El Salvador: A Testimony from Christians Who Accompany the People in Their Struggle *

No Christian ought to come easily to armed struggle, and the Christian community in El Salvador has been no exception to this rule. Although the popular organizations, many of whose leaders are practicing Catholics, and their respective guerrilla groups could boast of roots in Christian social action, even the Popular Church in El Salvador did not fully sanction violence by the opposition. Until several months before his assassination, Archbishop Oscar Romero condemned the violence of both the right and government security forces and that of the left. Only with the failure of all peaceful avenues to justice did a clear distinction begin to be drawn by some sectors of the church between the violence of the oppressed and that of the oppressors.

THE people of El Salvador are living a critical and decisive hour of their history. They are deciding to liberate themselves from

---

* *The Sign of Resurrection in El Salvador* was released just prior to the opposition offensive in January of 1981 by religious groups affiliated with the Popular Church in El Salvador. The groups were the Archdiocesan Caritas, a committee from the Health Ministry, the Conference of Men and Women Religious of El Salvador, the Federation of Centers of Catholic Education, the Archdiocesan Pastoral Council, the National Commission of Justice and Peace, Faith and Joy, Christian Life Com-

oppression, to regain dignity, and to organize a society that will be communal and just for the poor majorities. In these moments the Salvadoran people are preparing themselves for an insurrection as a last resort to obtain that justice and peace for which they have so yearned and which has so many times been denied them.

We as Christians, men and women religious and clergy, working in diverse areas of pastoral ministry, education, social development and humanitarian aid, want also to accompany the people in these moments, acknowledge the justice of their cause and their struggle, and recognize the legitimate right which moves them to insurrection.

For years we have been close to the suffering people, to the poor and oppressed; we have experienced their misery but also their hope and their decision for an authentic liberation. We have attempted to serve them according to the Gospel, but they also have showed us the ultimate truth of the Gospel—the love of God as the good news of the kingdom for the poor. In this hour of insurrection, full of suffering and hope, we want to be with the poor, we want to explain our option, and we want to see in the insurrection of the people the very signs of the time, the word that God addresses us as Christians.

History of the People's Suffering

For 50 years the Salvadoran people have lived under the oppression of gravely unjust economic, social and political structures, which in no way have promoted the common good of the poor majorities but rather have fostered the privileges and the domination of a few. At every level of life—health, nutrition, housing, employment and education—the horrible reality described by Puebla—"the distance between the many who have little and the few who have much"—has existed.

Human rights have been systematically violated under military regimes of national security. Freedom of expression, the right to vote, constitutional guarantees have all been violated. The legislative system and the administration of justice have been corrupted. The successive regimes have repressed the people, used illegal arrests and torture, murdered and brought about the disappearance of many of the poor of El Salvador and of many of those who have been in solidarity with their cause.

---

munities, the Foundation of Promoters of Cooperatives, the Federation of Cooperative Associations of Agriculture/Livestock Production, the Baptist Assembly, and the Christian Student Movement.

This long course of oppression and repression has in no way changed but rather worsened, even to the limits of genocide, with the present government born of the pact between the military and the Christian Democratic Party. Despite repeated democratic words and deceptive promises of reform, 1980 has witnessed the increase of misery and unemployment and, above all, the greatest repressive barbarity against the people. More than 10,000 Salvadorans have been assassinated by security forces, members of the army and paramilitary groups. Peasants, laborers, union members, students, teachers, professionals, doctors, hut dwellers have been murdered in horrifying numbers and with a cruelty unparalleled in the history of the country. El Salvador has turned, as Archbishop Romero used to say, into the empire of hell.

The church has also been persecuted as never before during this year. The assassination of Archbishop Romero has been the most significant crime, the most repugnant and provocative, showing the measure of the cruelty of the current system. And along with him this year have been assassinated four priests, bringing to 11 the martyrs of the Salvadoran clergy, three women religious and one social worker from North America,[1] numerous catechists, and a large number of the Christian faithful. In addition, the quarters of the Archbishop, the Legal Aid Office, the church shelters, the radio station, the Catholic press and libraries, the Christian educational institutions, the dwellings of priests and women and men religious and even churches have frequently been searched, machine-gunned and dynamited. . . .

The Present Conflict

The Salvadoran people have not chosen armed conflict. Rather, conflict has been imposed on them. Over the years they have sought peaceful solutions in elections and used social and political pressure to achieve their aspirations. Everything has proved futile. Elections have been systematically fraudulent, and political organizations and parties have been systematically harassed and threatened with annihilation.

The coup of October 15, 1979, which might have been a last peaceful resort to bring about a solution, soon betrayed its ineffectiveness. All the civilian and some of the honest military men have gradually abandoned the successive juntas and their governments. All of them have cited the same reasons: the impossibility of carrying out a genuine policy favoring the people and the impossibility of stopping the

---

[1] See Reading 17, above.—Eds.

Jose Antonio Morales Ehrlich, member of the junta and head of the land reform project

Jose Antonio Morales Carbonell, son of junta member Morales Ehrlich and militant of the FPL

José Napoleón Duarte, President of El Salvador

(from left) Mario Andino; Col. Jaime Abdul Gutierrez; Guillermo Manuel Ungo; Col. Adol Arnoldo Majano; and Ramon Mayorga. Original members of the junta that assumed power in October, 1979.

Col. José Guillermo Garcia,
Minister of Defense

Col. Eugenio Vides Casanova,
Director General of the National
Guard and Col. Adolfo Castillo.

Three guerrilleros from Guazapa Ridge combat zone, October, 1980

Bishop Rivera y Damas, acting Archbishop of San Salvador

The late Archbishop Oscar Romero

Members of the Atlacatl Battalion, El Salvador's elite counter-insurgency force, at the Playa de Suchitoto June, 1981.

Young woman fighting with the guerrilleros, carrying an Israeli-made Uzi submachine gun, and playing with a villager's child, October, 1980.

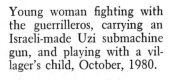

Literacy class conducted in Salvadoran refugee settlement at La Virtud, Honduras, May, 1981.

Children among the eight-hundred refugees at the seminary of San Salvador June 1981

repression, decidedly promoted by those entrenched in the armed forces, the government and the junta.

If the common good does not exist in El Salvador, if peaceful avenues have been continually closed, then we are in that situation in which the church admits the right of legitimate insurrection, "... *in the case of clear and prolonged tyranny which gravely menaces the fundamental rights of the person and injures the common good of the country ...*" (Paul VI, *Populorum Progressio*, n. 31; Medellín, Peace, n. 19).

As Salvadorans and Christians we are conscious of the tragedy of a war, of the human and material costs it brings with it. We are conscious of the fruitfulness of peace and we have worked for it. But we repeat, with Monsignor Romero, that if this is not possible, "*then it is a case of insurrection, which the church admits when all peaceful means have been exhausted*" (interview in the Caracas *Diario*, March 19, 1980).

The Salvadoran people have, besides, the right not only to their internal liberation but to their external independence. They have the right to decide their own destiny without the intervention of foreign powers to defend what they term their vital interests. For that reason we repeat what Monsignor Rivera recently affirmed and Monsignor Romero clearly expressed in a letter to President Carter: the United States is not supported by any right to interfere in the destiny of El Salvador in order to determine its future and still less to support militarily the current government. "*It would be unjust and deplorable if, because of the interference of foreign powers, the Salvadoran people were to be frustrated, were to be repressed and prevented from deciding autonomously the economic and political course which our nation must follow. It would suppose the violation of a right which we Latin American Bishops, gathered in Puebla, publicly acknowledged when we cited 'the legitimate self-determination of our peoples which will allow them to organize themselves according to their proper genius and the march of their history'*" (Puebla, 505; Letter to President Carter, February 17, 1980).

For that reason we join with many voices from across the world and especially with the declarations of bishops, priests, religious and Christians of the United States to demand of their government not to interfere in El Salvador.

An Uprising Speaks of Resurrection

An insurrection for the liberation of a people is not only a legitimate historical reality, but, for Christians, it is also a sign of the times through which God speaks to and calls us. The first thing that a just uprising tells us is that God's patience has run out. The experience of Israel in Egypt is being repeated: "I have seen the affliction of my people, I have heard their cry of complaint against their oppressors; I know well what they are suffering. Therefore, I have come down to liberate them" (Ex. 3: 7-8). The God of life, of justice and of liberation is once again present in the rebellion of a people against the sin of society. God is present defending the poor against the oppressors.

In this situation, an uprising speaks to us of Christian resurrection. An oppressed people, crucified like Christ, like the servant of Yahweh, sheds once again its blood for the life of the poor masses. And, like the cross of Christ, this is fruitful and salvific. Though in a tragic way, it does produce anew the paschal cycle of death and life, of suffering and hope. . . .

In an insurrection there is, above all, *hope*. Christian hope clearly does not reside in arms, even though these may be necessary and legitimate. Christian hope resides in the justice of a people's cause, in the generosity of their gift of self, in the nobility of their struggle. Hope is present when the heroism and valor characteristic of the armed struggle are afterwards transformed into generosity and commitment in the reconstruction of the country as expressed by Isaiah: that swords be turned into plowshares, that the wolf and the lamb shall graze together, that the poor shall live in the houses they build and eat the fruit of the fields they till (Is. 2:4; 65:21-25). Christian hope, finally, resides in there issuing from the uprising the real resurrection of the poor of El Salvador. . . .

With faith in God and in the blood shed by so many Salvadoran martyrs, we would like to end with the prophetic words of Monsignor Romero that we may not falter: *"The cry of liberation of this people is a cry that reaches up to God and one that nothing and no one can stop."* Over these ruins the glory of the Lord will shine.

PART FOUR

THE DECISION TO INTERVENE

EDITORS' INTRODUCTION

IN response to a penetrating question by CBS newsman Walter Cronkite, President Ronald Reagan in early March, 1981, made one of his few references to historical factors in the present conflict over the U.S. role in Central America. Reagan referred to the "memories . . . that our southern friends down there do have . . . of the great colossus of the north and so forth." The point of the reference was to *dismiss* history in the face of overwhelming imperatives of policy.

But history cannot just be waved aside at will. Current U.S. actions fall into a long pattern of intervention going back at least until the early nineteenth century, when the Central American isthmus was an attractive alternative to the long, arduous circumnavigation of South America for those who wanted to reach the Pacific coast, especially after the discovery of gold in California. Having warned European nations away from the area by invoking the Monroe Doctrine (announced, 1823), U.S. adventurers and capitalists felt free to explore possibilities for profit and empire in the region. The most spectacular of these forays was undertaken by a colorful group called the *filibusteros*,[1] who flourished chiefly in the 1850s. Financed by U.S. capitalists jockeying for control of transportation routes, these adventurers tried to carve out little empires for themselves in Central America. The most famous of these *filibusters*, William Walker, attempted to become potentate of Nicaragua and set up a Yankee colony in Central America in which slavery (long outlawed by local law) would be *restored* and U.S. exploitation of local inhabitants

---

[1] Although the word *filibuster* in English later came to mean a lengthy speech in the U.S. Senate to halt consideration of legislation, the term is originally derived from a Dutch word for freebooters, or pirates.

would be guaranteed. He was defeated by Commodore Cornelius Vanderbilt, the New York financier; but, undaunted, Walker made one last filibustering expedition in 1860 before he was captured and executed by Honduran armed forces.[2]

Later U.S. interventions in Central America cannot hope to escape being seen as anything but modern dress versions of the nineteenth century *filibusteros*. Twentieth century U.S. governments have come to recognize this; and, after a long series of armed incursions and occupations (the United States Marines occupied Nicaragua from 1912 to 1933!), President Franklin D. Roosevelt announced the Good Neighbor Policy in 1933 and pledged no further armed interventions by the United States in Latin America.[3] But this policy was significantly qualified by Washington's insistence that the unruly nations to the south maintain a friendly climate for North American business interests, and that local political authority be augmented by military officers trained in the U.S. and armed by Washington. This elaborately erected structure of the Good Neighbor Policy and Pan-Americanism began to crumble in the 1960s under the twin impact of popular unrest and the Cuban revolution, which was a dramatic demonstration of an alternative to the traditional cycle of poverty and exploitation.

Since then, U.S. policy has been marked by a series of attempts to find ways to counter popular insurgency and social revolution in the area. The designation of El Salvador as an arena for the suppression of rebel social movements was begun before Ronald Reagan became President; but under his administration a stepped-up effort has been made to fit the Salvadoran conflict into a readymade Cold War mold. The assumptions behind such a view include what we have already seen to be highly exaggerated notions of the role of external factors in guerrilla insurrections: the belief that the Kremlin is the mastermind behind most if not all of them. This book should help its readers to judge the validity of these Cold War doctrines, at least as

---

[2] The fullest account is William B. Scroggs, *Filibusters and Financiers* (New York, 1916), which is marred by the author's own uncritical identification with the aims of Walker and his fellow adventurers. A modern study of the *filibusteros*, and the lingering resentment they left behind in Latin America, is badly needed.

[3] Bryce Wood, *The Making of the Good Neighbor Policy* (New York, 1961). This nonintervention policy ended in 1954 with the U.S. involvement in the overthrow of the Arbenz regime in Guatemala, the Bay of Pigs invasion of Cuba in 1961, and the U.S. intervention in the Dominican Republic in 1965. Indirect intervention, it should be noted, in which U.S. political and economic pressure has helped overthrow regimes not to its liking, played a role throughout, notable examples being the Goulart government of Brazil (1964) and the Allende government of Chile (1973).

applied to Central America; to assess their more general validity it will be necessary to consult a wider range of sources. One highly respected recent survey of U.S. Cold War policy, Stephen Ambrose's *Rise to Globalism* (1980), cites Washington's belief that the U.S. has a special responsibility to create and sustain a world according to its image. But despite awesome military power at the disposal of the U.S. government, such a goal seemed unattainable because forces abroad in the world were too unruly to contain and control. Out of frustration at the thwarting of globalist aims, American policymakers ascribed responsibility to the Russians.[4] Soviet policy indeed has often supported national liberation struggles, but to suggest that such struggles are essentially *caused* by the Soviets is to stretch conspiracy notions beyond all empirical boundaries. Yet, by acting on the belief that El Salvador is part of Moscow's blueprint for world domination, the U.S. augments the very Third World anti-Yankeeism it seeks to avoid. Intervening in behalf of tyrannical local oligarchies, the North American colossus gives the citizens of such countries as El Salvador a narrow range of alternatives: either submit to oppression or join the insurgents. As these words are being written, many Salvadorans are making the fateful choice.

---

[4] Stephen E. Ambrose, *Rise to Globalism* (Second ed., Harmondsworth, England, 1980), esp. pp. 17–18.

Chapter I

THE U.S. GOVERNMENT'S COMMITMENT TO THE JUNTA

Editors' Introduction

MORE invoked than studied, President George Washington's "Farewell Address" of 1796 did *not* call for any general isolationism. (The statement, "No alliances, with any nation, at any time, for any purpose," did not appear in the Farewell Address, and was not something the outgoing first President would have urged on the fledgling nation in any case.) He did caution later U.S. policymakers "to steer clear of permanent alliances," but indicated that they "may safely trust to temporary alliances" if the diplomats who arrange such international commitments take care to keep the country's true interests in mind.[1] The commitment made by both the Carter and Reagan administrations to the Salvadoran junta, defended in the readings that follow, ought to be independently weighed by all concerned citizens according to George Washington's sensible criteria: is it a policy in accord with rationally determined U.S. interests, or is it the sort of hastily, ill-conceived entangling alliance that he warned us against almost 200 years ago?

33. Rationalizing The Winter 1981 Intervention *

BY THE U.S. DEPARTMENT OF STATE AND RONALD REAGAN

We present here, with some attempt to reduce duplication, statements from various levels of the U.S. government justifying military aid to the

---

[1] J. D. Richardson, ed., *Messages and Papers of the Presidents* (10 vols., Washington, D.C., 1907), I, pp. 221–23.

* From the *Department of State Bulletin* (April and May, 1981); *The New York Times;* State Department press releases (March-April-May, 1981).

junta, the coalition government in El Salvador. In some cases the govern-ment officials are subject to sharp questioning from journalists.

A WELL-ORCHESTRATED international Communist campaign
designed to transform the Salvadoran crisis from the internal
conflict to an increasingly internationalized confrontation is under
way. With Cuban coordination, the Soviet bloc, Vietnam, Ethiopia
and radical Arabs are furnishing at least several hundred tons of military equipment to the Salvadoran leftist insurgents. . . .

The Communist countries are orchestrating an intensive international disinformation campaign to cover their intervention while discrediting the Salvadoran Government and American support for that
Government. . . .

Our most urgent objective is to stop the large flow of arms through
Nicaragua into El Salvador. We consider what is happening is part of
the global Communist campaign coordinated by Havana and Moscow to support the Marxist guerrillas in El Salvador.

The policy implications are already clear:

First, the U.S.G. [United States Government] supports and will
continue to support the present Government in El Salvador. We
intend to work with that Government with the objective of achieving
social justice and stability in that strife-torn country.

Second, the U.S.G. is convinced that neither stability nor social
justice in El Salvador is possible as long as Communist subversion
continues.

Third, we will not remain passive in the face of this Communist
challenge, a systematic, well-financed, sophisticated effort to impose a
Communist regime in Central America.

This effort involves close coordination by Moscow, satellite capitals
and Havana, with the cooperation of Hanoi and Managua. It is a
repetition of the pattern we have already seen in Angola and Ethiopia, and, I may add, elsewhere. It is a threat, in our view, not just to
the United States but to the West at large.

We have not yet decided on the precise steps we will take to deal
with the situation; we will, however, in some way have to deal with
the immediate source of the problem—and that is Cuba.

Off the record, I wish to assure you we do not intend to have
another Vietnam and engage ourselves in another bloody conflict
where the source rests outside the target area.[1]

We believe in all sincerity we have no alternative but to act to

---

[1] See Readings 38-41, below, for the Vietnam analogy.—Eds.

prevent forces hostile to the U.S. and the West from overthrowing a government on our doorstep, particularly when that government offers the best hope of progress toward moderate democracy. . . .

We are faced with a four-legged stool:

One leg is what we should do in manifesting support of and encouraging reform in El Salvador.

The second leg is the problem of Nicaragua and the urgent need to put an end to the illicit arms traffic to El Salvador from Nicaragua—a country which has received millions of dollars in U.S. economic support.

The third leg I would call the external disinformation campaign designed to paint the revolutionary effort as distinctively apart from outside interventionist activity.

The fourth leg is the problem of Cuba. We do not anticipate dealing with that situation in the historic sense of what we did in Vietnam. We are studying a number of alternatives. I have nothing further to add on this except to assure you that we see happening here in El Salvador what happened in Africa and Southwest Asia— and that is dangerous not only for the U.S. but for all nations that share our values.

—U.S. Secretary of State Alexander M. Haig briefing to members of the North Atlantic Treaty Organization, February 17, 1981.

The government of El Salvador remains committed to carrying out basic economic and political reforms, including elections in 1982-83. The United States continues to support strongly these reforms, which include agrarian and banking reforms, promotion of employment, and encouragement of the private sector. . . .

Violence is the enemy of all democratic change, of individual rights, and of economic progress. Those who are responsible for the violence and terrorism, with arms support from Cuba and other countries, are the real obstacle to negotiations. We continue to impress upon the Government of El Salvador the importance of controlling violence, whatever its source.

In El Salvador, an end to the present suffering and violence would permit that nation to get on with the task of economic reconstruction and progress. The United States, with its long tradition of democratic change, recognizes the need for and supports peaceful and democratic change in El Salvador.

—U.S. State Department Press Statement, February 18, 1981.

Q. You are denouncing interventionism of the Soviet Union and their interference in certain countries. Aren't you about to do the same thing as you undertake to prevent attempts to take power in El Salvador? Aren't you promising to engage in your own kind of interventionism?

A. I think this is an important question, and again, I think the facts have to be maintained in the vision of your viewers.

As you know, there has just recently been concluded a major offensive by the so-called liberation forces in El Salvador. Prior to that time, and only in the last days of the Carter administration, did the United States provide any military equipment to the government of El Salvador, and that occurred at a time when they were racked in the final phases of the Cuban-sponsored and -supported offensive. So I do not believe that such a charge is either appropriate or correct.

I would also like to emphasize that it is not our intention in El Salvador to engage ourselves along the model of Southeast Asia. As we have said repeatedly, the problem must be dealt with at the source, and in this instance, clearly it's Cuba. . . .

—*Secretary Haig, interviewed for French television, Antenne 2, February 23, 1981.*

Q. Some Latin Americans feel that President Duarte [of El Salvador] has control of the situation. The people have not risen. This last offensive of the guerrillas did not work, and, therefore, aren't we likely to exacerbate the situation by American presence there now, therefore sort of promoting a self-fulfilling prophecy by coming down there and getting the guerrillas and people themselves upset about "big brother" intervention, and therefore losing the game instead of winning it?

A. No, and we realize that our southern friends down there do have memories of the great colossus of the north and so forth—but no, his government has asked for this because of the need for training against terrorist and guerrilla activities, has asked for matériel such as helicopters and so forth that can be better at interdicting the supply lines where these illicit weapons are being brought in to the guerrillas. . . .

Q. You've said that we could extricate ourselves easily from El Salvador if that were required at any given point in this proceeding. I assume you mean at any point. How could we possibly extricate ourselves? Even now, from this initial stage, how could we extricate ourselves without a severe loss of face?

A. I don't think we're planning on that—I think, to extricate ourselves from there. But the only thing that I could see that could have brought that about is if the guerrillas had been correct in their assessment and there had been the internal disturbance, well, then it would be a case of we're there at the behest of the present government. If that government is no longer there, we're not going there without an invitation. We're not forcing ourselves upon them, and you'd simply leave and there aren't that many people to be extricated.

Q. Even if the Duarte forces begin to lose with whatever military matériel assistance we give them, whatever training advisers we give them, are you pledging that we will not go in with fighting forces?

A. I certainly don't see any likelihood of us going in with fighting forces. I do see our continued work in the field of diplomacy with neighboring countries that are interested in Central America and South America to bring this violence to a halt and to make sure that we do not just sit passively by and let this hemisphere be invaded by outside forces. . . .

Walter Cronkite interviewing President Reagan, CBS News, March 3, 1981.

Q. Is the current level of American assistance to El Salvador likely to be the end of it, or is it likely to be more than you've done so far?

A. Well, I can't answer that question, and I think it would be foolish to attempt to do so. That would depend largely on the willingness of Cuba and the Soviet Union and those associated with them to continue to intervene illegally in the internal affairs of the member states of this hemisphere.

Q. Meaning that if they do more, we will too?

A. We feel that this is no longer an acceptable or tolerable kind of activity in this hemisphere. . . .

Q. Do you rule out the use of combat troops in El Salvador without qualification? Will you say definitely that there will be no U.S. combat troops in El Salvador?

A. No. I think it has been made very clear—and eloquently so—by the President last night in one of the most unusual and extensive interviews I've seen on national television in some time. I think the President addressed himself to that question explicitly and I refer you to it.

Q. Mr. Secretary, in that interview last night, there were some suggestions that the Duarte regime might be losing power [inaudible]. Do you see that happening? Do you see the threat either from the left or the right and the possibility of a coup shaping up?

A. Well I don't think it would serve any useful purpose for me to speculate on that—on issues of that kind. These are internal affairs within El Salvador. It is clear that we are supporting the government of El Salvador and the leadership of Duarte at this time. And I don't see any change in that. . . .

—Secretary Haig's remarks to journalists after meeting with Congressional leaders on Capitol Hill, March 4, 1981.

_____

On January 10, 1981, the Marxist guerrilla forces in El Salvador under the command of the Cuban-organized Unified Revolutionary Directorate, the DRU, began their so-called final offensive to topple the Duarte government. The DRU called for a popular insurrection to sweep the government from power, just as the Sandinista Front had been able to do in Nicaragua. The DRU said it wanted to present the Reagan administration with a "fait accompli," i.e. a revolutionary government in place, that could not be dislodged. But the situation in El Salvador was different from that of Somoza's Nicaragua. The Salvadoran people rejected the DRU's call for an insurrection in El Salvador. Unlike in Nicaragua, the government forces were not faced with entire cities rising up and workers striking in support of the Marxists. Instead the people of El Salvador chose to go to work, effectively turning their backs on the guerrilla groups who claimed to lead them. Government forces were able to block the guerrilla offensive, thus winning at least a symbolic victory over internationally supplied Marxist forces in El Salvador. . . .

The crucial question is why there was no popular uprising in response to the DRU's appeal. Where was the popular support that the Salvadoran left and its supporters here and in Europe claimed and apparently believed that they had? The explanation lies in the fact that the revolutionary civilian-military government of El Salvador, headed by Christian Democrat José Napoleón Duarte, has given El Salvador the hope for peaceful change, while the guerrillas have revealed themselves to be terrorists, interested only in obtaining power through brute force. . . .

We agree with President Duarte that his government is not a permanent repository of power in El Salvador. We look upon it as a transition to democracy. We believe the future of El Salvador should be determined at the ballot box not at the end of a gun. . . .

—Testimony of John A. Bushnell, Acting Assistant Secretary of State for

Inter-American Affairs, before a subcommittee of the U.S. House of Representatives Foreign Affairs Committee, March 5, 1981.

34. Beefing up the Salvadoran Military Forces: Some Components Of U.S. Intervention *

BY CYNTHIA ARNSON

Cynthia Arnson, whose analysis of the Salvadoran security forces appears earlier in this volume (Reading 15), has carefully researched the Pentagonal labyrinth as it relates to El Salvador. She tells us what military aid consists of, down to the last helicopter and hand grenade. For those interested, updates of her material are available from the Institute for Policy Studies, Washington D.C.

FROM the turn of the century until immediately after World War II, Chilean officers directed military training and operations for the Salvadoran armed forces. Chileans founded the first war college, later renamed the Command and General Staff School, and directed its activities until 1957. U.S. training and doctrine became increasingly important following World War II, when El Salvador received its first U.S. grants under the Military Assistance Program, as well as the first U.S. military mission.

Security assistance from the United States to El Salvador between fiscal year 1950 and fiscal year 1979 has totalled $4.97 million in Military Assistance Program grants, $3.479 million in Foreign Military Sales Agreements, $2.454 million in Excess Defense Articles, and $5.814 million in International Military Education and Training Program grants, all for a total of $16.72 million. The United States has trained a total of 1971 Salvadoran officers, including at least 17 in

---

* This reading is excerpted by permission of the author from various Resource Reports of the Institute for Policy Studies, Washington, D.C.: "Background Information on the Security Forces in El Salvador" (March 1980 IPS Resource Report), passim, and "Background Information on El Salvador" (IPS Resource Update #4, April, 1981), passim.

urban counterinsurgency, 14 in military intelligence, 108 in basic combat and counterinsurgency, and 124 in basic officer preparation. According to the Pentagon in 1977, ". . . our security assistance program facilitates our overall relations with the government of El Salvador and fosters useful professional contacts with key members of the Salvadoran armed forces."

Internal Security and the U.S. Office of Public Safety (OPS). To upgrade El Salvador's police and internal security forces, the United States instituted in 1957 a public safety program under the auspices of the Agency for International Development, ". . . to develop the managerial and operational skills and effectiveness of its civil police forces." Between 1957 and the program's termination in 1974, OPS spent a total of $2.1 million to train 448 Salvadoran police, and provide arms, communications equipment, transport vehicles, and riot-control gear.

Until 1963, the program was directed mainly at the National Police; from 1963 on, the program's emphasis shifted to the National Guard. At the height of U.S. involvement between 1963 and 1965, five U.S. advisers were stationed in the country to oversee training and program management. When Congress terminated the OPS program in 1974, U.S. A.I.D. analysts concluded that ". . . the National Police . . . has advanced from a nondescript, *cuartel*-bound group of poorly trained men to a well-disciplined, well-trained, and respected uniformed corps. It has good riot-control capability, good investigative capability, good records, and fair communications and mobility. It handles routine law enforcement well."

Graduates of OPS training, including those brought to the United States for studies at the International Police Academy (IPA) in Washington, D.C., occupied key positions in the Salvadoran security establishment. The assistant to the head of the Intelligence Division of the National Police was an IPA graduate; at various times the top positions in the Treasury Police, the Customs Police, and Immigration were U.S.-trained, as were the second and third in command in other security agencies.

Public safety advisers organized the Police School, prepared a standard textbook for the Treasury Police, and trained and equipped special riot control units in the National Police and National Guard. OPS created within the National Police a bomb-handling squad ". . . responsible for investigating terrorist activities . . . ," established a central police records bureau, and installed a teletype system linking El Salvador, Nicaragua, Honduras, Guatemala, Costa Rica, and Panama. Funds provided under OPS were used to purchase 2045 revolvers and carbines; 94 transport vehicles, including jeeps, sedans, and trucks; 208 mobile radio units and base radio stations; 755,000 rounds of ammunition; 950 tear gas grenades and projectiles; and assorted other riot control helmets, handcuffs, training films, cameras, and narcotic test kits.

Arms Sales. Until the mid-1970's, the Salvadoran armed forces were equipped primarily with surplus U.S. equipment, largely from World War II stocks, including 3 T-34, 10 T-6, and 6 T-41 trainers, and 6 C-47 helicopters. In 1975 the Israeli and Salvadoran governments concluded a package deal to re-equip the Salvadoran air force: Israeli sales of 18 refurbished French fighter bombers and trainers were the first jet aircraft operated by the Salvadoran air force. Since the Israeli sales in 1975, France has sold several more trainers, as well as light tanks, and the state-owned Brazilian firm EMBRAER has concluded a sale of 12 patrol aircraft, which use U.S.-designed engines and radar.

In 1977, El Salvador joined Argentina, Brazil, and Guatemala in rejecting proposed U.S. military assistance, in protest over U.S. criticism of its human rights record. No new requests for assistance were made in fiscal years 1979 or 1980, although deliveries of previously-authorized equipment and training have amounted to at least $1.04 million since 1978.

Arms sales by private U.S. firms, which must be licensed by the State Department's Office of Munitions Control, have totalled $2.0 million since fiscal year 1971. Increasingly, U.S. companies have been selling to private guard services in El Salvador, as well as to traditional security forces.

Current U.S. Arms Policy. On November 9, 1979, the U.S. government authorized a sale of $205,541 of tear gas, gas masks, and protective vests to El Salvador's security forces. Three days later, for a cost of $7,176, a six-man U.S. military training team arrived in El Salvador to train security forces in riot control. Between October 1, 1979 and December 31, 1979, El Salvador used $213,000 in Foreign Military Sales credits and purchased $801 worth of weapons through the Commercial Sales program.

On December 14, 1979, the Defense Department informed Congress of its intent to reprogram $300,000 in International Military Education and Training grants from fiscal year 1980 funds for El Salvador. These funds, which are now available to be spent, would go primarily for the purchase of U.S. Mobile Training Teams, placing U.S. military personnel in El Salvador for training purposes. On March 4, 1980, the Defense Department informed Congress of an additional reprogramming of $5.7 million in Foreign Military Sales credits for El Salvador. Congress has fifteen days in which to act on the administration's recommendation; otherwise, the reprogrammings become effective. In fiscal year 1981, the administration is asking for an additional $5 million in Foreign Military Sales credits and $498,000 in training grants, bringing total proposed assistance (reprogramming plus new funds) to a total of $11.5 million, or *69% of all military assistance El Salvador has received since 1950.* With no further authorizations of U.S. money, El Salvador still has $472,000 "in the pipeline" from authorizations from previous years.

Additional Emergency Aid. Within days after releasing the document [the "White Paper," Reading 35], the Reagan Administration announced major new increases in military assistance for El Salvador. A Pentagon assessment of the Salvadoran army had reportedly concluded in late February that the armed forces were "not organized to fight a counterinsurgency war," and had "no hope" of defeating the guerrillas with existing resources. The National Security Council met on February 27th, and approved the placement of additional U.S. non-combat advisers in El Salvador, as well as the provision of additional matériel.

The proposals were spelled out at a State Department briefing on March 2, 1981. They included:

• $25 million in Foreign Military Sales credits and loan guarantees to "permit the government of El Salvador to acquire additional helicopters, vehicles, radar and surveillance equipment and small arms."

• Four additional five-man teams to "train Salvadoran personnel in communications, intelligence, logistics, and in other professional skills designed to improve their capabilities to interdict infiltration and to respond to terrorist attacks."

Twenty million dollars of the arms credits came from a military aid contingency fund allowing the President to bypass Congress in sending emergency aid to foreign countries. Another $5 million was "reprogrammed" from fiscal year 1981 funds, and required Congressional approval. The Senate Appropriations Subcommittee on Foreign Operations approved the reprogramming on March 13. The House Appropriations Subcommittee on Foreign Operations approved the aid on March 24.

U.S. Military Personnel in El Salvador. As of late March, 1981, the Reagan administration had authorized the placement of 56 U.S. military personnel in El Salvador for training and administrative purposes. Their functions were as follows:

6—Staff of U.S. Military Group at the U.S. Embassy (raised from a level of 4).

5—Mobile Training Team acting as an adjunct to the MilGroup, for administrative, logistics, and command purposes related to the presence of additional U.S. personnel.

6—Naval training team "to assist the Salvadoran navy in improving its capability to interdict seaborne infiltration of arms destined for the leftist guerrillas" and to "survey the need for upgrading and refurbishing Salvadoran patrol boats and provide training in the maintenance of boats and other naval equipment."

14—Training in the use and maintenance of helicopters.

15—Three small unit-training teams of five men each to "provide in-garrison training for the Salvadorans' new quick-reaction force." The 15 are counterinsurgency specialists from the U.S. Army School of Special Forces, who had been stationed in Panama. They will provide basic, air mobile tactics, and counterinsurgency tactics training. The "quick-reaction force" envisioned by the Salvadorans involves an infantry unit of 2,000 men supported by helicopters for rapid mobility to points of conflict.

10—Two "operational and planning assistance teams" of five men each to aid each of El Salvador's five regional commands in planning specific operations. (One of these teams, authorized under Carter, was involved in "Operation Golden Harvest"—protecting the harvest against guerrillas.)

The War Powers Act and Other Legislation. The Reagan administration has taken care to point out that "U.S. personnel will not accompany Salvadoran units outside their garrison areas. Nor will U.S. personnel participate in any combat operations." Nevertheless, numerous members of Congress have charged that the administration has not adequately consulted Congress, and that the decision to send military personnel may be a violation of the War Powers Act of 1973. The Act requires that Congress be notified in writing within 48 hours of any situation ". . . in which United States forces are introduced into hostilities, or into situations where imminent involvement in hostilities is clearly indicated by the circumstances."

A section of the Arms Export Control Act, moreover, requires that ". . . personnel performing defense services . . . may not perform duties of a combatant nature, including any duties related to training and advising that may engage United States personnel in combat activities. . . ."

In early March, 45 members of the House of Representatives telegrammed President Reagan advising him that ". . . any involvement of military personnel in hostilities in El Salvador requires compliance with the War Powers Act." Senator John Glenn (D-OH), member of the Senate Foreign Relations Committee, has said he will "closely watch" administration compliance with the War Powers Act and the Arms Export Control Act.

Under pressure from Congress and the U.S. press to the effect that the presence of U.S. military advisers in El Salvador could lead to another Vietnam-like entanglement, the Reagan administration indicated in late March that most or all of the U.S. military personnel could be withdrawn from El Salvador by summer or fall of 1981. On March 13th, however, Under-Secretary of State for Political Affairs Walter Stoessel, Jr., told a Senate Subcommittee that ". . . El Salvador is not another Vietnam. . . . Experience has shown, however, that for our support to be credible, it must respond not only to the present situation but to the potential of the other side to create further violence. . . . We must anticipate future needs rather than being merely reactive. There is, thus, an element of deterrence built into our support."

EMERGENCY MILITARY AID TO EL SALVADOR
JANUARY–MARCH 1981

I. $5 Million sent by Carter January 17, 1981 **

Quantity	Item	Cost $
30,000	C rations	59,275
100	M79 grenade launchers	38,800
2,000	M-16 rifles	934,000
6	M-23 systems w/12 M60D machine guns	61,276
5,000 rds.	40 mm M79 ammunition	44,900
1,000,000 rds.	5.56 mm ammunition	220,000
38,340 rds.	7.62 mm linked ammunition	13,419
4,500,000 rds.	7.62 mm ammunition	1,080,000
2,000	hand grenades	18,000
10,000	smoke grenades	210,000
300 rds.	57 mm HE ammunition	11,000
5,000 each	helmets, liners, and headbands	80,750
5,000	flak jackets	180,450
10	AN/VRC-46 radio installation kits	2,620
3	helicopter training and maintenance teams	228,700
—	transportation, administrative and other costs	1,816,810
		5,000,000

II. $5 Million Reprogramming by Reagan, March 2, 1981

Training	$ 300,000
Communications equipment	200,000
Assorted vehicles	3,000,000
Upgrade Navy vessels	1,500,000
	5,000,000

** Special Executive authority granted under Section 506(a) of the Foreign Assistance Act.
Source: U.S. Defense Security Assistance Agency, March, 1981.

III. $20 Million sent by Reagan, March 2, 1981 **

Arms and ammunition	$8,000,000
Helicopters *	4,000,000
Training	1,000,000
Communications	3,000,000
Medical equipment	500,000
Individual equipment (uniforms, helmets, etc.)	1,500,000
Upgrade Air Force aircraft	1,500,000
Air defense	500,000
	20,000,000

---

* Four additional helicopters were delivered to El Salvador in March, 1981.

Editors' note: Though for reasons of space we must omit the extensive footnotes to Cynthia Arnson's well-researched article, we list here some of the sources she has drawn on. This is particularly to aid students who wish to penetrate the dense screen of official government pronouncements in order to find out what's really happening: Organization of American States, Inter-American Commission on Human Rights Report on the Situation of Human Rights in El Salvador, Washington, D.C., 1979; Howard Blutstein, ed., Area Handbook on El Salvador, U.S. Government Printing Office, Washington, D.C., 1971; U.S. Agency for International Development, Phase-out Study of the Public Safety Program in El Salvador, Washington, D.C., 1974; Amnesty International, El Salvador: General Background, London, December, 1977, and the International Institute for Strategic Studies, The Military Balance 1979-1980, London, 1979; U.S. Department of Defense, Foreign Military Sales and Military Assistance Facts, Washington, D.C., 1979; Michael Klare, Supplying Repression, Institute for Policy Studies, Washington, D.C., 1977; U.S. Department of Defense, Congressional Presentation Document: Security Assistance Fiscal Year 1978, Washington, D.C., 1977; Gen. David C. Jones, USAF, United States Military Posture for Fiscal Year 1982, U.S. Department of Defense, Washington, D.C.

Chapter II

THE WHITE PAPER AND ITS CRITICS

Editors' Introduction

ONE of the strongest Congressional proponents of an aggressive U.S. foreign policy is the arch-conservative Senator from North Carolina, Jesse Helms. In a recent issue of *The New Yorker*, Washington correspondent Elizabeth Drew presented a fascinating if chilling insight into Helm's political philosophy and that of the "new right" generally. The Senator's key legislative aide stated that only a small number of people approach politics rationally; most respond emotionally to basic questions, and Helms intends to lead this latter group by the techniques of emotive persuasion (augmented, of course, by the facilities of modern technology). His hope, it appears, is to reverse the whole course of western history since the eighteenth-century Enlightenment.[1]

If political life in the contemporary United States continues to be dominated by the Helmses of this country (and it looks as if we're in for it, for a while at least), then the function of policy rationales has to be reconceptualized. In the age of post-rational politics that people like Helms hope to initiate, rationales for political action (such as the decision to intervene in El Salvador) will no longer have to meet the test of traditional rational thought; it will be enough simply to invoke the emotional force of such symbols as God, Home, Country. People no longer will be under the obligation of *thinking* about government policies; they will only have to *feel*.

The Enlightenment belief of a statesman appealing to the best in people, raising up his constituency by rationally defensible leadership

---

[1] Elizabeth Drew, "A Reporter at Large: Jesse Helms," *The New Yorker*, July 20, 1981, pp. 78–95. (See especially, Drew's account of the views of James Lucier, Helms's chief legislative assistant, on pp. 85–86.)

is now under threat. Foreign policy initiatives that persist, *even when* their hastily-framed rationales are shown to be based on flimsy assumptions and fabricated data, suggest a thoughtless dogmatism—or cynicism—in U.S. foreign policy. How else is one to interpret the government's El Salvador White Paper of February, 1981,[2] and an aggressive foreign policy (supported by Jesse Helms and his cohorts) in the face of the public refutation of that White Paper? Does it herald a new age of international irrationalism? And what will be the domestic counterpart of the new irrationality? These are questions we ought to deeply ponder—rationally, it is hoped.

35. "Communist Interference In El Salvador": The U.S. State Department White Paper*

As early as 1681, according to the authoritative Oxford English Dictionary, official governmental reports in Great Britain were known as "White Papers." Along with much other political nomenclature and practice, the preparation of such reports became part of the political tradition of the United States. During the period of the Vietnam war, the U.S. government issued two notable White Papers on that fateful Indochina conflict: A Threat to the Peace: North Vietnam's Efforts to Conquer South Vietnam (U.S. Department of State Publication 7308, December, 1961); Aggression From the North: The Record of North Vietnam's Campaign to Conquer South Vietnam (U.S. Department of State Publication 7839, February, 1965). These White Papers share at least one important feature with this comparable State Department publication on El Salvador: the fervent, even obsessive attempt to link local insurgency with some nefarious outside conspiracy. Subsequent readings will subject the 1981 White Paper to careful scrutiny.

SUMMARY. This special report presents definitive evidence of the clandestine military support given by the Soviet Union, Cuba, and their Communist allies to Marxist-Leninist guerrillas now fight-

---

[2] Reading 35.

* United States Department of State, Special Report No. 80 (February 23, 1981).

ing to overthrow the established government of El Salvador. The evidence, drawn from captured guerrilla documents and war matériel and corroborated by intelligence reports, underscores the central role played by Cuba and other Communist countries beginning in 1979 in the political unification, military direction, and arming of insurgent forces in El Salvador.

From the documents it is possible to reconstruct chronologically the key stages in the growth of the Communist involvement:

• The direct tutelary role played by Fidel Castro and the Cuban government in late 1979 and early 1980 in bringing the diverse Salvadoran guerrilla factions into a unified front.

• The assistance and advice given the guerrillas in planning their military operations.

• The series of contacts between Salvadoran Communist leaders and key officials of several Communist states that resulted in commitments to supply the insurgents with nearly 800 tons of the most modern weapons and equipment.

• The covert delivery to El Salvador of nearly 200 tons of those arms, mostly through Cuba and Nicaragua, in preparation for the guerrillas' failed "general offensive" of January 1981.

• The major Communist effort to "cover" their involvement by providing mostly arms of Western manufacture.

It is clear that over the past year the insurgency in El Salvador has been progressively transformed into another case of indirect armed aggression against a small Third World country by Communist powers acting through Cuba.

The United States considers it of great importance that the American people and the world community be aware of the gravity of the actions of Cuba, the Soviet Union, and other Communist states who are carrying out what is clearly shown to be a well-coordinated, covert effort to bring about the overthrow of El Salvador's established government and to impose in its place a Communist regime with no popular support.

I. A Case of Communist Military Involvement in the Third World

The situation in El Salvador presents a strikingly familiar case of Soviet, Cuban, and other Communist military involvement in a politically troubled Third World country. By providing arms, training, and direction to a local insurgency and by supporting it with a global propaganda campaign, the Communists have intensified and widened the conflict, greatly increased the suffering of the Salvadoran people, and deceived much of the world about the true nature of the revolution. Their objective in El Salvador as elsewhere is to bring about—at little cost to themselves—the overthrow of the established government and the imposition of a Communist regime in defiance of the will of the Salvadoran people.

The Guerrillas: Their Tactics and Propaganda. El Salvador's extreme left, which includes the long-established Communist Party of El Salvador (PCES) and several armed groups of more recent origin, has become increasingly committed since 1976 to a military solution. A campaign of terrorism—bombings, assassinations, kidnappings, and seizures of embassies—has disrupted national life and claimed the lives of many innocent people.

During 1980, previously fragmented factions of the extreme left agreed to coordinate their actions in support of a joint military battle plan developed with Cuban assistance. As a precondition for large-scale Cuban aid, Salvadoran guerrilla leaders, meeting in Havana in May, formed first the Unified Revolutionary Directorate (DRU) as their central executive arm for political and military planning and, in late 1980, the Farabundo Martí People's Liberation Front (FMLN), as the coordinating body of the guerrilla organizations. A front organization, the Revolutionary Democratic Front (FDR), was also created to disseminate propaganda abroad. For appearances' sake, three small non-Marxist-Leninist political parties were brought into the front, though they have no representation in the DRU.

The Salvadoran guerrillas, speaking through the FDR, have managed to deceive many about what is happening in El Salvador. They have been aided by Nicaragua and by the worldwide propaganda networks of Cuba, the Soviet Union, and other Communist countries.

The guerrillas' propaganda aims at legitimizing their violence and concealing the Communist aid that makes it possible. Other key aims are to discredit the Salvadoran government, to misrepresent U.S. policies and actions, and to foster the impression of overwhelming popular support for the revolutionary movement.

Examples of the more extreme claims of their propaganda apparatus—echoed by Cuban, Soviet, and Nicaragua media—are:

• That the United States has military bases and several hundred troops in El Salvador (in fact, the United States has no bases and fewer than 50 military personnel there).

• That the government's security forces were responsible for most of the 10,000 killings that occurred in 1980 (in their own reports in 1980, the guerrillas themselves claimed the killings of nearly 6,000 persons including, noncombatant "informers" as well as government authorities and military).

In addition to media propaganda, Cuba and the Soviet Union promote the insurgent cause at international forums, with individual governments, and among foreign opinion leaders. Cuba has an efficient network for introducing and promoting representatives of the Salvadoran left all over the World. Havana and Moscow also bring indirect pressure on some governments to support the Salvadoran revolutionaries by mobilizing local Communist groups.

II. Communist Military Intervention: A Chronology

Before September 1980 the diverse guerrilla groups in El Salvador were ill-coordinated and ill-equipped, armed with pistols and a varied assortment of hunting rifles and shotguns. At that time the insurgents acquired weapons predominantly through purchases on the international market and from dealers who participated in the supply of arms to the Sandinistas in Nicaragua.

By January 1981 when the guerrillas launched their "general offensive," they had acquired an impressive array of modern weapons and supporting equipment never before used in El Salvador by either the insurgents or the military. Belgian FAL rifles, German G-3 rifles, U.S. M-1, M-16, and AR-15 semiautomatic and automatic rifles, and the Israeli UZI submachinegun and Galil assault rifle have all been confirmed in the guerrilla inventory. In addition, they are known to possess .30 to .50 caliber machineguns, the U.S. M-60 machinegun, U.S. and Russian hand grenades, the U.S. M-79 and Chinese RPG grenade launchers, and the U.S. M-72 light antitank weapon and 81mm mortars. Captured ammunition indicates the guerrillas probably possess 60mm and 82mm mortars and 57mm and 75mm recoilless rifles.

Recently acquired evidence has enabled us to reconstruct the central role played by Cuba, other Communist countries, and several radical states in the political unification and military direction of insurgent forces in El Salvador and in equipping them in less than 6 months with a panoply of modern weapons that enabled the guerrillas to launch a well-armed offensive.

This information, which we consider incontrovertible, has been acquired over the past year. Many key details, however, have fallen into place as the result of the guerrillas' own records. Two particularly important document caches were recovered from the Communist Party of El Salvador in November 1980 and from the Peoples' Revolutionary Army (ERP) in January 1981. This mass of captured documents included battle plans, letters, and reports of meetings and travels, some written in cryptic language and using code words.

When deciphered and verified against evidence from other intelligence sources, the documents bring to light the chain of events leading to the guerrillas' January 1981 offensive. What emerges is a highly disturbing pattern of parallel and coordinated action by a number of Communist and some radical countries bent on imposing a military solution.

The Cuban and Communist role in preparing for and helping to organize the abortive "general offensive" early this year is spelled out in the following chronology based on the contents of captured documents and other sources.

Initial Steps. The chronology of external support begins at the end of 1979. With salutations of "brotherly and revolutionary greetings" on December 16, 1979, members of the Communist Party of El Salvador (PCES), National Resistance (FARN), and Popular Liberation Forces (FPL) thank Fidel Castro in a letter for his help and "the help of your party comrades . . . by signing an agreement which establishes very solid bases upon which we begin building coordination and unity of our organizations." The letter, written in Havana, was signed by leaders of these three revolutionary organizations.

At the April 1980 meeting at the Hungarian Embassy in Mexico City, guerrilla leaders made certain "requests" (possibly for arms). Present at this meeting were representatives of the German Democratic Republic, Bulgaria, Poland, Vietnam, Hungary, Cuba, and the Soviet Union.

In notes taken during an April 28, 1980 meeting of the Salvadoran Communist Party, party leader Shafik Handal mentions the need to "speed up reorganization and put the party on a war footing." He added, "I'm in agreement with taking advantage of the possibilities of assistance from the socialist camp. I think that their attitude is magnificent. We are not yet taking advantage of it." In reference to a unification of the armed movement, he asserts that "the idea of involving everyone in the area has already been suggested to Fidel himself." Handal alludes to the concept of unification and notes, "Fidel thought well of the idea."

Guerrilla Contacts in Havana. From May 5 to June 8, 1980, Salvadoran guerrilla leaders report on meetings in Honduras, Guatemala, Costa Rica, and Nicaragua. They proceed to Havana and meet several times with Fidel Castro; the documents also note an interview with the German Democratic Republic (G.D.R.) Chairman Erich Honecker in Havana. During the Havana portion of their travels, the Salvadoran guerrilla leadership meets twice with the Cuban Directorate of Special Operations (DOE, the clandestine operations/special forces unit of the Cuban Ministry of Interior) to discuss guerrilla military plans. In addition, they meet with the Cuban "Chief of Communications."

During this period (late May 1980), the Popular Revolutionary Army (ERP) is admitted into the guerrilla coalition after negotiations in Havana. The coalition then assumes the name of the Unified Revolutionary Directorate (DRU) and meets with Fidel Castro on three occasions.

After the Havana meetings, Shafik Handal leaves Havana on May 30, 1980 for Moscow. The other Salvadoran guerrilla leaders in Havana leave for Managua. During the visit of early June, the DRU leaders meet with Nicaraguan revolutionary leaders (Sandinistas) and discuss: (1) a headquarters with "all measures of security"; (2) an "international field of operations, which they (Sandinistas) control"; and (3) the willingness of the Sandinistas to "contribute in material terms" and to adopt "the cause of El Salvador as its own." The meeting culminated with "dinner at Humberto's house" (presumably Sandinista leader Humberto Ortega).

Salvadoran Communist Party Leader's Travels in the East. From June 2 to July 22, 1980, Shafik Handal visits the U.S.S.R., Vietnam, the German Democratic Republic, Czechoslovakia, Bulgaria, Hungary, and Ethiopia to procure arms and seek support for the movement.

On June 2, 1980, Handal meets in Moscow with Mikhail Kudachkin, Deputy Chief of the Latin American Section of the Foreign Relations Department of the CPSU Central Committee. Kudachkin suggests that Handel travel to Vietnam to seek arms and offers to pay for Handal's trip.

Continuing his travels between June 9 and 15, Handal visits Vietnam where he is received by Le Duan, Secretary General of the Vietnamese Communist Party; Xuan Thuy, member of the Communist Party Central Committee Secretariat; and Vice Minister of National Defense Tran Van Quang. The Vietnamese, as a "first contribution," agree to provide 60 tons of arms. Handal adds that "the comrade requested air transport from the USSR."

From June 19 to June 24, 1980, Handal visits the German Democratic Republic (G.D.R.), where he is received by Hermann Axen, member of the G.D.R. Politburo. Axen states that the G.D.R. has already sent 1.9 tons of supplies to Managua. On July 21, G.D.R. leader Honecker writes the G.D.R. Embassy in Moscow that additional supplies will be sent and that the German Democratic Republic will provide military training, particularly in clandestine operations. The G.D.R. telegram adds that although Berlin possesses no Western-manufactured weapons—which the Salvadoran guerrillas are seeking—efforts will be undertaken to find a "solution to this problem." (NOTE: The emphasis on Western arms reflects the desire to maintain plausible denial.)

From June 24–27, 1980, Handal visits Czechoslovakia, where he is received by Vasil Bilak, Second Secretary of the Czech Communist Party. Bilak says that some Czech arms circulating in the world market will be provided so that these arms will not be traced back to Czechoslovakia as the donor country. Transportation will be coordinated with the German Democratic Republic.

Handal proceeds to Bulgaria from June 27 to June 30, 1980. He is received by Dimitir Stanichev, member of the Central Committee Secretariat. The Bulgarians agree to supply German-origin weapons and other supplies, again in an apparent effort to conceal their sources.

In Hungary, from June 30 to July 3, 1980, Handal is received by Communist Party General Secretary Janos Kadar and "Guesel" (probably Central Committee Secretary for Foreign Affairs Andras Gyenes). The latter offers radios and other supplies and indicates Hungarian willingness to trade arms with Ethiopia or Angola in order to obtain Western-origin arms for the Salvadoran guerrillas. "Guesel" promises to resolve the trade with the Ethiopians and Angolans himself, "since we want to be a part of providing this aid." Additionally, Handal secures the promise of 10,000 uniforms to be made by the Hungarians according to Handal's specifications.

Handal then travels to Ethiopia, July 3 to July 6. He meets Chairman Mengistu and receives "a warm reception." Mengistu offers "several thousand weapons," including: 150 Thompson submachineguns with 300 cartridge clips, 1,500 M-1 rifles, 1,000 M-14 rifles, and ammunition for these weapons. In addition, the Ethiopians agree to supply all necessary spare parts for these arms.

Handal returns to Moscow on July 22, 1980 and is received again by Mikhail Kudachkin. The Soviet official asks if 30 Communist youth currently studying in the U.S.S.R. could take part in the war in El Salvador. Before leaving Moscow, Handal receives assurances that the Soviets agree in principle to transport the Vietnamese arms.[1]

---

[1] Handal categorically rejected the State Department's charges of an arms agreement between him and Soviet-bloc countries, and countercharged that the White Paper "is a maneuver to justify the growing supply of U.S. arms and military personnel to the genocidal Christian Democratic military junta and prepare the ground for an eventual military aggression in Central America." See The New York Times, February 27, 1981, for Handal's full statement. Another Salvadoran insurgent leader reported to a Latin American correspondent of the Paris newspaper, Le Monde: "If we only had half the weapons the enemy attributes to us, we'd have no trouble overrunning several of its barracks and grabbing the matériel the Salvadoran army is receiving from the United States by plane and boat (via the Panama Canal)." Francis Pisani, "Where El Salvador's Guerrillas Get Arms," Manchester Guardian Weekly (March, 8, 1981).—Eds.

Further Contacts in Nicaragua. On July 13, representatives of the DRU arrive in Managua amidst preparations for the first anniversary celebration of Somoza's overthrow. The DRU leaders wait until July 23 to meet with "Comrade Bayardo" (presumably Bayardo Arce, member of the Sandinista Directorate). They complain that the Sandinistas appear to be restricting their access to visiting world dignitaries and demanding that all contacts be cleared through them. During the meeting, Arce promises ammunition to the guerrillas and arranges a meeting for them with the Sandinista "Military Commission." Arce indicates that, since the guerrillas will receive some arms manufactured by the Communist countries, the Sandinista Army (EPS) will consider absorbing some of these weapons and providing to the Salvadorans Western-manufactured arms held by the EPS in exchange. (In January 1981 the Popular Sandinista Army indeed switched from using U.S.-made weapons to those of Soviet and East European origin.)

The DRU representatives also meet with visiting Palestine Liberation Organization (PLO) leader Yasir Arafat in Managua on July 22, 1980. Arafat promises military equipment, including arms and aircraft. (A Salvadoran guerrilla leader met with FATAH leaders in Beirut in August and November, and the PLO has trained selected Salvadorans in the Near East and in Nicaragua.)

On July 27, the guerrilla General Staff delegation departs from Managua for Havana, where Cuban "specialists" add final touches to the military plans formulated during the May meetings in Havana.

Arms Deliveries Begin. In mid-August 1980, Shafik Handal's arms-shopping expedition begins to bear fruit. On August 15, 1980, Ethiopian arms depart for Cuba. Three weeks later the 60 tons of captured U.S. arms sent from Vietnam are scheduled to arrive in Cuba.

As a result of a Salvadoran delegation's trip to Iraq earlier in the year, the guerrillas receive a $500,000 logistics donation. The funds are distributed to the Sandinistas in Nicaragua and within El Salvador.

By mid-September, substantial quantities of the arms promised to Handal are well on the way to Cuba and Nicaragua. The guerrilla logistics coordinator in Nicaragua informs his Joint General Staff on September 26 that 130 tons of arms and other military material supplied by the Communist countries have arrived in Nicaragua for shipment to El Salvador. According to the captured documents, this represents one-sixth of the commitments to the guerrillas by the Communist countries. (NOTE: To get an idea of the magnitude of this commitment, the Vietnamese offer of only 60 tons included 2 million rifle and machinegun bullets, 14,500 mortar shells, 1,620 rifles, 210 machineguns, 48 mortars, 12 rocket launchers, and 192 pistols.)

In September and October, the number of flights to Nicaragua from Cuba increased sharply. These flights had the capacity to transport several hundred tons of cargo.

At the end of September, despite appeals from the guerrillas, the Sandinistas suspend their weapons deliveries to El Salvador for 1 month, after the U.S. government lodges a protest to Nicaragua on the arms trafficking.

When the shipments resume in October, as much as 120 tons of weapons and matériel are still in Nicaragua and some 300–400 tons are in Cuba. Because of the difficulty of moving such large quantities overland, Nicaragua—with Cuban support—begins airlifting arms from Nicaragua into El Salvador. In November, about 2.5 tons of arms are delivered by air before accidents force a brief halt in the airlift.

In December, Salvadoran guerrillas, encouraged by Cuba, begin plans for a general offensive in early 1981. To provide the increased support necessary, the Sandinistas revive the airlift into El Salvador. Salvadoran insurgents protest that they cannot absorb the increased flow of arms, but guerrilla liaison members in Managua urge them to increase their efforts as several East European nations are providing unprecedented assistance.

A revolutionary radio station—*Radio Liberación*—operating in Nicaragua begins broadcasting to El Salvador on December 15, 1980. It exhorts the populace to mount a massive insurrection against the government. (References to the Sandinistas sharing the expenses of a revolutionary radio station appear in the captured documents.)

On January 24, 1981 a Cessna from Nicaragua crashes on takeoff in El Salvador after unloading passengers and possibly weapons. A second plane is strafed by the Salvadoran Air Force, and the pilot and numerous weapons are captured. The pilot admits to being an employee of the Nicaraguan national airline and concedes that the flight originated from Sandino International Airport in Managua. He further admits to flying two earlier arms deliveries.

Air supply is playing a key role, but infiltrations by land and sea also continues. Small launches operating out of several Nicaraguan Pacific ports traverse the Gulf of Fonseca at night, carrying arms, ammunition, and personnel. During the general offensive on January 13, several dozen well-armed guerrillas landed on El Salvador's southeastern coast on the Gulf of Fonseca, adjacent to Nicaragua.

Overland arms shipments also continue through Honduras from Nicaragua and Costa Rica. In late January, Honduras security forces uncover an arms infiltration operation run by Salvadorans working through Nicaragua and directed by Cubans. In this operation, a trailer truck is discovered carrying weapons and ammunition destined for Salvadoran guerrillas. Weapons include 100 U.S. M-16 rifles and 81mm mortar ammunition. These arms are a portion of the Vietnamese shipment: A trace of the M-16s reveals that several of them were shipped to U.S. units in Vietnam where they were captured or left behind. Using this network, perhaps five truckloads of arms may have reached the Salvadoran guerrillas.

The availability of weapons and matériel significantly increases the military capabilities of the Salvadoran insurgents. While attacks raged throughout the country during the "general offensive" that began on January 10, it soon became clear that the DRU could not sustain the level of violence without suffering costly losses in personnel. By the end of January, DRU leaders apparently decided to avoid direct confrontation with government forces and reverted to sporadic guerrilla terrorist tactics that would reduce the possibility of suffering heavy casualties.

III. The Government:
The Search for Order and Democracy

Central America's smallest and most densely populated country is El Salvador. Since its independence in 1821, the country has experienced chronic political instability and repression, widespread poverty, and concentration of wealth and power in the hands of a few families. Although considerable economic progress took place in the 1960s, the political system remained in the hands of a traditional economic elite backed by the military. During the 1970s, both the legitimate grievances of the poor and landless and the growing aspirations of the expanding middle classes met increasingly with repression. El Salvador has long been a violent country with political, economic, and personal disputes often resulting in murders.

The Present Government. Aware of the need for change and alarmed by the prospect of Nicaragua-like chaos, progressive Salvadoran military officers and civilians overthrew the authoritarian regime of General Carlos Humberto Romero in October 1979 and ousted nearly 100 conservative senior officers.

After an initial period of instability, the new government stabilized around a coalition that includes military participants in the October 1979 coup, the Christian Democratic Party, and independent civilians. Since March 1980, this coalition has begun broad social changes: conversion of large estates into peasant cooperatives, distribution of land to tenant farmers, and nationalization of foreign trade and banking.

Four Marxist-Leninist guerrilla groups are using violence and terrorism against the Salvadoran government and its reforms. Three small non-Marxist-Leninist political parties—including a Social Democratic Party—work with guerrilla organizations and their political fronts through the Democratic Revolutionary Front (FDR), most of whose activities take place outside El Salvador.

The government of El Salvador—headed since last December by José Napoleón Duarte, the respected Christian Democrat denied office by the military in the Presidential elections of 1972—faces armed opposition from the extreme right as well as from the left. Exploiting their traditional ties to the security forces and the tendency of some members of the security forces to abuse their authority, some wealthy Salvadorans affected by the Duarte government's reforms have sponsored terrorist activities against supporters of the agrarian and banking reforms and against the government itself. ·

A symbiotic relationship has developed between the terrorism practiced by extremists of both left and right. Thousands have died without regard for class, creed, nationality, or politics. Brutal and still unexplained murders in December of four American churchwomen—and in January of two American trade unionists—added U.S. citizens to the toll of this tragic violence. The United States has made clear its interest in a complete investigation of these killings and the punishment of those responsible.

Despite bitter resistance from right and left, the Duarte government has stuck to its reform programs and has adopted emergency measures to ease the lot of the poor through public works, housing projects, and aid to marginal communities. On the political front, it has offered amnesty to its opponents, scheduled elections for a constituent assembly in 1982, and pledged to hand power over to a popularly elected government no later than mid-1983.

The government's pursuit of progress with order has been further hampered by the virtual breakdown of the law enforcement and judicial system and by the lack of an effective civil service.

The introduction of the reforms—some of which are now clearly irreversible—has reduced popular support for those who argue that change can only come about through violence. Few Salvadorans participate in antigovernment demonstrations. Repeated calls by the guerrillas for general strikes in mid- and late 1980 went unheeded. The Duarte government, moreover, has made clear its willingness to negotiate the terms of future political processess with democratic members of all opposition forces—most notably, by accepting the offer of El Salvador's Council of Bishops to mediate between the government and the Democratic Revolutionary Front.

In sum, the Duarte government is working hard and with some

success to deal with the serious political, and economic problems that most concern the people of El Salvador.

.U.S. Support. In its commitment to reform and democracy, the government of El Salvador has had the political support of the United States ever since the October 1979 revolution. Because we give primary emphasis to helping the people of El Salvador, most of our assistance has been economic. In 1980, the United States provided nearly $56 million in aid, aimed at easing the conditions that underlie unrest and extremism. The assistance has helped create jobs, feed the hungry, improve health and housing and education, and support the reforms that are opening and modernizing El Salvador's economy. The United States will continue to work with the Salvadoran government toward economic betterment, social justice, and peace.

Because the solution in El Salvador should be of the Salvadorans' own making and nonviolent, the United States has carefully limited its military support. In January, mounting evidence of Communist involvement compelled President Carter to authorize a resupply of weapons and ammunition to El Salvador—the first provision of lethal items since 1977.

IV. Some Conclusions

The foregoing record leaves little doubt that the Salvadoran insurgency has become the object of a large-scale commitment by Communist states outside Latin America.

• The political direction, organization, and arming of the insurgency is coordinated and heavily influenced by Cuba—with active support of the Soviet Union, East Germany, Vietnam, and other Communist states.

• The massing and delivery of arms to the Salvadoran guerrillas by those states must be judged against the fact that from 1977 until January 1981 the United States provided no weapons or ammunition to the Salvadoran armed forces.

• A major effort has been made to provide "cover" of this operation by supplying arms of Western manufacture and by supporting a front organization known as the Democratic Revolutionary Front to seek non-Communist political support through propaganda.

• Although some non-Communist states have also provided material support, the organization and delivery of this assistance, like the overwhelming mass of arms, are in the hands of Communist-controlled networks.

In short, over the past year, the insurgency in El Salvador has been progressively transformed into a textbook case of indirect armed aggression by Communist powers through Cuba.

36. Blots on the White Paper: The Reinvention Of The "Red Menace" *

BY JAMES PETRAS

Responsible journalists during the Vietnam war, such as I. F. Stone, refused to take government pronouncements at face value. Stone in particular subjected the 1965 Vietnam White Paper, Aggression From the North, to withering analysis in I. F. Stone's Weekly (March 8, 1965), reprinted in M. E. Gettleman, ed., Vietnam (1965, 1970). In a similar spirit, Latin American expert James Petras subjects the 1981 El Salvador White Paper to close scrutiny in this reading. Professor of Sociology at the State University of New York, Binghamton, Petras has written Politics and Social Forces in Chilean Development (1969); Latin America: Reform or Revolution, with Maurice Zeitlin (1968); and Class, State and Power in the Third World (1981). He was also a member of the international People's Tribunal on El Salvador that met in Mexico City in February, 1981.

THE State Department's white paper entitled *Communist Interference in El Salvador* [1] purports to provide evidence demonstrating:

(1) "the central role played by Cuba and other Communist countries . . . in the political unification, military direction and arming of insurgent forces in El Salvador";

(2) that "the insurgency in El Salvador has been progressively transformed into another case of indirect armed aggression against a small Third World country by Communist powers acting through Cuba"; and

(3) that "Cuba, the Soviet Union and other Communist states . . . are carrying out what is clearly shown to be a well-coordinated, covert effort to bring about the overthrow of El Salvador's established gov-

---

* The Nation [New York] (March 28, 1981), pp. 353, 367–372, by permission.
[1] See Reading 35.——Eds.

ernment and to impose in its place a Communist regime with no popular support."

The white paper fails to provide a convincing case for any of those propositions. On the contrary, its evidence is flimsy, circumstantial or nonexistent; the reasoning and logic is slipshod and internally inconsistent; it assumes what needs to be proven; and, finally, what facts are presented refute the very case the State Department is attempting to demonstrate. The document, in a word, has the aura of a political frame-up in which inconvenient facts are overlooked and innuendoes and unwarranted inferences are made at crucial points in the argument. In demonstrating this, I will follow the format of the white paper, discussing the sections in order, under their original titles, and making cross-references to material in other sections where it is warranted; for example, when the authors contradict themselves.

I. A Case of Communist Military Involvement in the Third World

The first technique that is employed in the white paper is to conflate what is happening in El Salvador with other alleged examples of Soviet and Cuban military involvement. The political opposition is reduced to a group of extreme leftist guerrillas manipulated by Cuba and in turn manipulating "small, non-Marxist-Leninist parties" in order to deceive public opinion. Opposition activity is labeled terrorist. Journalists who describe the U.S.-backed regime's behavior as terrorists are labeled as witting or unwitting dupes of an orchestrated Communist propaganda effort.

What is most striking about this description of the opposition to the junta government is the complete absence of even a minimal account of the numerous social, political and civic movements that has developed in El Salvador over the past decade, which represent a wide range of political views and social strata. This collective omission on the part of the State Department is necessary if one is bent upon labeling the opposition as Soviet-Cuban manipulated and if one wishes to reduce the conflict to an East-West military confrontation.

The fact of the matter is that over the last decade an enormously rich variety of social organizations have emerged in El Salvador, embracing the great majority of professional and technical workers, peasants, labor and business people. Their membership is in the hundreds of thousands and they are an integral part of the main political opposition group, the Revolutionary Democratic Front (F.D.R.).

Almost all union members, peasant associations, university and professional people are members or supporters of social and civic organizations that are sympathetic to the front. The white paper clearly falsifies the political and social realities by excluding an account of the social forces involved with the opposition. Moreover, the origins of the opposition are clearly rooted in the social realities of the country—a point which the document admits in Section III in a politically vague and unspecified fashion when it notes that: "during the 1970's, both the legitimate grievances of the poor and landless and the growing aspirations of the expanding middle classes met increasingly with repression."

What the paper fails to acknowledge is that these "legitimate grievances" and "growing aspirations" found expression and were embodied in the mass organizations which are the essential components of the opposition groups that make up the F.D.R. The guerrilla movement is part and parcel of a larger political and social movement that has been and is repressed. Its activities stem from social realities of Salvadoran history, which the paper concedes is one of "repression, widespread poverty and concentration of wealth and power in the hands of a few families." Because it is intent on demonstrating that the problem is Soviet-Cuban intervention, the paper fails to examine the crucial relationship between the repressive nature of the state, social inequalities and the growth of opposition and guerrilla movements.

The "Non-Marxist" Opposition. The striking feature of the Salvadoran revolution is the broad array of political forces that have united to oppose this regime—Christian Democrats, Social Democrats and Liberal Democrats, as well as independent Marxist groups and pro-Moscow coalitions. What is particularly unique in the Salvadoran case is the substantial leadership and its popular base of support that has developed among Christian communities. In all areas of social and political organization, a plurality of political tendencies are represented—among peasants, workers, professionals and so on. The attempt by the white paper to reduce the opposition to a handful of Marxist guerrillas manipulating the "non-Marxists" is a crude oversimplification and gross distortion of reality. What is remarkable in the document is the systematic exclusion of any mention of the mass-based Christian opposition, the twenty-eight Christian priests, nuns and community leaders murdered by the regime for their opposition activities. A discussion of these facts would complicate the State Department's job of selling intervention to the U.S. public.

In describing the emergence of the guerrilla forces, the document downgrades accounts of repressive political conditions under the junta. Yet detailed descriptions are available from the Organization of American States, the United Nations and, most comprehensively, from the Legal Aid Commission of the office of the Archbishop of El Salvador, which has compiled a lengthy dossier of the regime's systematic violence against all legal public organizations opposed to it in any way. Churches, trade unions, independent newspapers and peasant co-ops have been assaulted and bombed, leaving almost 9,000 dead between January 1980 and January 1981. The precondition for the growth of guerrilla activity was the closing of political channels by the U.S.-backed regime—not Soviet intervention.

Shortly after the first junta was established in October 1979, and before the rightist military took over, the guerrillas and political opposition groups offered a cease-fire. The rightists in the armed forces responded by escalating the number of assassinations, which touched off renewed hostilities. The decision to seek a military-political solution was forced upon the opposition by the military regime when it murdered Archibishop Oscar Romero on March 24, 1980, and then the six leaders of the F.D.R. meeting in San Salvador on November 27, 1980. The subsequent purge of the moderate Christian Democrats and reformist military officers from the first government junta is further proof that political options had been taken away. The white paper overlooks this context of regime violence in order to invent a Cuban-inspired conspiracy and to impute the violence of the regime to its victims. The killings by the military regimes increased from 147 in 1978 to 580 between January and October of 1979 and to 8,952 between January 1980 and January 1981. This increasing reign of terror clearly was instrumental in lowering the rate of popular participation in public activity and swelling the numbers of clandestine groups. Oblivious to this reality, the white paper describes the increase in guerrilla activity as a willful act of the "extreme left."

In its attempt to cast doubt on the opposition's legitimacy, the paper omits any mention of centrist defections from the U.S.-backed junta to join the leadership of the Revolutionary Democratic Front. The shift of a significant body of centrist opinion to the opposition is described disparagingly in the following fashion: "For appearances' sake, three small non-Marxist-Leninist political parties were brought into the front, though they have no representation in the D.R.U. [Unified Revolutionary Directorate]." These former Christian and Social Democratic allies of the U.S.-backed coalition had been described by U.S. officials a few weeks earlier as major political forces representing significant reform-minded sectors of Salvadoran public opinion. The fact that the pro-Moscow Communist Party of El Salvador is a marginal political force in the opposition coalition is never discussed by the white paper, nor is the fact that three of the four major leftist groups are critical of the Soviet Union.

Moreover, the paper's charge that Fidel Castro was responsible for unifying the left overlooks the fact that the unity of the leftist forces was under way prior to December 1979 as a result of increasing repression by the regime and pressure from the rank and file of all the groups. The F.D.R. was formed in El Salvador, not in Cuba, and was supported and promoted by European social-democratic forces. It was certainly not a product of the alleged machinations of Castro. As the participants stated at the time, the needs of the popular struggle, the limited options open to all opposition groups and the example set by the success of the Nicaraguan revolution were the main impulsions to unity.

Conspiratorial Hypothesis. The effort by the white paper to discredit the F.D.R. by describing it as a "front" disseminating propaganda for the guerrillas systematically ignores the popular support that these groups draw away from the junta, the internal political debates within the front and between the front and the guerrillas and the influence they have had in shaping the program in a reformist direction. The white paper's conspiratorial view requires that its authors overlook the importance of these moderates and their internal and external influence. The paper says nothing about the widespread international support for the front and the isolation of the junta. Indeed, it expands its conspiratorial hypothesis to find Cuban and Soviet-sponsored deception behind the front's success.

The numerous and detailed accounts of repression by the regime compiled by the Archbishop's Legal Aid Commission which have swayed world public opinion are not mentioned; nor are Amnesty International's publicized accounts of widespread systematic torture. In place of careful consideration of these documents, the white paper labels the 10,000 deaths attributed to the junta (13,000 by the time the paper appeared) an "extreme claim" of the guerrilla propaganda apparatus, which is parroted by the Cuban, Soviet and Nicaraguan media. Actually, the principal source of data collected on the regime's repression is non-Communist, Catholic and respected by most non-U.S. government sources. In summary, through omissions and distortions, through labeling and simplification, the white paper early on fabricates a case against a broad-based popular revolutionary movement in order to prove "Communist military involvement."

II. Communist Military Intervention:
A Chronology

This section is the longest and most convoluted. It is also the section that is supposedly based on secret documents purporting to demonstrate Soviet-Cuban intervention and direction in El Salvador. We have no way of authenticating the documents—nor the particular quotations which are cited.[2] Nevertheless, even in the terms in which the documents are presented, there is serious doubt that they make the case the white paper claims, despite the self-serving assertions by the authors that the evidence is "incontrovertible."

In the first section, the white paper describes the revolutionaries prior to September of 1980 as "diverse guerrilla groups . . . ill-coordinated and ill-equipped, armed with pistols and a varied assortment of hunting rifles and shotguns." In effect, the document affirms that up to a few months ago, the guerrilla movement consisted of local forces employing their own resources and forging their own programs with no outside support, let alone control. The subsequent aid then is directed toward a leadership and organization that has been shaped by organizational and political experiences rooted in many years of independent activity. It is highly unlikely that such groups would suddenly submit themselves to foreign tutelage or be subject to foreign manipulation. The initial document which purports to "demonstrate" Cuban involvement is a letter of salutation from the guerrillas to Castro thanking him for help. There is no mention of arms, political direction or military coordination; rather, the emphasis is on the need for Salvadoran groups to build and coordinate their activities among themselves. The next reference is to a meeting of guerrillas at the Hungarian Embassy in Mexico City at which the word "requests" was apparently mentioned. Without any rhyme or reason, the white paper extracts the word and appends a parenthesis: "(possibly for arms)." To this gratuitous appended parenthesis is added a list of the Eastern European ambassadors present, presumably to suggest a neo-Comintern conclave.

Alleged Soviet Help. Inadvertently, however, a document cited by the white paper does demonstrate the *absence* of pro-Soviet forces within the actual guerrilla struggle. It quotes Shafik Handal, secretary

---

[2] For subsequent examination of these documents and the White Paper arguments they purport to substantiate, see Reading 37 below.—Eds.

general of the Salvadoran Communist Party, as mentioning the need to "speed up reorganization and put the party on a war footing." As late as April 28, 1980, the Salvadoran Communist Party is not yet prepared to engage in the ongoing guerrilla struggle. Then the white paper quotes Handal as saying, "I'm in agreement with taking advantage of the possibilities of assistance from the socialist camp. . . . We are not yet taking advantage of it." From this we can deduce incontrovertibly that, the socialist camp was not involved at all up to then in El Salvador; that any assistance was a "possibility"; and that the overriding concern of the Salvadoran Communist Party was how to use the "socialist camp." This is hardly the attitude of a docile tool of Moscow conspirators.

Finally, regarding unification of the left, Handal mentions that "the idea for involving everyone in the area has already been suggested to Fidel himself. . . . Fidel thought well of the idea." In other words, the idea of unifying the left did not even initiate with Castro; it came from the Salvadorans and Castro merely granted his approval.

What the white paper fails to mention in all its accounts of guerrilla and leftist meetings with the Communists are the frequent contacts among all the opposition groups—including centrist Social Democrats and Christian Democrats—and their political counterparts in other countries, from Stockholm to Mexico City, from Washington, D.C., to Bonn. Requests for aid and support were laid before U.S. State Department officials and European Social Democrats. Outside the United States these ideas have, at least in part, met with favorable responses. Europeans favor a "Zimbabwe solution" in El Salvador—unifying the opposition and working for a center-left regime. The white paper's attempt to attribute this idea to secret Communist cabals is willful ignorance. The paper's selective discussion of meetings between guerrillas and Communists and its omission of meetings by other opposition forces in the European and Latin American left is a tactic more appropriate to a lawyer's brief.

Handal is also supposed to have visited Nicaragua to hold discussions about setting up an office there from which to disseminate propaganda and make political contacts. Such overtures from dissidents in one country to officials in another are commonplace the world over. In this case, the possibility was merely *discussed*—which would seem to be within the bounds of propriety for officials of a sovereign government.

Handal's Travels. The heavy stuff is still to come. The next itinerary for the peripatetic Handal is listed as "travels in the East." During his stop in Moscow, supposedly in search of arms, Handal, we are told, met with a Soviet official. This official merely suggested that

Handal travel to Vietnam and offered to pay for his trip. (The white paper's sources apparently could not determine if it was one way or round trip.)

The white paper goes on to claim that in Vietnam Handal gained concrete support—sixty tons of arms. The East Germans told him they would put out a search for available arms, as did the Czechs, Bulgarians, Hungarians and Ethiopians. Lieutenant Colonel Mengistu, chairman of Ethiopia's Provisional Military Administrative Council, we are told, promised "several thousand weapons." The white paper adds that the Russians asked if they could send thirty student volunteers to take part in the "war," and agreed to ship the Vietnamese arms. Eventually, even the Palestine Liberation Organization and Nicaragua pledged arms. According to the white paper, a total of 780 tons of arms were to be transported to Nicaragua via Cuba, and then to El Salvador. By September 26, there were supposedly 130 tons of arms cached in Nicaragua. The paper claims that "in September and October the number of flights to Nicaragua from Cuba increased sharply. These flights had the capacity to transport several hundred tons of cargo."

Yet we learn that at the end of September the Sandinists "suspend their weapons deliveries to El Salvador for one month. . . . When the shipments resume in October, as much as 120 tons of weapons and matériel are still in Nicaragua and some 300–400 tons are in Cuba." There are curious discrepancies in this account. For example, we are told that there were 130 tons of arms in Nicaragua by September 26. We are also informed that shipments to El Salvador were "suspended" for one month at the end of September but the flights from Cuba continued through October. Yet when the shipments resumed in October "as much as 120 tons of weapons and matériel are still in Nicaragua. . . ." Since no weapons were going to El Salvador and presumably loaded planes were continuing to arrive from Cuba, it seems odd, to say the least, that at the end of the one month's suspension, Nicaragua had a net loss of ten tons of arms in its stores for shipment. Apparently, the white paper's several authors didn't bother to coordinate their stories.

Swamped with Arms. After reporting that only about 2.5 tons were shipped in November, the white paper authors step up the pace dramatically. In December, we are told, there was such a deluge of arms that the Salvadoran insurgents complained that they could not absorb them. Yet earlier in the white paper we were told how poorly armed the 4,000 to 5,000 guerrillas were in September 1980 ("ill-coordinated and ill-equipped, armed with pistols and a varied assortment of hunting rifles and shotguns"). Is it conceivable that within a few weeks in December the guerrillas were inundated with arms? What is more, the flood mysteriously turned into a drought, because in the March 1 *New York Times* the guerrilla leaders are said to be complaining that they do not have an adequate supply of arms, a shortage that hindered their January offensive.

During this period of supposedly massively flowing arms, no specific figures are ever given, nor is there any detailed explanation of how so many (undisclosed) arms flowed into El Salvador. There are only references to a Cessna that crashed, and it is *speculated* that it had arms ("unloaded passengers and possibly weapons"). A second plane strays into government hands, and "numerous weapons are captured." We are told of shipments in motor launches and overland, but there is no evidence that any of these were captured, even though the roads and seaways are easily policed and at least some large shipments should have been intercepted. But the security forces' total bag is one trailer truck carrying 100 U.S. rifles and some mortars. The Honduras-El Salvador border is heavily patrolled, and needless to say the roads that would be passable by trucks loaded with arms are closely watched. The paucity of evidence suggests that the arms flow is minimal; thus, the claims of massive outside intervention are unsubstantiated. The failure of the guerrilla offensive in January was in part the result of inadequate armaments coupled with massive infusions of U.S. arms to the regime's forces. Even junta spokesman José Napoleón Duarte and former U.S. Ambassador Robert White (who originally promoted the story of a massive weapons influx) would question the need for further U.S. arms.

The white paper's evidence of outside Communist arms shipments supports only a small fraction of its claims. Such shipments as there were did not approach the flow of weapons, advisers, napalm, helicopter gunships and the like to the military-civilian dictatorship from the United States.

III. The Government:
The Search for Order and Democracy

The massive propaganda efforts to focus attention on outside Communist intervention is a way of diverting attention from the repressive regime that the United States is supporting. The Reagan administration's tactic is to win backing for the junta not because of what it stands for (few democratic governments would support a government whose army has killed 13,000 civilians) but to "draw the line" against "outside intervention."

In its opening section the white paper claims that El Salvador experienced "considerable economic progress" during the 1960s, "although . . . the political system remained in the hands of a traditional economic elite backed by the military." The facts are that between 1961 and 1975 the proportion of landless laborers rose from 11 percent to 40 percent; the level of unemployment climbed from 10 percent in 1960 to 25 percent in 1979. Whatever economic progress took place did not benefit the workers and the peasants. Rather, the growth of El Salvador's gross national product was intimately tied to its repressive system. Prosperity for some was matched by the repression of the many. The white paper notes that the "legitimate grievances of the poor and landless and the growing aspirations of the expanding middle classes met increasingly with repression." The paper does not go on to identify the organizations and leaders which come to express these "legitimate grievances" and middle-class "aspirations" because they are not found in the current junta but among the opposition. Moreover, these aspirations and grievances are not answered by the military measures and repressive forms of rulership undertaken by the current regime. The document's systematic evasion of the sources of violence and the U.S. Government's responsibility is revealed in its attempt to blame it on everyone: "El Salvador has long been a violent country."

In fact, El Salvador has not been a violent country—its U.S.-backed oligarchical-military regimes have been violent, killing 30,000 people in 1932 and running the country with an iron fist ever since. Between 1946 and 1979, the United States has provided Salvadoran military dictatorships with more than $17 million in military assistance and trained 2,000 military officers while providing the ruling oligarchy with $157.7 million in economic aid.

The "Progressive" Coalition. The white paper describes the governing coalition that took over after the coup in October 1979 as being made up of progressive civilian and military officers. Yet the great majority of these progressives defected to the F.D.R. or were killed by the rightist faction which is now in control. The "three small non-Marxist-Leninist political parties" that the white paper earlier dismisses as window-dressing in the F.D.R. leadership are later portrayed as significant progressives when they were in the first coalition. The white paper's inconsistency is apparent in the way it attempts to reclaim the progressive character of the original junta while discrediting the genuine progressives who resigned from it in protest or were pushed out. The systematic purge of the progressives by the rightist faction within the junta between October 1979 and March 1980 is described in the same vacuous, euphemistic language that is used throughout the white paper when the authors wish to cover their tracks: "After an initial period of instability, the new government stabilized around a coalition that includes military participants in the October 1979 coup, the Christian Democratic Party and independent civilians." The white paper leaves out the purge of the Majano reformists, and the bulk of the Christian Democrats who are now in opposition, along with the university faculty and students. It does not say that ultra-right forces deeply involved in repressive actions are all that remain of the original junta that took power in October 1979.

The white paper claims that "since March 1980, this coalition has begun broad social changes." Actually, the number of peasants killed and co-ops that fell under military occupation rose sharply: peasants killed increased from 126 per month in February, to 203 in March, to 423 in July, totaling 3,272 for the glorious year of agrarian reform! The paper then repeats the falsehood that the opposition to this "reform" consists of Marxist-Leninist guerrilla terrorists and the three significant non-Marxist-Leninist political parties operating outside of the country. Once again, the authors omit mention of the absence of any political rights in El Salvador, and the state of war that the junta has declared against all opposition.

Extremist Symbiosis. The white paper then proceeds to argue that the government "faces armed opposition from the extreme right as well as from the left. . . . A symbiotic relationship has developed between the terrorism practiced by extremists of both left and right." This notion has been systematically refuted by the Archbishop's Legal Aid Commission report on repression, which adduces evidence showing that in 1980, 66 percent of the assassinations were committed by government security forces, and 14 percent were committed by right-wing death squads. Moreover, voluminous testimony, documents and photographs have emerged to substantiate the frequent and close collaboration between the death squads and the regime's security forces. The "symbiosis" causing most of the violence is between the regime and the death squads, not the right and left.

In this regard it is important to note that not one right-wing death squad assassin has ever been apprehended, let alone prosecuted, despite the public nature of most of the killings. This in itself should dispel any notion that the regime is innocent in the activity of the death squads. The Legal Aid Commission study further demonstrates that the bulk of victims were poor peasants, students and wage workers—the groups in whose names the purported reforms were carried out. In fact the reforms were mere facades for the militarization of the country. The escalation of regime terror against the peasants is the surest indication of this.

The white paper voices concern about the murder and rape of the U.S. nuns, but it fails to mention the fact that the nuns were opposed to U.S. policy, and were murdered by the junta along with more than a score of other church people working for the poor. While the white paper claims to be interested in a complete investigation of these killings, former Ambassador White stated emphatically that Washington has not made any effort to pressure the junta and has effectively collaborated with the regime in covering up the murders—rewarding its perpetrators with additional arms and economic aid.

In one of its more cynical statements, the paper notes that "few Salvadorans participate in anti-government demonstrations"—implying that they support the government. The scores of dead protesters, including mutilated and decapitated corpses that appeared in the wake of every protest march, have no doubt had a dampening effect on demonstrations. But to equate a terrorized population with one that approves the government is a grotesque distortion which only indicates how out of touch this administration is with the political reality in El Salvador and the rest of the Third World. There is not only an absence of all forms of political protest in El Salvador, there is an absence of all forms of political expression; the dictatorship is total. The support for the front and the guerrillas has not diminished—it has gone underground. The white paper's claim that U.S. aid "has helped create jobs and feed the hungry" is belied by the accounts of church sources. U.S. economic aid has contributed to massive military corruption; military aid hardens the resolve of the military dictators and increases the rate of killing. U.S. economic aid does not keep up with the massive flight of private capital estimated at more than $1.5 billion during the past year. The collapse of the Salvadoran economy and the massive exodus of refugees from repression in rural areas hardly testifies to the "success" of what the paper describes as the "Duarte government." The latter is a figment of the State Department's imagination, for real power continues to be vested within the military—a point emphasized by a military official in an interview in *Le Monde* recently.

Conclusion. The white paper is a thin tissue of falsifications, distortions, omissions and simplifications directed toward covering up increased U.S. support for a murderous regime. It has sought to transform a war between the regime and its people into an East-West struggle and to deny the internal socioeconomic and political roots of the struggle. The purpose of these distortions is to mobilize U.S. public opinion behind the new administration's policies not only in El Salvador but throughout the Third World. The hypocrisy suffusing the white paper is vice's tribute to virtue, for it tacitly recognizes that if the truth were presented, the American people would balk at supporting a regime that is rewarded for killing its noblest sons and daughters who seek social justice in El Salvador.

37. Further Blots on the White Paper: Doubts About Evidence and Conclusions *

By ROBERT G. KAISER

Fresh information on the preparation of the El Salvador White Paper, reviewed here by a Washington Post *staff correspondent, suggests a complex process that included several drafts less dogmatic than the final version with its claim to present "definitive evidence." It may be some time before the full story of how the White Paper came to be written appears. Until then, this provisional report, in which Mr. Kaiser had the assistance of Karen DeYoung and Lewis H. Diuguid of the* Washington Post's *foreign bureau, is the fullest account available. The major press and television media in the U.S. played, after a slow start, an important role in undermining Washington's justification for intervention in Vietnam.[1] After a long period during which the media uncritically swallowed official U.S. positions, such events as the publication of the full "Pentagon Papers" by The New York Times in 1971 proved devastating to Washington's credibility. The Salvadoran intervention has been marked by a shorter period between media acceptance and media criticism of official rationalizations. The response of the* Washington Post *and even The Wall Street Journal, as suggested in this Reading, may mean that U.S. journalists are aware of how the press was manipulated during the early days of American involvement in the Vietnam conflict, and are determined not to be taken in again. Within the limits of historic patterns of journalistic deference to government versions of truth, the U.S. press may have already put an end to its foreign policy honeymoon with the Reagan administration.*

THE State Department's white paper on El Salvador, published in February, contains factual errors, misleading statements and

---

* From *The Washington Post* [Washington, D.C.] June 9, 1981. *Post* librarian Carmen Chapin helped with translations from the Spanish.

[1] See on this, David Halberstam, *The Making of a Quagmire* (New York, 1964), but especially I. F. Stone, "Vietnam: An Exercise in Self-Delusion," *New York Review of Books,* April 22, 1965. For a comprehensive report on El Salvador and the press, see "Operation El Salvador: The American Press Falls into Line," by Jonathan Evan Maslow and Ana Arana, *Columbia Journalism Review,* May/June 1981.

unresolved ambiguities that raise questions about the administration's interpretation of participation by communist countries in the Salvadoran civil war.

The white paper was the first significant initiative from the Reagan administration in the field of foreign policy.

The document, and the supporting evidence described as "incontrovertible," were taken by administration emissaries to many countries of the world last winter.

When the white paper was published, the major news media tended to accept the document at face value, but it has subsequently been challenged in several analyses, primarily by individuals and journals critical of American policy in El Salvador. Yesterday, *The Wall Street Journal* added its reservations in a front-page story that said the white paper was flawed by errors and guesses.[2]

The *Journal*'s article prompted a statement from the State Department yesterday defending "the conclusions of the white paper," without replying to specific criticisms.

The Washington Post has been conducting its own inquiry into the white paper and the captured documents on which it was based. The inquiry was initiated to determine whether the evidence released by the State Department actually supported the department's sweeping conclusions.

This was a textual analysis, not an attempt to determine the extent of communist involvement in El Salvador, which cannot be determined from Washington.

The Post's inquiry indicates that on several major points, the documents do not support conclusions drawn from them by the administration. On other points the documents are much more ambiguous than the white paper suggested. Many of the documents contain no

---

[2] "Tarnished Report?" by staff reporter Jonathan Kwitny (*Wall Street Journal*, June 8, 1981) was based on a three-hour interview with the principal author of the White Paper, 37-year-old Jon D. Glassman, a U.S. Foreign Service officer with a Ph.D. in Soviet studies. Glassman conceded that parts of the report were "misleading" and "overembellished," and that it included a number of "mistakes," and examples of "guessing." He also acknowledged misattribution of a number of key documents upholding the White Paper's main thesis of outside military support for the Salvadoran guerrillas. "We completely screwed it up," Glassman admitted to Kwitny. Apparently skeptical himself of some of the documentation, Glassman submitted the material to the U.S. Central Intelligence Agency (CIA) with the question, " 'Did you fabricate any of the documents, or is there any indication they were fabricated by anyone else?' And the answer was no to both." Glassman still held that the White Paper was, according to a later State Department briefing, "an accurate and honest description of the development of communist support for the Salvadoran insurgency," and that the very shortcomings of the documents on which it was based testify somehow to its truthfulness.—Eds.

identifying markings whatsoever, though the State Department gives them concrete identifications.

In one key document, the State Department dropped a sentence from its translation into English, which undermines the department's characterization of the document.

The documents released by the State Department were only a small portion of the total found in two "caches." Both were found by police in San Salvador, one in November behind an art gallery, the second in January behind a false wall in a grocery store. Other documents from the same sources made available to *The Post* by the State Department actually contradict or differ substantially from the picture of the Salvadoran insurgency that is painted in the white paper.

Some of the broad conclusions in the white paper were simply not supported by the documents released with it. For example, the white paper made a much-publicized accusation that nearly 200 tons of arms had been delivered covertly to El Salvador, mostly through Cuba and Nicaragua. There is no concrete evidence to support this claim in any of the documents released with the white paper.

Some critics have charged that the documents were forged, but their evidence is essentially circumstantial, and the documents carry such meager identification that it would be hard to say just what had been forged if they were made up. The inconsistencies between the documents and the white paper do not prove that the white paper's conclusions are wrong, but they do raise questions about those conclusions and how they were reached.

The most substantial of the documents published with the white paper was a partial account of a trip purportedly taken by Shafik Handal, secretary general of the small Salvadoran Communist Party, which is part of the front of opposition groups now backing the guerrillas in the civil war.

Last summer, according to the document, Handal visited Moscow, Hanoi, the major East European captials, Addis Ababa and Havana. The purpose of his trip was to line up donations of arms and equipment for the Salvadoran rebels, according to the captured document.

In the book of documents the State Department released with its white paper, this one was described as an "excerpt of report on trip to the socialist countries . . ." by Handal. The document carries no identification of any kind, nor any signature, but its contents do describe a trip taken by an unnamed "comrade" who was apparently seeking military aid for the Salvadoran rebels.

The white paper, in summarizing this document, makes it appear that Handal wrote it. In the book of documents released with the white paper, this document is not attributed to any specific author. A quick reading might suggest that it was produced by someone close to Handal in the Salvadoran Communist Party. But the one sentence in the Spanish original (also released by State), which the department dropped in its English translation of the document, seems to confirm numerous other hints within the document that it was written by a Cuban.

The dropped sentence comes at the end of a paragraph describing what is purported to be Handal's visit to Ethiopia last July. The document says the Ethiopians promised to contribute arms to the Salvadoran rebels, listing types of weapons. The last sentence says that this cargo of arms "will leave in our ship the fifth of August."

Since the Salvadoran rebels have no navy of their own, it is unlikely that this was written by Handal or one of his associates. The State Department indirectly acknowledges that the document in question was written in Havana by translating its many references to "here" as meaning Cuba.

If this was a Cuban report on Handal's trip, why was it found in a cache of rebel documents in Salvador? This would seem to be a significant point, but the State Department ignored all questions about the origins of this untitled, unsigned document.

The white paper makes Handal's trip around the Soviet bloc, Vietnam and Ethiopia sound like an idyllic journey on which the traveler always got what he wanted (mostly arms, uniforms and equipment). Summarizing this document, the white paper recounts Handal's two visits to Moscow, one in early June and the other in late July. As the white paper notes, on the second visit Handal raised an issue that had come up earlier in his travels—whether the Soviets would provide aircraft to transport arms that Vietnam planned to donate to the Salvadoran rebels.

In the white paper's summary, this is how that is described: "Before leaving Moscow, Handal receives assurances that the Soviets agree in principle to transport the Vietnamese arms."

The document itself tells a different story. According to it, Handal was repeatedly frustrated in Moscow, and reported his frustration candidly to whomever wrote the document. A senior Soviet communist party official told Handal, the document says, that, "In principle, there is opinion in favor of transporting the Vietnamese weapons, but there has been no approval on the part of the leadership organs."

Handal, apparently angry, "made known through other channels his disagreement with the . . . lack of decision concerning the requests for assistance."

After two more weeks without a reply from Moscow, the document says, Handal began "expressing concern as to the effects that the lack

of decision by the Soviets may have, not only regarding the assistance
that they themselves can offer but also upon the inclination of the
other parties of the European socialist camp to cooperate. . . ."

Neither this nor any other document released by the State Department indicates that the Soviets ever did provide the requested air
transport. And this document is the only one that linked the Soviets
directly to the Salvadoran civil war.

The white paper also suggests that the account in this document of
Handal's visit to Hanoi (which, the document says, the Russians suggested and financed) plus the later capture of U.S. M16 rifles that
could be traced back to Vietnam demonstrated conclusively that
Vietnam was providing weapons to the Salvadoran guerrillas.

The evidence presented, however, does not confirm this. According
to this document, Handal was promised a wide variety of arms in
Vietnam, but the M16 assault rifle—the basic weapon used by American infantrymen in the Vietnam war—was not on the detailed list
given in the document.

The M16s in question were found in a truck that was captured in
Honduras en route to El Salvador, according to the State Department. "Approximately 100 M16 rifles, some of which were traceable
to Vietnam," were found in the truck, the department said. Why
only "some" could be traced to Vietnam was not explained.

On another point in this document, the white paper says: "The
Soviet official [who dealt with Handal in Moscow] ask[ed] if 30 communist youth currently studying in the U.S.S.R. could take part in
the war in El Salvador." In fact, the document says, it was Handal
who asked the Soviets to give military training to 30 youths then
studying in Moscow who wanted to fight in the war, a request the
Soviets approved after repeated prodding.

Another document in the collection is described as a "trip report"
recounting a visit by Salvadoran rebels to Managua, Nicaragua, last
summer. The white paper draws on this document to describe a meeting between the Salvadorans and Yasser Arafat, leader of the Palestine Liberation Organization. "Arafat promises military equipment,
including arms and aircraft," according to the white paper.

The document, however, includes only this parenthetical reference:
". . . On the 22nd there was a meeting with Arafat." There is not a
single word in the document about Arafat promising arms and aircraft. Nor is there any information in the white paper about where
the PLO might acquire aircraft to donate to the Salvadoran rebels.

One handwritten document in the batch is described by the State
Department as notes on an April, 1980 meeting of the Salvadoran
Communist Party written by the same Shafik Handal. On the face of

it this is an implausible description: even to an amateur eye, it is obvious that the document is written in two distinctly different hand-writings. The document contains no reference to Handal or to a meeting of the Communist Party, and it is not dated.

According to the State Department's translation of this document, its author says it is necessary to "put the party on a war footing." In fact the author of this part of the document did not use the phrase for war footing ("estado de guerra") but refers instead to a state of struggle or dispute ("estado de pelea"). The translation quotes the author as saying that the attitude of the socialist camp "is magnifi-cent." He adds: "We are not yet taking advantage of it." In fact, though, the word "yet" does not appear in the original Spanish.

Another questionable translation appears at the end of another unsigned, undated document headed "Logistical Concepts," which outlines plans for intensified rebel activity inside El Salvador (among other things). According to the State Department's translation, the document ends with this sentence: "This plan is based on there being an excellent supply source in Lagos [said to be a code name for Nicaragua]."

In fact, this document ends with this Spanish sentence: "Este plan partiria de que exista una real fuente de abastecimiento en Lagos." This is a conditional construction that should be translated: "This plan is based on the suppositon that there exists a real source of supplies in Lagos," or, "This would be the plan if there is a real source of supplies in Lagos." The State Department removed this conditional sense, and changed the word "real" to "excellent."

Besides the documents published with the original white paper, the State Department's El Salvador working group allowed two *Washington Post* reporters to leaf through a batch of other docu-ments captured in the same caches, including full versions of docu-ments that were excerpted for release earlier. Read together with the documents released originally, these others draw a picture that differs in significant ways from the one in the white paper. These documents portray a guerrilla movement that is chronically short of arms and scrounging for more of them.

For example, among the documents released by the State Depart-ment is one described as an excerpt from a report on a meeting of the Salvadoran Unified Revolutionary Directorate (DRU), the leading body of the guerrilla movement. In the book of released documents it is dated Sept. 30, 1980, though the original (made available by the State Department later) is dated Aug. 30. In the English translation of the excerpt provided by State, the date is Sept. 1.

Whatever the right date, the short excerpt released by State is a list of weapons that Salvadoran communist party's "secretary general" [Handal] reported had been shipped to them by Soviet-bloc countries, which are said to be arriving in Nicaragua on Sept. 5. This is an impressive list of military hardware and supplies, including the weapons purportedly promised to Handal in Vietnam, Ethiopia and Eastern Europe.

Curiously, the list of weapons coming from Vietnam seems to be describing the same shipment listed in the report of Handal's trip discussed above; most of the items listed are the same on both lists. But inexplicably, this one differs on many details. For example, the trip report list said Vietnam offered 15,000 7.62 mm. cartridges for M30 and M60 machine guns; this second document says 480,000 such cartridges are coming from Vietnam.

In any event, the State Department included this small excerpt from a much longer document in its book of documents released with the white paper. It is obviously a list of equipment that Handal says is coming to Nicaragua for the Salvadoran rebels.

The full version of this document includes another section about the difficulties the rebels are having getting arms out of Nicaragua. It paints a picture that contradicts flatly the impression left by this other list. (This section was not released publicly, though it was made available to reporters who asked to see more of the captured documents.) Here are some excerpts:

"With regard to bringing weapons from Lagos [described by State as the rebels' code name for Nicaragua]:

"a) The E.R.P. [The Popular Revolutionary Army in Salvador] has made two serious attempts and the F.S.L.N. [the ruling Sandinista front in Nicaragua] has stood in its way for reasons which in the opinion of the E.R.P. are subjective and at times wrong.

"The E.R.P. has air, water and land resources and is ready to make two trips per week.

"One reason for not using the maritime route is that the F.S.L.N. [the Sandinistas] says that the E.R.P. should not touch its shores; the E.R.P. agreed to stay out at sea but even this did not work.

"The F.S.L.N. [Sandinistas] claimed that by land the weapons the E.R.P. would bring in would be too few (it was 200 rifles). It also said that it would no longer allow the F.P.L. [the Farabundo Martí Popular Liberation Forces, the largest rebel group in El Salvador] to bring weapons by the methods it has been using.

"b) The P.C. [presumably the Communist Party] has reported that it cannot bring in large quantities but that it can bring in small quantities. . . ."

In other words, the State Department selected for public release a section of a document listing large quantities of arms due to arrive in Nicaragua, according to the report of the man alleged to have arranged for their shipment. Another section of the same document reporting on the actual troubles the rebels were having bringing arms into El Salvador was not selected for public release.

The contention of the white paper that the Salvadoran rebels were enjoying the benefits of "nearly 200 tons" of communist-supplied arms and matériel is not supported anywhere in these documents, and is implicitly refuted by many of them. In document after document there are reports of rebels short of arms, or looking for ways to buy arms, or exhorting comrades to produce home-made arms, or plotting to kidnap wealthy Salvadorans thought to have access to private arsenals.

Document number 48 in the State Department's files (not released with the white paper) is described as a war plan of the Farabundo Martí Peoples' Liberation Front, described by State as "the coordinating board" of the principal leftist guerrilla groups. The document anticipates a military campaign that would last from Nov. 25 to Dec. 10 of last year. The document says it should be possible to bring 30 tons of arms into the country during November to prepare for this, but that the campaign could go forward even with less.

This document, dated Nov. 18, listed these guerrilla needs as of that time: 1,000 automatic rifles, four 50-cal. machine guns, 16 30-cal. machine guns, six M79 grenade launchers—in other words, modest needs indeed compared to the huge numbers of weapons emphasized in the white paper.

Document 83 in the State Department's files, unsigned and undated, is a description of arms and equipment available to the guerrillas. The file copy includes this notation from a U.S. government official who read and evaluated it: "From this," the American wrote, "it would appear they had only 626 weapons for more than 9,000 men." This document was omitted from the collection released to the press with the white paper.

The heart of the white paper is the accusation that "over the past year, the insurgency in El Salvador has been progressively transformed into a textbook case of indirect armed aggression by communist powers through Cuba."

This is a characterization that the Salvadoran government does not accept; on a recent visit to Washington, the foreign minister, Fidel Chavez Mena, said the war in his country was first of all an internal conflict, and secondarily an arena for the East-West contest.

The idea that the war in El Salvador is an internal, factional struggle does not appear in the Reagan administration's white paper. The anti-government guerrillas are described as part of the Salvadoran "extreme left"; and the white paper ignores the moderate elements, including former government ministers who belonged to the Christian Democratic Party of President José Napoleón Duarte, who have joined the guerrilla cause.

Instead of the civil struggle described by Salvador's own government, the white paper perceived "a textbook case of indirect armed aggression by communist powers through Cuba."

Chapter III

THE LEGACY OF VIETNAM

Editors' Introduction

HAS the specter of Vietnam come back to haunt us in the small Central American republic of El Salvador?

There is a familiar ring to what is going on in El Salvador: military advisers have been sent but never—of course—to go out on combat missions; Roy Prosterman is with us once again, engineering a "land-to-the-tiller" reform; a White Paper shows aggression from the east (Cuba)—in Vietnam it was from the north (North Vietnam). It is a sign of progress that a White Paper is being discredited by *The Washington Post* and *The Wall Street Journal* rather than by the lonely and courageous voice of dissenter I. F. Stone.[1]

There are massacres to rival My Lai; questionable body counts; zones of control where guerrillas melt away only to return again after government soldiers leave; and analogies of guerrillas and peasants as "fish" and the "ocean," and the inability of the junta to distinguish between guerrilla and peasant. Once again there are search-and-destroy missions, refugees, and reports of napalm and guerrilla tunnels. One can almost hear the dominoes falling.

The Vietnam era was marked by massive antiwar protest. Senator Jesse Helms (Rep., NC) has mocked the "nervous Nellies" who oppose U.S. policy in El Salvador as Lyndon Johnson before him did those opposed to the Vietnam War. The first massive demonstration in Washington against the latter took place in 1965, four years after the number of advisers in Vietnam were significantly increased by President Kennedy in 1961. The process of protest has speeded up:

---

[1] See Marvin Gettleman, *Vietnam: History, Documents, and Opinions on a Major World Crisis*, Fawcett, New York, 1965. See also Marvin Gettleman, "Vietnam War," *Academic American Encyclopedia*, Vol. 19, pp. 584-591.

months after military "advisers" have been introduced in El Salvador, upwards of 100,000 demonstrated in Washington, on May 3, 1981.

More than 50,000 Americans were to die in Vietnam (not to speak of the vastly greater losses suffered by the Vietnamese). Opinion polls and Congressional mail both attest to most Americans' not wanting U.S. troops sent to El Salvador, no doubt a fear that many will return, as they did from Vietnam, in body bags. Vietnam created a legacy of constraint. It is a legacy to be overcome by those who want a free hand to intervene globally, where necessary, on behalf of their anticommunist crusade. Walter LaFeber shows how history is being rewritten to accommodate this need.[1]

From the perspective of the Reagan administration, the Vietnam War was a "noble" endeavor, a war the U.S. could have won had it not been hamstrung in its use of force by civilian opposition in the form of the peace movement. LaFeber rightly dismisses the "new revisionists" who contend that victory only required an appropriate military escalation. Such a view, LaFeber points out, ignores the military reality that existed in Vietnam as well as the unacceptable domestic consequences another escalation would have touched off.

In the course of his argument, but not central to it, LaFeber states that "the effectiveness of the antiwar movement has been greatly overrated by the new revisionists." LaFeber is undoubtedly correct when he argues that the majority of Americans, as measured in polls, rallied round the President, who himself was draped in the flag, after every escalation from the invasion of Cambodia to the mining of Haiphong. But the protest after the invasion of Cambodia and after the shootings at Kent State (and Jackson State) was so intense, so extensive and so prolonged, it wrested from President Nixon an unqualified pledge of withdrawal from Cambodia.

The "domestic crisis of unprecedented proportions" that Secretary of Defense Clark Clifford warned of, and which stayed the hand of President Lyndon Johnson and caused him to reject the 200,000 additional troops requested of him by General Westmoreland, included "defiance of the draft," "growing unrest in the cities," and businessmen who "suddenly became scared and dovish." LaFeber downgrades the role of "campus protesters"—why only campus?—in these crucial responses to escalation.

But surely the specific domestic costs of further escalation that LaFeber cites were closely related to the accelerating level of protest. The Vietnamese withstood the most savage barrage of destructiveness ever unleashed in the history of war and yet managed to fight the

---

[1] See Reading 41.

U.S. to a draw. That the United States could not win on the field of battle without nuclear weaponry meant it had to lose. No society with free elections is going to permit an endless war on behalf of principles so vague that in the end the pathetic justification reduced itself to "we're there because we're there."

To the extent that the Reagan administration is sincere when it denies that there is a parallel to Vietnam in El Salvador, it is based on the belief that sufficient force can be mobilized against the guerrillas by the Salvadoran military (aided perhaps by Honduran proxies) and that no need will exist for the employment of U.S. troops. But "Vietnamization" was an utter failure in Vietnam. Is it likely to succeed in El Salvador? Is the United States willing (and able) to pull out all stops in its support of the junta, to bounds it was unwilling to attempt in Vietnam? Is the United States, in other words, literally willing and ready to destroy El Salvador in order to save it?

What follows is material directed toward understanding the continuing legacy of Vietnam in the American consciousness and in the formulation of foreign policy.

38. No Vietnam Parallel *

By Ronald Reagan

Following are excerpts from an interview of President Reagan by Walter Cronkite for CBS News (broadcast on March 3, 1981), and from a presidential press conference held on March 6, 1981. Additional comments from the Cronkite interview are included in Reading 33.

CRONKITE: With your administration barely 6 weeks old, you're involved now in, perhaps, the first foreign policy crisis, if it can be called a crisis yet—it probably cannot be, but it's being much discussed, of course—much concern about El Salvador and our commitment there. Do you see any parallel in our committing military advisers and military assistance to El Salvador and the early stages of our involvement in Vietnam?

Reagan: No, I don't. I know that that parallel is being drawn by many people. But the difference is so profound. What we're actually

---

* From the *Department of State Bulletin*, Vol. 81, No. 2049, April, 1981, pp. 8-9, 12.

doing is at the request of a government in one of our neighboring countries helping—offering some help against the import or the export into the Western Hemisphere of terrorism, of disruption, and it isn't just El Salvador. That happens to be the target at the moment.

Our problem is this whole hemisphere and keeping this sort of thing out. We have sent briefing teams to Europe, down to our Latin American neighbors with what we've learned of the actual involvement of the Soviet Union, of Cuba, of the PLO [Palestine Liberation Organization], of even Qadhafi in Libya, and others in the Communist bloc nations to bring about this terrorism down there.

You used the term military advisers. You know, there's a sort of a technicality there. You could say they are advisers in that they're training, but when it's used as adviser, that means military men who go in and accompany the forces into combat, advise on strategy and tactics. We have no one of that kind. We're sending and have sent teams down there to train. They do not accompany them into combat. They train recruits in the garrison area. And as a matter of fact, we have such training teams in more than 30 countries today, and we've always done that; the officers of the military in friendly countries and in our neighboring countries have come to our service schools—West Point, Annapolis, and so forth. So I don't see any parallel at all.

And I think it is significant that the terrorists—the guerrilla activity—in El Salvador was supposed to cause an uprising that the government would fall because the people would join this aggressive force and support them. The people are totally against that and have not reacted in that way. . . .

Q. Secretary of State Haig has said that we'll not have a Vietnam in El Salvador because the United States will direct its action toward Cuba, which is the main source of the intervention, in his words. But Cuba is a client state of the Soviet Union. It's not likely to stand by and let us take direct action against Cuba, is it?

A. A term "direct action," there are a lot of things open: diplomacy, trade, a number of things and Secretary Haig has explained the use of the term. The source with regard to Cuba means the intercepting and stopping of the supplies coming into these countries—the export from Cuba of those arms, the training of the guerrillas as they've done there, and I don't think in any way that he was suggesting an assault on Cuba.

Q. An intercepting and stopping means blockade. And isn't that an act of war?

A. This depends. If you intercept them when they're landing at the other end or find them where they're in the locale, such as, for example, Nicaragua, and informing Nicaragua that we're aware of the part that they have played in this, using diplomacy to see that a country decides they're not going to allow themselves to be used anymore—there's been great slowdown. We're watching it very carefully—Nicaragua—of the transfer of arms to El Salvador. This doesn't mean that they're not coming in from other guerrilla bases in other countries there.

Q. [At press conference] The United States role [in El Salvador] is being compared with its role in Vietnam 15–20 years ago. Do you think that's a valid comparison? And also, how do you intend to avoid having El Salvador turn into a Vietnam for this country?

A. I don't believe it is a valid parallel. I know that many people have been suggesting that. The situation here is, you might say, our front yard, it isn't just El Salvador. What we're doing, in going to the aid of a government that asked that aid of a neighboring country and a friendly country in our hemisphere, is try to halt the infiltration into the Americas by terrorists, by outside interference and those who aren't just aiming at El Salvador but, I think, are aiming at the whole of Central and possibly later South America—and, I'm sure, eventually North America. But this is what we're doing, is trying to stop this destabilizing force of terrorism and guerrilla warfare and revolution from being exported in here, backed by the Soviet Union and Cuba and those others that we've named. And we have taken that evidence to some of our allies. So, I think the situation is entirely different.

We do not foresee the need of American troops, as I said earlier, in this, and we're sending, what, some 50-odd personnel for training. We have such training squads in more than 30 countries today, so this isn't an unusual thing that we are doing.

39. Some Differences Between U.S. Involvement in Vietnam and El Salvador *

By the U.S. Department of State

THE political and military situation in El Salvador and the nature of U.S. support for that country differ in a number of important ways from the situation we faced in Vietnam in the 1960's and 1970's.

---

* From a U.S. Department of State press release, May 12, 1981.

Vietnam was nearly half-way around the globe from the continental United States. El Salvador is less than two hours by air from the United States, in the Caribbean, the maritime frontier of the U.S. and an area traditionally of priority concern to us.

El Salvador is bordered by friendly noncommunist states that fully share the interest of the Salvadoran government in curbing the Marxist-Leninist guerrilla insurgency. Lacking an adjoining communist country, the Salvadoran insurgents can receive supplies and replacements only through indirect, clandestine means. South Vietnam was bordered by North Vietnam, a country openly committed to its conquest which served as a safe haven and resupply base for guerrillas and which even sent its regular army units into the conflict in the south. El Salvador is a small country in population and area. The number of combatants in the present fighting and the areas in which they operate are correspondingly small. Most of the territory is well suited for guerrilla concealment and operations. Vietnam was a considerably larger and more populous country, with large areas of jungle there and in neighboring states suitable for guerrilla concealment operations. Vietnam also has much longer land and sea borders than El Salvador and more difficult to patrol.

Historically, the origins of the conflict in Vietnam were interlinked with the struggle for independence from French colonial rule following World War II. El Salvador won its independence from Spain in 1821 and has been an independent republic since 1838. The conflict there had a basis in domestic grievances, but has been internationalized by the Cubans and other communist and radical states that assisted and armed the insurgents.

We have 57 military training personnel in El Salvador, with the intention of reducing that number this summer. These personnel are prohibited from accompanying Salvadoran troops on patrols or combat operations of any kind. In contrast there were 525,000 military personnel in 1968 in Vietnam in a combat role. For every military training personnel the U.S. has in El Salvador there were 10,000 combat personnel assigned to Vietnam at the peak of American commitment there.

Unlike our aid to Vietnam, the major emphasis of our assistance program for El Salvador is economic rather than military. In fiscal year 1980 we provided roughly $58.8 million for the government's reforms and its programs for the most needy. In FY 82, we will provide an additional $126.5 million in economic assistance.

We are providing military assistance to the government of El Salvador with the greatest prudence and caution. Our objectives are limited; to help the government with its problems of training, equipment repair and maintenance, mobility and resupply. This year we have made grants of articles and services valued at $25 million and are providing an additional $10 million in foreign military sales loan guarantees. This additional assistance includes sending a small number of U.S. personnel in temporary duty who are remaining in military garrisons and regional command centers. The activities assigned to our military personnel do not call for them to "command, coordinate, participate in the movement of or accompany Salvadoran forces at any time or place where involvement in hostilities is imminent." President Reagan has promised that no American personnel will be sent into combat in El Salvador, now or in the future.

The United States supports the established government of President Napoleón Duarte as it implements economic and social reforms, moves toward free and open elections, and eliminates terrorism, whatever its source.

40. El Salvador: Which Vietnam?*

BY WILLIAM E. COLBY

William E. Colby is a former director of the Central Intelligence Agency. He is officially described as having directed "multiagency advisory teams in the Civil Operations and Rural Development Support (CORDS) mission in Vietnam from 1968 to 1971." Under Colby, an objective was the systematic elimination of National Liberation Front cadres, a program known more familiarly as Operation Phoenix.

DEBATE over American action in Central America is dominated by the specter of Vietnam. Some call for a bold stance to exorcise the American defeat there. Some fear that sending the first few advisers will start a certain descent toward a pit of hundreds of thousands of American soldiers locked in a fruitless and bloody jungle battle. Some predict the inevitability of revolutionary success against a corrupt and brutal government. And some decry the analogy, saying El Salvador and Vietnam have little in common, so that the earlier experience does not augur the result in a new area.

The common measuring stick of these contending points of view is

---

* From *The Washington Post*, April 20, 1981.

an image of Vietnam emanating from the Tet attack of 1968—masses of guerrillas outwitting a corrupt local government and a ponderous and yet deadly American fighting force. With this image, the condition is inevitable that we should not repeat the experience.

But there were several "Vietnams." A blind application of only one in our decision-making process today only exacerbates the cost of Vietnam and its wounds upon the American body politic. Identification of these quite different "Vietnams" forces attention to real policy alternatives rather than obliterating the process by emotion and imagery.

John Paul Vann, a leading figure in our effort in Vietnam from 1960 to his death in 1972, once commented that Americans did not have 10 years' war experience in Vietnam (1960-1970) but rather one year repeated many times, due to the short tours most Americans spent there. But those with a longer perspective can clearly identify four distinct periods of the American wartime experience in Vietnam, each with its own characteristics.

The first period, 1960 to 1963, marked the start of Hanoi's effort to overthrow the South, launched by a call by the Lao Dong Party for the overthrow of President Ngo Dinh Diem and his American allies. This was implemented by the reactivation of dormant Communist nets in South Vietnam and the infiltration of organizers and guerrilla leaders. After an initial period of indecision, the South Vietnamese developed the Strategic Hamlet strategy, to gather the smallest local communities for self-defense, with the military's role being to support these communities and act against regular forces. The American role was one of advice and support.

This program had its failings, but it seized the momentum of the "people's war" to the extent that Wilfred Burchett, an Australian communist apologist, later commented that "1962 belonged to the government [of South Vietnam]." At this point, a combination of urban political oppositionists, Buddhist religious frenzy and Mandarin repression led to American encouragement of a junta of generals to revolt against President Diem. Diem might have won or might have lost the people's war on his own, but America's complicity in his overthrow produced instant turmoil and cemented America's responsibility for Vietnam's fate.

The second "Vietnam" is closest to the one commonly perceived, from 1964 to 1968. Most Americans served then as our involvement increased to 550,000 men. Instructed to find, fix and fight the enemy, they reacted with frustration and frequently fury before an enemy that only occasionally could even be found. The side effects of this massive military force in a tiny land dominate most fictional and theatrical representations of Vietnam, making this period the basic reference point of Vietnam for most Americans. Its culmination was the Tet attack of 1968, whose media drama so overshadowed its military failure as to win for the Vietnamese communists a psychological victory.

The third "Vietnam" appeared between 1968 and 1972. The rural countryside was rebuilt and pacified by a revival of reliance upon village participation in defense and development. The combat was turned on the secret political enemy, not just his military forces. The contrast with the earlier period became dramatic in the opening of the Delta to land reform and commerce, the arming of local security and self-defense forces for village protection and the resettlement of millions of refugees in the villages from which they had been driven by the war. And most of America's military force was withdrawn from the country.

Vietnamese communists are quite frank today in recognizing this period as the lowest point of their effort to defeat South Vietnam. The shift from the earlier period was best illustrated by the large North Vietnamese military attack in the spring of 1972, which took place only at three points along South Vietnam's borders (Quang Tri, Kontum and An Loc), with no countrywide guerrilla assault. South Vietnamese, not American forces, fought back and stopped the attacks, helped by reinforcements from the Delta where they were not needed to defend against local forces and guerrillas. The American contribution was limited to advisers, extensive logistics support and B-52 bombardment from the sky, with almost no combat force participation on the ground.

The fourth "Vietnam" appeared between 1973 and 1975. A "peace" treaty was pressed by the United States upon South Vietnam, which left North Vietnamese forces in place in South Vietnam and the border areas of Cambodia and Laos. American logistics support of South Vietnam's forces was cut back so that President Thieu's American-advised forward defense strategy became impractical. When in 1975 North Vietnam made a major assault at almost the same point as in 1972, American logistics were held back by Congress, and B-52s did not fly. South Vietnamese tactical errors, not substantially different from some in 1972, led this time to total collapse before the oncoming North Vietnamese armor, artillery and regular forces. But even the North Vietnamese commander acknowledged that guerrillas played no part in his final victory. The boat people have dramatized the human dimension of the outcome; the degree to which it cast doubt on America's will and ability to stand by its allies is more ambiguous.

The question then is: Which "Vietnam"? There is little doubt that no one wishes to see another Vietnam of the turmoil and blood from 1964 to 1968. Neither should we repeat the 1960 to 1963 period of America's turning against a friendly president and government for their imperfections and producing something worse. Nor, one hopes, do we want to see a Vietnam of 1973 to 1975, misusing aid to a nation battling a foe that makes no secret of its hostility to the United States. But the Vietnam of 1968 to 1972 offers a positive model of a leading role for political, economic and social programs to enlist a nation to develop and defend itself, with American advice and assistance in doing both.

41. The Last War, the Next War, and the New Revisionists *

By Walter LaFeber

Walter LaFeber, Professor of History at Cornell University, is the author of America, Russia and the Cold War, 1945–1966 *(New York, Wiley, 1967) and* The Panama Canal: The Crisis in Historical Perspective *(New York, Oxford University Press, 1978).*

AS if to prove Lord Acton's dictum that "the strong man with the dagger is followed by the weak man with the sponge," a remarkable rewriting of the Vietnam war's history is under way. It is especially remarkable because the new revisionists are either ignorant of American policy in the conflict or have chosen to forget past policies in order to mold present opinion. More generally, they are rewriting the record of failed military interventionism in the 1950 to 1975 era in order to build support for interventionism in the 1980s. More specifically, the new revisionists are attempting to shift historical guilt from those who instigated and ran the war to those who opposed it.

Immediately after South Vietnam fell in 1975, Secretary of State Henry Kissinger urged Americans to forget the quarter-century-long war. That advice was no doubt related to his other concern at the time: committing U.S. military power to Angola and the Horn of Africa. Congress had fortunately learned from experience and stopped Kissinger from involving the country in an African Vietnam.

---

* From *democracy*, Vol. 1, No. 1, January, 1981.

The next year, however, influential authors began to discover that Vietnam's history was more usable than Kissinger had imagined. General William Westmoreland, who commanded U.S. forces during the worst months of fighting in the 1960s, set the line when he argued in his memoirs and public speeches that the conflict was not lost on the battlefield, but at home where overly sensitive politicians followed a "no-win policy" to accommodate "a misguided minority opposition . . . masterfully manipulated by Hanoi and Moscow." The enemy, Westmoreland claimed, finally won "the war politically in Washington."

Part of Westmoreland's thesis was developed with more scholarship and cooler prose by Leslie H. Gelb and Richard K. Betts in *The Irony of Vietnam: the System Worked*. It was not the "system"—that is, the Cold War national security establishment—that failed, the authors argued. Failure was to be blamed on the American people, who never understood the war and finally tired of it, and on the Presidents who supinely followed the people. Thus the "system" worked doubly well: the professional bureaucrats gave the correct advice, as they were paid to do, and the Presidents followed the public's wishes, as democratic theory provides that they should.

Westmoreland's argument that the antiwar groups wrongly labeled Vietnam an illegal and immoral conflict was developed by Guenter Lewy's *America in Vietnam*. Lewy, however, was so honest that his own evidence destroyed the thesis. Although he wrote that U.S. soldiers followed civilized modes of war even though this sometimes meant virtual suicide, Lewy also gave striking examples of how the troops ruthlessly destroyed villages and civilians. "It is well to remember," he wrote, "that revulsion at the fate of thousands of hapless civilians killed and maimed" because of American reliance upon high-technology weapons "may undercut the willingness of a democratic nation to fight communist insurgents." That becomes a fair judgment when "thousands" is changed to "hundreds of thousands." Lewy nevertheless held grimly to his thesis about the war's morality and legality, even as he reached his closing pages: "the simplistic slogan 'No more Vietnams' not only may encourage international disorder, but could mean abandoning basic American values." It apparently made little difference to Lewy that those basic American values had been ravaged at My Lai, or at Cam Ne, where a Marine commander burned down a village and then observed in his after-action report that "It is extremely difficult for a ground commander to reconcile his tactical mission and a people-to-people program." Lewy's conclusions, not his evidence, set a tone that was widely echoed, particularly after the foreign policy crises of late 1979.

The Soviet invasion of Afghanistan was seized upon with almost audible sighs of relief in some quarters. *Commentary*, which had publicly introduced Lewy's argument in 1978, published a series of essays in early 1980 that developed some of his conclusions, especially the view that if the Vietnam experience inhibited future U.S. interventions, it "could mean abandoning basic American values." In an essay that thoughtfully explored the meaning of his own antiwar protests in the 1960s, Peter Berger nevertheless drew the conclusion that the American defeat in Vietnam "greatly altered" the world balance of power, and that "American power has dramatically declined, politically as well as militarily." Charles Horner condemned President Jimmy Carter's early belief that Vietnam taught us the limits of U.S. power. "That view," Horner claimed, "is the single greatest restraint on our capacity to deal with the world, and that capacity will not much increase unless the view behind it is changed, thoroughly and profoundly." Horner did his best to reinterpret the meaning of Vietnam, but it was *Commentary*'s editor, Norman Podhoretz, who best demonstrated how history could be rewritten to obtain desired conclusions.

"Now that Vietnam is coming to be seen by more and more people as an imprudent effort to save Indochina from the horrors of Communist rule rather than an immoral intervention or a crime," Podhoretz wrote in the March 1980 issue, "the policy out of which it grew is also coming to be seen in a new light." He believed that the "policy—of defending democracy [sic] wherever it existed, or of holding the line against the advance of Communist totalitarianism by political means where possible and by military means when necessary," was based on the Wilsonian idea that "in the long run," U.S. interests depended on " 'the survival and the success of liberty' in the world as a whole." This revisionist view of Vietnam, Podhoretz argued, is helping to create a "new nationalism"—the kind of outlook that "Woodrow Wilson appealed to in seeking to 'make the world safe for democracy' and that John F. Kennedy echoed."

Podhoretz's grasp of historical facts is not reassuring; the essay has three major errors in its first three pages. George A. Carver, Jr.'s essay subtitled "The Teachings of Vietnam," in the July 1980 issue of *Harper's*, only adds to that problem. An old CIA hand who was deeply involved in Vietnam policy planning, Carver is identified in *Harper's* only as "a senior fellow" at Georgetown University's Center for Strategic and International Studies. That identification is nevertheless of note, for the Center serves as an important source of personnel and ideas for what passes as Ronald Reagan's foreign policy program. In the article, Carver set out to "dispel Vietnam's shadows" so the United States could again exercise great power and influence.

When he mentioned earlier policy, Carver simply postulated that South Vietnam fell to North Vietnamese conventional forces, not to "any popular southern rebellion," and that "the press and media, and their internal competitive imperatives" misrepresented the real progress the U.S. forces were making in the war. Beyond that, the analysis consists of empty generalizations (Americans are encumbered in their foreign policy by "theological intensity" and "childlike innocence"), and it climaxes with the insight that "the world is cruel."

Read closely, Carver's warning about the dangers of "theological intensity" contradicts Podhoretz's call for a new Wilsonianism. But in the wake of the Iranian and Afghanistan crises, few read these calls to the ramparts of freedom very closely. The essays were more valuable for their feelings than for their historical accuracy. The new revisionists wanted to create a mood, not recall an actual past, and their success became dramatically apparent when that highly sensitive barometer of popular feelings, commercial television, quickly put together a new sitcom on the war, "The Six O'Clock Follies." One reviewer labeled it a "gutlessly cynical comedy," signaling that "suddenly we are supposed to be able to laugh at Vietnam." As the *Washington Post*'s critic observed, however, since the conflict has "been deemed a safe zone . . . all three networks have Vietnam sitcoms in the works" for 1980–1981. Television was placing its seal of approval on a revisionism that promised to be commercially as well as ideologically satisfying.

Given this new mood, it was natural that those who wielded, or planned to wield, power were also prepared to help wring the sponge. In 1978 Zbigniew Brzezinski had lamented privately to Senate staff members that the floundering administration needed a *Mayagüez* incident so Carter, as Ford had in 1975, could get tough with Communists (preferably, apparently, from a small country), and rally Americans behind a battle flag. By the end of 1979, Carter had not one but two such opportunities with the Iranian hostage issue and the Soviet invasion of Afghanistan, and as usual Americans indeed closed ranks behind the President. In mid-December, Brzezinski observed that the country was finally getting over its post-Vietnam opposition to military spending and overseas intervention.

Three months later, Ronald Reagan, in his only major foreign policy speech prior to the Republican Convention, urged a return to Wilsonianism—what one reporter characterized as a belief that Americans have "an inescapable duty to act as the tutor and protector of the free world in confronting . . . alien ideologies." To carry out this mission, Reagan proclaimed, "we must rid ourselves of the 'Vietnam syndrome.'" He of course meant the old "syndrome," not the new syndrome of the revisionists that the war was to be admired for its intent if not its outcome. A frustrated job seeker at the Republican Convention best captured the effects of the new revisionism. A reporter teased Henry Kissinger about his prediction in the early 1970s that if the war did not end well for Americans there would be a fierce right-wing reaction. "It turned out just about the way I predicted it would," Kissinger replied. The former Secretary of State, however, contributed to the mood that threatened to confine him to academia. In recent writings and speeches, Kissinger has argued that if the Watergate scandal had not driven Nixon from office, South Vietnam would not have been allowed to fall. His claim cannot, of course, be completely disproved, but it is totally unsupported by either the post-1973 military and political situation in Vietnam, or the antiwar course of American policies, including Nixon's, that appeared long before the Watergate scandal paralyzed the administration.

The arguments of the new revisionists—or the new nationalists, as some prefer to be called (in perhaps unconscious reference to the New Nationalism of Theodore Roosevelt and Herbert Croly that pledged an imperial "Big Stick" foreign policy)—dominated the foreign policy debates and, indeed, the Carter-Brzezinski foreign policies in early 1980. Because those arguments rest heavily on interpretations of the Vietnam conflict, their use of the war's history deserves analysis. This can be done on two levels: the new revisionists' explicit claims, and the events they choose to ignore.

The most notable explicit theme is captured by Westmoreland's assertion that the war was lost because of pressure from a "misguided minority opposition" at home, or by Peter Berger's more careful statement that "the anti-war movement was a primary causal factor in the American withdrawal from Indochina." Since at least the mid-1960s, detailed public opinion polls have existed that show that Americans supported a tough policy in Vietnam. In this, as in nearly all foreign policies, the public followed the President. As Herbert Y. Schandler concluded after his careful study of public opinion between 1964 and 1969, "If the administration is using increasing force, the public will respond like hawks; if it is seeking peace, the public responds like doves." When Lyndon Johnson tried to convince doubters by whipping out the latest opinion polls showing support for the war, he did not have to make up the figures. George Ball has testified that the antiwar protests only "dug us in more deeply" and intensified the administration's determination to win. Ball, who served as Under Secretary of State under Johnson, rightly calculated that "only late in the day did widespread discontent . . . appreciably slow the escalation of the war." Even those who dissented in the

1960s were more hawk than dove. Richard Scammon and Ben Wattenberg's analysis of the 1968 election concluded that a plurality of the Democrats who voted for Eugene McCarthy in the primaries supported George Wallace in November, and that finding is corroborated by polls revealing that a majority of those who opposed the conduct of the war also opposed protests against the war. Westmoreland's "misguided minority opposition" was of significantly less importance than a much larger group that wanted him to have whatever he needed to end the war. It simply is not true as Barry Goldwater claimed at the 1980 Republican Convention, that the "will" to win the war was missing in the 1960s.

By 1970–1971, antiwar opposition had increased, but it did not stop Nixon from expanding the conflict into Cambodia and Laos. One statistic stands out: before Nixon sent in the troops, 56 percent of college-educated Americans wanted to "stay out" of Cambodia, and after he committed the forces, 50 percent of the same group supported the Cambodian invasion. When Nixon carpet-bombed North Vietnam two years later and for the first time mined the North's ports, 59 percent of those polled supported the President, and only 24 percent opposed him, even though it was clear that the mining could lead to a confrontation with the Russians and Chinese, whose ships used the harbors.

The effectiveness of the antiwar movement has been greatly overrated by the new revisionists, and the movement has consequently served as the scapegoat for them as well as for the national security managers whose policies failed in Vietnam. Given the new revisionist arguments, it needs to be emphasized that the United States lost in Vietnam because it was defeated militarily, and that that defeat occurred because Americans could not win the war without destroying what they were fighting to save—or, alternatively, without fighting for decades while surrendering those values at home and in the Western alliance for which the cold war was supposedly being waged. The antiwar protesters only pointed up these contradictions; they did not create them.

The new revisionists argue that the nation has largely recovered from the disaster. Carl Gershman writes that "as the polls reveal, the American people have now overwhelmingly rejected the ideas of the new [Carter-Vance-Young] establishment." The strategy of the post-Vietnam "establishment" is to contain communism only in selected areas, and by using nonmilitary means if possible. The polls actually reveal considerable support for this strategy. In January 1980, after the invasion of Afghanistan, a CBS/*New York Times* survey showed that about two-fifths of those polled wanted to respond with nonmilitary tactics, two-fifths wanted to "hold off for now," and less than one-fifth favored a military response. Lou Harris discovered that within six weeks after the seizure of the hostages in Iran, support for military retaliation dropped off sharply. Quite clearly, if the new nationalists hope to whip up public sentiment for using military force wherever they perceive "democracy" to be threatened, they have much work yet to do. Most Americans have not overwhelmingly rejected nonmilitary responses, even after being shaken by the diplomatic earthquakes of 1979–1980. And they appear too sophisticated to agree with Podhoretz's Wilsonian assumption that "American interests in the long run [depend] on the survival and the success of liberty in the world as a whole." A majority of Americans seem to agree with that part of the post-Vietnam "establishment" represented by Vance and Young that it is wiser to trust nationalisms in the Third World than to undertake a Wilsonian crusade to rescue those nationalisms for an American-defined "liberty."

There is a reason for this confusion among new revisionist writers. They focus almost entirely on the Soviet Union instead of on the instability in Third World areas that the Soviets have at times turned to their own advantage. Such an approach allows the new revisionists to stress military power rather than the political or economic strategies that are most appropriate for dealing with Third World problems. The new nationalists, like the old, pride themselves on being realists in regard to power, but their concept of power is one-dimensional. Once this military dimension becomes unusable, nothing is left. A direct military strategy is appropriate for dealing with the Soviets in certain cases—for example, if the Red Army invaded Western Europe or Middle East oil fields. That strategy, however, has existed since the days of Harry Truman; the Vietnam war, regardless of how it is reinterpreted, has nothing new to teach us about that kind of massive response. A quarter-century ago, when the United States took its first military steps into Vietnam, Reinhold Niebuhr warned that the policy placed "undue reliance on purely military power" and therefore missed the fundamental political point: a U.S. military response was incapable of ending "the injustices of [Asia's] decaying feudalism and the inequalities of its recent colonialism." Niebuhr's advice was of course ignored. The supposed realists of the day proceeded to commit military power in Vietnam—to contain China. For, in the mid-1960s, China was the villain for the national security managers, as the Soviets are now for the new revisionists.

The reason for the failure of U.S. military power was not that it was severely limited. Lyndon Johnson bragged that he put 100,000 men into Vietnam in just one hundred and twenty days. Those troops were supported by the most powerful naval and air force ever used in Asia. Laos became the most heavily bombed country in history, North Vietnam's ports and cities were bombed and mined almost yard by yard, and Nixon dropped a ton of bombs on Indochina for every minute of his first term in the White House. Neither the will nor the power was missing. As Michael Herr wrote in *Dispatches,* "There was such a dense concentration of American energy there, American and essentially adolescent, if that energy could have been channeled into anything more than noise, waste and pain, it would have lighted up Indochina for a thousand years." Vietnam provides a classic lesson in the misuse of military power, but that lesson is being overlooked by the new revisionists.

And if they have misunderstood the conflict's central political and military features, so have the new revisionists lost sight of the historical context. They stress that Vietnam caused the decline of American power. It is quite probable, however, that when historians look back with proper perspective on the last half of the twentieth century, they will conclude that U.S. foreign policy problems in the 1970s and 1980s resulted not from the Vietnam experience, but more generally from political misperception and from an overestimation of American power. The *hubris* produced by the American triumph in the Cuban missile crisis contributed to such misestimation, but the problems also resulted from the failure to understand that U.S. power began a relative decline in the late 1950s and early 1960s. It was during those earlier years that the American economy and international trade began a decline that only accelerated—not started—in the 1970s; that such important allies as Japan and West Germany directly attacked American markets and helped to undermine the dollar; that the Western alliance displayed its first signs of slipping out of Washington's control; and that the Third World rapidly multiplied its numbers and decided—as the creation of OPEC in 1960 demonstrated—that it no longer had to join either one of the superpower camps. Future historians will consequently see the Vietnam war as one result, not a cause, of the relative decline of American power that began in the late 1950s. They will also probably conclude that space ventures, and the achievement of independence by nearly one hundred nations in the Third World, were of greater historical significance than the Vietnam conflict or the U.S.-USSR rivalry that obsesses the new revisionists.

Even with their narrow focus on the lessons of Vietnam, it is striking how much the new revisionists omit from their accounts of the war. They say relatively little about the South Vietnamese. The war is viewed as an eyeball-to-eyeball confrontation between Americans and Communists, and the turn comes when the Americans, undone by what Carver calls their "childlike innocence," blink. This approach resembles watching two football teams but not noticing the ball that is being kicked and passed around. The new revisionists have downplayed the inability of the South Vietnamese to establish a stable and effective government amid a massive U.S. buildup, the Vietnamese hatred for the growing American domination, and the massive desertions from the South's army in 1966-1967, even when the U.S. forces arrived to help. As early as 1966, non-Communist student leaders accurately called the country's presidential elections "a farce directed by foreigners." By 1971, a Saigon newspaper ran a daily contest in which readers submitted stories of rape or homicide committed by Americans. As Woodrow Wilson learned in 1919, some people just do not want to be saved—at least by outsiders with whom they have little in common.

The new revisionists also overlook the role the allies played in Vietnam. There is a good reason for this omission: of the forty nations tied to the United States by treaties, only four—Australia, New Zealand, South Korea, and Thailand—committed any combat troops. The major European and Latin American allies refused to send such forces. We later discovered that the South Koreans, whom Americans had saved at tremendous cost in 1950, agreed to help only after Washington bribed them with one billion dollars of aid. The key Asian ally, Japan, carefully distanced itself from the U.S. effort. This was especially bitter for American officials, for Truman and Eisenhower had made the original commitment to Vietnam in part to keep the area's raw materials and markets open for the Japanese. Relations between Tokyo and Washington deteriorated rapidly. When Lyndon Johnson asked whether he could visit Japan in 1966, the answer came back, "inconceivable." An article in the authoritative *Japan Quarterly* stated that if the United States became involved in another war with China, divisions in Japanese public opinion "would split the nation in two" and lead to "disturbances approaching a civil war in scale."

As Jimmy Carter admitted in early 1980, the United States needs strong support from allies if it hopes to contain the Soviets in the Middle East. It would be well, therefore, to note carefully the allied view of U.S. policy in Vietnam and elsewhere before embarking on a Wilsonian crusade to make "democracy" safe everywhere. Having chosen to ignore the lesson that Vietnam teaches about the allies, the new revisionists resemble traditional isolationists, who, as scholars have agreed, were characterized by a desire for maximum freedom of action, minimum commitment to other nations ("no entangling alliances"), and a primary reliance on military force rather than on the compromises of political negotiations.

Finally, these recent accounts neglect the war's domestic costs. The new revisionists stress the decline of the American "will" to win, but they say little about how the economic disasters and a corrupted presidency produced by the war influenced that "will." As early as January 1966, Lyndon Johnson admitted that "Because of Vietnam we cannot do all that we should, or all that we would like to do" in building a more just society at home. As the phrase went at the time, Americans—those "people of plenty"—suddenly discovered they could not have both guns and butter. The butter, or, more generally, the Great Society program, was sacrificed. A Pentagon analysis drawn up under the direction of Secretary of Defense Clark Clifford after the 1968 Tet offensive faced the problem squarely. It concluded that militarily the war could not be won, "even with the 200,000 additional troops" requested by Westmoreland. A drastic escalation, moreover, would result not only in "increased defiance of the draft," but in "growing unrest in the cities because of the belief that we are ignoring domestic problems." A "domestic crisis of unprecedented proportions" threatened. If the new revisionists and Reagan Republicans plan to manipulate the war's history to obtain higher defense budgets and unilateral commitments overseas, they should discuss this crucial characteristic of the war's course: it was determined less by campus protesters than by the growing realization that the costs worsened the conditions of the poorest and most discriminated against in American society until an "unprecedented" crisis loomed. Clifford turned against the war after businessmen he respected suddenly became scared and dovish. Clifford learned, but there is little evidence that the new revisionists understand the choices that were embedded in what they dismiss as the "Vietnam syndrome."

As persons who attack centralized power in the federal government, the new revisionists and the Reagan Republicans should at least discuss the effect of Vietnam on the imperial presidency. They could note, for example, that nothing centralizes power more rapidly than waging the cold war militarily, unless it is waging hot war in Korea and Vietnam. In 1967, Under Secretary of State Nicholas Katzenbach told the Senate that the power given by the Constitution to Congress to declare war was "an outmoded phraseology." In 1969–1972, Nixon used "national security" as the rationale for ordering a series of acts that resulted in nearly forty criminal indictments. Vietnam raised the central question in American foreign policy: How can the nation's interests be defended without destroying the economic and political principles that make it worth defending? In their extensive study of Vietnam, the new revisionists have chosen to ignore the question.

They have instead concentrated on an objective that is as simple as it is potentially catastrophic: the removal of the restraints of history, so that the next war can be waged from the start with fewer limitations. They are offering a particular interpretation of the last war, so the next war can be fought differently. This purpose helps explain why these writers stress the narrow military aspects of the war and ignore the larger problems of historical context, the Western allies, economic costs, and political corruption. Westmoreland again set the tone with his remark that "If we go to war . . . we need heed the old Oriental saying, 'It takes the full strength of a tiger to kill a rabbit,' and use appropriate force to bring the war to a timely end." In his reassessment of the tragedy, Ambassador Robert Komer condemned the "institutional factors—bureaucratic restraints" that made success impossible. Lewy argued that the struggle was considered a mistake at the time because of "the conviction that the war was not being won and apparently showed little prospect of coming to a successful conclusion." If only the restraints had been lifted, the new revisionists imply, the war—which they consider morally and politically justified—could have been fought to a successful conclusion. This inference is drawn with little attention to either the inherent contradictions in Vietnam military strategy (for example, that villages had to be destroyed to be saved) or the nonmilitary aspects of the conflict. It comes perilously close to an end-justifies-the-means argument.

By trying to make the last war more acceptable, the new revisionists are asking us to make the next war legitimate, even before we know where it will be or what it will be fought for. A Chinese official once told Henry Kissinger that "One should not lose the whole world just to gain South Vietnam." Nor, it might be added, should men with sponges try to legitimize their global cold-war policies by whitewashing the history of the war in South Vietnam.

Chapter IV

TOWARD A
NEGOTIATED SETTLEMENT?

Editors' Introduction

THE major basis for settlement is the announced commitment of all sides—the junta, the U.S. government, the rebel *frente*—to a "political" resolution of the conflict. Of course, there are sharply divergent notions of the components of such a "political settlement." The coordinated position of the Salvadoran governing junta and the U.S. (as of the late summer of 1981) was that a political settlement meant elections in 1982-3, the holding of which would restore political legitimacy to an "elected" government in El Salvador, and thus end the armed conflict. The speech of U.S. Assistant Secretary of State Thomas O. Enders, delivered in mid-July, states Washington's view of the conditions;[1] José Napoleón Duarte, a month and a half earlier, stated the junta's position in an interview with an Argentinian journalist. It is necessary, Duarte said, "to reestablish law in the country" before the new elections take place. As for the left opposition, it too can participate in the electoral process, "but with one condition: [it] will have to accept democratic rules."

We do not want any type of totalitarianism, neither leftist nor rightist [Duarte continued]; if the Democratic Revolutionary Front defines itself as a democratic political party, there will be no problems.[2]

---

[1] See Reading 43, below.

[2] Duarte, interview in Buenos Aires *La Nación*, June 2, 1981 (Foreign Broadcast Information Service, Daily Reports, June 9, 1981). Soon after the joint French-Mexican declaration of August 28, 1981, recognizing the opposition in El Salvador as a "representative political force," Duarte repeated his demand that opposition groups lay down their arms and form parties to participate in assembly elections scheduled for March 1982. See *The New York Times*, September 17, 1981.

What the junta expects from the *frente's* redefinition of itself was further clarified by Hector Jorge Bustamente, head of the Salvadoran electoral commission: the FDR can participate in the preliminaries "if it puts down its weapons and publicly states that it has broken away from, and does not support, any guerrilla group. It must also express its intention of seeking power through free and democratic elections." [3] In evaluating such wholesome-sounding proposals one must keep in mind that a fierce daily struggle wracks El Salvador, and that the *frente's* leaders are marked for death by the armed forces (many have already been killed), and that open participation in electoral activity is tantamount to suicide.

The *frente*, therefore, has another scenario for a political settlement, which involves bringing the conflict to an end through international mediation, or through negotations involving all participants as in Zimbabwe (formerly Rhodesia). Such efforts have already been made by the Socialist International and by the mediation committee sent in June, 1981, by the European Parliament.[4] These efforts failed, chiefly because of opposition of the junta, and its U.S. backers, to what Duarte called "foreign interference" in El Salvador.[5] Some in the rebel *frente* too favor reliance on guerrilla struggle rather than resort to negotiated settlement, but the main line of thinking in the opposition is expressed by Guillermo Ungo, FDR president, who in an interview with an Italian newspaper, stressed the international context of any settlement.[6] This position has also been advanced in the United States by critics of the Reagan administration's policy of military support for the junta, and for the junta's position of no negotiations with the rebels. It is hard to see how the conflict in El Salvador, viewed by the U.S. government as an international confrontation, can be solved in any other way than by internationally-generated negotiations. The only alternative, it would seem, is the prolongation of an armed struggle that has already cost the lives of thousands of Salvadorans.

---

[3] San Salvador, *El Diario de Hoy*, June 3, 1981 (Foreign Broadcast Information Service, Daily Reports, June 4, 1981).

[4] A good summary of these futile negotiation efforts may be found in "Central America Watch," *The Nation*, July 11–18, 1981, and in National Public Radio, "All Things Considered," June 27, 1981.

[5] Duarte, interview in *La Nación*, June 2, 1981.

[6] See Reading 44, below.

42. El Salvador: Why Not Negotiate? *

By Robert E. White

Robert E. White was the Ambassador to El Salvador during the Carter administration, and was removed from that position by the Reagan administration. He is now a senior associate at the Carnegie Endowment for International Peace.

White's position is unique. A critic of Reagan's foreign policy and the Salvadoran military, he argues that both the Christian Democrats and President Duarte personally favor negotiations and independence for El Salvador. In his view, the Christian Democrats and the Duarte forces can in fact be separated from the interests and concerns of the Salvadoran army. White's more recent assessment appears in Reading 52.

THE poverty of this administration's policy toward El Salvador becomes clearer every day. The government of El Salvador is going nowhere. The violence continues. The reforms have stopped. The economy is foundering. The extremes are gathering strength. Yet the only response from this administration has been to discourage diplomatic initiatives from friendly governments, to spin tall tales about massive arms shipments from Nicaragua and to point the Salvadoran military toward search and destroy missions against *campesino* towns suspected of containing guerrillas.

To a government pleading for economic assistance to carry out its reform programs, we have provided unneeded armaments. To a people crying out for an end to the violence, we have furnished unwanted military advisers. To moderate civilian and military leaders trying desperately to contain the slaughter practiced by the security forces, we have given an abandonment of our human rights policy and a justification for government-sponsored terrorism. To friendly governments seeking to encourage a negotiated solution, we have trumpeted unsupportable charges of a "textbook case of indirect armed agression by communist powers." And to world leaders who believed that the United States had finally learned that counter-revolution is not an adequate response to a people determined to transform their country, we have responded with Cold War rhetoric.

If U.S. policy toward El Salvador continues to exclude a political

---

* From *The Washington Post*, June 9, 1981.

solution to that country's tragic civil war, the inexorable result will be to drive the moderate element—the Christian Democrats—from the government. This has long been the objective of the economic elites that regard the commitment of the Christian Democrats to profound reform as far more dangerous than the threat posed by the guerrillas of the far left.

The Reagan administration has thrown its weight behind a military solution to the Salvadoran tragedy. This has forced the Christian Democrats to equivocate regarding their long and strongly held position in favor of a negotiated solution to the conflict, and threatens their ability to govern. Two public examples that bear witness to the Christian Democrats' commitment to negotiation come to mind.

In October 1980, the bishop of San Salvador, Arturo Rivera y Damas, speaking in the name of the entire episcopate, offered to mediate between the government and the Democratic Revolutionary Front (FDR). While the FDR turned its back on the bishops' initiative, the government immediately accepted the mediation offer. A few weeks later, at a ceremony in the headquarters of the Organization of American States, Foreign Minister Fidel Chavez Mena stated unequivocally the government's willingness to "meet with all groups and sectors at the negotiating table."

It is important to be clear on this essential point. The Christian Democrats want to enter into negotiations with the FDR. It is the Salvadoran military that opposes any accommodation with the left, preferring instead to kill them with the assistance of our arms and our military advisers. Unless the United States uses its influence in favor of negotiation, the Christian Democrats have no choice but to temporize. They are not powerful enough to move the military toward a political solution without the solid backing of the United States. The Christian Democrats' only hope is that the nations of Western Europe and this hemisphere will persuade the United States to adopt a more responsible and humane course.

It is not only the Reagan administration that treats the Christian Democrats as expendable. Leaders of the FDR have persistently underestimated the importance of the Christian Democrats. FDR President Guillermo Ungo has spoken contemptuously of President Napoleón Duarte and other party leaders, describing them as nothing more than a facade for repression. This is both factually wrong and morally unfair. Men such as junta member José Antonio Morales Erhlich and Minister of Planning Atilio Vieytez, as well as Duarte and Chavez Mena are authentic democrats committed to a new deal for their country. More than the others, perhaps, Duarte may be tempted to use every device available to stay in office even after any real hope of transferring power from the military to the civilian institutions of the country has disappeared.

Ultimately, however, Duarte is a disciplined Christian Democrat. Should the party decide to leave the government, he will comply. And there is solid evidence of a sentiment building within Christian Democracy that the party can expect no support from the Reagan administration and would do well to leave the government in order to salvage what they can of its reputation. When Minister Atilio Vieytez said publicly that, while he did not dress in olive drab, he was as much a revolutionary as any guerrilla, he spoke for the great majority of the party.

The government of El Salvador contains worthy people, both uniformed and civilian. It also contains some of the most brutally repressive military in the world. Although the FDR counts many committed democrats in its ranks, it also contains armed guerrillas led by Marxist-Leninists who are guilty of unacceptable violence. It may be that any negotiation would both drive hard-line military elements into opposition to the government and induce some Marxist-led guerrilla groups to break away from the FDR. Both results should be welcomed. The repressive elements of the military, which regularly torture and kill, constitute a fatal weight around the neck of the government. The FDR must also decide which route it favors—negotiations, guarantees and elections, or a continuation of armed struggle. Each side must face the reality that it contains extremist elements which cannot be assimilated.

In a recent message to his confreres, the director general of the Jesuits, Pedro Arrupe, said, "Even when Christians recognize the legitimacy of certain struggles and do not exclude revolution in situations of extreme tyranny that have no other solution, they cannot accept that the privileged method for ending struggle is struggle itself. They will rather seek to promote other methods of social transformation calling for persuasion, witness, reconciliation."

Profound words. World leaders who profess Western values should indeed prefer negotiation over violence. It is therefore discouraging that the Reagan administration has set its face against a political solution for El Salvador. If it continues to follow this course it will alienate not only the Western community of nations but also the crucial civilian component of the government of El Salvador. For the Christian Democrats are not only tough, pragmatic politicians, they are also idealists who have more in common with much of the FDR leadership than they do with those whom professor Thomas J. Farer eloquently and correctly condemned as "an alliance of corrupted soldiers, industrialists and landowners [who] would rather fight to the last worker, peasant, politician and priest than accept reform." [1]

43. El Salvador:
We Favor a Political Solution *

BY THOMAS O. ENDERS.

Thomas O. Enders is Assistant Secretary of State for Inter-American Affairs. He presented this assessment to the World Affairs Council in Washington, D.C. on July 16, 1981.

WHAT I would like to talk about today: A political solution. For just as the conflict was Salvadoran in its origins, so its ultimate resolution must be Salvadoran.

El Salvador, however, remains a divided country. It is divided between the insurgents and a great majority that opposes the extreme left's violent methods and foreign ties. It is divided between an equally violent minority on the extreme right that seeks to return El Salvador to the domination of a small elite and a great majority that has welcomed the political and social changes of the past 18 months.

The insurgents are divided within their own coalition between those who want to prolong their ill-starred guerrilla campaign and those who are disillusioned by their failure to win the quick military victory their leaders had proclaimed inevitable, between those who despise democracy as an obstacle to their ambitions to seize power and those who might be willing to engage in democratic elections.

Finally, the majority of Salvadorans in the middle are also divided—over whether to emphasize the restoration of the country's economic health or the extension of the country's social reforms, between those who honor the army as one of the country's most stable and coherent institutions and those who criticize it for failing to prevent right-wing violence, between those who see the need to develop participatory institutions, and those who maintain that there is no alternative to the old personalistic politics.

Only Salvadorans can resolve these divisions. Neither we nor any

---

[1] See Reading 5, above.—Eds.

* *The New York Times,* July 17, 1981.

other foreign country can do so. It is therefore critical that the Salvadoran Government itself is attempting to overcome these divisions by establishing a more democratic system.

We wholeheartedly support this objective, not out of blind sentiment, not out of a desire to reproduce everywhere a political system that has served Americans so extraordinarily well and certainly not because we underestimate the difficulties involved.

Rather, we believe that the solution must be democratic because only a genuinely pluralistic approach can enable a profoundly divided society to live with itself without violent convulsions, gradually overcoming its differences.

Violence of the left and violence of the right are inextricably linked. Since the failure of the January offensive, the tragic cycle of violence and counterviolence has been most evident in Chalatenango and Morazán, the remote areas where guerrilla forces are concentrated and where most of the violent incidents recently attributed to the far right and to government forces have taken place. Elsewhere, the violence has tended to fall as the level of nationwide insurgent activity has declined. The investigations into the murders of the four American Catholic women and the two A.I.F.L.D. experts, though still unfortunately incomplete, have led to detentions. But more needs to be done.

Cuban and Nicaraguan supplies to the guerrillas must stop. There is no doubt that Cuba was largely behind the arms trafficking that fueled the guerrilla offensive this winter. In April, when Socialist International representative Wischnewski confronted Castro with our evidence of Cuban interference, Castro admitted to him that Cuba had shipped arms to the guerrillas—just as we had said.

After their arms trafficking was exposed, Cuba and Nicaragua reduced the flow in March and early April. Recently, however, an ominous upswing has occurred, not to the volume reached this winter, but to levels that enable the guerrillas to sustain military operations despite their inability to generate fresh support.

This brings me to my third point, that all parties that renounce violence should be encouraged to participate in the design of new political institutions and the process of choosing representatives for them.

The government of El Salvador has announced that it will hold presidential elections in 1983. Prior to that a constituent assembly to be elected in 1982 will develop a new constitution. Four months ago, in March, President Duarte appointed an electoral commission to develop the necessary procedures. Last week, the government officially approved measures recognizing the legal status of registered parties and setting the procedures whereby these parties and any new parties that come legally into existence can participate in the election.

But it is only realistic to recognize that extremists on both left and right still oppose elections and that an army suspicious that its institutional integrity might not be respected could itself become a destabilizing element. In this regard, we should recognize that El Salvador's leaders will not and should not grant the insurgents through negotiations the share of power the rebels have not been able to win on the battlefield. But they should be and are willing to compete with the insurgents at the polls.

Elections are quintessentially matters of internal policy, but there may be ways other nations can assist. If requested by the government of El Salvador—and desired by those involved—other countries might be invited to facilitate such contacts and discussions or negotiations on electoral issues among eligible political parties. The United States is prepared, if asked, to join others in providing good offices to assist the Salvadorans in this task, which could prove critical to the search for a political solution to the conflict.

We have no preconceived formulas. We know that elections have failed in the past. We have no illusions that the task now will be anything but difficult. But we believe that elections open to all who are willing to renounce violence and abide by the procedures of democracy can help end El Salvador's long agony.

The culmination of the search for peace is necessarily the responsibility of Salvadorans, but Salvadorans look to us for understanding and assistance. We can help by:

 • Extending economic and military assistance to counter the disaster visited upon El Salvador by enemies of democracy;
 • Standing by our friends while they work out a democratic solution, and
 • Identifying and seizing opportunities to help such a solution actually take shape.

44. Crumbs and Shattered Illusions *

BY GUILLERMO UNGO

Guillermo Ungo is president of the Democratic Revolutionary Front (FDR). Ungo, who resigned on January 3, 1980, from the junta set up after

* From an interview which originally appeared in La Republica (an Italian daily), March 24, 1981. It was translated and reprinted in Newsfront International, June 1–15, 1981.

the October 15, 1979 coup, which deposed General Romero, is also the leader of the National Revolutionary Movement (MNR), a constituent member of the FDR. The MNR represents El Salvador in the Socialist International, whose president is Willy Brandt of West Germany.

Q. WHAT are the chances for a political solution to the crisis in El Salvador?

A. A "democratic" or "political" solution. . . . We use these words as tools in our struggle. These words have brought us many bitter experiences. Every two years since the military dictatorship was first established 50 years ago, we have told ourselves that democracy would return, that free elections would be held, and that we were fighting for national unity, national conciliation, and the depoliticization of the military. José Napoleón Duarte, the current president, is now using this same language—a language which he once rejected as misleading and deceitful. We know now that we can gain nothing by negotiating, nothing but crumbs and shattered illusions. Power has become the central question for us.

Q. But you don't win power by putting absolute faith in old formulas. No revolution has ever succeeded by simply following the model of the previous revolution.

A. There are two rather simplistic viewpoints prevalent today. The military sees all opposition as coming from the left and therefore being subversive. It equates subversion with Marxism-Leninism and Marxism-Leninism with the desire for power—and the military, of course, doesn't negotiate over power. The opposite view equates the government with fascism and the right, associates the right with oligarchy, and ties oligarchy to the dictatorship of the past 50 years. These simplifications capture a part of the reality, but only a part.

We in the MNR have said since 1977 that El Salvador is under an oligarchical military regime, with an army directly serving minority interests. Thanks to a series of fraudulent elections, the majority of the people has always been excluded from the country's political, economic and social life. Until recently, labor unions were all but nonexistent, encompassing less than 10% of urban workers; there were no legal unions whatsoever in the countryside, where 60% of the population lives. Since they've been legalized, the unions have organized, at most, three strikes. The proletariat—persecuted, manipulated, and co-opted—has nevertheless attained a level of consciousness. It has engaged in practical politics and has understood that dialogue means death, rigged elections and persecutions. An organized popular response has thus finally developed. Understanding that legal means have always been less effective, people now have developed a non-conventional civil resistance. At the same time, the system, founded on a minority dictatorship, is generating increasing violence. The two positions play off one another: a war of extermination is met by a war of resistance and insurrection.

Q. But a war of extermination doesn't necessarily generate a growing spirit of revolt. It may also lead to discouragement, desperation, and rejection of the struggle.

A. Civilians, especially those who support or are active in the resistance, suffer most from the violence. The harshest repressive measures are directed against the poorest sectors of the population, against those who live in the countryside, where the struggle for power becomes a matter of life or death. Guerrilla activities concentrate in the center of an area of popular support, which is in turn surrounded by a larger circle of sympathizers or "potential supporters." The army must kill large numbers of people in these circles of pro-guerrilla sentiment before it can strike at the guerrillas themselves. This explains why more than 200,000 refugees have fled the zones of army dragnets and police activities. It is inevitable, given our situation. It is our task to carry on with the politics of resistance in the midst of this military campaign.

Q. But your public statements mention a military solution, and one senses that there is a strong military component in your movement.

A. The military component won't go away overnight, but we're interested in a political, not a military, solution. Even as we draw closer to forming a democratic and revolutionary government, our political objective, threatened by military development, seems further away than before. As U.S. military intervention escalates, the political and human costs rise and the conflict threatens to explode past our borders and through all of Central America. We believe that this regionalization of the conflict is against both U.S. and our own interests. All the political movements and the different guerrilla forces in the FDR and in the Farabundo Martí National Liberation Front agree on this point.

Q. What factors favor a political solution?

A. Everyone recognizes that we must co-exist with the United States. This in itself has contributed to the search for a political solution. After a democratic victory, the country's development will take place within the sphere of the western capitalist system: coexistence with the U.S. will then become a matter of necessity, not mere tactics. Our primary objective in itself favors a political solution. We are working for a democratic and revolutionary government, and will not accept a government which is only democratic or only revolutionary. Indeed, such a government would be unworkable given the plurality of the forces in the struggle.

The present oligarchy has proved that democracy is not enough, that we need an anti-oligarchical program which will clear out the Christian Democrats and change the armed forces. On the other hand, there isn't any single political force capable of providing El Salvador with a stable government. Preserving the FDR's unity and its pluralism is therefore a strategic and historical necessity, but it isn't enough. We also need to extend our network of alliances and agreements and to consider the international context.

Q. Why does the U.S. oppose such a pluralistic program?

A. Historically, the U.S. has always committed the same error. They cannot tone down their anti-communism. The Europeans are different. Europeans and Third World nations could help modify U.S. policies. Members of the British Parliament, for example, came to El Salvador in 1978, and stated very clearly that a major transformation of the oligarchical structure was necessary. Washington could learn from this example that it need not choose between the two blocs, East and West. Unfortunately, Reagan only sees the East-West axis, not that which connects the North and the South. For us, hope for a political solution rests upon international collaboration, and we are seeking it among the three major currents of European politics: Social Democracy, Christian Democracy, and liberalism.

Q. So you think it is impossible to reach an accord with the present junta?

A. We don't believe in their modifications and formulas. As long as the body is a military oligarchy, the head remains anti-democratic. We must form a new government, in which, however, the FDR will not claim exclusive powers. In the current government, power resides in the military structure, and more particularly in its right-wing, which prefers military solutions to political ones. Duarte speaks for this group. But the technocracy, which tends to be reformist and democratic, is responsible for many recent government dismissals. It, like the Christian Democrats, is an important political sector with which we must collaborate. The political solution will be achieved through struggle, not by following a formula.

Q. Is U.S. intervention the major obstacle?

A. Repression serves to push the country to the right. The more we move to the right, the stronger the oligarchical sectors become, and the more quickly the reforms fail. U.S. military aid strengthens the right, even if it does not support an ultra-right-wing coup. They say there are only 54 military advisers in El Salvador, but 54 advisers constitute 20% of the total military authority in a country with 500 officers, half of whom are no longer in active service. And the U.S. advisers are all specialists; they direct the repression.

PART FIVE

THE "DOMINOES" OF CENTRAL AMERICA

EDITORS' INTRODUCTION

Fidel Castro . . . said, "Now there are three of us," meaning Cuba, Nicaragua and Grenada. He went on to suggest there would be 4, 5, 6, 7, 8, 9, 10 more. Not 4, 5, 6, 7, 8, 9, 10 "Vietnams," but 4, 5, 6, 7, 8, 9, 10 advanced Soviet bases in our hemisphere. . . .

—Jeane Kirkpatrick, 1981

A Hit List! Completamente loco. . . . How can anyone take this Haig seriously? I mean, anyone who knows Central American history? . . . Hit list! . . .

—A Mexican delegate to the U.N., 1981

The "hit list" that so angered the Mexican U.N. delegate was Secretary of State Haig's picturesque way of describing Soviet intentions in Central America. Secretary Haig assured a House panel in March, 1981 that Moscow was engaged in a "four-phased operation"—first Nicaragua, next El Salvador, then Honduras and Guatemala—"for the ultimate takeover of Central America."

The idea of a "hit list" is cousin to the "domino theory." In supporting U.S. assistance to the French in the Indochinese War, President Dwight Eisenhower popularized the concept, citing the "broader considerations that might follow what you would call the 'falling domino' principle. You have a row of dominoes set up, you knock over the first one, and what will happen to the last one is the certainty that it will go over very quickly. So you could have a beginning of disintegration that would have the most profound influences." [1]

The metaphor of dominoes is borrowed from the laws of physics, and that of the hit list from the laws of the Mafia and the criminal underworld; unfortunately, neither dominoes nor hit list have much to do with the laws of international politics in Central America. And

---

[1] From a presidential press conference, April 7, 1954. Cited in Walter LaFeber *America in the Cold War: Twenty Years of Revolution and Response, 1947–1967* (New York, 1969), p. 96.

underlying current U.S. policy there may be several political misconceptions that find expression in irrelevant metaphors.[2]

One misconception is that of a Central America politically activated by external forces, identified with Cuba and the U.S.S.R. (In Indochina, in Washington's view, forces in South Vietnam were set into motion by North Vietnam; Vietnam as a whole was a pawn of Communist China; and manipulating China—until the Sino-Soviet break rendered such a connection absurd—was the U.S.S.R.) In Part Four, above, we have seen critics question the accuracy of that assumption as applied in Washington's White Paper on "Communist Interference in El Salvador." In the following material, the social and political complexities of some of the individual Central American "dominoes" are examined to reveal how internal pressures generate revolutionary situations. As recently elected French Socialist President François Mitterrand said in an interview, "The people of the region want to put an end to the oligarchies that, backed by bloody dictatorships, exploit them and crush them under intolerable conditions." Commenting that he had "serious reservations" about U.S. policy in Central America, Mitterrand asked, "How is it posssible not to understand this popular revolution?"[3]

A second misconception relates to the source of the external force that activates the dominoes or draws up the hit list, sometimes referred to as "communism" but more concretely as the U.S.S.R. or its Cuban "proxy." Judging by published scholarly and political analyses, there is considerable debate within the Soviet establishment on defining social formations in Latin America, on the nature of revolutionary movements there, and on the extent to which Moscow should

---

[2] Falling dominoes may be an appropriate figure of speech for describing military conquests from region to contiguous region, as areas fell to German armies in Europe and Japanese armies in Asia during WW II. Transferred to Central America, the domino theory in this sense would reflect Washington's fear that revolutionary Nicaragua, say, might send its armies into Honduras to assist armed struggle in that country. A second reading of a domino theory, one with considerable merit, focuses on the power of political/ideological inspiration and emulation. Clearly, the Sandinista rebels in Nicaragua were animated by the original victory of the Cuban revolution; the Salvadoran rebels are fortified by the success of the Sandinistas, and so on—revolutionary movements freely borrow the symbols, the language and the hopes of other revolutions. But revolutionary situations are never exactly alike; they are not, in other words, uniform entities that might be called dominoes. Michael Harrington employs the domino concept in a novel way in Reading 46, below.

[3] Interview in Le Monde, July 2, 1981; cited in The New York Times, July 2, 1981.

support this or that tendency.[4] Judging by actual policy, there is no evidence of some coordinated plan, much less of some strategy for "takeover." Soviet policy in Latin America as a whole has ranged from active support for a revolutionary regime—Cuba's, *after* that regime was in place; to indifference to the fate of a Marxist government—the Allende coalition in Chile; to consolidating friendly commercial and other ties with an anti-communist dictatorship—the present Argentine junta. There is no pattern here save that of a great power engaged in an active global competition with the U.S., seeking opportunities for trade and influence, and occasionally covering its actions with revolutionary rhetoric. As for the Cuban "proxy," its Latin American strategies have fluctuated considerably over the years, reflecting internal problems in Cuba as well as evolving, perhaps even maturing, perceptions of hemispheric realities. The Havana that once preached militant resistance to U.S. imperialism, now advises the Sandinista rebels in power in Nicaragua to practice caution and pragmatism in domestic and foreign affairs.[5]

A third misconception is illustrated in Ambassador Kirkpatrick's formulation, quoted above, that a revolutionary regime in Latin America is by definition an "advanced Soviet base" threatening U.S. security. This misconception recapitulates and crystallizes several related assumptions—that regimes brought to power by popular movements are simply passive agents for Soviet geopolitical intentions; that Soviet capacities for influencing such regimes are absolute; and, most peculiar of all, that the U.S. has no choice but to resist those popular movements. We say peculiar because it is an assumption underrating the number of choices available to the U.S. beyond support for tyrants and juntas, and because the assumption skimps on the power of the U.S. to affect the revolutionary course without antagonizing the revolution. The Soviet Union has discovered that allies, even some on its borders, have minds of their own—China broke away altogether, Yugoslavia has kept its distance, and the Poles are now working on another variant of independence within the Soviet bloc. For geographic, economic, political, and cultural reasons the U.S.S.R.'s impact on Latin America is bound to be even less, much less, than on other zones of the world. By contrast, and for the same

---

[4] See Jerry F. Hough, "The Evolving Soviet Debate on Latin America," *Latin American Research Review*, Vol. XVI, No. 1, 1981, pp. 124–43.

[5] Castro now even looks favorably on the role of Social-Democratic parties, once denounced as "revisionist," in popular opposition movements throughout Latin America. See Reading 51, below.

reasons, the U.S. impact on Latin America has been and will continue to be immense. The Readings that follow suggest the dangers
and dynamics of social change in Central America, and the problems
they pose to U.S. policy. The problems are great, but so are the
opportunities—not for countering hit lists and falling dominoes, but
for assisting the people of Nicaragua, Guatemala, Honduras and El
Salvador in their struggle to end political terror, build civil peace, and
establish economic and social justice.

45. Freedom and Unfreedom in Nicaragua *

By Shirley Christian

Shirley Christian went to Nicaragua and reported on a new, less euphoric stage in the development of the Sandinista revolution, a stage filled with contradictions that confound all attempts at classification. Christian, a Latin American correspondent for the Miami Herald, *won the Pulitzer Prize for Central American coverage in 1980.*

MANAGUA. Not too long ago, hundreds of women in frayed dresses and aprons, many of them toting children, stormed the glass doors of the government headquarters here. At first, those inside the small, modern building locked the doors and tried to ignore the shouting, placard-waving crowd. After a few hours, a delega-
tion was admitted, and Daniel Ortega, a former Sandinista guerrilla
who is now the "coordinator" of the governing junta, came down-
stairs to talk to the women. The conversation was not pleasant. The
women, sellers of beans, rice, and other basic foods in the city's de-
lapidated Eastern Market, claimed that for political reasons they had
been denied stalls in recently opened new markets and that the government now was trying to drive them out of business at the old
market by cutting off the bus routes. They complained of being
called *somocistas* and thieves by government bureaucrats and of
being pressured to join the Sandinistas' neighborhood committees.

* The New Republic, Vol. 185, No. 3, July 18, 1981, pp. 15–20.

Finally, they said, word had reached them that Ortega had referred to them as "scum." None of this was pleasing to women who said they had been among the earliest supporters of the Sandinista cause. The meeting ended when Ortega stormed off after a dispute about whether a photographer from the opposition newspaper *La Prensa* should be allowed to take pictures. "If you like *La Prensa*, then take your problems to *La Prensa* to resolve," he said.

But Ortega, a 35-year-old high school dropout who still dresses in the olive fatigues of his guerrilla days and wears a handgun on his hip, ended up facing the women twice more, on television. In a tone alternately pleading and frustrated, he denied the government had used politics in assigning new market stalls and said the problem was that the women had been afraid to try the new sites. Finally he committed the government to keeping the Eastern Market open and to improving the facilities there. As for the "scum" charge, he first denied using the term, then changed his mind and said maybe he had. In case he had, he was now taking it back. That was his privilege, he said.

This episode may not appear important in the greater scheme of things, but it says a great deal about how things function in Nicaragua two years after the Sandinista National Liberation Front, backed by a popular insurrection, ended the 45-year reign of the Somoza family and its National Guard. It demonstrates that the Sandinistas are capable of making arbitrary, authoritarian decisions, then backing off from them. It demonstrates that the Sandinistas would like to control all of the press, but don't. It demonstrates that they wish everybody would line up behind their revolution, but don't force the issue. It demonstrates that the Sandinistas are willing to face the people and practice give-and-take on practical matters. Most of all, it demonstrates that Nicaraguans do not fear the Sandinistas, that people are willing to talk and fight back.

Nicaragua today is a country where East German troop carriers are a common sight, where an Aeroflot cargo plane lands every morning, carrying such items as AK-47 rifles for the growing Sandinista army, and where 5,000 or more Cubans are at work. It is a place where elections are an almost forbidden topic, where the vast majority of the top leadership is Marxist, and where the measure of patriotism is the degree of tongue-lashing an official can mete out to a visiting U.S. congressional delegation. It is also a country with many of the functional trappings of liberty: a press that operates in a free and aggressive manner, opposition political parties that generally speak their minds, and a church-going population that has been trekking in droves to a village where the Virgin Mary was reported sighted. And it is a country where those who want out can get out, but where it is a test of faith among the opposition to stay.

The government's foreign policy is "nonaligned," with the kind of alignments that term has come to signify: it disapproves of the Pinochet regime in Chile, but abstained in the U.N. vote condemning the Soviet Union for invading Afghanistan. It has developed excellent relations with the likes of Kampuchea and Libya, which recently provided a $100 million loan to Nicaragua, while verging on war with one of its neighbors, Honduras, and giving at least some sustenance to insurrection movements in Guatemala and El Salvador.

It adds up to a situation that provides justification to those who argue that Nicaragua is inevitably bound for totalitarianism and to those who argue that political and economic pluralism is alive and well. Both of these concepts are abstractions, however, and Nicaragua is not a place of abstractions. It is a place where what matters are human dealings, where people carry their individual ideas into face-to-face encounters, as did Daniel Ortega and the market women, and where what emerges is either accommodation or blows. In a region where *personalismo* is always a key factor in determining outcomes, Nicaragua is perhaps the country where personal dealings and personal ties matter the most. It has fewer than two and a half million people in a territory the size of Iowa. It is often said that one reason the Nicaraguan revolution has been occurring in a largely civilized manner is that every family has its own Sandinista commander, as it also has its own *somocista*, perhaps exiled now in Miami, or living quietly in Nicaragua.

Thus, Nicaraguans are threading their way through the maze caused by the juxtaposition of conflicting ideological abstractions as if it were business as usual, while the outside world ponders the great issues of where they are headed. Even the formal structure of the government is a maze. At the top are nine Sandinista *commandantes*, most of them in their early and mid-30s, who comprise the Directorate of the Sandinista National Liberation Front. Acting together, they constitute the executive power, but the Nine also have individual constituencies or ministerial empires that they largely control on their own. It has long been expected that the Front will evolve into a political party, and the opposition already calls it that, but the Sandinistas have taken no known steps so far in that direction, except for issuing membership cards to about 150 of the highest-ranking Sandinistas.

Below the Sandinista Directorate is the junta, recently reduced from five men to three. Its role is that of a sort of general manager, running the country on a day-to-day basis under guidelines laid down by the Sandinista Directorate. But in the crossover style typical of the Nicaraguan government today, Daniel Ortega, the junta member who dealt with the angry market women, is also one of the Nine and therefore the dominant member of the junta. A second junta member, writer and intellectual Sergio Ramírez, is a member of the Sandinista Front, though a civilian, and functions as Ortega's counselor. The third junta member, Rafael Córdova Rivas, is a member of the opposition Democratic Conservative party and provides one of the few remaining signs of formal pluralism in the government.

The reduction in the size of the junta was brought about by the resignation in late February of Arturo J. Cruz, another member of the Democratic Conservative party. Cruz, a former official of the Inter-American Development Bank who is highly regarded by the Sandinistas, had become the focal point in the struggle between the Marxists and the bourgeoisie, the one man with considerable government influence whose door was always open to those with complaints. His resignation was brought about by a combination of family pressures and a conviction on his part that it was better for the Sandinistas and the opposition to confront each other head to head instead of having him deflect things. Not wanting to lose his prestige and counsel, however, the Sandinistas made him ambassador to Washington. The fifth junta member, Moises Hassan, a civilian Sandinista, was removed for reasons of balance and named minister of construction.

Cruz and Córdova Rivas actually constituted the second generation of non-Marxists on the junta. They were selected after negotiations between opposition leaders and Sandinistas that followed the resignations in April 1980 of Alfonso Robelo and Violeta Chamorro. Robelo, a millionaire businessman and political leader who had helped mount business opposition to Somoza, quit the junta because he felt the Sandinistas were breaking their promise to establish a democratic process. Mrs. Chamorro, the widow of assassinated newspaper publisher Pedro Joaquín Chamorro, reportedly was having health problems, but she had sided with Robelo on the issues that led to his resignation.

Theoretically below the junta are the government ministers, but since the most important ministries are held by various members of the Nine, it is difficult to determine who responds to whom. Other ministers include three Roman Catholic priests and various civilians, among them the son of a former U.S. Marine from the occupying force of 50 years ago. Those from the Sandinista Directorate who are cabinet ministers are Tomás Borge, the Sandinista elder at 51, who is minister of interior, a post that includes state security; Humberto Ortega, Daniel's brother, who is minister of defense and army commander; Jaime Wheelock, the minister of agriculture and agrarian reform; and Henry Ruíz, minister of planning.

In addition to the Directorate, the junta, and the ministers, Nicaragua has a Council of State with quasi-legislative functions. Established by decree, it has been expanded twice and now has 52 members representing various elements in Nicaraguan society, ranging from the Sandinista Front and its mass organizations to the clergy, organized labor, private enterprise, and the political parties. However, when the council opened its second session on May 4, 1981, a dozen non-Marxist delegates stayed away to underscore their demand for an election timetable and guarantees of formal democracy. In theory the Council of State can initiate legislation, but in practice most of what it takes up seems to come from the junta or, unofficially, from the Directorate through the president of the state council, Carlos Núñez, another of the Nine.

On paper this system of Directorate, junta, ministries, and Council of State looks like a formula for tight control. Nine men, who to the casual observer look and act alike, constitute the executive power, then in their individual capacities control the organisms that are responsible to the general management, and even control the legislative body by a form of gerrymandering in assigning seats. Sometimes it all works that way; usually it doesn't. The thing to remember is that power emanates not from one man but from nine. As the *comman- dantes* distance themselves more and more from the bush life that once united them, they develop individual ways of working. Although remarkably adept at presenting a united face when necessary, the Sandinista Front comes from three guerrilla tendencies, which were the product of early dissension within the insurrection movement. These differences were bandaged over, not healed, to form the Front. The tendencies, however, represented different ways of fighting Somoza more than different ways of governing. So while the signs of the tendencies remain today, there are also signs of a reordering of the division into two camps that have to do with style of governing. One we might call the pragmatists, the other the ideologues.

In this division, the pragmatist camp, supposedly people who recognize the non-Marxist nature of the Nicaraguans and are willing to accommodate themselves to it, is made up of the Ortega brothers and Jaime Wheelock. In the U.S. context, these are the moderates, or the potential ones. Those who seem to put ideology first are Tomás Borge and his protégé, Bayardo Arce. Whether this breakdown results from genuine feelings or from the division of labor within the regime is an unanswered question.

Borge and Wheelock seem to represent the extremes among the Nine. While Wheelock looks for ways to keep private farmers and professionals in place and producing, Borge says if they don't like the way things are going they can leave any time. The only surviving founder of the Sandinista movement, Borge is the standup comic of the revolution, a man who tosses out rapid-fire one-liners about his friendships with Fidel Castro, the Libyans, and the PLO, and his disdain for Yankee imperialism. An example: "The North Americans say that if we'll behave ourselves they will loan us money again. But we intend to continue behaving badly." Wheelock, a self-critical intellectual who charms nearly everyone he meets, doesn't utter such things. He received his university education in Chile and lived in Western Europe before founding one of the branches of the guerrilla movement, the Proletarian tendency. He organized this splinter group after being thrown out of the Prolonged Popular War tendency by Borge. Many private-enterprise Nicaraguans, as well as some Sandinistas, have come to believe that Wheelock is not a Marxist. "Watch what we do, not what we say," he admonishes anyone trying to analyze the Sandinista Front.

The Sandinistas promised political democracy and a mixed economy before reaching power, and they supposedly committed themselves in a secret accord more than a year ago to establish a timetable leading to national elections. But Nicaraguan democrats take more encouragement from the divided nature of power in Nicaragua than from any signed document. In general, the state of relative freedom that exists today in Nicaragua reflects the ability of freedom's advocates to wheel and deal within a system that is more accurately described as a nine-headed authoritarian one than as a totalitarian one. In trying to assess whether the Nicaraguans are establishing totalitarian or democratic institutions, the first question is whether they are going to establish real institutions of any kind, or whether the country will just continue to operate as an interplay of personalities.

The judiciary, for example, was completely restaffed, but the new judges are the product of the same legal educational system that trained the old judges, and the laws that they enforce are still largely the ones they inherited. Like Somoza, the Sandinistas have shown a willingness to bend the legal system to their purposes. In December 1979, the Sandinistas created nine special tribunals of three people each to try thousands of former Somoza followers as war criminals. At least half the prisoners were members of the National Guard who had thought their records were clean and, as a result, had gone to Red Cross camps or stayed in their homes when other guardsmen fled to Honduras and Miami. The existing criminal code, under which there was no death penalty, was the basis for judging them. During the course of the trials, the International Commission of Jurists and the Inter-American Human Rights Committee sent delegations to Nicaragua and made reports critical of the trial process. The jurists' commission said many former National Guardsmen were being convicted of guilt by association rather than of actual crimes. In a private section, intended only for the Nicaraguan government, the commission criticized the lack of judicial experience of the tribunal members and the absence of normal legal processes, and alleged that the tribunals were not impartial. Some of the tribunal members were said to be relatives of people who had suffered at National Guard hands.

More criticism came from José Esteban González, head of the Nicaraguan Permanent Commission of Human Rights, an independent organization that was founded in the twilight of the Somoza regime and that gets some of its financial support from groups such as the World Council of Churches. González complained of the slowness of the process and charged that some prisoners were mistreated, that others had disappeared, and that some were in jail without justification. When the Sandinistas tired of listening to the man who had once defended them, they set up a rival human rights organization, denied him access to the jails, and finally arrested him and charged him with violation of state security. Conviction would have carried a maximum penalty of three years in jail, but González's friends talked to the right Sandinistas and the charges were dropped within a week.

In February of this year, justice officials brought the war crimes trials of the Somoza followers to an abrupt close. They said 6,310 people had been tried or investigated in the preceding 14 months. Of that number, they said, 4,331 people were now serving sentences ranging from one to 30 years. They said about 1,700 people had been freed, because they were found innocent, were pardoned, or had the charges dismissed. They said about 300 cases had appeals pending. No complete list was ever made public of the names of those arrested, pardoned, released, or sentenced.

Among the institutions whose condition gives clues to the state of freedom in Nicaragua is the beleaguered and divided, but surviving, Roman Catholic church. Many people think of the Nicaraguan revolution as the church's revolution, but two years after the triumph, most of the church hierarchy looks with skepticism on the process over which the Sandinistas are presiding. Archbishop Miguel Obando y Bravo has become one of the forces around which the opposition rallies. Although there is no indication that the existence of the church itself is threatened, the archbishop dislikes the practice of sending young Nicaraguans to Cuba for several months of schooling during their formative years. Information is scarce on this, but at least several hundred—and perhaps more than 1,000—Nicaraguan children have studied on Cuba's Isle of Youth. The archbishop also worries about plans to "reform" the educational system toward emphasis on the class struggle.

Another major institution, the press, is a mixed bag of regime-controlled organs, Sandinista sympathizers, and outright opposition. There are decrees that restrict news coverage of food shortages, politics, and armed clashes, but in practice these do not seem seriously to hamper the flow of information. All television is controlled by the Sandinistas and used accordingly. On July 7, for example, the director of the Sandinista television system banned Archbishop Obando y Bravo from Nicaraguan TV. The regime also controls two radio stations outright and influences several others through the adept placing of advertising and patronage. Opposition political parties can buy radio time, but they may find it being allotted at, say, six A.M. on Sundays. Only two stations of any significance can be considered to be either independent or of the opposition. Two other stations that were associated with the opposition but presented almost no news lost their transmitters to political violence in March, but one of them has been collecting money to rebuild.

The press in Nicaragua is synonymous with the Chamorro family, and they are print people. They are, in fact, a family newspaper monopoly, though hardly a monolith. Family members publish all three daily newspapers that appear in Nicaragua, with attitudes toward the Sandinistas that range from love to hate. It was the assassination of *La Prensa* publisher Pedro Joaquín Chamorro in January 1978 that provided the catalyst in uniting most Nicaraguans against Anastasio Somoza. Today *La Prensa* is flourishing under Pedro Joaquín Jr. and criticizing the Sandinistas at every turn. One brother of the martyred publisher and the majority of his employees left more than a year ago to found *El Nuevo Diario*, which gives what is termed "critical support" to the government. Younger son Carlos Fernando Chamorro is editor of the official Sandinista newspaper, *Barricada*. Both of the new papers make a practice of criticizing the bourgeoisie, the traditional political parties, private enterprise groups, Yankee imperialism, and, especially, *La Prensa*.

La Prensa, however, gives as well as it takes. The paper's style is traditionally flamboyant and combative. It was that way 50 years ago under the ancestors of today's Chamorros, and it is that way today. The 45 years of Somoza family rule were 45 years of Chamorro family opposition. The two years of Sandinista rule have entailed nearly two years of criticism from *La Prensa*. The paper uses its news pages to report the story or the angle the other media ignore. It uses its editorials and columns for strong commentary by the newspaper's staff, by outsiders such as the archbishop, and by diplomats and politicians from Latin American countries with undisputed democratic credentials, such as Venezuela and Costa Rica. *La Prensa's* cartoons often take digs at the Sandinistas.

At one point, Carlos Fernando Chamorro suggested in an editorial in *Barricada* that *La Prensa* had become so reactionary that it ought to close down. That is the last thing his brother has in mind. Pedro Joaquín Jr. likes to say that the truth lies in the press run. By that standard, Nicaraguan readers are unquestionably with *La Prensa*. Reliable estimates place *La Prensa's* paid circulation at 70,000 to 75,000, which is thought to be three or four times the paid circulation of *Barricada* and *El Nuevo Diario* combined.

The only concession the Sandinistas make to the usual idea of political liberty is the continued existence of a half-dozen non-Sandinista political parties, five of them in open opposition. One of them is the Nicaraguan Democratic movement of Alfonso Robelo. Robelo describes his party as social democratic, but it has been unsuccessful in efforts to join the Socialist International because of the SI's support for the Sandinista Front, which maintains observer status there. The other significant party is the Democratic Conservative party, descendant of what was traditionally the leading opposition to Somoza. There are also a Social Christian party, a social democratic group separate from Robelo's, and a splinter of Somoza's old Liberal party that began opposing him a number of years ago. In addition, there is the Popular Social Christian party, which gives partial support to the Sandinistas. Politicians are prohibited from declaring themselves candidates for office, but the parties are free to do other things, such as criticize the government, hold membership drives, and advertise on billboards. Almost any public event they attempt, however, produces some kind of clash with Sandinista police or members of the Sandinista youth movement. Robelo's party has suffered the most from these groups, being forced by mass violence to cancel two major rallies in the past year. The Democratic Conservatives have held several rallies on a smaller scale, proceeding despite some opposition from police officials on the spot.

What is alternately called a "dialogue" or "forum" is under way between the Sandinista Front and the five opposition parties, but it is given little chance of achieving anything. The Sandinistas and the five parties can't even agree about what they are negotiating. The parties want to talk about changing the domestic political environment and the Sandinistas want to convince the parties to join their campaign against alleged U.S. intervention in Nicaragua.

The wrinkle in this is that those campaigning for traditional political democracy and those who make up the leadership of private enterprise are essentially the same people. In the declining days of the Somoza dynasty, they learned to use economic power to achieve political ends. It was the joining of most of Nicaraguan private enterprise to the guerrilla battle that produced the potent mix of money and guns that Somoza's National Guard could not contain. Over the past two years, in dealings with the Sandinistas, Nicaragua's politicians and private enterprise people have again mixed their economic and political ends, calling for guarantees against confiscations at the same time that they demand elections and guarantees of free press and religious thought.

To realize the now discarded election promise of a year ago, the cotton growers hinted that they would not plant cotton, Nicaragua's leading export. The Sandinistas finally promised, and the farmers planted, but after the seeds had sprouted, the Sandinistas said there would be no elections before 1985 and hinted that the electoral system might be different from the traditional Western variety. Since then, however, the Sandinistas have gone out of their way to assure private farmers that their role in Nicaraguan life is secure and, to a lesser extent, have done the same with business and industry. Confiscations and the fear of them have virtually ended in agriculture, leaving private farmers in control of 80 percent of the country's production. Confiscations also are supposed to be over in industry but still occur intermittently.

It appears the Sandinistas are gambling that the private sector will be quiet about formal political liberty once it is obvious that pocketbooks are secure, though they never have given a clear explanation of why they don't want to put their popularity on the line in elections. At times they say it is a question of the lack of electoral infrastructure and tradition and the necessity to accomplish more important reconstruction tasks first. At other times they say "the people already voted" by supporting them against Somoza. It requires no sophisticated polling, however, to conclude that the majority of Nicaraguans are disillusioned today with the young men they swept into power and would vote against them if given the chance. The other argument against general elections, from the Sandinista standpoint, is that it would force their differences into the open once campaigning began.

The Sandinistas like to say that they did not fight for nearly 20 years to rid Nicaragua of one kind of foreign influence, the United States, only to turn it over to another, the Soviet bloc. At the same time, however, Tomás Borge is busy beefing up his state security operation with Cuban expertise, something he acknowledges by saying the Cubans know a lot about state security. Humberto Ortega is also using large numbers of Cubans in training an army and police force that already numbers at least 30,000 and is expected to grow to 50,000. The remainder of the Cubans in the country are primarily doctors and teachers working in isolated areas that lacked medical care and education before, plus some who work in the cultural ministry. In relative terms, the Cuban presence is strongest on the Atlantic coast, where the population is a mixture of indigenous tribes, English-speaking descendants of black West Indians, and people of Spanish descent. The reputedly strong Cuban presence at military posts in that area set off disturbances last October in the town of Bluefields in which several people died. In the succeeding months, dissatisfaction with the Sandinistas over a number of issues, including food distribution and governmental efforts to alter the communal pattern of land ownership, has caused about 3,000 indigenous people, primarily Miskito Indians, to flee across the border into Honduras.

The United States is trying to balance the Cuban influence and the less obvious Soviet presence with a large aid program, though a substantial portion of it was suspended recently by the Reagan administration. Among other Western governments, Venezuela and Mexico have a significant presence with their oil assistance. Mexico and Venezuela both theoretically want to serve as moderating influences on the Sandinistas, but in practice Mexico often seems to be giving them unreserved backing. For example, when the Reagan administration decided to withhold aid over the issue of arms supplies to Salvadoran guerrillas, Mexico quietly doubled the amount of its oil assistance. At the same time, Mexico maintains only superficial contacts with the internal opposition. By contrast, Venezuela, through an active ambassador with direct access to Venezuelan president Luis Herrera Campins, provides strong public support for Alfonso Robelo and other opposition figures, the church hierarchy, and *La Prensa*.

The U.S. embassy, though supporting the goals of the opposition in Nicaragua, often has played a mediating role by maintaining contact with some of the top Sandinistas, particularly Jaime Wheelock and the Ortega brothers, and non-Sandinistas who have served in the government. To a large extent, it has been the existence of the aid program that has kept the door to these people open for the United States. It is significant that when the first major crisis occurred in the government with the resignation of Alfonso Robelo from the junta more than a year ago, the Sandinistas, despite their anti-Yankee rhetoric, turned to the American ambassador, Lawrence A. Pezzullo, to open a line of communication to the opposition. When they might have chosen a Cuban, a Venezuelan, a Mexican, or even a Nicaraguan, they chose the ambassador from the United States.

46. The Good Domino *

By Michael Harrington

Michael Harrington is National Chair of the Democratic Socialist Organizing Committee, a successor organization to Norman Thomas's and Eugene Debs's old Socialist Party. He is also the North American member of the Socialist International Committee to Defend the Nicaraguan Revolution. Harrington recently traveled to Nicaragua as part of this committee

Harrington is the author of scores of books and articles, including Socialism; The Twilight of Capitalism; *and* The Vast Majority: A Journey to the World's Poor. *He is also author of* The Other America, *the book that helped trigger the 1960s' "war on poverty."*

His analysis suggests some possible outcomes of the current crisis and assesses the U.S. role.

THE Nicaraguan revolution may well be a paradigmatic event in Central America. Perhaps it is the *good domino.*

That is, of course, a reference to the *bad domino* theory of Ronald Reagan and Alexander Haig: that Nicaragua is the first phase in a Soviet and Cuban takeover of the entire region, which will then move to El Salvador.[1] "Consider the effect of the U.S. failure in Nicaragua to play a strong role in the transition from the detested regime of dictator Antastasio Somoza Debayle," writes the Reagan adviser W. Scott Thompson in the Summer, 1981, issue of *Foreign Policy.* "The fact that during 1979 El Salvador's insurgency rocketed from obscurity to full-scale fighting must be seen as related to events in Nicaragua." From El Salvador, this theory argues, the Soviet conspiracy will go on to take over Guatemala and Honduras and, finally, the greatest prize of all, Mexico.

This is analytic nonsense. It explains revolutions which rise out of

---

* Copyright 1981 by Michael Harrington. This essay was written expressly for this volume.

[1] See the Editors' Introduction to Part Five, above.——Eds.

indigenous conditions of repression and exploitation as if they were plots hatched in the Kremlin or Cuba. Worse, by ignoring the possibility that there may be democratic alternatives to the dictatorships of the right and left, Reaganism makes a self-fulfilling prophecy. For if the United States continues its support of the right in Central America, it can drive the Nicaraguan and Salvadoran revolutions toward the dictatorial, "Marxist-Leninist" "left." I use all of these quotation marks simply to signify that terms like "Marxist-Leninist" and "left" can be used to express the most varied contents and that if such dictatorships are indeed established in this region, in considerable measure because of American policy, that will certainly be a defeat for freedom and democracy but not necessarily a victory of Soviet conspirators.

The London *Economist* understands at least part of my point for utterly conservative reasons. "Nicaragua may not yet be lost," it editorialized in June 1981 ("lost" by Somoza, the United States—or by democracy?). "The continued existence of a large private sector shows that the Sandinistas are still in a dither about their revolution. The United States could yet follow Mexico's sound advice to stick a fistful of dollars through a door that remains even a quarter open." That is said in the traditional tone of *The Economist* when it speaks of the Third World: a contemptuous colonialism, Colonel Blimp for sophisticates. And yet there is a sense of the complexity of the situation which is so much greater than anything found in Washington.

Even *The Wall Street Journal*, which editorially has been acting as a house organ for Ronald Reagan since his election, is worried that "a combative U.S. stance could alienate Nicaragua and drive it toward the very nations the U.S. wants it to avoid. . . . If relations should break down, the administration could lose all hope of influencing events in Nicaragua, thereby thwarting its goal of cutting into Cuba's influence in Central America. (The quotations are from an editorial page article by Gerald Seib, a foreign affairs specialist in the *Journal's* Washington Bureau.)

But I do not want to remain at the level of *The Economist's* shrewd multinational corporationism or *Wall Street Journal Realpolitik*. Rather, I propose to explore a radical possibility: that Nicaragua is indeed a domino, but a good domino, a new model of a democratic alternative to the American-backed dictatorships of Central America, the image of a possible future, not only for El Salvador, but for Guatemala and Honduras as well. But it should be carefully noted that I am talking about a *possibility*. For, as my analysis will show, there are immense forces at work, built into the very structure of the world economy, which militate against that outcome. There-

fore a rightist victory is possible, only it would not provide the relatively stable fascism of the Somoza years (or of Guatemala since the
American inspired coup of 1954) but rather the institutionalization
of a civil war. And "left" dictatorship is possible, too, but not on the
relatively stable Cuban model since it is unlikely that the Soviet
Union would provide the massive, and ongoing, subsidies it has given
to Castro.

I am talking, then, about one *possibility*—but, I trust one has
noted—the *only* progressive possibility. My attitudes were not determined, but were most certainly given an emotional coloration, by a
very brief visit to Nicaragua as a member of the Socialist International Committee to Defend the Nicaraguan Revolution in June,
1981. Several days hardly gives one first-hand knowledge of a complex
revolution; but it does give one an impression of it. Moreover, I had
the opportunity to participate in a closed, frank meeting with the
Political Committee of the Frente Sandinista, to talk to various
members of the Council of State, to wander freely around Managua
and to spend time with revolutionists in provincial centers. I am
excruciatingly aware of the dangers to the Nicaraguan project of a
democratic and pluralist restructuring of the society, and some of
them could come from within (both on the right and left), as well as
from without. But I must confess to have been deeply moved by the
sincerity and passion of those with whom I talked. We made a completely unscheduled and accidental visit to what turned out to be the
blessing of a neighborhood center in León by the bishop. The
bronzed, lined and sometimes toothless faces of men and women
filled with evident hope had not been conjured up in Moscow or
Havana.

To begin with, there is an enormous economic limitation facing
the people of Nicaragua because this is a dependent country in the
world capitalist economy.

It is not just that the civil war destroyed half a billion dollars worth
of industrial and social infrastructure, pushing living standards back
to 1962 levels and raising unemployment to 25%. And it is not even
mainly a consequence of the fact that the Somocistas looted the
country during more than forty years of dictatorship and particularly
during their last days in power, transferring a good portion of the
national patrimony to banks in Miami and elsewhere. Even if those
intolerable conditions did not exist, Nicaragua would be in deep trouble. They do exist, which makes the creation of a new model of
political and economic development even more difficult.

The interest on the Somocista thefts has been postponed. Even so,
the Sandinista economists told us in Managua, the service on the

foreign debt requires 9% of the gross national product and 43% of the income from exports. If one then adds to that 43% figure the cost of oil imports—in a society which has long had enormous potential for geothermal energy—then the debt/oil total comes to 90% of the projected export income for 1981. These difficulties are exacerbated by some other trends. The increase in production is taking place more in the sphere of domestic consumer goods and services than in the export sector. The private sector, which is still dominant, is not meeting its investment targets, while the public sector is overfulfilling its goals; and the commitment of the revolution to raise the living standards of the masses places further burdens on the import system.

All of these tendencies remind one, in a chilling way, of the brilliant analysis of the Chilean Revolution and *coup d'état* made by the French economist, Serge-Christophe Kolm, in *La Transition socialiste* (Paris, 1977). There was in that case, Kolm suggests, a contradiction between the policy of egalitarianism in consumption and continued market domination (or rather, corporate—and multinational corporate—domination) of production. The Chilean economy had not been designed to produce consumer goods for the masses; it was set up to minister to a class society. Therefore, when Allende decreed a doubling of the income of the poorest workers along with price controls, it was impossible to meet the resultant demand from within the system. Goods were brought in to meet needs, which further worsened the international economic position of Chile at a time when the Nixon administration was working for counterrevolution by means of an international financial blockade. Eventually, these and other pressures saw the real living standard of the people decline even before the fascist coup.

In the case of Nicaragua all of this was made even more difficult by the American refusal to come through with credits for basic food needs (that increased the importation of consumer goods by almost 10%). All of this took place when there was a sharp downturn in the terms of trade for almost all of the poor countries. In Nicaragua, that meant that in 1980 exports fell from a historic level of $650 million to $450 million—just when they were more desperately needed than ever before. The result, as the Sandinistas themselves stress, is that if import capacity declines along with production and the deficit increases, then inflation will reach the 1980 level of 27% in 1981. "This translates into a deterioration of the real wages of the workers, even though there are planned increases in pay for the low-income sectors of 20%."

These are the impossible conditions under which the revolution labors to remain democratic and pluralist. In all of our conversations with the Sandinista leaders in 1981, the formula "mixed economy, democracy and pluralism" came up again and again. There are, I suspect, a number of reasons for this policy. First, it is now clear that the Cuban model will only "work" in an economic sense with Soviet subsidies (and "payments" to Moscow in the form of troops for Soviet purposes and political backing for repression in Afghanistan and Poland). Secondly, there are at least some signs that Fidel Castro realized this fact and advised the Sandinistas to avoid his own errors. Thirdly, the revolution was incredibly broad, included significant elements from business and the church, and quite consciously sought to be "generous" after the victory. Finally, there are international pressures, not only from a hostile United States, but even from countries sympathetic to Nicaragua, like Mexico and France under Mitterrand, to maintain a pluralist society.

All of this, however, puts the Nicaraguans in an extremely difficult position. A kind of "dual power" exists in the country: a leftist government and a conservative—and massive—private sector. This is compounded by the fact that the Sandinistas have found it difficult, or even impossible, to control the flow of funds in and out of Nicaragua. Economic autarchy is not a plausible alternative; but economic openness is fraught with risks. That problem is political, too. For some time now, there are important elements within the private sector attacking the regime as "Stalinist"—in open television debates, in press conferences, *i.e.*, in actions which are totally unthinkable in a genuinely Stalinist society. In June, 1981, one of those press conferences came very close to declaring that life had been better under the Somoza dictatorship.

It is, of course, impossible to define where political opposition to the government merges into a counterrevolutionary willingness to join with the exiled Somocistas (and their American supporters) in a military action to overthrow the Sandinistas. In democratic theory—but not in the U.S. Supreme Court decisions of the McCarthy era—there is a necessary distinction between the *advocacy* of violent overthrow and the *action* of violent overthrow. It was clear at the time, and is even clearer now, that the American Communist Party of the late forties and early fifties was utterly incapable of insurrection if it contemplated such a course (and there is no evidence that it did). It was, in fact, punished under the Smith Act for advocating the teaching of the desirability of overthrowing the government at some future date, which was McCarthyite law. But in Nicaragua the situation is different.

There, it is not at all to be excluded that the agents of violent overthrow are using democratic freedoms to prepare their conspiracy.

This is where the United States could play an enormously progressive role if, but only if, it completely reverses the Reagan policy. If this country made it emphatically clear that it will not support any armed attempt to overthrow the revolutionary government, that would work to decrease those tensions in Nicaragua which provide the impetus for curtailing existing freedoms. Up until now, the United States, for all of its insistence on the rights of a free press and of opposition in Managua, has done more to threaten those institutions than Fidel Castro and Leonid Brezhnev.

More broadly, this raises the point which Willy Brandt [2] and the Socialist International have insisted upon, in Central America and elsewhere. Brandt and the SI are giving political support to the Sandinistas. François Mitterrand, a vice-president of the SI, reiterated that point shortly after he was inaugurated as President of France. But in addition to this political support, Brandt and the SI have a vision of a program to create the economic conditions for democratic change in the world. In the report of his international commission on North-South relations—a commission which included liberals like *Washington Post* publisher Katherine Graham of the United States and conservatives like Edward Heath, the former Tory Prime Minister of the United Kingdom—Brandt stressed the benefits which would flow, not simply to the poor, but also to the affluent, from an international campaign for justice in the Third World.[3] If there were a vast transfer of wealth from the advanced to the developing societies—if those economic constraints which straitjacket the Nicaraguan revolution were removed—where would that money be spent? Much of it would return to the donors as the recipients bought the technology for their own economic growth. That happened in the case of the Marshall Plan: the United States "made money" on its generosity and its Cold War politics. Why not, Brandt is arguing, repeat that positive-sum game, but this time do it for the Third World?

Thus far, however, Reagan has been maneuvering to use any development funds in Central America and the Caribbean for blatantly political purposes, *i.e.*, for strengthening the Seaga government in Jamaica (which took over from a socialist administration under Michael Manley that faced many of the problems now confronting the Nicaraguans—like an intolerable balance of payments situation—and which may well have been deliberately destabilized by the

---

[2] Former West German Chancellor, presently head of the German Social-Democratic Party and of the Socialist International.—Eds.

[3] *North-South*, familiarly known as the "Brandt Report" (Cambridge, Mass., 1980).—Eds.

United States in a "Chilean" tactic). It is possible that Seaga will receive certain rewards for reducing his nation to a client of Washington (when I interviewed him in 1979, that was what he was proposing as far as I am concerned). Jamaica could become Washington's satellite. But that is not merely an outrageous form of neo-colonialism; it is also unworkable on any large scale in Central America and the Caribbean.

That fact was brought home in an excellent report made by Ed Broadbent, the leader of the Canadian New Democratic Party and a vice-president of the SI, when he completed a tour of Central America in May-June of 1981.[4] Broadbent wrote: "Central America as a whole in the post-war period, and specially in the 1970s, has not been a region characterized by the development of economic justice and the expansion of political liberty. Exactly the opposite process has been the rule in most countries, as the tragic recent events in El Salvador illustrate. In the coming decade, the key foreign player in the region, the United States, must recognize serious forces for change are now underway.

"The plain fact," Broadbent continued, "is that intense social conflict arising out of maldistribution of wealth and power is likely to have one of three possible results in the 1980s: The result can be a radically changed regime of a moderate left type, more or less evolving democratically, with a mixed private and public sector economy, and which will likely be neutral to the U.S. and non-aligned with other power blocs. The result can be a regime which is radically Marxist-Leninist, undemocratic, state-dominated, hostile to the U.S. and aligned with the Communist world. The result can also be the emergence of a repressive military oligarchy, where social change is held in check by brute force which will violate every notion of human rights to maintain the status quo. Such a regime, as long as it inflicts enough terror, may well be friendly to the U.S., but just the opposite to its own population."

And, of particular importance, Broadbent concluded, "It is my belief that there is no likely fourth tendency in the region. Specifically, I mean that the post-war models of Venezuela and Costa Rica are not now likely to be repeated. The forces of social change have been repressed too long for this type of moderate government to be seen by those affected as desirable models."

I think that is accurate. I call that first choice the "good domino," which is a possibility in Nicaragua today and, if it were to succeed, could become a model for a free El Salvador, Guatemala and Hon-

---

[4] Unpublished report to the Socialist International, 1981.

duras tomorrow. The third choice is the one which the United States under Reagan favors—and the second choice is likely to be the outcome it will produce. I therefore think that it is profoundly in the national interest of the United States—the genuine national interest of the United States—that the Sandinista revolution accomplish its work as it wants to do, that it not be driven to either the second or the third choice.

But finally, I do not want to end with a theoretical judgment. In those several days in Nicaragua I met a good number of people. I am sophisticated enough to know that revolutionary tourists often come back starry-eyed, having seen what they are supposed to see. And yet, talking to a young woman, the Sandinista political leader in the city of León, and hearing her story—how the daughter of a Somoza functionary became a guerrilla through participation in the student Catholic movement, was imprisoned for eighteen months, including a long stretch of solitary in a "tiger cage" kind of cell—and then watching her participating in the religious ceremony at the neighborhood center, singing the hymn, making the sign of the cross, at ease but respectful toward the bishop: after these things I felt that there was and is something decent and good struggling to be born in this land and that my country is shamefully working against it. I believe in my theories; I also believe in that emotional judgment.

47. Guatemala: The Coming Danger *

BY MARLISE SIMONS

Marlise Simons is a Mexico-based journalist who reports on Latin American affairs for The Washington Post *and other publications.*

The real test of the Reagan administration's Central America policy will come in Guatemala, not El Salvador. The reason is simple: In El Salvador the administration has been able to disguise its raw anticommunism by pointing to the ruling junta's commitment to democracy and social reform.

In Guatemala, terror is institutionalized. The right-wing death squads responsible for more than 3,000 murders last year are directed from the office of President Romeo Lucas García himself, according

* Foreign Policy, no. 43, Summer 1981.

to Amnesty International.[1] The repression has ignited a civil war, and there is little pretense that any political middle ground exists.

The notion, developed by U.S. Ambassador to the United Nations Jeane Kirkpatrick, that "moderately repressive" allies deserve U.S. support faces a severe test in Guatemala. How far is Washington willing to back a military dictatorship that adamantly opposes reform and is committed, in the name of "fighting communism," to a policy of political assassination?

The Reagan administration indicated in May 1981 that it was inclined to provide military aid to Guatemala. But even months after Secretary of State Alexander Haig, Jr., declared Guatemala the next nation after El Salvador on the "hit list" of Soviet expansionism, the administration still had no coherent Guatemala policy. In many ways Guatamala is more important than El Salvador or any other Central American nation. With 6.9 million people, it has the largest population and economy in the region; it borders on four countries, including Mexico and its vital oil fields. Direct U.S. investment of $221 million—double the amount in El Salvador—is the highest in the region. In the past 25 years, the United States has played a far more important role in Guatemala than anywhere else in Central America.

Whereas the Reagan administration cites outside agitation as the chief cause of the Salvadoran conflict, such claims will be far more difficult to support here. When analyzing the Guatemalan civil war, the history of U.S. policy and of indigenous reform movements is impossible to discount.

The most important U.S. interference in Guatemalan politics occurred in 1954, when the Central Intelligence Agency engineered the overthrow of Guatemala's reform-minded president, Colonel Jacobo Arbenz. A former defense minister, Arbenz had taken office peacefully and punctually, the first president to do so in more than a century. His labor and land reforms were tepid by the standards of what the United States recommended in El Salvador last year. However, when Arbenz began legal proceedings to expropriate 178,000 acres owned by United Fruit Company, offering to pay the company's own book value of the land as compensation, the company skillfully converted a business dispute into an ideological conflict. The U.S. government and media presented Arbenz's reforms not as populist attempts to move Guatemala from feudalism to modern capitalism, but as militant communism.

The coup, which cost the United States less than $10 million,

---

[1] See the Amnesty International report *Guatemala: A Government Program of Political Murder* (New York, 1981).—Eds.

marked the return of the Big Stick policy toward Latin America that Franklin D. Roosevelt had abandoned 20 years earlier. It also became a model for U.S. response to revolutionary change in Latin America. The language, arguments, and techniques of the Arbenz episode were used in Cuba in the early 1960s, in Brazil in 1964, in the Dominican Republic in 1965, and in Chile in 1973.

In Guatemala itself, the coup cut short the beginning of a natural process of modernization. Since 1954 the U.S. government and Guatemala's ultraconservative landed gentry and its military allies have time and time again spurned opportunities for peaceful change.

No sooner had Arbenz been overthrown than his CIA-picked successor, Carlos Castillo Armas, dismantled the budding labor movement, the literacy campaign, the peasant cooperatives, and revoked all land reform measures. This aggravated the overcrowding of the several million Indians living on tiny plots on the highland plateaus. Anticommunism became the ruling norm, and it still is today.

After the 1959 Cuban revolution, conditions seemed ripe for guerrilla warfare in Guatemala too. Led by dissident army officers, several guerrilla groups appeared in the early 1960s in the eastern region of the country. Guatemalan ruling groups again looked to Washington for help. In 1966 the United States responded with large numbers of military advisers, weapons, and Green Berets to stop the guerrillas. Guerrilla attacks resulted in the deaths of a U.S. and a West German ambassador, and two U.S. military attachés. The counter-insurgency program escalated into "indiscriminate terror," according to a 1980 State Department study. "To eliminate a few hundred guerrillas," the report concluded, "the government killed perhaps 10,000 Guatemalan peasants."

The elections of 1974 marked another lost opportunity and a new turning point. The liberals and leftists who wanted change, not bloodshed, supported a reformist coalition. To accommodate the military, they chose an army officer, the moderately progressive General Efraín Ríos Montt, as their presidential candidate. However, then-President Carlos Arana Osorio decided that the general he favored had to win. The election results were held up just long enough for the military to fix the ballots. U.S. diplomats admitted an "embarrassing" and "counterproductive" fraud had taken place, and several urged Washington to protest. As in El Salvador two years earlier, where a similar reformist coalition had been cheated of victory, Washington did not raise its voice. In both countries, the blatant fraud convinced many young people, who saw all political doors closed, to go underground.

As Guatemala prepares for elections in March 1982, revolution is brewing once more. Almost every day there are guerrilla actions: an ambush of an army convoy, an attack on a police station, or a take-over of a village to hold political meetings and kill army informants. As in the 1960s, right-wing death lists are circulating, and mysteriously named murder squads have reappeared.

Wiped out completely a decade ago, the left-wing guerrillas have been able to return because of three factors: the radicalization of the Roman Catholic church, the ability of the guerrillas to mobilize the Indians for the first time, and the inevitable demonstration effect of events elsewhere in Central America.

In contrast to the defeated guerrillas of the 1960s, the Guatemalan leftists in the 1970s decided no revolution would be possible without the participation of the country's Indians, who make up 53 percent of the population. Descendants of the Mayans, the Indians have protected one of the oldest and most coherent cultures in the Americas by rejecting the values of the society imposed by the Spanish conquest. Their tight social organization also protects them against Guatemala's pervasive racism. Divided into 18 language groups, the Indians follow a conservative, contemplative, and deeply religious life-style. Despite years of political pressure, they had always remained aloof from right and left.

Undismayed by the challenge, young members of the Guerrilla Army of the Poor (EGP) moved into the El Quiché area in 1975, learned Indian languages, gave the people legal and marketing advice, became involved in cooperatives, and slowly gained their confidence. Catholic priests, many of them foreigners, served effectively as a bridge between the guerrillas and the Indian population by raising the Indians' consciousness and eventually endorsing—thereby legitimating—the revolutionary path.

These efforts found strong popular support. The Kakchikel, Kekchi, and Quiché peoples have long resented "the army of the whites," which forcibly recruits Indian boys. The Guatemalan military has also made a policy of seizing Indian land on behalf of the powerful, particularly in a new oil, nickel, and forestry development area known as the Transversal Zone. The army has also kidnapped, tortured, and killed local leaders, often entire families, in its hunt for subversives.

In the 1970s, the living conditions of the impoverished Indians worsened. Population growth put more pressure on the short supply of land, services, and employment. Illiteracy remained at more than 60 percent. Light industry and tourism created a boom in Guatemala City. But every year half a million Indians in the countryside are forced to migrate to the cotton, sugar, and coffee plantations along the Pacific coast, where they often work for less than the minimum wage of $3.20 a day.

Official terror and desperation have pushed many Indians to cooperate with the guerrillas or actually to join their ranks. Of the four armed leftist groups in Guatemala, the EGP and the Organization of People in Arms have the largest Indian following. Although they are kept small for tactical reasons, these groups can now draw on a vast, invisible support network on a terrain that the Indians know intimately and the army does not.

If the Indians are a key to possible change in Guatemala, the military is the key to the status quo. The military's strategy for preserving power is to terrify the villagers and to put the guerrillas in a moral bind by punishing innocent civilians for guerrilla actions. Frequently, after guerrillas have ambushed a military convoy or taken a village for a political meeting, the army or one of the death squads retaliates by raiding the town. They leave maimed bodies lying in public to underline their warning. If at all reported in the press, these raids are described usually as an armed clash between the army and subversives.

Increasingly, the army feels that it stands alone in the way of revolution. Encouraged by U.S. military support and equipment and dissatisfied with the role of protecting other people's fortunes, the military began to acquire its own wealth in the early 1970s. Modeling themselves after Brazil's powerful military, the officers decided to build economic muscle to increase their independence. The 14,000-man Guatemalan armed forces now own a bank, an investment fund, and have launched industrial projects. Top military leaders own vast stretches of land. They earn extra income selling protection to the large landowners. As in El Salvador, much of the high command is U.S.-trained. Between 1950 and 1977, according to Pentagon statistics, 3,334 Guatemalan officers attended U.S. military academies.

Three years ago, Guatemala rejected U.S. military aid to protest Carter's human rights criticism. Since then, Guatemala has spent more than $89 million on military purchases, mainly in Israel and Argentina.

Guatemala had seemed the sort of country where the Carter administration human rights program might have had some impact. Between 1974 and 1978, fraudulently elected President Kjell Laugerud García proved surprisingly tolerant of the newly emerging trade union and Indian cooperative movements. And there were hopes that his successor, Lucas, and his social democrat civilian running mate, Francisco Villagrán Kramer, would insure continuation of the *apertura* or political opening.

Relations, however, between Guatemala and Washington deteriorated sharply within months of the Lucas takeover. Lucas believed that Washington's policies in Nicaragua and El Salvador were destabilizing the entire region and encouraging the extreme left. As the

Sandinistas gained strength in Nicaragua, the army command decided to end the *apertura* and demobilize the opposition. In its siege mentality, the right began identifying all non-rightists—teachers, union leaders, students, priests, journalists, Christian Democrats, and social democrats—as communist threats. Within two years, repression had become so extreme that even Vice-President Villagrán resigned and fled the country.

The United States was snubbed. The Carter administration's human rights representations were totally ignored. High-ranking State Department envoys to Guatemala were refused audiences with the president, while the local press taunted them as "moderate Marxists." When Washington decided in 1980 to replace meek Ambassador Frank V. Ortiz, Jr., with a more assertive career diplomat, George Landau, it was met with defiance. Guatemala refused to accept Landau. For the past year, the fortress-like U.S. embassy in Guatemala City has been without an ambassador.

Although U.S. officials now hope that a political solution can be shaped around the March 1982 elections, it is difficult to imagine how Guatemala's political direction could change sufficiently in the coming months to make elections remotely credible. The far left abandoned elections as a political tool after the 1974 fraud. The murders of union and peasant leaders have forced popular organizations to go underground, if not to take up arms, at least to provide support for the armed guerrilla forces.

Two of the country's most respected and popular opposition leaders have been murdered by the rightist death squads, which enjoy official protection. Former Foreign Minister Alberto Fuentes Mohr, head of a socialist party, was assassinated in early 1979. Manuel Colom Argueta, the popular former mayor of Guatemala City, was shot to death six days after his left-of-center party had been granted registration with the government.

The left-of-center and centrist groups that have survived the assassination campaign find it impossible to operate publicly. Even the Christian Democrats, whose Salvadoran colleagues are allied with the right-wing military there, feel terrorized in Guatemala. Since last summer, 76 party leaders have been murdered, seven of them in one day. The Christian Democrats are threatening to boycott the elections unless the repression eases.

The Reagan administration has quietly started to encourage Christian Democratic leader Vinicio Cerezo to run party candidates next March. Yet Cerezo himself receives frequent death threats and has narrowly escaped three assassination attempts in recent months. And by early May, Washington had done nothing to help create conditions that would make Christian Democratic participation more than an act of political—and actual—suicide.

With the political center virtually extinct, the elections are very likely to be another squabble for power among the rightists. Besides Lucas, two men count in the jockeying for the presidency. One is former Vice-President Mario Sandoval Alarcón, head of the fiercely rightist National Liberation Movement (MLN), who has already announced his candidacy. The MLN calls itself the "party of organized violence" and claims to maintain a 3,000-man paramilitary force. Its party headquarters are painted with images of the sword and the cross, the symbols of the warrior monks of the Middle Ages. Representing Guatemala's powerful land-owning classes, the MLN is perhaps closest to the European fascist parties. Sandoval himself has expressed great admiration for Spain's fascist Falange and Chile's neofascist organization, Patria y Libertad.

Sandoval's primary rival is Arana, who cannot become president again, but is expected to offer his own candidate. As tough as Sandoval, Arana earned the nickname "the Jackal" for his fierce repression of the left. Architect of the economic boom of the past decade, he has a strong following among the military and the conservative but more modern business community, which does not like to be identified with the fanaticism of the MLN.

Although both groups have supported and encouraged repression, they are being hurt by the current instability. Investment has slowed dramatically, and capital flight has been such that the government was forced to impose exchange controls a year ago. Although the nation's reserves stood at $741 million at the end of 1978, better interest rates abroad and political panic at home brought them down to $444 million at the end of 1980. Scared by the left's assassination of government officials and members of their own community, many businessmen have begun to use heavy security for themselves and their property.

The Guatemalan establishment overestimated how willing the Reagan administration would be to provide support once it took office. Reagan's nomination last summer had encouraged Guatemalan hostility toward the Carter administration on both official and private levels. Ultraconservative Guatemalan groups made early contact with the Reagan camp and persuaded hard-line congressmen, retired U.S. military officers, and academics to visit Guatemala City. The visitors, in turn, reassured their Guatemalan hosts that U.S. policies in Central America would be radically different under a Reagan presidency. Members of a conservative group called Amigos Del País—represented at the time by the public relations firm of Michael Deaver, now assistant to the president and deputy chief of staff—even boasted that Guatemalan businessmen had made substantial contributions to the Reagan campaign.

Visibly cheered by Reagan's El Salvador policy, the military in Guatemala hoped for similar aid. The government even came up with purported guerrilla documents proving Cuban arms shipments in the hope of panicking Washington. All of this failed to trigger any immediate U.S. policy commitments. The Reagan administration has not yet responded to requests for the spare parts needed to repair Guatemala's grounded, U.S.-made helicopters.

The administration is in a bind. Although sympathetic to Guatemala's anticommunism, Washington cannot afford to ignore its brutal repression. The administration's professed support for reform in El Salvador is likely to be undermined by open support of reaction in Guatemala.

Whereas the administration has good contacts with the Guatemalan elite—Sandoval and Arana mixed with the Reagan inner circle during inauguration week—U.S. influence on the military is minimal. Even the kind of nominal leverage for reform that the United States has in El Salvador does not exist in Guatemala. If the administration were to push the military regime to reform, knowledgeable insiders doubt that there is even a faction of progressive officers willing to support reform-minded policies. In fact, one of the strongest opponents of a more reformist policy would be the ultraconservative U.S. business community in Guatemala City. The local American Chamber of Commerce has become a vocal defender of the Lucas regime, both in Guatemala and in the United States.

Supporting the current government would mean renewed U.S. acquiescence in the senseless brutal policies of the past. The wide-scale political murder—30,000 killings since 1954—has done nothing to resolve Guatemala's true problems. And it has prevented the formulation of reform policies more in harmony with long-term U.S. interests.

Outside communist involvement is no pretext for U.S. involvement in Guatemala. Contrary to recent State Department allegations, Guatemalan rebels were not created by Cuban agents, nor are they challenging the United States. Cuban Premier Fidel Castro reportedly did intervene to help the four guerrilla groups form a unified command, much as he did in El Salvador. An unknown number of Guatemalan guerrillas have visited Cuba, and some have received Cuban training. U.S. officials say privately they have no evidence of significant arms shipments to Guatemala from Cuba or Cuban-linked sources.

Betting on the 1982 elections as an avenue of meaningful change is wishful thinking. To rebuild the political center is nearly impossible at this late stage. Even among moderates, U.S. credibility is low.

The only way that the Reagan administration can avoid repeating the mistakes of the past is to show that it opposes government-sponsored terrorism. Without extracting significant concessions from the current ruling groups in Guatemala, the United States will not obtain the measures essential to long-term stability here.

The administration should not go ahead with plans to resume military assistance. The Guatemalans are hurting without U.S. aid. In rejecting military support in 1977, the Guatemalans figured that they could ride out the Carter years and gain friendlier treatment from a Republican administration, without having to curtail their human rights violations. An indefinite military cutoff now could induce the armed forces to revise its reactionary policies.

The United States has not halted Agency for International Development support, which in 1979 amounted to $24.7 million. By denying the portion of this aid earmarked for public works projects, Washington would offer evidence of its determination to promote change.

Communist involvement should be countered diplomatically, not militarily. If the United States finds legitimate proof of large Cuban arms shipments, it should move quietly to cut them off at their source. To respond with an embrace of the Guatemalans would not necessarily stop the shipments and would jeopardize U.S. leverage for reform. Such an embrace would also be impossible to repudiate.

The Reagan administraion has the advantage of being known and trusted in Guatemala. Ruling groups know that they will have nowhere else to turn if they alienate a conservative U.S. administration. Given the choice of facing a hostile United States or instituting genuine reforms, Guatemalan leaders might grudgingly accept the latter. But the United States should not pretend that it can accomplish anything easily in Guatemala. Creating an atmosphere for reform will be very difficult; real arm-twisting will have to take place.

The impasse here is proof of the failure of past U.S. policies and symptomatic of U.S. myopia throughout Central America. The United States needs to design a consistent policy instead of reacting—often belatedly—to emergencies. It needs to confront the economic sources of instability and help form political systems flexible enough to prevent the enormous tensions that exist today.

In Guatemala, change is inevitable; to live with long-term stability, the United States will have to live with short-term upheaval. The issue in Guatemala is, once again, not how to prevent change, but how to guide it. The problem is that it may be too late for the United States to play a constructive role. "If only we had an Arbenz now," a State Department official lamented recently. "We are going to have to invent one, but all the candidates are dead."

48. We Have 12 Helicopters in Honduras— Is It the Next El Salvador? *

By Peter Shiras and Leyda Barbieri

Peter Shiras, whose critique of land reform in El Salvador appears earlier in this volume, recently traveled through Central America. Leyda Barbieri is a staff member of the Washington Office on Latin America, a non-governmental information resource agency (110 Maryland Ave., N.W., Washington, D.C. 20002).

APPEARING before the House Appropriations Subcommittee last February 25th, ex-U.S. ambassador to El Salvador, Robert White, wondered out loud, "I don't know why we have twelve [U.S. Army] helicopters in Honduras at this time." White could have asked why Honduras, a country of three million inhabitants, was the second largest recipient of U.S. economic assistance to Latin America last year, receiving almost one-fifth of all aid to Latin America. Why has Honduras received over $3.5 million in U.S. military aid since April of last year as well as increased military training funds? Why is all of this American largesse and military hardware going to a country traditionally exempt from the violent upheavals of its Central American neighbors: Guatemala to the west, El Salvador to the south, and Nicaragua to the east?

White's query went unanswered and ignored by the press. The question, however, of U.S. policy towards Honduras and the role of Honduras in the Central America drama is becoming increasingly important. It has implications both for Honduras's internal evolution towards civilian democracy and for the eventual scope and outcome of the war in El Salvador.

Part of the answer to the sudden U.S. interest in Honduras lies in the geography of Central America. Honduras occupies a strategically

* *Democratic Left*, Vol. IX, no. 5, May 1981.

vital position bordering on all three of the region's actual or potentially explosive nations. Honduras's border with Nicaragua has been the scene of numerous confrontations between ex-Somocista National Guardsmen and the Nicaraguan armed forces. Along the Honduras-Salvadoran border, thousands of refugees have fled in terror from the counterinsurgency tactics of the Salvadoran military. Recently, the U.S. State Department charged that Honduras is being used as one of the major routes for arms deliveries from Nicaragua to the Salvadoran insurgents. Finally, along the Guatemalan border, officials from Honduras, Guatemala and El Salvador regularly meet to discuss their respective security needs and problems.

Immediately following the election of Ronald Reagan in November, U.S. Ambassador to Honduras Jack Binns said that "the United States is looking for a vigorous Honduran role in Central America." The nature of that role has been twofold. On the one hand, U.S. officials cite Honduras as a model of peaceful social change and laud the transition process underway from military to civilian rule. On the other hand, the U.S. has been fortifying the Honduras military with large amounts of new assistance and weaponry, thereby strengthening the role of the military both in the region and within Honduras itself.

Honduras is beset with an array of economic and political problems that are rapidly polarizing political forces within the country and show signs of leading to the same kind of political violence that has convulsed other Central American nations. U.S. policy, as it has consistently done in other parts of Latin America, contributes to this polarization by strengthening the hand of the military as opposed to civilians and forcing concessions from Honduras to shore up the faltering Salvadoran regime. The dangers of this policy are not only that of increasing the threat of a regionalization of the war in El Salvador, but of threatening the process of democratization underway in Honduras. Indeed, much evidence indicates that these threats have already become realities.

The roots of Honduras's current crisis date most immediately to the elections for a constitutional assembly held in April 1980. Under pressure from the Carter administration, the military allowed free elections to be held and voters turned out in record numbers. The provisional military regime, which still rules under the leadership of General Policarpo Paz García, was duly rewarded with large amounts of military assistance from Washington.

Since then, the elected constitutional assembly has been working under the shadow of constant threats and rumors of a military coup d'état that would interrupt if not terminate the democratization process. As a result, the process has gone very slowly and large segments of Honduran society, particularly trade unions, student groups, peasant organizations, and opposition political parties, have been excluded from the transition process. The military has purged from its ranks left-leaning military officers and has kept the political "opening" within the limits it finds acceptable. Whether the military will honor its pledge to hold presidential elections this year is debatable; what is clear is that despite public statements to the contrary, the U.S. is strengthening the military's position and thus no government will rule without its approval.

Opposition to the government has galvanized around two issues: the Honduras-El Salvador peace treaty and the treatment of the Salvadoran refugees entering Honduras. That these involve neighboring El Salvador testifies both to the key role that El Salvador plays in Honduran politics and the importance of Honduras in the region.

The circumstances surrounding the signing of the peace treaty on October 30, 1980, indicate that the United States exerted strong pressure to bring the two countries to terms. After eleven months of frustrated talks, the treaty was rushed through hurriedly as a diplomatic feather in El Salvador's otherwise unadorned hat. The Hondurans caved in on their demand that the border issue be resolved and agreed to the terms of the treaty that were highly favorable to El Salvador. El Salvador gained Honduran markets for its cheaper manufactured products, use of Honduran highways, and an escape valve for its burgeoning population by reopening the border between the two countries. In addition, the treaty grants both armies license to clear the border zone of guerillas, thus creating the kind of anti-guerrilla united front the U.S. hoped to achieve in bringing the two sides to the bargaining table. In short, the treaty bestows on the Salvadoran government a certain political legitimacy, may alleviate its immediate economic crisis, and strengthens its military position.

The Honduran military and elite have also benefited from increasing military and economic aid, but this has come at the cost of strong domestic protest from opposition groups and some business sectors. The business sectors fear the economic consequences of cheap Salvadoran products flooding the Honduran market. Other protests have focused on the U.S. military aid to Honduras that has come as a result of the treaty and these sectors oppose Honduran involvement in the U.S. and Salvadoran war against the insurgents. As former ambassador White said, "Why do we have twelve helicopters in Honduras?" The reason can only be understood in the context of Honduran military actions against Salvadoran guerillas in the border zone. By sealing off the border, the Salvadoran military forces can more effectively combat the insurgency.

The irony and tragedy of the peace treaty is its role in broadening and internationalizing the war in Central America. Immediately before the treaty was signed, in anticipation, Honduran and Salvadoran troops collaborated in "rastreos," cleanup operations, against suspected guerrilla bases. Refugees along the border report that since the treaty was signed there have been more attacks in the zone as well as incursions by Salvadoran troops into the refugee centers themselves to attack alleged guerrilla sympathizers. Furthermore, American and Chilean officers attached to the Organization of American States (OAS) observer force make weekly flights across the border and maintain constant communication between the two armies. Whereas this communication served to mediate past disputes, the OAS force is now acting as a bridge between two armies carrying out joint military activities against what they perceive as a common enemy. In attempting to justify such military actions, the U.S. military representative to the OAS force in Honduras explained, "Although I hate to raise the specter of Southeast Asia, the guerrillas are using the 'bolsones' exactly the way the Viet Cong used Cambodia for base camps."

While it is still too early to assess the economic impact of the treaty, the Honduran economy is already in deep trouble. The International Monetary Fund (IMF) issued a report late last year indicating that Honduras's foreign reserves had decreased by $50 million in the preceding two months and that as a result no new aid would be forthcoming. The report generated widespread concern among Honduran businessmen and reports of large-scale capital flight have been circulating once again.

Meanwhile, for the general population, prices are climbing, shortages of some basic products are appearing, demands for higher salaries are increasing, and strikes becoming more widespread. Symptomatic of the malaise of the Honduran economy is the 75,000 ton short-fall in domestic basic grain production for a country with tremendous agricultural potential. As a result, Honduras is having to import food and increase taxes.

The foreign debt of $550 million is almost as great as export revenues of $575 million in 1980 and public debt servicing accounts for 15 percent of government expenditures. For 1981, it is expected that fully 25 percent of the government budget will be derived from foreign loans which, although they might relieve short-term budget problems, will contribute to large budget deficits, indebtedness and dependency. A report in the Mexican daily *Excelsior* blamed the present economic crisis on increased imports, administrative corruption (particularly notorious among the military), and beefing up of the military budget. Despite an IMF-approved stabilization plan instituted in 1979, economic minister Rubén Mondragón admits to an inflation rate of 50 percent and a 1981 budget deficit of $175 million. For the Honduran peasantry and working class, already suffering from the lowest per capita income in Central America, the IMF plan is likely to bring no relief, but only more hardship. From 1971-1978, the real wages of Honduran workers declined by 30 percent.

On May 14, 1980, some 300 to 600 Salvadoran refugees were killed at the Sumpul river along the Honduran-Salvadoran border in a joint military action by the two countries. Local priests in the Santa Rosa de Copán diocese learned of the massacre and, after being unable to attract serious press coverage, published a statement on the massacre implicating Honduran forces.[1] The government reacted angrily, charging the priests with being leftist sympathizers and threatening to expel all foreign priests. One priest, Father Earl Gallagher, an American, received death threats over Radio El Salvador and another, Father Fausto Milla, was recently arrested and detained for three days for allegedly carrying subversive material. Clashes between the church and the government have become increasingly bitter this year, with even the conservative Archbishop of Tegucigalpa calling for fundamental changes in the society.

Underlying the conflict between the priests of Santa Rosa and the military government is the highly politically sensitive issue of the Salvadoran refugees and the strategically important border area between El Salvador and Honduras. In 1969, the two countries fought the famous "Soccer War" over a border dispute and the influx of Salvadoran settlers into Honduras. Now, even with the peace treaty signed, the border disputes have yet finally to be settled. A six-kilometer-wide demilitarized zone along the border is still under OAS observation to guarantee its neutrality. It was, however, in that zone that the massacre of the refugees occurred, despite the statements of the head of the OAS force at the time to the contrary.

According to U.S. military intelligence, the Salvadoran guerrillas have established bases in the demilitarized zone which they are using as supply camps. Honduran officials are concerned about not only arms shipments across the border which were recently described in the State Department's White Paper, but also about shipments of food and medicines that refugees may be supplying to the guerrillas. According to relief workers in the area as well as the testimony of the refugees themselves, the food distributions do not even meet the needs of the refugees, let alone allow them to transport supplies to the guerrillas. According to a report in a Honduran newspaper, the

---

[1] See Reading 20, above.—Eds.

weapons that the State Department claims were destined for El Salvador were in fact for Honduran rebels.

The refugees are undeniably sympathetic towards the left because it is the government security forces and right-wing paramilitary forces that have made them refugees in the first place. A recent congressional delegation visited the border area and though members questioned the refugees as to who was committing the acts of terror found no evidence that leftist guerrillas were engaged in such actions. According to their report, the Salvadoran strategy, as articulated by one commander, runs as follows: "The subversives like to say that they are the fish and the people are the ocean. What we have done in the north [of El Salvador] is to dry up the ocean so we can catch the fish easily." "Drying up the ocean" entails waging a campaign of terror against the rural population which has resulted in approximately 500,000 refugees, 30,000 of whom have entered Honduras.

Recently, the Honduran government has come up with its own plan to "dry up the ocean," a plan to move all the refugees away from the border area and into tightly controlled camps. This would remove the refugees from the border and rid the area of troublesome journalists and relief workers who act as witnesses to military actions. Without these constraints, closer coordination would be possible between the two armies in mopping up any guerrilla bases on either side of the border. Such a scenario of increasingly regionalized conflict would be met with strong protest within Honduras but would probably be supported in Washington. After all, to paraphrase Lyndon Johnson, why not let Central American boys fight the war instead of American boys?

Salvadoran guerrilla leaders and Guillermo Ungo, head of the Democratic Revolutionary Front, have already charged that Honduran troops are massing along the border and operating in collusion with Salvadoran troops. In Marcala, some 50 kilometers from the Salvador border, a major counter-insurgency force has been assembled and a military airstrip built in the last six months. Significantly, Marcala is located on the major highway into El Salvador's northern region where the fiercest battles between government troops and leftist insurgents have occurred. Recently, General Wallace Nutting, commander of the Southern Command, visited Honduras and made a special trip to Marcala.

The signs of domestic polarization in Honduras are unmistakable. The first right-wing death squad, appropriately named MACHO (Movimiento Anti-comunista Hondureño Organizado) recently made its presence known—threatening students supporting the Salvadoran struggle and peasants complaining about their conditions. In December, unknown assailants kidnapped Paul Vinelli, a high-level banker who had spoken out against government policies. New leftist groups have split off from the traditional left opposition parties to form groups advocating armed insurrection and have been organizing to prepare for such an eventuality. It is all too reminiscent of Nicaragua, El Salvador, and Guatemala.

The aspirations and legitimate rights of the Honduran people, and one might add, the Salvadoran people also, are being sacrificed to achieve U.S. geopolitical objectives. At the same time that the U.S. attempts to crush the guerrilla offensive in El Salvador, it is sowing the seeds of revolution in Honduras. By frustrating genuine reform and blocking expression of popular will, U.S. policy can hope to keep the lid on the explosive situation in Central America from one election year to the next, but it is a policy in the long run that can only lead to increased instability in the region, and more spilling of blood.

49. A Note on U.S. Economic Interests in Central America and El Salvador

By DAVID MERMELSTEIN AND LOUIS MENASHE

I spent 33 years and 4 months in active service as a member of our country's most agile military force—the Marine Corps. I served in all commissioned ranks from a second lieutenant to Major-General. And during that period I spent most of my time being a high-class muscle man for Big Business, for Wall Street and for the bankers. In short, I was a racketeer for Capitalism. . . .

Thus I helped make Mexico . . . safe for American oil interests in 1914. I helped make Haiti and Cuba a decent place for the National City Bank boys to collect revenues in. . . . I helped purify Nicaragua for the international banking house of Brown Brothers in 1909–12. I brought light to the Dominican Republic for American sugar interests in 1916. I helped make Honduras "right" for American fruit companies in 1903. In China in 1927 I helped see to it that Standard Oil went its way unmolested.

During those years, I had, as the boys in the back room would say, a swell racket. I was rewarded with honors, medals, promotion. Looking back on it, I feel I might have given Al Capone a few hints. The best he could do was to

operate his racket in three city districts. We . . . operated on three conti-
nents.
                              —U.S. Major General Smedley D. Butler, *Common Sense*, 1935

R EVOLUTIONARY regimes in Latin America—or the threat of
  such regimes coming to power—always send waves of anxiety
throughout sections of the U.S. business community. Such regimes
are committed to taking hold of their national economies through
planning and nationalizations, and to breaking traditional ties of dependence to external markets and sources of capital. By definition,
this implies a confrontation with U.S. firms having substantial interests south of the border. Expropriations of U.S. holdings in sugar
processing, petroleum refining, nickel mining and other sectors in
Cuba soon after the assumption of power by Fidel Castro contributed to the tensions resulting in a total break between Washington
and Havana. U.S. copper interests and ITT had a direct hand in
destabilizing the radical coalition headed by the Marxist Salvador
Allende in Chile. Encouraged by such activity and abetted by the
CIA the Chilean military executed a bloody *coup d'état* in 1973 that
unseated Allende and installed the present Pinochet dictatorship.
The latter has restored U.S. business confidence in Chile.

There are many who attribute the Reagan administration's obsessive concern with the Central American region, and the Salvadoran
"domino" in particular, to anxiety over the safety of U.S. business
interests there. After all, the Reagan administration is the businessman's regime: Then is the Reagan State Department a throwback to
earlier State Departments whose chief role was protecting U.S. economic interests abroad, especially in Latin America? Reasons of space
have limited this book to political and policy issues primarily. The
volume and character of U.S. business activity in Central America
and its possible role in shaping Washington's thinking about the region are subjects we can only probe lightly in this note.

Less than 20% of all U.S. investment abroad in 1977, or $27.7
billion, was accounted for by Latin America. Of this, Central America's share came to less than one billion dollars. Investment in El
Salvador is a slight $100 million, down some from an earlier peak.
Apart from investments in Guatemalan oil and nickel, it appears that
Central America in general, and El Salvador in particular, are primarily of geopolitical value to the U.S.

But in a number of respects, conclusions based only on volume of
direct investment are misleading. For one thing, it should be noted
that Third World investment is extremely profitable. Sales by U.S.

subsidiaries should also enter the picture. Sales by such firms based in Latin America exceeded $60 billion—no small amount. In El Salvador, dozens of large corporations have this kind of financial stake, including Texas Instruments, Chevron, Phelps Dodge, Kimberly-Clark, Texaco, Datarama and Crown Zellerbach.

In some cases, it is difficult to separate economic interest from geopolitical concern. What was more important in Cuba—the extent of Castro's expropriations or its location "ninety miles from home"? From the State Department point of view, Mexico is strategically placed and is potentially an endangered "domino." The vast amount of oil and natural gas are also of strategic concern. But how would U.S. corporations feel about a threat to their direct investment (as of 1976) of $2.2 billion?

There is another dimension to the problem. Even if U.S. investment to the south doesn't amount to much when measured against U.S. global investment aggregates, its role in El Salvador's economy may be decisive. This may be true even if there is no U.S. investment at all in coffee, El Salvador's chief source of income, or in agriculture in general. While early U.S. investment in El Salvador was in gold and silver mines (since shut down) and railroads, recent investment has been—as elsewhere in the Third World—increasingly channeled into manufacturing. In Central America virtually all of what is manufactured, in contrast to what is mined and pumped, is sold domestically.

Post-World War II "modernizers" in El Salvador were puzzled by the problem of finding a domestic market for a small country characterized by dazzling wealth for a few at the top and numbing poverty for the many on the bottom. The redistribution of wealth and income certainly was not on their agenda. Economic integration provided a partial solution to the problem: In 1961, the Central American Common Market (CACM) was formed. Economic integration led to swamping backward Honduras with Salvadoran goods, and to general economic strains that radicalized the growing urban labor force. A result of these developments was the five-day "Soccer War" of July 1969 between Honduras and El Salvador. Repression was one reaction to urban unrest in El Salvador, but it backfired. The impact of the world economic crisis in the 1970s, along with other political developments discussed elsewhere in this book, helped create a full-scale insurgency.

U.S. investment in El Salvador is less than 1% of total U.S. investment in Latin America. But its importance to El Salvador, to repeat, should not be underrated. Overall foreign investment plays a role in virtually every industrial branch, except possibly brewing and cement.

More than 50% of that investment comes from the U.S., mostly in the form of joint ventures, followed by Japan, 14%, Mexico, 9%, and the United Kingdom, 7%.

Although a few U.S. firms have pulled out of El Salvador (notably Beckman Instruments after their executives were kidnapped), others report minimal disruption by the civil strife. On the other hand, even after an average annual rate of growth between the years 1960–78 of 5.3%, the 1981 economic situation tells of deepening crisis: GNP is off 5%; the construction industry has just about come to a halt; exports and imports are down more than 10%; capital formation, especially in the private sector, is off 40%; foreign reserves are dangerously low; the flight of capital is accelerating; internal and external debt is rising; and inflation is approximately 20%. It is obvious that the increased U.S. military commitment has to be complemented by increased economic aid if Washington is to keep the junta afloat. This is still another consideration shaping U.S. intervention policies in El Salvador.[1]

---

[1] Based on: Business Week, April 13, 1981. James Petras, Class and Power in the Third World: With Case Studies of Class Conflict in Latin America (Montclair, N.J.: Allanheld, Osmun, 1981). NACLA Report on the Americas, Vol. XIV, No. 2, March–April, 1980, "El Salvador—Why Revolution?"; Vol. XIV, No. 4, July–Aug., 1980, "El Salvador—A Revolution Brews"; Vol. XV, No. 3, May–June, 1981, "Central America: No Road Back." Marc Herald, unpublished paper on direct U.S. investment in El Salvador (March 1980). Latin American Weekly Report and Latin America Regional Reports, Mexico and Central America (London), various issues. Carlos Vela, Symposium on El Salvador and U.S. Policy in the Region, January 16, 1981, U. of California, Berkeley, available from Faculty Committee for Human Rights in El Salvador. E. Torres-Rivas, "Ocho Claves Para Comprender La Crisis en Centroamerica," Centro de Capacitación Para el Desarrollo, Doc. A 29 (unpublished), 1981.

PART SIX

POLICY PERSPECTIVES ON EL SALVADOR AND CENTRAL AMERICA

Editors' Introduction

The United States has no interest in Central America more important than that of aiding the five republics to become strong, prosperous and well-governed commmonwealths, and it is therefore impossible to suppose that it will be hostile to any movement which promises to improve their situation.

—Dana Munro, *The Five Republics of Central America* (1918)

THE crux of the U.S. effort in El Salvador, ominously reminiscent of what went on in Vietnam, is the attempt to uphold by military aid and U.S. advisers a regime nominally headed by civilian "reformers" and pledged to carry out a U.S.-designed program of agrarian reform. Just as these proved insufficient in Vietnam,[1] they seem to be deficient in El Salvador as well. The possibility that sizeable detachments of U.S. troops might have to come into play in Central America should not be ruled out. Direct military intervention may have to be used to prop up the sagging Salvadoran junta, an even more brutal regime in neighboring Guatemala,[2] or to overthrow the leftist Sandinista government of Nicaragua. The Reagan Administration, however, seems to be keeping its options open. In mid-August, 1981, the Assistant Secretary of State for Inter-American Affairs, Thomas O. Enders, met privately with Nicaraguan officials during a 30-hour visit to Managua, suggesting a possible softening of the new Administration's line.[3]

In spite of rumors that the Reagan Administration may announce a far-reaching plan for the economic development of the Caribbean basin, as of late summer 1981, none has been forthcoming. If Reagan's complete program for Central America, therefore, is yet to be revealed, its opening thrusts are evidence enough that he has taken a hard line in which a military component to any policy is central. For

---

[1] On U.S. policy in support of "reformer" Ngo Dinh Diem, and Diem's agrarian reform program in Vietnam, see Marvin E. Gettleman, *Vietnam: History, Documents and Opinions* (New York, 1970), Part VI; Frances Fitzgerald, *Fire in the Lake: The Vietnamese and the Americans in Vietnam* (Boston, 1972), Chap. 3.

[2] See Reading 47.

[3] See "U.S. Official, in Nicaragua, Ties Aid to Policy Shifts," *The New York Times*, August 13, 1981. For a statement by Enders on El Salvador, see Reading 43.

one whose budgetary commitment to the military at the expense of the civilian sector is without precedent, this comes as no surprise.[4]

His predecessor, to be sure, had begun the military build-up, and in adopting a tough—some might say hysterical—response to the Soviet invasion of Afghanistan, had all but scuttled detente. By his appeasement of hawkish views, and by simple ineptitude, Carter managed to undermine the Salt II agreement he had signed and send it to a political purgatory from which it may never return. Still, Carter's dedication to the symbolism of human rights, and occasionally its reality; [5] his willingness to consider a relationship with the fledgling Sandinista government; his relatively sober treatment of the Iranian hostage crisis (notwithstanding the provocation that started it—admitting the Shah to the United States); his suspension of military aid to the Salvadoran junta, temporary though it was, after the military murdered four U.S. religious women; and, finally, his support, however attenuated, of SALT II—all attest that the Carter Administration maintained, in the final analysis, and however hesitantly, a policy within the framework of détente.

Carter may have been troubled by indigenous Communist "subversives" playing in or near "our" Caribbean waters but, unlike Reagan, he did not attempt to create an international crisis by claiming that Moscow is in the mountains directing each guerrilla raid. By both its rhetoric and its actions, the Reagan Administration appears to be a throwback to an earlier Cold War era with all its mischief and dangers.

As the Carter administration passed out of power, a "Dissent Channel Paper," possibly drafted by officers in the State Department, the Central Intelligence Agency, and the Defense Department, began to circulate in Washington, airing fears of renewed Cold War and setting out alternative policies.[6] Spokesmen for the Reagan administration dismissed the document as "unofficial" and "spurious," as it went about doing precisely what the "dissidents" warned against—

---

[4] Emma Rothschild, "Reagan and the Real Economy, New York Review of Books, February 5, 1981; Lester Thurow, "How to Wreck the Economy," ibid., May 14, 1981.

[5] See the remarks of Patricia M. Derian in Reading 50.

[6] We regret that space limitations prevented our reprinting the "Dissent Channel Paper." Interested readers may obtain the document from CISPES (see the list of Resources, below). For arguments similar to those in the "Dissent Channel Paper," see Richard E. Feinberg, "Central America: No Easy Answers," Foreign Affairs, Summer 1981. (Feinberg was a member of the Policy Planning Staff of the State Department from 1977 through 1979 and is editor and co-author of Central America: International Dimensions of the Crisis, forthcoming.)

applying Cold War doctrines of a conspiracy by the Soviet Union and its "surrogate," Cuba, to subvert Central America. Since Washington now believes Cuba to be a key link in the Soviet plan to dominate Latin America, the views of Fidel Castro have been included here so that the Cuban leader's response to—and fears about—Reagan policies may be gauged (Reading 51). By contrast, many figures who are not on the Left and who are apprehensive of Soviet power argue that the stiff Reagan posture toward El Salvador is counterproductive and inconsistent with the real security interests of the U.S. In this category are the views of Robert E. White, whose dissenting arguments cost him his ambassadorship to El Salvador and forced his retirement from the State Department (Reading 52). (One analyst, Robert S. Leiken, has argued that attempts to pursue military rather than political solutions in Central America could estrange Mexico and cripple U.S. influence in a number of other Latin American countries, including Venezuela, as well as ignite a regional war that might tie down U.S. resources already stretched to the limit.)[7] From a perspective with which the editors of this volume are in general agreement, American University professor William LeoGrande concludes this section with a comprehensive survey and analysis (Reading 53) that ought to be on the Reagan State Department's reading list as the crisis in El Salvador continues to yield its daily harvest of deaths.

50. Debate Over U.S. Policy on Human Rights *

BY JEANE KIRKPATRICK AND PATRICIA M. DERIAN

The publication of Jacobo Timerman's Prisoner Without a Name, Cell Without a Number *(New York, 1981) added to the public debate over the Reagan administration's new policy on human rights. Timerman, editor and publisher from 1971 to 1977 of* La Opinión, *a Buenos Aires daily newspaper, described his arrest, incarceration, and torture at the hands of Argentine*

---

* Reprinted from *U.S.News & World Report*, March 2, 1981, pp. 49–50.

[7] Robert S. Leiken, "Eastern Winds in Latin America," *Foreign Policy*, No. 42 (Spring 1981). For a liberal Congressional view that vigorously dissents from current U.S. policy, see Gerry E. Studds, *Central America, Report to the Committee on Foreign Affairs*, U.S. House of Representatives, March 1981.

*military authorities. He has spoken widely against an official policy of si-
lence when serious human rights violations take place under "friendly" authoritarian regimes.[1] Timerman attended the confirmation hearings of
Ernest Lefever, President Reagan's controversial choice for the post of Assistant Secretary of State for Human Rights and Humanitarian Affairs. The
Senate Foreign Relations Committee voted against Lefever—perhaps Timerman's presence affected the conscience of Committee members. Lefever,
like Ambassador Kirkpatrick, has taken the position that the U.S. should
speak out against human rights violations in the U.S.S.R. but engage in
quiet diplomacy when they occur in Guatemala, Chile or Argentina. This
reflects the now-familiar "totalitarian"/"authoritarian" distinction cham-
pioned by the ambassador in the interview below (and originally articulated
by her in Reading 3, above)—a formulation that has become the official
policy of the Reagan administration.[2]*

*Patricia M. Derian was Human Rights Secretary in the Carter administra-
tion and is generally credited with having helped obtain Timerman's release
from prison and perhaps saving his life. As this book was going to press, three
related developments in the human rights arena came to light: 1. Former
President Carter broke his policy of silence on the new administration's
policies and ridiculed an "ephemeral tightwire between proper torture by
'friendly' dictators and unacceptable torture by others less favored." 2. The
administration is now supporting international development loans to Chile,
Argentina, Paraguay and Uruguay, something that many critics deem in
violation of a 1977 law that instructs the U.S. government to oppose international bank loans to countries engaging in "a consistent pattern of gross
violations of human rights." 3. The administration is considering eliminating
the position of Human Rights Secretary. Meanwhile, Mr. Lefever has been
hired as a special consultant by the State Department.*

1. Interview with Jeane Kirkpatrick

Q. Ambassador Kirkpatrick, the crisis in El Salvador raises the
question of how the U.S. should deal with human-rights violations.
Why do you favor discarding the Carter administration's approach
abroad?

---

[1] See his address to the Annual General Meeting of Amnesty International U.S.A.,
June 14, 1981, available from Amnesty, 304 West 58th Street, New York, New York
10019.

[2] See the excerpts from the speech by Secretary Haig on Human Rights and Foreign Policy before the Trilateral Commission in Washington, March 31, 1981, in
The New York Times, April 21, 1981.

A. Because it was utopian, because it was conducted outside of the political and historical context, and because it didn't work. It used a concept of human rights that was far too broad. It included not only legal and personal rights, such as freedom from arbitrary arrest and torture and a guarantee of due process, and a full range of democratic political rights, such as freedom of speech, press, assembly, elections, but also a full range of economic rights—the right to food, shelter, education, medical care—which amounted to the demand that all countries become affluent social democracies.

Q. You see that as an unrealistic standard?

A. Yes. That is a standard which virtually no country in the world can meet. Some people think Sweden or Denmark might. West Germany and France don't. We ourselves don't. And when you set up a standard that no real country meets, you end up with no standard at all and you operate, instead, on the basis of arbitrary judgments.

So arbitrariness became, along with utopianism, a leading characteristic of the Carter policy. It became a policy of being *selectively* unfriendly to autocracies. Moreover, it encouraged us to wrap ourselves in a mantle of righteousness while pursuing hypocritical policies.

Q. You said the Carter administration ignored the political context of rights issues—

A. It measured all countries by the same standards—disregarding differences in history, political traditions and social conditions. If, for example, a country was combatting dissidents, no account was taken of whether that country had a tradition of democracy and due process, or had ever been anything but autocratic; of whether it was miserably poor or had an affluent economy; of the fact that it might be in the midst of a civil war or under guerrilla attack. Political thinking that takes no account of the concrete circumstances and traditions and values of a people not only is useless but usually turns out to be damaging.

Q. Specifically, what damage did it do?

A. By helping to destabilize the Somoza regime in Nicaragua, for example, it fanned the flames of a civil war in which some 40,000 Nicaraguans lost their most basic human right—the right to life. Another 100,000 were left homeless, and some 2 billion dollars' worth of destruction was wrought. A Sandinista regime was ushered in which instituted measures more repressive than those of Somoza. Similar mistakes were made in El Salvador, Guatemala and Bolivia.

Our position in the Western Hemisphere has deteriorated to the point where we must now defend ourselves against the threat of a ring of Soviet bases being established on and around our borders. I'm not saying that the Carter human-rights policy was the only factor in bringing this about, but it certainly played a role. One reason for the failure of the Carter policy was the belief that you can influence governments and people more effectively by hitting them over the head with a two-by-four, excoriating and humiliating them publicly and treating them like moral pariahs than by using quiet persuasion and diplomacy.

Q. Defenders of the Carter approach argue that it resulted in an improvement of conditions in Argentina and Chile——

A. To think that such improvements were the result of our policy is a good example of the arrogance of power, of a colossal overestimation of our influence. In both of these countries, as well as in Brazil and other Latin American countries, there is a long tradition of swings between military dictatorship and constitutionalism. It is this and not our policy that explains the current movement in these countries toward a return to government by law.

Q. Didn't the Carter policy help some individuals?

A. It did. But, by and large, it failed in its goal of leaving more people more free and better off than they were. During the Carter years, the boundaries of freedom were constricted in as many places as they were expanded.

The principal function of the policy has been to make us feel good about ourselves. But that is not an appropriate foreign-policy goal.

Q. Will the new administration turn its back on human rights?

A. Absolutely not. But our approach will be different.

First, the concrete circumstances in which a human-rights violation takes place will be taken into account. Take El Salvador. It is engulfed in civil war, and I know of no country which has ever successfully carried out reforms while fighting a civil war. Besides, Napoleón Duarte, the junta leader, is and has always been known as a social reformer. The junta *is* a reform government. But as to how and when to carry out these reforms, I'd rather trust his judgment than yours or mine or that of our government.

Or take Africa. It is filled with moderately repressive autocracies—governments headed by military men who came to power by military coup. Does anyone seriously believe we should therefore not have relations with those governments?

We're not free to have relations only with the democratic countries of this world. And in governments, as in life, there are degrees of evil. To say that measles is less bad than meningitis doesn't make you promeasles, does it?

Q. Where will the Reagan administration draw the line?

A. Speaking generally, we must make it perfectly clear that we are revolted by torture and can never feel spiritual kinship with a government that engages in torture. But the central goal of our foreign policy should be not the moral elevation of other nations, but the preservation of a civilized conception of our own national self-interest.

2. Interview with Patricia M. Derian

Q. Ms. Derian, why do you oppose abandonment of the Carter approach to human rights abroad?

A. I oppose it for three good reasons. First, the Carter approach is in our long-range national interest. Second, we must conduct our foreign policy in a way consistent with our sense of ourselves. We are people who value human rights. Third, we are signatories of international documents that obligate us to further human rights.

Q. Haven't there been instances where our emphasis on human rights proved detrimental to our national interest?

A. I know of none.

Q. How do you answer arguments that our stand encouraged the overthrow of pro-U.S. governments in Iran and Nicaragua?

A. In both instances we put those dictatorial, tyrannical leaders—the Shah and Somoza—into power and kept them there for 30 years with our support. Finally, the people who had to live under the tyranny of each of these despots reached the point of revolution. It was not the human-rights policy of our government that brought about the revolutions.

Q. Some critics say that human rights are an internal matter for each country and therefore none of our business—

A. I can't believe that in 1981 anyone would advance such an argument. Internal matters affect the world community. Was it none of our business when Hitler decimated the Jews? When Stalin, who killed millions inside the Soviet Union, was, in the name of *Realpolitik*, effectively given Eastern Europe? And when today many people who want to leave the Soviet Union are still prevented from doing so? Or when millions were killed in mainland China? Curiously, I find people applying this argument of "none of our business" only to right-wing dictatorships—not to the Soviet Union.

In addition, a roomful of documents makes human rights a matter of international law and concern: The Helsinki Final Act of 1975, the Inter-American Declaration of the Rights and Duties of Man, the United Nations Universal Declaration of Human Rights.

Q. How should the U.S. protect human rights in the world?

A. There is a whole arsenal of tactics to be used. One is quiet diplomacy. You are sitting across a table from representatives of another government to discuss an official agenda, one item of which is human rights. Then there is the way you vote in the United Nations and what you say in lobbying for support of the U.S. position. There's also what you do in the Inter-American Human Rights Commission, in the U.N.'s Human Rights Commission and in the casting of U.S. votes in the international banks.

Q. When would you withhold economic and military aid?

A. U.S. law says that gross violators of human rights are not eligible for U.S. economic and military aid unless the President determines that a cutoff would be detrimental to U.S. national security or the aid goes to assist the poorest of the poor.

A good example of such a national-security exception is South Korea. As bad as its government's human-rights policies are, we certainly don't want the North Koreans to come in and take over. It would jeopardize regional security and our own, since we have a stake in the Pacific.

Q. Just how successful was the Carter administration in reducing repression around the world?

A. Very successful. Countless numbers of people are alive today because of our policy. Torture has been reduced somewhat. A number of countries have returned to civilian government. Thousands and thousands of people who were in prison are now free.

Indonesia is one example. In 1977, there were 30,000 people in jail who had been there for about 13 years—never charged, never tried, never sentenced; just stashed away. And now they're out. In Argentina, thousands of people had disappeared. Many of their bodies were found in the streets. Now, summary execution has practically stopped, though there is still torture, and disappearances do continue, but at a lower rate. In South Korea, opposition leader Kim Dae Jung is alive today largely because of the U.S. emphasis on human rights. There is almost no country where we cannot see some favorable consequences for individuals.

Q. What other effects did the policy have?

A. It strengthened human rights in a global way. The Inter-American Human Rights Commission is much stronger—largely due to the support of the United States. The U.N.'s Human Rights Commission, which for more than 10 years had done virtually nothing, has become an effective mechanism. The Organization of African Unity is now working diligently to establish a regional human-rights organization.

Also, as a result of the Carter policy you cannot now find a leader of any country who does not place hand on heart and swear fidelity to human rights. Such words are an important first step, even if actual progress is slow.

Q. In what way did the Carter policy help the U.S. national interest?

A. It greatly improved our image abroad. In 1977, citizens of many other countries tended to view our policies as completely self-centered. Now, as a result of four years of the Carter policy, much of that bad feeling about the U.S. has been washed away. This shows up clearly in international polls and in the attitude of foreign diplomats toward us.

Q. What will happen to the human-rights policy under Reagan's administration?

A. I can't predict. I keep hearing administration people say, "Well, we're going to practice quiet diplomacy," as though they were inventing the electric light for the first time. Until recently, human rights has not been a partisan political issue. It has had Republican as well as Democratic supporters. To turn it into a political football is to do a disservice to the country.

---

51. Some Advice for President Reagan *

BY FIDEL CASTRO

In this reading, Cuban President Fidel Castro's fears of a threatening turn in U.S. foreign policy toward the hemisphere were expressed after Reagan's electoral victory and before he assumed office. In an assessment four months later, Castro charged the Reagan administration with turning Central America and the Caribbean "into a hotbed of tension" and of attempting to "attack, to isolate and to impose a policy of pressure and blackmail against Cuba." (Address to the World Council for Peace, Havana, April 21, 1981, as reported in The New York Times, *April 22, 1981.)*

REAGAN'S electoral victory has serious immediate implications for Latin-American political life. In its international approach to the major problems of war and peace, the United States will be

---

* Report to the Second Congress of the Cuban Communist Party, Havana, December 1980, *Cuba Update* [Center for Cuban Studies, New York City], II, Summer 1981.

forced to take into account the real factors of the world situation, the undeniable potential of the socialist countries and the cautious stand of its allies. On the Latin-American scene, however, the U.S. imperialists feel freer to carry out their reactionary schemes. Therein lies the evident danger for Latin America of Reagan's election to the presidency.

Reagan has not hesitated to proclaim that he considers reactionary oligarchies and fascist military dictatorships to be valuable allies who should not be needlessly harassed with the mention of human rights and with whom it is recommended that tolerance be used.

He has questioned the validity of the Panama Canal treaties. He has used a threatening tone when talking about Cuba. He has shown hostile ideological, political and economic intentions against Nicaragua and has wielded the threat of intervention over Central America, starting off with offers of economic, military and technical aid to the brutal rulers of Guatemala and El Salvador. He also expressed the wish to enlist support for his policy from the three most powerful countries in the area: Argentina, whose violations of democracy and liberty he offers to ignore; Brazil, whom he courts; and Mexico, whom he seeks to force together with Canada into an undesirable and unequal political and economic alliance with the U.S. in order to bring both countries under perpetual U.S. domination.

Reagan's Latin-American policy is all the more dangerous as it expresses the aspirations and intentions of an important section of the U.S. finance capital and transnationals, of aggressive wings within the Pentagon and the CIA, and is presented to the people of the United States as being in the U.S. interest for reasons of national security, allegedly threatened both by Latin-American "subversion," wherein Cuba plays an outstanding role, and by a secret and ominous intervention of the Soviet Union in the area.

It is evident that these positions of the incoming U.S. administration encourage and inspire the confidence of military fascists in Chile, Uruguay and Bolivia. They encourage those who refuse to democratize the Argentine process and cater to the interests of the genocidal regimes of Guatemala and El Salvador. The defeat of Manley's government in Jamaica provides imperialist plans with a useful tool in the Caribbean.

However, events also show that it is no easy task for imperialism to impose itself in its former backyard. The resounding victories of the peoples of Nicaragua and Grenada and the irrepressible struggle of the peoples of El Salvador and Guatemala should be taken into account together with other factors when analyzing the situation in Latin America and the Caribbean.

The readiness of the masses to fight—which has reached unprecedented levels—should be especially underscored. . . .

The unity of the revolutionary forces in some countries and the progress achieved in this respect in others have been significant factors in the triumphs and advances of the Latin-American revolutionary movements for national and social liberation. This unity has also prompted solidarity with the struggle in various countries.

In Latin America the active participation of the Christian forces which go beyond the conservative—at times reactionary—stands of the Christian-Democratic parties in the region and actively join the struggle for national liberation, democracy and social change of our peoples, becomes increasingly important. The fact that leftists are joined in the shoulder-to-shoulder battle by Christian revolutionaries, including occasionally Catholic priests and high-ranking clergy, is a notable aspect of the great historic changes that are taking place in our countries.

When referring to the revival of the people's forces we must not overlook another new element in the Latin-American situation: the presence of the Social Democrats. . . . In spite of the well known ideological differences we find between Marxist-Leninist revolutionaries and Social Democrats, in the first analysis, under today's historical condition the participation of Social Democrats and the social democratization of old bourgeois and oligarchic Latin-American parties shows a positive balance. They join forces and extend the battlefield against the U.S. imperialist domination in Latin America.[1] Moreover, Social-Democratic propaganda contributes to the sociopolitical awakening of the masses, where Marxist-Leninist ideas are totally repressed. . . .

Relations with the United States sum up our major contradictions in the international arena. Although there are permanent and unsurmountable elements in those contradictions, resulting from the socialist character of the Cuban state and the imperialist nature of the United States ruling system, it does not justify the extreme hostility by successive U.S. governments towards Cuba, which is most of all the result of their obstinacy in rejecting the slightest possibility of existence of socialist countries in the area, and their hopeless stubbornness to sweep revolutionary Cuba off the map of Latin America and the Caribbean. The first Congress adopted the principled policy of the Central Committee of the Party, based on our willingness to settle the historical differences created by the acts of aggression of the

---

[1] On the wide composition of the revolutionary groups in El Salvador, illustrating Castro's point, see Readings 9 and 10 above.—Eds.

United States imperialist governments and, consequently, on the possibility of discussing the normalization of our relations with that country, as well as on Cuba's firm stand not to take official steps to that end unless the United States is willing to lift the blockade, discuss the issue of Guantánamo and refrain from violating Cuba's sovereignty.

Some time during the early stage of Carter's administration, there seemed to be a certain inclination among the leaders of the United States along the path of negotiations. Carter, no doubt, made some gestures toward Cuba: at the beginning of his term he cancelled spy flights, allowed United States citizens to travel to Cuba and proposed the creation of an interests section.

Cuba was receptive to these gestures, but in the end the reactionary ideas of some of his advisers prevailed over the less aggressive trends in the State Department under Vance and Muskie, and the relations became tense once again.

Reagan's election introduces an element of uncertainty—rather of danger—in U.S.-Cuban relations. . . .

Statements have been made threatening the world, Latin America and Cuba in particular.

Reagan and his advisers are trying to attain military superiority and negotiate with the socialist camp from a position of strength, but this idea is simply absurd. This would lead to an unbridled arms race in the midst of the worst international economic crisis the world has recently had to suffer. It would be equivalent to declaring that the peoples are fatally doomed to destroy themselves mutually. This might apply when muzzle loaders and catapults were in use, but not in our era of thermonuclear arms. Does anyone have the right to play with the survival of the human race? . . .

Reagan and his advisers have announced that they intend to establish an alliance with the rightist, reactionary and fascist forces in this continent. But the peoples of our America will never submit themselves to this ignominious subjugation. The workers, the peasants, the intellectuals, the students will know how to resist such cruel fate. Our hemisphere's recent history has demonstrated our peoples' combat capacity. It is useless to despise, ignore and underestimate them; Nicaragua, El Salvador, Grenada and Guatemala have proven that doing so is an error.

How many Yankee and fascist soldiers will be needed to subjugate hundreds of millions of Latin Americans? There are no longer any Switzerlands in our America. Chile and Uruguay are eloquent examples of such illusions. There are no longer any masks to disguise our oppression. There are no longer military or repressive mechanisms developed by the U.S. intelligence agencies—no matter how cruel and sophisticated they may be—capable of curbing the insurgency of the peoples. Who can prevent our peoples from fighting sooner or later? Oppression will not last forever, terror and fear will not rule forever. The awakening of the peoples has become more frightening than anything the oppressors have devised to submit them. One must be blind not to see that. The crueler internal tyranny is, the stronger imperialist oppression becomes, the more rebellion there will be! And this rebelliousness will be invincible!

It is truly incredible that in today's world some should speak of military interventions and of applying the "big stick" policy again in our continent. They should best awake from such dreams. Others also dreamed of dominating the world and turned into ashes.

Reagan has said that in Vietnam the mistake was not making war but losing it. In Latin America the mistake of making war might represent a greater defeat than that of Vietnam. Who has told Mister Reagan that making war means the right to win it?

Cuba believes that for the world it is a historical necessity that normal relations exist among all countries, based on mutual respect, on the acknowledgment of the sovereign right of each one and on non-intervention. Cuba considers that the normalization of its relations with the United States would improve the political climate in Latin America and the Caribbean and would contribute to world détente. Cuba, therefore, is not opposed to finding a solution to its historical differences with the United States, but no one should expect Cuba to change its position or yield in its principles. Cuba is and will continue being socialist. Cuba is and will continue being a friend of the Soviet Union and of all the socialist states. Cuba is and will continue being an internationalist country.

Principles cannot be negotiated.

52. The Day of Reckoning Is Coming: An Interview with Robert E. White *

BY JEFF STEIN

Jeff Stein's interview with Robert E. White, former Ambassador to El Salvador, took place the same day that Thomas O. Enders of the State Department was delivering a speech advocating a "political solution" to the

---

* From *The Progressive*, September, 1981.

Salvadoran civil war (See Reading 43). Stein's first question asked for White's reaction to Enders's speech. Jeff Stein is Washington Correspondent for The Progressive.

I N February, the Reagan Administration removed career Foreign Service officer Robert E. White from his post as U.S. ambassador to El Salvador and forced him to retire from the State Department. That move turned out to be the opening shot in what White now says is a "political purge"—the removal from the Department of any officers the Administration identifies with the "traitorous" human rights policies of the Carter Administration.

Urbane, articulate, and considered widely to be one of the State Department's most knowledgeable and thoughtful specialists on Latin America, White vigorously pursued a policy which he thought would lead to negotiations between El Salvador's revolutionary forces and the Christian Democratic Party—a political solution that has been rejected by the Reagan Administration in favor of military victory and "elections" that exclude rebel leaders.

Besides his ambassadorship to El Salvador, White has held several other prestigious posts in his twenty-five-year career; he has been Latin American director of the Peace Corps, deputy permanent representative to the Organization of American States, and ambassador to Paraguay. In light of the escalating violence and U.S. military involvement in El Salvador, we thought White's views would be useful for understanding the past and current situation there.

On the day we spoke in his new office in the modernistic Carnegie Endowment for International Peace headquarters off Washington's Dupont Circle, Thomas O. Enders, the State Department's chief of Latin American policy, was delivering a speech across town that advocated a "political solution" to the war but, at the same time, seemed to reiterate a stance of no negotiations with declared revolutionary forces in El Salvador. The current Reagan strategy, White declared, can't help but support the "creeping coup" from El Salvador's rightist and military elements, which are out to eliminate the reformist Christian Democrats as a factor in a peaceful solution to the civil war now raging.

We began our one-hour talk—wedged into White's grueling schedule of writing articles, giving speeches, meeting with delegations from Central America, and preparing for his own trip to the region—with White's reaction to Enders's major speech.

WHITE: In what it says, the speech represents a positive change. It invites other countries to participate in negotiations leading to elections. And although it appears to exclude the revolutionaries of the Left from the negotiations, I believe there may be some flexibility there. But the most important thing about the speech is what it does not say. As you know, [junta president José Napoleón] Duarte and the Christian Democrats have been under attack from the rightist business forces. They have announced their intention to eliminate the Christian Democrats from the government. Logically, therefore, the Enders speech should have contained a ringing affirmation of our support for Duarte and the Christian Democrats. But it said nothing, and I think this seals the fate of the Christian Democrats as an effective reform component in the government of El Salvador.

Therefore, the "creeping coup" is going to continue, and in all probability is going to succeed, because the far Right has a stranglehold on the economy, and they have a deliberate policy of ceasing economic activity until they get their price. And that price is the exit of Christian Democrats.

JS: That presents the United States with a *fait accompli*, right? And then what? Won't we likely be locked into a succession of Saigon-style governments?

WHITE: Not necessarily. But what it does lock us into is a traditional combination that has driven El Salvador into the ground over the last fifty years. The day the Administration decided to support the government of Guatemala was, in effect, the day it wrote "finish" to any serious reform in the rest of Central America that depends on U.S. support, because the military of El Salvador are perfectly able to catch the nuances in the messages from Washington. If the Guatemalan military can get anything it wants—a government that has to have one of the most repressive policies in the world—then what incentive does the Salvadoran military have to clean up its act?

JS: At first, the idea that El Salvador was "another Vietnam" didn't quite fit for me, for several reasons. But as I listen to you, and as time passes, it does begin to take shape. Is El Salvador "another Vietnam" to you?

WHITE: The really crucial place where the analogy fits is the inability of the United States Government to face up to what the reality is and come to grips with it. Instead, what you've got are U.S. domestic forces—the left wing of the Democratic Party and the right wing of the Republican Party—fighting out their ideological battles with El Salvador as the ploy. And what each is advocating has little relationship to what's going on in El Salvador.[1]

---

[1] For additional discussion of the Vietnam analogy, see Readings 38-41, above.—Eds.

JS: The Right sees the guerrillas as Soviet proxies. . . .

WHITE: Right. And the Left sees the guerrilla forces as just the result of historical injustices and the growing up of a group of dedicated patriots.

That, of course, is closest to reality. But there's a very great potential for those guerrillas, should they win, to bring the Soviet presence into El Salvador. I don't exclude it. At all. I don't think the national security argument can be dismissed.

You know, in Nicaragua all the people were against Somoza. In El Salvador, what you have had building up is a real class war. Look, Somoza was a liberal compared to the Salvadoran military. Somoza used to tell me, "Those Salvadoran fourteen families give me hell because they say I'm too soft, because I'm too liberal," and I believe he was telling me the truth when he said that. So I think the class hatred that has admittedly been engendered by the military and the economic elites which have been supported in the past by the United States has created a situation that is really very dangerous.

The far Left are just totally dedicated revolutionaries who, if they came into power, would reject the United States. Their program would be to eliminate all U.S. power from the area and counter the United States by bringing in Cuba and perhaps the Soviet Union. I can't be sure, but I think that would be the way they would act.[2]

JS: Well, look, without romanticizing the guerrillas at all . . . they just may have earned their revolution at this point, don't you think?

WHITE: I don't think there's any question about that. Mind you—

JS: Who are we after all these years of silent acquiescence to say they can't have it now just because they've taken the revolutionary road after other avenues were denied them?

WHITE: It's hard to make that argument stick with anybody who's got a responsibility for administering the national security of the United States.

JS: I agree only to an extent. I agree that it's hard to make it stick for a party that wants to keep itself in power.

WHITE: All right. Had the Carter Administration been more intelligent a year and a half, two years ago, instead of—but this is what happens when you become captive of a weak, vindictive oligarchy and a brutal military. If we had, at the beginning of 1980, really made a commitment to negotiations and seeking out [Social Democrat Guillermo] Ungo and company, and bringing in Mexico, West Ger-

---

[2] Michael Harrington hopes for an alternative solution, based on the Nicaraguan situation, in Reading 46, above.—Eds.

many, Venezuela, and others, we could have brought about some sort of commonsense solution.

I think there was still a chance to salvage something right up until a couple of months ago. There may even still possibly be a chance today, if the Reagan Administration would turn on a dime and come out in favor of negotiations.

JS: They seem to have taken exactly the opposite tack.

WHITE: Oh, absolutely. When you advocate sending arms to Guatemala, you doom El Salvador. I mean, when the Guatemalan military can have everything it wants and be nakedly brutal—even take credit for it! No one in the Guatemalan government has even bothered to deny charges that they deliberately target moderate leaders and kill them in order to destroy any possible bridge between the Left and the Center.

JS: The Reagan team seemed to think El Salvador was an easy hit.

WHITE: They thought it was like rolling a drunk. You know, "There's El Salvador, and we can dramatize the difference between us and the soft-headed Carter Administration." And, of course, when you're so wildly wrong in your analysis, the chance that you'll hit on the right prescription to bring about a solution is very doubtful.

JS: If there is some blame for that kind of strategy, doesn't the Carter Administration share some of it by its decision to ship arms to the junta just before it left office? And can't the Reagan Administration claim that it is continuing what Carter began?

WHITE: I agree—and I thought exactly along those lines at the time. But the thing that really licked us was that Nicaragua had permitted its territory to be used to supply the guerrillas for the January "final offensive." There's no doubt about that. So it was impossible to make the argument in Washington that the guerrillas can get their supplies from Nicaragua but the government we're supporting can't get its supplies from the United States. It was tough to fight, but even so, we tried to fight it.

But what happened? At that time, Carter, Mondale, and Muskie were totally involved in the Iranian hostage crisis—right through the Administration's last three days, and the pressure increased dramatically for the kind of policy that you're now seeing. And career officers—who are vulnerable to political revenge—whether at State, CIA, or the Pentagon, started to say, looking toward the Reagan Administration, "Well, we'd better try and burnish our image with the new fellows." The Pentagon never supported the human rights policy anyway, and when the restraining hand of Muskie was gone, you had them gaining increasing power.

JS: One had the feeling here that the Pentagon almost attempted a coup on El Salvador policy in the last days of the Carter Administration.

WHITE: They did. No question about it. They tried to take advantage of the confusion during the transition period and have seventy-five U.S. military advisers in place when Reagan came in. I wouldn't accept it. I stopped it. It amounted to a Pentagon take-over of U.S. foreign policy on El Salvador.

JS: What is the effect of the militarization of El Salvador policy now?

WHITE: The second stage of the land reform had been explicitly canceled with U.S. approval. And the powers that be are refusing to accept the first phase of land reform as a *fait accompli*—they want to roll it back.

JS: So where are we now?

WHITE: The United States now can only postpone the inevitable day of reckoning when the Right exacts its price, and that price is either the elimination or the total neutralization of the Christian Democrats. That day is coming. Whether it will be in two months or six months. I don't know.

JS: Will the time ever come when the United States will see it in its own interest to throw in with the other side—the one that we're fighting?

WHITE: Well, I don't think so. I think that—

JS: I mean, considering that it may be in everyone's best interest in the long run.

WHITE: The best policy for the United States to advocate is negotiations. Duarte and Ungo [who resigned from the junta last winter] have far more in common than Duarte has with Colonel Moran of the Treasury Police, or than Ungo has with the guerrilla leader [Salvador Cayetano] Carpio. Both sides have to face the fact that they've got indigestible, antidemocratic elements of considerable power within their coalitions, and the way to isolate those is to get together. But the United States has taken that option away from Duarte by refusing to permit negotiations.

JS: In January, there was a big splash in the newspapers about Nicaraguans landing in force on an El Salvador beach. That turned out to be false, and it seemed—even at the time—to have been a deliberate attempt to spread a false report and smear Nicaragua. You stood behind the initial reports. Do you think you were misled?

WHITE: Two members of the Salvadoran government called me the night this was allegedly happening. I trusted these people to tell me the truth. This was the day of the "final offensive," also, and I was quick to use anything I could to try to demonstrate that Nicaragua was involving itself when it shouldn't, because it was a mistake for Nicaragua to do it. Later, I sent my military attaché down to the area, and he couldn't find anything. And so, whatever happened, there was no big battle, and they never captured one Nicaraguan, and no one could even find evidence of a battle.

JS: What do you think of it all now—was it a plant?

WHITE: I'm suspicious. Perhaps it was an exaggeration by my sources. On the other hand, it is an interesting coincidence that all this happened when it did, and it could have been designed to dramatize the involvement of Nicaragua. So, I'm suspicious.

JS: That leads me to the State Department's White Paper on El Salvador. What is your estimate of the influence of Cuba or the Soviet Union as alleged in its conclusions?

WHITE: Well, if you regard Cuba as a total surrogate of the Soviet Union, that Cuba's a marionette and the Soviet Union pulls the strings, then you could say that any place that Cuba is involved, the Soviet Union is involved. If you want to make that equation, then indeed the Soviet Union is involved. That Cuba is involved there's no doubt. I *think* they've trained somewhere between 1,000 and 2,000 Salvadoran revolutionaries in Cuba. And they have undoubtedly sent some arms to the Salvadoran revolutionaries. But none of that is proved by the captured documents which served as the basis for the White Paper.

I believe that the documents are genuine if only for the reason that they prove so little. They tend to prove only (1), that [Communist Party chief Shafik] Handal went to Moscow, that he got what you might call a mixed reception there, and that from Moscow he jumped—presumably at Soviet expense—to a number of other countries, such as Vietnam, Libya, and Ethiopia, and that he obtained promises of support from them; (2), that he did obtain some support from them; and (3), that some Cuban and Nicaraguan leaders met with Salvadoran revolutionaries to talk about a common strategy.

That's all you can say the White Paper and the documents prove. So what it asserts in addition to that is wildly off mark.

JS: What was your reaction when the White Paper was published?

WHITE: To me it was just an inept and hastily thrown together piece of propaganda. I think some of the things the White Paper says are probably true, but there aren't any documents which justify the conclusions.

JS: This was the premier document laying down the rationale for U.S. military intervention and placing El Salvador squarely on the East-West Cold War chessboard, right? Why, if there were people around like yourself drawing these conclusions, did it take one free-lance reporter [John Dinges for Pacific News Service] three months to provoke the rest of the media into taking a critical look at the White Paper?

WHITE: Well, your question really is, why didn't I come out and say this was ridiculous. Look, I am—or at least I *was*—a disciplined Foreign Service officer. I don't go out looking for windmills to joust. And the idea that I'm some sort of martyr—well, I'm not. I just wanted to keep working in the State Department, pursuing my career. Nobody elected me to anything.[3]

JS: Is there a political purge going on in the State Department right now?

WHITE: There's something very close to it. Very close to it. It is unheard of for assistant secretaries and deputy assistant secretaries not to receive onward assignments as ambassadors. In this Administration, the whole front office of the Latin American region has been removed, and none of them has received an ambassadorial assignment. I'm sure it's a purge.

JS: It seems very similar to what happened in the State Department after the Chinese revolution.

WHITE: Yes, but there's a big difference. In those days, the ideologues of the Right were much more naive, open, and honest. They were out to get those guys in the State Department because they had "sold out China." They said so, and they went after them. The present tactic is much more insidious because they're pretending that everything is just normal and going forward routinely, and that no one is being "purged." This purge, though, is even more complete because the number of people at senior levels who know or are involved in Central America are really very few. The Reagan team has gotten rid of all of them, and in a very shameful and vengeful way.

JS: The new metaphor for "losing China" seems to be being in favor of a human rights policy.

WHITE: You're absolutely right.

JS: That is, if you're for human rights you're "soft on communism."

WHITE: They even talk about the "traitorous" Carter Administration.

JS: Traitorous?

WHITE: Yeah, that word has been used.

JS: On the seventh floor [Haig's executive offices]?

WHITE: I can't pin it to one person. But in meetings, Reagan people are actually using that phrase. My real argument with the Reagan Administration is that they threw away a very useful tool

---

[3] For the "White Paper" and its critics, see Readings 35-37, above.—Eds.

without even applying the pragmatic test of whether the policy was good or bad. If you want to reject morality in foreign affairs, fine, that's one approach. But obviously the human rights policy was a very useful tool in some cases, as I think it was to some extent in El Salvador.

JS: There are reports that Guatemala, Honduras, and El Salvador are cooperating in a policy of arrests, detentions, and "disappearances." Can you comment?

WHITE: There was very little of that when I was there. But there is obviously increasing cooperation between Honduran and Salvadoran forces, such as the forcible removal of refugee camps from the Honduran frontier.

JS: Is the Chilean military aiding the Salvadoran military?

WHITE: The Chilean government has always had a team of military advisers in El Salvador, and they are now increasing their numbers. But actually, the Chilean officers are probably a positive element in the sense that they have professional qualifications and they look down their noses in horror at some of the Salvadoran military's barbarous practices, and they talk about Central Americans as—

JS: Chilean military officers look down on Salvadorans for barbaric practices?

WHITE: Yeah. You may find that hard to believe, but it's true. They have been shocked by some of the things going on.

JS: There were reports that Venezuela was training Salvadoran police.

WHITE: There was hope for that, but as far as I know it didn't happen. Venezuela's involvement is more Christian Democrat to Christian Democrat.

JS: Argentine involvement?

WHITE: Very little. In Guatemala, yes, a lot.

JS: How about U.S. training of Salvadorans in the Canal Zone—so-called human rights training? Wasn't that just a bunch of nonsense?

WHITE: Well, yes, but look: There was increasing pressure from the Pentagon to get into El Salvador with training programs, groups, and so on, and I just resisted, because I didn't think this was the right idea. But the pressure grew very great, so I said to them, "Look, I don't object to your giving them technical training provided they get some really solid training in civilized conduct, you know, that you don't treat citizens as potential people to be killed, but you treat them as citizens, people who are supposed to be respected." In other words, I wanted them to understand who they're supposed to be fighting for. And conditioned on that, we persuaded the Salvador military to write and issue a code of conduct for the security forces. It seemed to me that if you first got a theoretical base, then you might start getting some kind of military justice. But I admit that this was a forlorn attempt. You plow with what you've got.

JS: In thinking about the possible long years of bloodshed ahead, it seems tragic to have missed an opportunity for negotiations.

WHITE: It really is tragic. I think that under the Carter Administration, we had a chance, because we were constantly pushing, every day pushing the Salvadoran military to improve, every day saying, "No, you can't have these goodies until you accomplish this, accomplish that, accomplish the other things." The Reagan Administration has rushed in headlong to prove how macho they are. It won't work.

JS: One last question: Is the Reagan Administration trying to overthrow the government of Nicaragua?

WHITE: Well, I don't know. I know that there are a number of very worrisome reports about activities going on, both in this country and in Honduras, that I think bear looking at. I won't make any accusations. I'd just say that there are some reports that really do concern me about what's taking place.

53. A *Splendid Little War:* Drawing the Line in El Salvador *

BY WILLIAM M. LEOGRANDE

William LeoGrande is Professor of Political Science, and Director of Political Science in the School of Government and Public Administration at the American University in Washington, D.C.

He is author of Cuba's Policy in Africa, 1959–1980, *published by the Institute of International Studies at the University of California, Berkeley; and, with Carla Robbins, "Oligarchs and Officers: The Crisis in El Salvador," which appeared in the Summer 1980 issue of* Foreign Affairs.

IN the midst of the presidential campaign, a skeptical reporter asked one of Ronald Reagan's foreign policy advisers whether he and his candidate really believed their own rhetoric about the communist menace in El Salvador. "El Salvador itself doesn't really matter," the adviser replied, "we have to establish credibility because we're in very serious trouble."

* From *International Security*, Summer 1981.

The Reagan administration has moved quickly to establish that credibility by "drawing the line" against "communist aggression" in El Salvador. During his first two months in the Oval Office, President Reagan fired the Carter administration's reformist ambassador to that country; launched a major political offensive in Europe, Latin America, and on Capital Hill to convince anyone who would listen that the insurgency in El Salvador is "a textbook case of indirect armed aggression by the communist powers"; and moved to more than double both economic and military assistance to the beleaguered Salvadoran government.

A nation of virtually no inherent strategic or economic interest to the United States, El Salvador has suddenly become a symbol—a vehicle through which the Reagan administration hopes to set the tone, by dint of example, for its whole foreign policy. Because the war in El Salvador looks like an easy victory, it provides a perfect opportunity for the new administration to demonstrate its willingness to use force in foreign affairs, its intent to de-emphasize human rights, and its resolve to contain the Soviet Union. In short, the conflict in El Salvador is a splendid little war, made to order for an administration determined to repudiate much of its predecessor's foreign policy.

There is no doubt that Ronald Reagan intends to vanquish the incipient regionalism of the Carter administration's international outlook and restore globalism to its traditional place of pre-eminence in America's strategic thinking. Whether reality will be so amenable is less clear.

Human Rights in Central America: The Reformist Interlude. Jimmy Carter's decision to make the promotion of human rights a major objective of U.S. foreign policy was at once the most celebrated and excoriated of his international initiatives. From the outset, the policy was presented in moral terms—it was an approach to the world as good and decent as the American people themselves.

It was also intended to distance the United States from the brutal excesses of decaying autocracies, rather than wager the prestige and interests of the nation on their doubtful survival. It made more sense, according to Carter's analysts, to adapt U.S. policy to the currents of history than to try vainly to stem the tide. They argued that right-wing dictatorships bent on preserving anachronistic social orders make bad security risks; that the more they rely upon brute force to sustain themselves, the more rapidly they mobilize and radicalize their opponents. For the United States to enlist wholeheartedly in support of right-wing dictatorships would actually endanger national security; ultimately, such regimes would collapse, and an angry populace would bitterly recall—as it did in Iran—that the United States had sided with the tyrants. The Carter administration believed that the best strategy for preserving national security was to help create pluralist democracies with relatively egalitarian social structures. Such states would tend to be culturally and philosophically closer to the United States than to the Soviet Union and, moreover, would be politically stable.

Despite the complaints of Carter's conservative critics, human rights were never allowed to overshadow immediate national security concerns of a more traditional kind. When crucial allies were involved (e.g., South Korea, the Philippines, the Shah's Iran), the issue of human rights was always muted. But in Latin America, where there appeared to be no immediate security threats in 1977, the human rights policy was applied full force. This was especially true in Central America, where the four nations of the northern tier (Nicaragua, Honduras, El Salvador, and Guatemala) were all ruled by military dictatorships notorious for their systematic repression. By reducing or terminating economic and military assistance to these regimes Washington sought to force them to improve their human rights practices.

The revolution in Nicaragua threw the Carter administration's human rights policy into crisis. As stability slipped away in Nicaragua after the assassination of opposition leader Pedro Joaquín Chamorro, the objective of promoting human rights was forced once again to compete with the desire to preserve order. Washington could not bring itself to break completely with Somoza, but was equally unwilling to re-enlist wholeheartedly on the side of his increasingly brutal National Guard. During the last eight months of the Nicaraguan insurrection, the unambiguous objective of U.S. policy was to prevent a Sandinista victory. Only the means for achieving this were at issue: should Somoza be forced out in favor of a government of moderates or should he be given the military wherewithal to defend himself, whatever the cost in bloodshed? The failure of policy in Nicaragua was the failure to actually select one strategy or the other. For nearly a year, leaders of Nicaragua's moderate opposition waited in vain for Washington to call for Somoza's resignation, while the Carter administration persisted in the naïve hope that it could somehow conjure up a reformed Somoza to reign over a stable Nicaragua.[1]

The Sandinista victory in Nicaragua set in motion a full-scale review of U.S. policy toward Central America—a review aimed at devising a more effective strategy for preventing similar leftist victories in

---

[1] For a different critique of Carter's Nicaraguan policy, see Ambassador Kirkpatrick's Analysis, Reading 3, above.—Eds.

El Salvador, Guatemala, and Honduras. At issue was the question that had not been adequately addressed during the Nicaraguan crisis: how could the administration reconcile its commitment to human rights with its desire to preserve political stability? Hardliners within the government argued that these objectives were inherently contradictory, and that stability ought to take precedence even at the expense of human rights. They argued for restoring military aid to the region's anticommunists—in essence, a return to the Kissingerian policy of supporting dictators so long as they were "friendly" ones.

Defenders of the human rights policy replied that military aid could not buy stability in the region and that Washington should instead press for progressive social and political reforms. As in the Alliance for Progress, evolutionary change was prescribed as the antidote to revolutionary upheaval. This option won the bureaucratic battle in Washington, and was put into effect almost immediately in an effort to avert the approaching civil war in El Salvador.

Carter and the Search for Order in El Salvador. For generations, the government of El Salvador served as the guardian of the landed oligarchy, suppressing by force of arms any challenge to the nation's rigid social order. The army seized power in 1932 in order to crush a peasant rebellion, which it did successfully at the cost of 30,000 lives. The military's monopoly on political power was retained for the next half century through alternating periods of modernization and retrenchment. But throughout these five decades, two political characteristics held constant: the policies of the regime never threatened the socio-economic foundations of oligarchic power and the military never allowed the political system to become so open that reformist civilians might actually win control of the government. . . .

By the summer of 1977, political order in El Salvador was decaying rapidly. Washington, armed with its new reformist strategy for the region, began pressuring General Romero to ease the strictures of his military rule and to initiate social and economic reforms to stem the growing strength of the revolutionary opposition. Romero refused, and in October was ousted by progressive military officers who promised the sorts of changes he had resisted. The new junta quickly incorporated civilian leaders from the centrist opposition parties and even suggested its willingness to reach some sort of accord with elements of the radical left. The regime promised to create democratic institutions and to enact social reforms that would break the socio-economic dominance of the landed oligarchy. This government was a seemingly perfect vehicle for Washington's new regional policy of reformism; the Carter administration quickly pledged to support it.

Unfortunately, the October junta proved to be incapable of carrying out its promises—a failure due largely to the internal politics of the Salvadoran armed forces and to the reticence of the United States to carry its support for reformism to its logical conclusion. While the Salvadoran military had traditionally governed in ways congenial to the oligarchy, it also had a tradition of allowing progressive officers to initiate modernizing reforms as long as they did not threaten the basic structure of the existing social order. The October coup was very much in this tradition, but the reforms it promised were more radical than those of the past. Whenever the progressive officers and their civilian allies proposed reforms of any significance, rightists within the armed forces blocked them as being too extreme. The result was paralysis of the government, which could only have been overcome if the progressive officers had been willing to break with their rightist brethren and take full control of the ideologically divided military. This they were unwilling to do—partly because of institutional loyalty and partly because the United States was unwilling to stand behind them. Though Washington favored social reform, it balked at the October junta's willingness to bring elements of the radical left into partnership with the government. The Carter administration's strategy was to isolate the radical left politically, not to allow it to share power.

The October junta's paralysis demolished any hope of accord with the radical left, which proceeded to escalate its insurrectionary activities. The mere suggestion of real socio-economic change terrified the oligarchy, which in turn escalated its paramilitary terrorism. Amidst this spiral of political violence, the moderate civilians within the government sought a showdown with the officers, demanding that reforms be implemented and that the rightist Defense Minister, General José Guillermo García, be removed. The military refused, the civilians resigned, and the government moved sharply to the right. At this critical juncture, the United States did nothing to preserve the moderate reformist character of the government. In fact, despite this fundamental shift in the balance of political forces within the government, U.S. policy changed not at all. The Carter administration continued to provide both economic and military aid to the regime, justifying its policy with claims that it was supporting a moderate centrist government under attack from extremists on both the left and the right.

Reform With Repression: Land Reform and the Rightward Shift of the Junta. Since January 1980, the moderation of the Salvadoran government has been more chimerical than real. The key difference between the junta formed in January and its predecessor lies in their strategy for resolving the nation's political crisis. While the October junta sought to create a political opening to the left, the January government has sought to defeat the left militarily. At the insistence of the United States, the government grudgingly undertook some social reforms, the most touted of which has been the agrarian program, but this strategy of "reform with repression," as Archbishop Oscar Romero characterized it, has been considerably more repressive than reformist.

Under the stewardship of Ambassador Robert White, the U.S. pursued four interrelated objectives during 1980:

•To pressure the government into implementing real social reforms designed to undercut the left's popular support.

•To urge the government to reduce the level of official terrorism by reining in its own security forces, even if that required the removal of some rightist officers.

•To protect the government from a coup by the extreme right.

•To entice the moderate left away from its alliance with the guerrillas, thus opening the way for a negotiated settlement that would leave the radicals isolated on the political periphery.

By year's end, it was apparent that this reformist strategy had failed. The agrarian program, the cornerstone of an otherwise modest package of reforms, was at a standstill. The level of official violence had risen dramatically rather than subsiding, and there was no evidence whatsoever that the government was making any serious effort to curtail it or to bring its perpetrators to justice. The extreme right had not overthrown the government, but the government itself had moved so far to the right that its extremist opposition was quiescent.

The agrarian reform program had come to symbolize the moderation of the Salvadoran government, but its progress offers a microcosm of the political dynamics blocking real social reform. . . .[2]

Though the Salvadoran land reform has not significantly altered the socio-economic condition of the nation's 2.5 million peasants, it has nevertheless been, in a perverse sense, a success. From the outset, the principal objectives of the reform package were political rather than socio-economic. For the Salvadoran government, it was a way of satisfying U.S. demands for reform without alienating rightist officers like Defense Minister García who hold the real reins of power. For the United States, it was tangible "proof"—indeed, the only proof—that the government of El Salvador was truly as moderate and reformist as the administration portrayed it. For if the agrarian reform is a sham or a failure, it is difficult to imagine on what grounds the Salvadoran government might qualify as either moderate or reformist.

---

[2] See Readings 23-28, above for a full explanation of the land reform.—Eds.

Certainly not in the political sphere. Ambassador White's hope of consolidating the position of the moderates within the government had even less success than the agrarian reform.

The Loosening Grip of the Moderates. The pivotal political issue over the past year has been whether the Christian Democratic civilians and the progressive military officers within the government could muster the influence to win control of the security forces away from the right. Such control would have allowed the moderates to remove extremist officers from command positions, punish those guilty of political murders, crack down on the death squads, and thereby curb the repression which took some 10,000 lives, 80 percent of which were civilian deaths ascribed to state security forces.

Not only were the moderates unable to restrain the security forces; they were unable even to maintain what little influence they had. The right-wing coup, which Ambassador White labored so diligently to prevent, occurred slowly, by degrees, not in the streets but in the high councils of the officer corps. As the rightist officers lost patience with reform, they slipped quietly into agreement with their more extremist compatriots, becoming convinced that the only way to meet the challenge of the left is with violence—however much violence that might take.

Over the past year, the rightist officers—the same officers who blocked the reforms of the October 1979 government—have consolidated their hold on power by reducing the Christian Democrats and the progressive officers to impotence. The steady stream of resignations by Christian Democrats over the last twelve months stands as testimony of the rightist character of the regime. Almost without exception, each letter of resignation has cited the intransigence of the rightists and the inability of the moderates to circumvent them.

The progressive officers within the government have fared worse than the Christian Democrats. In mid-summer of 1980, the rightist officers began a campaign to systematically strip the progressives of their command positions, demoting or reassigning them to diplomatic posts. Shortly thereafter, several of the most prominent progressives were assassinated by death squads, and in November their leader, Colonel Adolfo Majano, was finally removed from the five-member governing junta. Majano was later arrested and sent into exile. The progressive faction within the officer corps, which was powerful enough in 1979 to overthrow Romero's government, has now ceased to be a significant political force.

Without allies in the armed forces, the Christian Democrats serve at the pleasure of the rightist officers. The appointment last November of Christian Democratic leader Napoleón Duarte as president should not be mistaken for a significant realignment of political forces. The leadership shuffle that placed Duarte in the presidency left the senior military command basically intact, leading one diplomat to describe Duarte as an "adornment."

Duarte may have his own agenda, but he does not have the political power to carry it out. This is apparent by his inability to act in his own interests: for example, Duarte can neither proceed with the agrarian program nor can he dismiss his military opponents. Like the agrarian reform, the restructuring of the government came at the insistence of the United States. The Carter administration needed it to preserve the centrist image of its client in the wake of the murders of four North American women religious, and the Salvadoran officers acquiesced in it in order to mollify the State Department. But the reorganization has not altered the structure of political power in El Salvador one iota. The government was and remains a rightist military regime with a civilian facade.

Nothing demonstrates this more clearly than the practices of the government itself. The violence of the security forces accelerated in 1980; despite the pleas and promises of the Christian Democrats, the reign of official terror was much worse than under the openly reactionary government of General Humberto Romero. So too, the atrocities committed by the death squads. Not one person has been arrested for the hundreds of murders of Salvadorans for which the extreme right took "credit" in 1980. Officers on the extreme right who have been caught plotting against the government have not even been punished. Major Robert D'Aubuisson, who led a coup attempt last May, was arrested and then released after the officer corps voted not to place him on trial. The Vice-Minister of Defense, also implicated in the plot, was not even removed from his post.

The Opposition of the Left. Despite U.S. efforts to portray the Salvadoran regime as a centrist government beset by both the left and the right, there are really only two sides to the conflict in El Salvador: the rightist government and its leftist opposition, which is no more a "Pol Pot" left than the government is "centrist." The opposition includes a broad, politically heterogeneous array of groups organized under the political rubric of the Revolutionary Democratic Front (FDR), and the military command of the Farabundo Martí Front for National Liberation (FMLN). The FDR unites middle class social democrats, Christian Democrats who have split from Duarte, professional associations, trade unions, and the popular organizations whose ideology is best described as a homegrown amalgam of Marxism and liberation theology. The FDR's President, Guillermo Ungo, was Napoleón Duarte's vice-presidential running mate in the election of 1972.

The FMLN unites the various guerrilla armies which span the ideological spectrum of Marxism from Trotskyist to Castroist to orthodox Marxist-Leninist. Since early 1980, the FDR and the FMLN have pursued a coordinated political, diplomatic, and military strategy to defeat the rightist government. This collaboration has resulted in a moderation of the guerrillas' socialist political program and the joint adoption of a social democratic platform for a revolutionary government modeled on the Nicaraguan example. The platform calls for radically redistributive socio-economic reforms, but promises an economic role for the private sector, the preservation of political pluralism, and a foreign policy of nonalignment. The viability of such a program is by no means certain, but would depend, as in the Nicaraguan case, upon a host of internal and external circumstances.

The left clearly failed to create an irreversible military situation before Ronald Reagan entered the Oval Office, but the January 1981 offensive was hardly a great victory for government forces either. Though the guerrillas were unable to defend any of their initial territorial gains, they demonstrated their ability to launch coordinated assaults throughout the country and to operate with impunity in many rural areas. Never before had the various guerrilla groups demonstrated such a capacity for coordinated action. Indeed, the threat posed by the January offensive was severe enough to prompt the Carter administration to radically reverse its own policy. Lethal military aid had been withheld from El Salvador since 1977 on human rights grounds, and $5.7 million in "nonlethal" aid was suspended in November pending the outcome of the investigation into the murders of the North American clergywomen. On the very eve of leaving office, the administration restored the "nonlethal" aid and rushed an additional $5 million in lethal matériel to the Salvadoran armed forces, though the offensive was thwarted before the aid arrived.

Ironically, the Carter administration's decision to restore military aid came on the same day as Carter's farewell address, in which he offered a stirring rhetorical defense of his human rights policy. Nothing could have better symbolized the contradictions of Carter's policy in Central America. Ultimately, the administration's commitment to social and political reform could not compete with Washington's traditional fear of leftist governments.

The current military situation appears to be one of stalemate: the left does not yet have the capacity to defeat the armed forces, but neither do the armed forces have the capacity to exterminate the guerrillas. The January offensive was by no means the final battle of El Salvador's civil war—more likely, it was only the opening shot fired. The future course of the war could well depend as much upon external actors as upon the domestic principals, and a great deal more than the tranquility of El Salvador may be at stake.

Regional/International Alignments. The conflict in El Salvador has never been a purely domestic affair. The long succession of rightist regimes there have always relied upon Washington's military and political support to help cow their opponents. As political strife escalated in 1980, so too did the level of international involvement, and no external actor was more prominent than the United States. In addition to providing nearly $100 million in aid, Washington was intimately involved in the internal politics of both the Salvadoran government and its armed forces.

The United States has not been the only patron of the Salvadoran government; support from Venezuela and Costa Rica have been crucial for maintaining the regional legitimacy of U.S. policy. Venezuelan President Herrera Campins has lobbied hard within the international Christian Democratic movement to gain acceptance for Duarte's government, and Venezuela has provided considerable economic assistance to San Salvador. Venezuelan opposition leaders accuse their government of covertly shipping arms to the Salvadoran security forces, but Herrera Campins denies the charges. Costa Rica's Christian Democratic president, Rodrigo Carazo, has also been supportive of U.S. policy and maintains cordial relations with Duarte's government, though Costa Rica does not have the resources to make any major material contribution to the conflict.

Guatemala and Honduras are allies of the Salvadoran regime, a fact which the U.S. government has been less than eager to spotlight. Both nations are ruled by right-wing military governments which perceive the possibility of a leftist victory in El Salvador as a threat to their own internal security. Over the past year, both have sought closer ties with the rightist officers in the Salvadoran armed forces rather than with the government *per se.* During the left's January 1981 offensive in El Salvador, Honduran and Guatemalan forces were mobilized along the border, ostensibly to prevent the fighting from spilling across the frontiers. In effect, however, they were providing an anvil against which the Salvadoran military hoped to pound guerrillas. There were numerous though unconfirmed reports that some Honduran and Guatemalan units crossed the frontier to operate jointly with their Salvadoran allies.

Whether or not such reports are accurate, there is little doubt that the Guatemalans are predisposed to intervene in El Salvador if the left appears to be gaining militarily. The Guatemalan armed forces have a history of coming to the aid of the Salvadoran right in times of crisis (in 1932 and again in 1972), and the Guatemalan government has spoken openly of the need to halt the "communist tide" before it reaches Guatemalan shores. Finally, U.S. intelligence reports reveal that both the Guatemalan and Honduran governments are assisting in the creation of paramilitary groups within their territories, groups composed of former Nicaraguan National Guardsmen and anti-Castro Cubans whose objective is to wage war against communism on a regional scale.

The left, too, has its international allies, among whom Mexico, Nicaragua, and Cuba have been the most vocal.[3] Though Mexico has not formally broken relations with El Salvador, the Mexican government and ruling Institutional Revolutionary Party (PRI) are firm supporters of Salvadoran leftists. Mexico City is the principal base of operations for the FDR's efforts to build diplomatic support.

Mexico and the United States are farther apart on the issue of El Salvador than on any other. Within hours of Reagan's election, President José López Portillo publicly warned the incoming administration against intervention in Central America. Mexican protests escalated in January when the Carter administration restored military aid to El Salvador; Foreign Minister Jorge Castaneda warned the United States to let the Salvadorans "solve their own problems," and PRI President Gustavo Carvajal promised that the party would support any people that "fights for its freedom." That same week, 25,000 Mexicans marched against U.S. intervention in El Salvador—the largest such demonstration in recent years. In February, when General Vernon Walters traveled to Mexico City to present Washington's evidence of Cuban involvement in El Salvador, he was denied an audience with President Portillo. Portillo then followed Walters' visit with a speech in which he went out of his way to stress Mexico's close relations with Cuba, calling it the Latin American state "most dear" to Mexico.

Mexican policy is based upon an assessment of Central American reality not so different from that of the Carter administration. The Mexicans are convinced that the military governments of El Salvador, Guatemala, and Honduras cannot long survive the growing demands of the poor for social change. Stability in the region therefore requires that these narrowly-based dictatorial regimes be replaced with popular governments willing to dismantle the oligarchic land-owning systems and distribute the benefits of development to a broader cross-section of the populace. While the Mexicans have no desire to see pro-Soviet Marxist-Leninist regimes predominate in Central America, they see fundamental change as inevitable and believe that strong international support for social democratic opposition elements offers the best hope for long-term stability. The Mexicans, unlike the Carter administration, have not been afraid to

---

[3] And, since spring, 1981, France under the Mitterand government.—Eds.

carry this policy through to its logical conclusion, i.e., supporting the revolutionary oppositions in El Salvador and Guatemala. Based upon their experience of peaceful coexistence with Cuba, the Mexicans are confident that they can live cordially with whatever form of revolutionary government emerges.

Mexico's view is widely shared within the Socialist International, which has provided financial assistance and diplomatic support to the FDR. A number of key European Social Democratic parties, including those in Germany, Sweden, Holland, and Norway, are on record supporting the FDR and opposing any deeper U.S. military involvement in El Salvador. Sweden's support for the left has been so vocal that the Reagan administration was moved to lodge a formal protest in February—the first such protest made to a West European nation since the war in Vietnam.

The breadth of the FDR's European support prompted Washington to launch a major diplomatic offensive on the continent in an effort to counter it. Assistant Secretary of State for European Affairs Lawrence Eagleburger was dispatched to Germany, France, Belgium, the Netherlands, and the United Kingdom to convince the allies that Cuban and Soviet arms shipments to the Salvadoran left constituted a "textbook case of indirect armed aggression" requiring a coordinated allied response. He did not meet with stirring success. Most of the Europeans were unwilling to enter in the administration's crusade against communism in El Salvador until the administration provided more detail on how it proposed to respond. None of the Europeans were anxious to see the United States escalate its military involvement; all expressed support for a negotiated political settlement rather than a military solution.

The role of socialist and radical states, expecially Cuba and Nicaragua, has received great attention because of the State Department's report on "communist interference" in El Salvador. Up until the last few months of 1980, Cuban and Nicaraguan aid to the left was more political than military. Both states had openly endorsed the Salvadoran opposition and were routinely providing it with advice. Managua, like Mexico City, served as an important center of diplomatic and political activity for the FDR and FMLN, but U.S. intelligence could discern only a trickle of arms from Nicaragua to El Salvador. As late as September, 1980, Washington certified that the Nicaraguan government was not materially promoting the revolution in El Salvador and was therefore in compliance with the Congressionally imposed condition for the release of $75 million in economic aid.

The Tide Turns: Presidential Transition and Communist Involve-

ment. In the midst of the guerrillas' January offensive, the Carter administration reversed itself, claiming that it had "compelling evidence" that Cuba, Vietnam, and the Soviet Union had begun channeling massive arms shipments into El Salvador via Nicaragua. This sudden flood of arms, along with the exigency of the guerrilla offensive itself, were cited as justifications for the resumption of U.S. military aid to the Salvadoran armed forces. At the same time, economic aid to Nicaragua was suspended in an effort to force the Nicaraguans to close the arms conduit.

In February, the Reagan administration released a White Paper documenting the charges initially leveled by Carter. . . . The White Paper serves effectively as a justification for the Reagan administration's decision to escalate U.S. military involvement in El Salvador. Armed with the report, briefing teams were dispatched to Europe, Latin America, and Capitol Hill in a well-orchestrated effort to build domestic and international support for a change in U.S. policy. But the basic thrust of this new policy was determined long before the arms buildup described in the White Paper. Early in the presidential campaign, Reagan and his foreign policy advisers targeted Carter's human rights policy, especially as applied in Central America, as a major focus of attack. The insurgency in El Salvador was portrayed as resulting primarily from Cuban and Soviet subversion rather than domestic social and political conditions, and Carter's strategy for achieving stability through reform was denounced as idealistic and foolish, merely aiding the cause of international communism.

The administration's new policy for El Salvador is one of keeping the left from coming to power, whatever the cost. Within days of assuming office, Reagan increased economic aid by 63 percent and began a full review of policy toward the Salvadoran government. Shortly thereafter, Ambassador White, who was closely identified with the Carter administration's effort (albeit unsuccessful) to promote reform, was fired. He was replaced by Chargé d'Affairs Frederic Chapin, reassigned from the Defense Department where he had been preparing contingency plans for a major increase in U.S. military aid to the Salvadoran armed forces. Secretary of State Alexander Haig's pledge to shift the focus of U.S. policy away from human rights toward the battle against "international terrorism" was quickly followed by an announcement that U.S. aid to El Salvador would no longer be contingent upon either reforms or human rights. The next day, Department of State's William Dyess tried to dispel the impression that the Reagan administration was indifferent to reforms in El Salvador, but the afterthought served only to reinforce the obviously tertiary nature of the concern.

The likelihood that this new policy will have the effect of curtailing social reform and encouraging the terrorism of the security forces seems beside the point for the Reagan administration. The administration appears to be less interested in El Salvador *per se* than in creating a symbol of U.S. resolve to use military force abroad and to get tough with the Soviet Union. El Salvador provides what appears to be a geopolitically safe testing ground on which the United States can probe the depths of Soviet commitment to national liberation struggles, assess the cooperativeness of the allies, and begin to purge the national psyche of the "Vietnam syndrome" that Reagan has so denounced. . . .

El Salvador and the Lessons of Vietnam. The parallels between El Salvador and Vietnam apply not so much to the military circumstances of the two cases, which are quite different, but to the way in which U.S. policy is unfolding. El Salvador, like Vietnam before it, is being transformed from an internal war into an international test of will between East and West. The domino analogy has been resurrected to characterize the nations of Central America, falling in chain reaction from El Salvador north to Guatemala and Mexico, south to Costa Rica and Panama. As candidate Reagan warned, "We are the last domino."

Claims of an East-West confrontation distort reality in two ways—by making it sound as if the Salvadoran revolution is a Cuban creation, and as if it is a purely military struggle that can be won merely by countering the flow of arms from abroad. The revolution in El Salvador began long before the first Cuban arms shipments and it will not fade away if those shipments are halted. By failing to focus on the socio-economic causes of political turmoil, the Reagan administration betrays a narrowly military conception of national security and a preference for using military means to manage political problems. Revolutions spring from deep social and political fissures in the very foundations of a society—problems that cannot be solved by simply throwing guns at them. Though massive firepower failed to bring about victory in Vietnam, Administration policies reflect a considerable faith in the efficacy of arms.

By declaring El Salvador to be a test of will with international communism, the Reagan administration is wagering U.S. prestige and credibility on the survival of one of the weakest, most brutal, and least popular governments in the hemisphere. A nation of virtually no inherent strategic or economic interest to the United States is thus cast, like Vietnam before it, onto the world's center stage, and the success or failure of U.S. policy takes on implications it would never have otherwise. Once begun, the process of investing blood and treasure in this exemplary case provides its own rationale for incremental escalation.

Policymakers in Washington have already been seduced by the view that just a little more aid, a few more advisers, or one additional reorganization of the government will somehow produce success. Since January 1980, the United States has been drawn almost imperceptibly into a position so totally identified with the Salvadoran government that to disassociate from it would be viewed as a radical change in policy.

American aid has not produced a strong, stable government, it has only fostered dependency. The Salvadoran economy is already comatose, surviving solely on the life support system of U.S. largesse. With the munificence of the United States as a crutch, the rightist military regime has no incentive to make the kinds of political concessions and compromises necessary to achieve a lasting peace. Large-scale military aid to the Salvadoran armed forces will not strengthen them, it will only allow them to continue to ignore political reality. The Reagan administration promises that it will never send American troops to fight in El Salvador. But if, a year from now, the Salvadoran government is on the verge of collapse, as Saigon was in 1965, how will this adminstration respond?

One of the clearest parallels between El Salvador and Vietnam is the way in which the Reagan administration, and the Carter administration before it, have waged the public-relations war at home. The selling of the war began, as in Vietnam, with a natural effort to put the best possible face on U.S. policy. The Salvadoran government was described as "centrist" even as it engaged in repression worse than its "rightist" predecessor; the opposition was labeled a "Pol Pot left," even though it bore closer resemblance to the Sandinistas than to the Cambodians.

At some point in mid-1980, the Carter administration evolved a conscious policy of attempting to manage U.S. public opinion on El Salvador by encouraging media coverage favorable to the government. The objective, according to a dissent document purportedly prepared by foreign policy analysts within the administration, was to prevent the creation of a positive image for the Salvadoran left of the sort enjoyed by the Sandinistas. It was then that truth became hostage to policy; the Carter administration began making public pronouncements sharply at variance with internal reports—on the effectiveness of the agrarian reform, for example.

The Reagan administration has continued in this vein. Throughout 1980, Carter's State Department acknowledged that the right in El Salvador was responsible for the overwhelming majority of political murders. One official called the mortality statistics gathered by the Salvadoran Catholic church "the best data we have." Reagan's State Department now claims that the guerrillas have been committing most of the atrocities, and the same official who acknowledged the veracity of the church's data in January now solemnly contends that the church's figures are unreliable because it sympathizes with the communists. Truth has indeed become the first casualty.

Despite strenuous efforts, the Reagan administration's public relations campaign to justify American involvement in the Salvadoran conflict has not met with overwhelming success. Domestic opposition to the war is mounting and is already greater than was opposition to Vietnam at a comparable stage of the war. On May 3, 1981, [at least] 25,000 people marched in Washington in an antiwar demonstration reminiscent of the 1960's. The Reagan administration appears to recognize that it cannot sustain U.S. military involvement in El Salvador without the support of the U.S. public. What the administration appears not to recognize is that public support cannot be manufactured by good public relations; it is inextricably tied to a nature of the conflict itself. A massive counterinsurgency effort against a popular insurgency inevitably requires widespread brutality against the civilian populace if it is to succeed. The lesson of Vietnam at home is that the people of the United States will not long tolerate a policy that necessitates such brutality.

The Reagan administration's narrow military view of the domestic political situation in El Salvador is matched by its narrow geopolitical view of the conflict's international context and the implications of committing massive economic and military resources there. The administration seems to believe it can confront the Soviet Union in Central America with relatively little risk—that the Soviets will retreat rather than try to match U.S. escalation in a region far from the areas vital to Soviet national interest. All this is true enough, but it by no means follows that a major U.S. economic and military commitment in El Salvador bears no serious cost. On the contrary, its cost is potentially immense.[4]

The U.S.-Latin American Relations Angle. Reagan's policy places the United States on a collision course with Mexico at the very time that Mexico is unveiling a more activist foreign policy that seeks to extend Mexican influence throughout its "area of concern"—Central America and the Caribbean. While Mexico wants to maintain good relations with the United States, President López Portillo has repeat-

---

[4] Additional discussion of the Vietnam analogy appears in Readings 38-41, above.—Eds.

edly warned against the very policy Washington now seems intent on pursuing. A direct American intervention in El Salvador would demolish relations with Mexico just when it has emerged as the most important Latin American nation for the United States.

Even Venezuela and Costa Rica, two principal regional supporters of the United States on the issue of El Salvador, could not suffer U.S. intervention in silence. In both countries, the social democratic oppositions have harshly criticized their ruling Christian Democratic parties for supporting the Salvadoran government. Deeper U.S. involvement will intensify that opposition and could easily lead those governments to begin distancing themselves from American policy. A direct U.S. intervention could cause their support to evaporate immediately. Indeed, the Organization of American States would probably condemn such an intervention with only a few nations dissenting.

American relations with Nicaragua would probably not survive a major escalation of U.S. involvement in El Salvador. The insurrection there has already become the principal flash point in bilateral relations, with the Reagan administration charging that Nicaragua has served as a conduit for arms shipments to the FMLN, and threatening to cut off economic aid to Nicaragua in reprisal. Virtually all observers agree that a cutoff of aid would provoke a severe deterioration of U.S.-Nicaraguan relations, a rapid radicalization of domestic Nicaraguan politics, an unavoidable economic dependence on the Soviet Union, and an increased Nicaraguan role in El Salvador.

Diplomatic Costs of American Involvement: Europe and the Third World. The repercussions beyond the hemisphere of escalating U.S. involvement in El Salvador would be no less damaging. The cool reception encountered by emissaries sent to brief the allies on the Cuban and Soviet role in El Salvador suggests that Reagan will find little support for his policy in Europe. Most of the western European states would probably be content to leave El Salvador to the United States, but if Washington continues to insist that events in El Salvador will determine whether the United States enters in arms limitation talks with the Soviet Union, the issue will cease to be one which the allies can afford to ignore. Given the strength of European social democracy and its support for the Salvadoran opposition, Reagan may well find that his policy exacerbates tensions within the North Atlantic Community rather than forging a new unity and resolve to resist "communist aggression" in the third world.

In the third world, Reagan's policy of deepening U.S. involvement in El Salvador will undo most of the diplomatic gains accruing from Carter's human rights policy. Third world suspicions, focused in recent years upon the Soviet Union because of its interventions in

Ethiopia and Afghanistan, would shift back to the United States if Reagan were to intervene directly in El Salvador. The Soviets have had the good sense not to stake their prestige or credibility on the Salvadoran left, so its defeat would damage the Soviet Union not at all. But the sort of commitment by the United States required to defeat the left (if that is possible at all) would damage U.S. relations with the rest of the hemisphere, strain the Western Alliance, erode U.S. prestige in the third world, and prompt a new wave of domestic recriminations in the United States itself. Not incidentally, it would hand the Soviet Union a custom-made sphere of influence argument to justify its policy in Afghanistan and Poland.

The Costs of Military Involvement: Tumbling Into War. The military implications of Reagan's policy are even more sobering than the diplomatic ones. By siding with the right in El Salvador and justifying a deeper U.S. military involvement with claims of Cuban intervention, the United States, intentionally or not, lowers the barriers against direct intervention by Honduras and Guatemala. If massive U.S. aid can be justified as merely a necessary response to Cuban subversion, cannot Guatemalan or Honduran intervention be similarly justified? The Guatemalan government is faced with a major guerrilla insurgency of its own, and the Guatemalan left would surely respond to Guatemalan intervention in El Salvador by escalating its activities and extending its cooperation with the Salvadoran left. The Salvadoran war would thus become a transnational war of left against right in which national boundaries would cease to have any practical meaning.

The danger in Honduras is somewhat different since guerrilla forces there still number only a handful. But Honduras borders Nicaragua, and relations between the two states are strained because of attacks launched on Nicaraguan border areas by former National Guardsmen based in Honduras and clashes between Honduras and Nicaraguan border guards. Guatemalan or Honduran intervention in El Salvador would be viewed by Nicaragua as a clear and present threat to its own internal security. In such an atmosphere, the former Guardsmen might well try to provoke a conflict between Nicaragua and Honduras by launching a major border attack. If they should succeed, the whole northern tier of Central America would be engulfed by war.

Unfortunately, the danger does not end there. Nicaragua at war would be forced to turn to Cuba and the Soviet Union for major infusions of military aid. If the war were to go badly and Nicaragua were to call for Cuban troops to help defend Nicaraguan territory, Cuba would probably provide them, for the scenario would fit exactly the circumstances under which Cuba has in the past deployed combat troops abroad—at the request of a friendly government threatened by external attack. The arrival of Cuban troops amidst war in Central America would surely call forth a response by the United States—most probably a naval blockade. The stage might then be set for a re-enactment of the Cuban missile crisis, but without the 3-to-1 U.S. nuclear superiority that is thought to have determined the outcome in 1962.

Is There No Exit? Pursuing the "Zimbabwe Solution." Ironically, all the actors in the Salvadoran drama profess to recognize the need for a political rather than military solution to the civil war. Thus far, the obstacle to negotiations between the government and opposition has been the conviction of each party that the other lacks sincerity. Such suspicions produce negotiating proposals which are so clearly unacceptable that they must be understood as propaganda ploys rather than as serious initiatives. Yet even these spurious overtures serve to place the combatants on record favoring some sort of negotiations, thereby opening the possibility, however remote, that an appropriate coalition of international actors might be able to devise a workable negotiating formula.

There is little doubt that most of the international supporters on both sides in the civil war truly desire a political solution, and several have been actively pursuing a way to get the process started. Social Democrats in Western Europe, led by the Germans and Swedes, have attempted to cast themselves and their Christian Democratic counterparts in Germany and Italy as intermediaries between the Salvadoran government and opposition, thus far to no effect. In Latin America, Mexico, Venezuela, Brazil, Costa Rica, and even Nicaragua are also searching for an acceptable mechanism to initiate a dialogue.

Since there is no measure of trust whatsoever between the Salvadoran government and opposition, three necessary conditions must be met before negotiations can begin: 1) each side must be convinced that it has no hope of winning a military victory in the near term: 2) each must be certain that its opponent will not be able to gain military advantage during the negotiations themselves; and 3) each must be assured that the other will have to abide by the outcome of whatever political process emerges from a peace conference. Even then, substantial political pressure will probably have to be exerted by the international allies of both sides to bring them to the bargaining table.

The military statemate that currently exists in El Salvador provides what may be the last opportunity for arranging a political solution, but it is fleeting. As the Reagan administration begins to provide massive amounts of economic and military aid to the Salvadoran government, the armed forces there become increasingly convinced that their drive for military victory will be underwritten by Washington. By announcing that aid will no longer be tied to reforms or human rights practices, the administration is sending the Salvadoran security forces the message, whether intended or not, that the United States will tolerate and abet whatever level of violence pacification requires. Instead of providing unconditional military support of the Salvadoran government, the Reagan administration ought to be co-operating with European and Latin American efforts to convene a peace conference modeled loosely on the Lancaster House negotiations which produced peace in Zimbabwe.

Indeed, the role of the United States is crucial to meeting all the conditions necessary to launch such a conference. As the premier foreign source of material aid to the Salvadoran government, only the United States has the ability to restrain the Salvadoran army's quest for military victory, to bring the Salvadoran government to the negotiating table, and to assure that it will abide by any agreements reached (on pain of a cutoff of aid). Germany, Mexico, and Nicaragua can probably bring the FDR–FMLN to the bargaining table, just as the "front line states" brought the Patriotic Front to the Lancaster House conference; only the United States can play the role of Britain by assuring the participation of the Salvadoran government.

Unfortunately, the Reagan administration's determination to make El Salvador a global example of U.S. resolve probably makes negotiations impossible. Indeed, for Washington, they are counterproductive. It would hardly do to "draw the line" against communism in El Salvador and then fail to win a clear victory. The Reagan administration gives every indication of believing it can "win" in El Salvador, even if it has to destroy the country in order to save it. As Washington maps this initial gambit in its game of global chess with the Soviet Union, it is Salvadoran pawns that stand in the front rank, about to be sacrificed.

Epilogue: FAREWELL, MONROE DOCTRINE

54. Three Dates of Change in Latin America *

BY CARLOS FUENTES

The author of many articles, short stories, and novels, Carlos Fuentes is former Mexican ambassador to France.

IN 1961, C. Wright Mills [1] visited the newly created school of political science at the National University of Mexico. For most of the students and teachers of government of my generation, this was their first contact with the intelligentsia of the United States. The residue of good feeling left by the Roosevelt era had died in Guatemala; the majority of universities and scientific and cultural organizations in Latin America had sided with the Guatemalan revolutionaries and had decided to shun their U.S. counterparts after the invasion of 1954. This was the result of disillusionment, of outrage, and even of a certain confusion.

In 1954 [Fuentes' first "date"] an invasion of Guatemala had taken place. It was nominally headed by a putschist colonel, Carlos Castillo Armas. It had been carefully planned by the American ambassador, John Peurifoy. It was armed, launched, and then consolidated in power by the United States Central Intelligence Agency. It permitted the secretary of state, John Foster Dulles, to gloat over what he called "a glorious victory."

A "glorious victory" over what? According to the U.S. government it was communist influence in Guatemala, the communist-inspired government of Jacobo Arbenz Guzmán. A "glorious victory" for what? For the unilaterally proclaimed Monroe Doctrine—this Monroe Doctrine that periodically and conveniently pops out of the ghost closet of the U.S. government until it meets its spectral sibling, the Brezhnev Doctrine; this Monroe Doctrine that would ban extracontinental interventions in this hemisphere but not extracontinental in-

---

* Harpers, Vol. 263, No. 1,575, August 1981, pp. 29–35.
[1] Late U.S. radical sociologist, best known for his studies *The Power Elite* (1956) and *White Collar* (1953). In *Listen, Yankee* (1960), Mills sought to explain the Cuban revolution to the U.S. public as a Cuban might see it.— Eds.

terventions by the United States in other hemispheres and most assuredly not in this one, its backyard, its most immediate sphere of influence, Latin America; this Monroe Doctrine that ironically and conveniently forgets that if a Monroe Doctrine had been in effect in 1776, the United States would not exist. There was more evidence of French intervention in the North American War of Independence than there is or, I fear, ever shall be of Soviet intervention in the Salvadoran civil war.

1954: a glorious victory against democracy in the name of democracy. The victory of that extraordinary mixture of malice and innocence, arrogance and ignorance that has, as a rule, characterized Washington's policies in Latin America.

How many people in this country, except a few specialists (certainly not the policymakers themselves), knew the political traditions and cultural realities of Guatemala in 1954 or know those of El Salvador in 1981? How many were aware of Guatemala's troubled history, the background it shared with Latin America: conquest and colonization in the sixteenth century, legal independence and economic dependency since the nineteenth century, and, also since the nineteenth century, the heritage of our perennial struggle between civilization and barbarism—the basic dilemma of our nations, far beyond ideological nitpicking and strategic posturing—this demand that we choose between civilization, the respect due to a man's hands, a woman's sex, or a child's eyes, or barbarism and the brutality that humiliates, tortures, and then murders us all?

How many citizens of this country were aware, in 1954 or today, of the dramatic struggles in Guatemala, throughout the first half of the nineteenth century, between the liberalism of Francisco Morazán and the return to colonial privilege and exploitation under the military chieftain and lifetime president, Rafael Carrera; of the liberal reforms introduced by Justo Rufino Barrios after Carrera's death; of the fight against aristocratic privileges, for the separation of church and state, and for universal education?

And if these realities were ignored, how dare the faraway government of the United States rush in as if it knew them intimately and were capable of acting in the best interests of a people who alone understood the dynamics of their own history, their own contradictions, their family affairs?

How many people in the United States, as Dulles celebrated the "glorious victory," could recall the twenty-two-year-long dictatorship of Manuel Estrada Cabrera, built on repression and the piecemeal surrender of the country to the United Fruit Company—until in 1920 Congress declared the president insane? How many could remember the fourteen-year-long dictatorship of Jorge Ubico, the gerontocratic "easy rider" who militarized Guatemala on Mussolini's model, right down to the elementary schools?

How many, finally, knew and understood that the general strike of 1944, the Central American "Solidarity" movement of its day, gave birth to the first twentieth-century democracy in Guatemala, the successive governments of Juan José Arévalo and Jacobo Arbenz Guzmán, the creation of a labor code, social security, a free school system, and agrarian reform?

Democracy in Guatemala in the 1940s and 1950s meant the massive transfer of power from the army to the labor and peasant organizations. I stress its importance because if Guatemalan democracy had been allowed to persist it would have influenced democracy in El Salvador, Honduras, and Nicaragua, and would then have met Costa Rican democracy; perhaps a truly Central American model would have been born of this experience. Instead, the experience was aborted with callous, imperial blindness; the price is being paid today, in money and blood, in El Salvador.

Democracy in Guatemala, democracy in Nicaragua, democracy in El Salvador was born, is being born, shall be born of the local experiences of Spanish conquest and colonization, formal independence, economic dependency, liberal reforms, and dictatorial repression. In 1954, these Guatemalan experiences were violated and corrupted by the CIA invasion. This was the *only* non-Guatemalan experience suffered by Guatemala. The rest was, as ever, malice and ignorance, innocence and arrogance.

1954 was an important year for the men and women of my generation because the hopes for Franklin Roosevelt's Good Neighbor Policy—which, with political imagination and pragmatic respect for nonintervention, had met the dramatic challenge of the Mexican revolution under President Lázaro Cárdenas, thus ensuring collaboration within the Western hemisphere against the Axis—were now buried inside an iceberg that not even the warm waters of the Caribbean could melt.

It was an important year, because it proved how uneven was the balance of forces in the hemisphere at the time. The Dulles resolution against Guatemala at the Caracas Inter-American Conference was approved almost unanimously, with only two abstaining votes: those of Mexico and Uruguay. Mexico paid for its unruliness with the economic pressures exerted on it by the Eisenhower administration: the flight of capital and the devaluation of the peso.

It was an important year, 1954, because political development in Guatemala was not merely interrupted by violent foreign intervention; it has been continually perverted and poisoned down to this very day. Today Guatemala is a terrorist nation; the principal terrorist is the government of General Lucas García, and the violence that exists there stretches to the extremes of indiscriminate murder of political leaders, abduction of dissidents, torture of their families, torture of missionaries and other social workers, the moral prostitution of young Indians forced to deny their heritage, insult their parents in public, and become murderous goons of the dictatorship.

When some of us met C. Wright Mills in Mexico in 1961, my second date, we realized that we should distinguish between the actions of the U.S. government and those of the democratic polity in this country. We realized that the best interests of democracy in the U.S. and Latin America were served not by isolation but rather by a willingness to build bridges and make sure that communication was kept alive above and beyond visa restrictions, prejudices, and honest differences of opinion.

"Keep in touch," said Mills back in 1961. "We need you and maybe you'll need us." He added: "I tell gringos that when they come to Mexico they should keep away from the stones. There are too many beautiful stones in Mexico and they distract you from the people. Stick to the people." And he also said, "Do things your way. Don't sit forever waiting to see what the U.S. will do or won't do. To hell with the United States: do your own stuff."

Aye, there's the rub: that when Latin America does *not* "do its own stuff," it is accused of being composed of a bunch of shiftless, whining, grumbling, irresponsible beggars who throw all the blame for their native problems on the shoulders of the United States.

But when we do do something about our condition, we are accused of being communist agents and Soviet-trained terrorists, a subversive menace in the very backyard of the United States. We are then worthy only of being bombed back into the underdevelopment we should never have left. If ever there was an international Catch-22, it is surely this one.

At the beginning of the 1960s, the Cuban revolutionaries were experimenting with self-government. Instead of respecting them, as the Roosevelt administration had done in Mexico's case, the Eisenhower administration slammed the door in Cuba's face, countered every internal revolutionary reform with U.S. sanctions and propaganda, and prepared the invasion plans, again conceived by the CIA, which the Kennedy administration inherited and sent to defeat at the Bay of Pigs.

But as 1962 dawned, the balance of power had changed. At the Punta del Este Conference in late January, the United States tried to ram through the collective decision to break relations with Cuba, expel her government from the OAS, and launch a barrage of economic and political sanctions against the Castro regime.

Once again it was Mexico, this time standing quite alone, which refused to go along with a decision it judged legally unfounded and politically foolish. But this time the distribution of forces in the world was different. The López Mateos administration in Mexico could make a show of alliance with Gaullist France and with the leaders of the nonaligned movement, establish trade with communist bloc countries, and nationalize American-owned utilities.

I was in Havana the day the first Soviet tanker sailed into the harbor, bringing the Cuban government the oil it would otherwise have been denied. This was the price of its refusal to knuckle under to U.S. sanctions. I said to myself then that the history of our continent, for better or worse, had changed forever. The cold war had killed the Good Neighbor Policy. Its consequences became frighteningly evident during the October missile crisis.

I also told myself that Latin America should never again allow itself to be put in the quandary of having to choose between the United States and the Soviet Union; that the next revolution should find conditions that would offer a choice among different sources of economic and political support. Those revolutions have now come, first in Nicaragua and now in El Salvador. They have come about for the same reasons that they came to the thirteen colonies in 1776, to France in 1789, to Mexico in 1910, to Russia in 1917, to Guatemala in 1944, to China in 1949, to Bolivia and Cuba in the 1950s, and to the whole colonized world in the aftermath of World War II; for reasons rooted in the local culture, history, and economy; in the heavens and hells of a people's imagination, its memory, its hopes, its self.

The problems in El Salvador in 1981, my third date, have been around for five centuries; their name is colonialism, the internal colonialism of the traditional ruling class and the external colonialism inherent in client-state relations.

El Salvador shares with Guatemala, and Nicaragua under the Somozas—indeed, to some degree, with all of Latin America—problems that existed a long time before the United States or the Soviet Union came into being, problems as old as the discovery of the New World. Our lands were not only discovered and colonized; they were conquered, and conquest plus colonization spells what Max Weber called patrimonialism, a condition brought on by the confusion of all public and private rights in favor of the chieftain and his clan of relatives, favorites, sycophants, and hangers-on. Patrimonialism—the right of the conquistador—precludes competent administration or economic planning: it is based on obedience and whim, not law. This state of things requires a standing patrimonial army—thugs, mercenaries, death squads, responsible to no law save that of the caprice of the ruling clan.

This patrimonialist confusion of public and private functions and appropriations has been the style of governance in Latin America almost constantly, from the Indian empires to the Spanish colonies to the Republican nations. We in Latin America understand this. We know intimately that if we do not abolish these conditions ourselves, we shall never be viable societies and harmonious communities, minimally prosperous, sufficiently independent.

Many men and women have tried to change this barbaric order through reform: Juárez in Mexico, Sarmiento in Argentina, Battle in Uruguay, Arévalo in Guatemala, Allende in Chile. Others have had to use arms: Morelos and Morazán, Juárez when conservative militarism allied itself with French intervention to oppose the reform laws, Zapata, Sandino, and Guevara. The United States, too, knows this conflict between reform and revolution. Jackson and the two Roosevelts and Kennedy were able to reform; Washington and Lincoln had to fight, and their fights were cruel, bloody, and necessary. But they never had to reform or revolutionize such a persistent, ancient, slow-moving creature as this turtle of Latin American patrimonialism, protected by its standing army.

Today there are deep inequalities and staggering poverty in many other nations of Latin America, Africa, and Asia; but there is not always an accompanying revolutionary situation. Sometimes, as in Mexico or India, nationalist revolutions have created political institutions that cushion class warfare, permit policies of mediation and even of postponement, and are at times capable of effectively and flexibly reforming themselves. In Algeria and Zimbabwe, Tanzania and Nigeria, institutions are being fashioned out of the anti-colonial experience, and many of the problems of those new nations will surely find political solutions.

In El Salvador political development was brutally interrupted in 1932, when the army, under the command of General Maximiliano Hernández Martínez, surrounded and massacred 30,000 people in order to crush a rebellion of peasants and proletarians who were simply asking for a minimum wage. Political freedom in El Salvador has been smothered ever since, from coup to rigged election to counter-coup and through a constant unresponsiveness to the needs of the people. Who cared? Who knew anything about this nation, the smallest, the most densely inhabited, and one of the poorest nations in our hemisphere?

I shall tell you who knew. Father Rutilio Grande knew, who was killed because he said that poverty is not the will of God but the greed of a few. Archbishop Oscar Romero knew, who was killed because he found it intolerable that illiteracy in El Salvador affected nearly half of the population. Four American missionaries knew, who went to work and help so that the level of infant mortality in El Salvador should not be three or four times higher than that of any other Western nation. President José Napoleón Duarte should know, he who was tortured by the same thugs with whom he shares power today, who was deprived of his electoral victory in 1972 by the same gorillas with whom today he offers free elections to a population that has seen its brothers and sisters and fathers and mothers and children die, assassinated by the same death squads that are supposed to guarantee free elections in El Salvador.

Yes, those who knew have been silenced. The political opposition has been decimated. Yet a revolution of complex composition—Catholic, agrarian, and nationalist in its roots, but also with strong Marxist, democratic Christian, and social-democratic elements, with militant students and accountants, printers and bank clerks—has claimed the right to do for El Salvador what has not been achieved in nearly five centuries: the abolition of colonialism, and at the very least the creation of a few conditions that might permit some evolution of the political structure.

They have met the army. I suppose they have found out what every Latin American democratic movement has had to find out for itself: that as long as the army protects the fortress of colonialism, conditions will continue as they traditionally always have. Perhaps the problem for El Salvador is not the overthrow of this or that junta, but the overthrow of the army. For the army is the only obstacle standing between the congealed colonialism that feeds its own vicious circle and any form of evolutionary democracy. In order to exist, colonialism needs an army to protect it by repression; in order to exist, the army needs a colonial structure, which it must defend and preserve through repression.

The problem is there. It has been there for nearly five centuries. But it has been forgotten. It is conveniently forgotten every time Latin America makes a move toward independence.

When the U.S. ambassador to the United Nations, Jeane Kirkpatrick, says that violence in El Salvador is created by outside intervention, not by social injustice, which has "existed for decades," she forgets that *violence* has also existed for decades; that it has, in fact, co-existed with social injustice for centuries. And when Secretary of State Alexander Haig says that "we are not going to be dragged into another Vietnam, but the problems will be dealt with at the source of the difficulty," it is to be hoped that he understands that the "source of difficulty" in El Salvador is military and paramilitary repression, the prevention of political evolution by the army.

Perhaps Mr. Haig and Ms. Kirkpatrick, if they are real anticommunists, will come to understand that by helping the military in El Salvador they help communism in El Salvador; that by identifying the Soviet Union with the revolution in El Salvador they hand the Soviet Union a moral victory that belongs only to the Salvadoran people. And that even if Cuba and the Soviet Union did not exist, there would still be a revolution in El Salvador. And that if it were true that arms are flowing into El Salvador from Hanoi and Havana and Managua, and should they then cease to flow, the civil war would continue in El Salvador, because it depends on historical factors that have nothing to do with communism—and because most of the arms that flow in come from private sources of contraband in Florida, Texas, and California.

The State Department White Paper on communist intervention in El Salvador proves nothing. The same arms have been photographed over and over, for Indochinese and Cuban and now Salvadoran effect; the captions and the photographs do not coincide; an example of what, ludicrously, does coincide is the sinister "meeting" between Salvadoran communists and Sandinistas in Managua on a particular date, which happens to be the date of the anniversary of the Nicaraguan revolution. So that [U.S.] Ambassadors McHenry and Pezzullo, who were also present, stand accused as well.

What can be proved is that if the Salvadoran rebels had half the arms that the State Department credits them with, they would by now have swept the army barracks and captured the abundant U.S. matériel shipped into El Salvador; that the army commanders themselves smirk at the allegations of the State Department, because they know the rebels have mostly old rifles and bazookas and whatever they can get on the international black market. But they will not say so publicly; they need arms to control El Salvador and repress, again and again, any attempt at even minimal change. For how long would the present agrarian reforms outlive the triumph of the army and the death squads in El Salvador? Two sets of figures tell the tale: 240 members of the new agrarian cooperatives have now been murdered by the paramilitary forces; eighty co-ops are paying "protection" to the army. Protection from what? From the death squads trained, armed, and financed by the army itself, of course.

The way out of this mess is by not identifying military success in El Salvador with the prestige of the United States. For whether the

United States loses or wins militarily in El Salvador, it will always lose in the end. It loses because if it thinks it has won it will have done so at the expense of the social and economic self-determination of the Salvadoran people. It will only have strengthened the prevailing official brutality and postponed the next insurrection. But it also loses if it thinks it has lost militarily, because it will then have passed up the opportunity to help El Salvador in the only way it can be helped by the United States. This way is for the United States to swallow hard and choose to become simply one among many participating forces in the solving of El Salvador's economic and social problems, according to El Salvador's needs.

For 1981 is not 1954; it is not even 1961. The opposition in El Salvador knows, as the revolutionaries in Nicaragua have learned, that once in power it can and should choose a plurality of sources of support—financial, technological, political. The choice for Nicaragua and El Salvador, the choice for all the underdeveloped nations, is not between the United States and the Soviet Union. It is between cold-war submission to one of the superpowers and the new, freer polity taking shape in spite of Moscow and Washington.

The balance of forces in 1981 is not what it was in 1954 or in 1961. The U.S. should take a good hard look at the Central American and Caribbean area; link the realities there to those of the emerging nations in Asia and Africa, especially after the election of François Mitterrand in France; understand western Europe's desirable role as an enlightened broker in the relations between the developing and the industrialized worlds; glance at the severe tensions within the Soviet bloc; and conclude, with true courage, with true self-interest, that nobody's welfare can be furthered by inventing a fictitious fulcrum of East-West confrontation in a small country where, even if it should "go communist," the Soviet Union would be unable to maintain it within its orbit without paying an exorbitant material price. I suspect, however, that the Soviet Union does not want El Salvador in its orbit. The Soviet Union prefers to wink at the United States and say: "We have understood you. You can do whatever you like in your sphere of influence. We can do whatever we like in ours. We strangle Afghanistan. You strangle El Salvador. We strangle Poland. You strangle Nicaragua. And if it comes to the crunch and you want to strike at sources not outside the target area, here goes Cuba and here comes West Berlin. Okay?"

No, it is not okay; the balance has changed because Mexico and Venezuela have emerged as important economic and political powers in the Americas. They have a role to play in Central America and the Caribbean. They are playing that role, and their message is, Hands off

El Salvador, everyone. Negotiate. Do not internationalize an internal conflict. Do not invent an East-West confrontation in a land that only requires North-South cooperation. The United States has a role to play, too, but only if it is in concert with the other nations of the area. What no one will tolerate is a proconsular attitude from Washington.

What we expect of the United States is loyal participation in our own Latin American policy of shifting power from the army to the people; of ending the long rule of the army; of cooperating with Mexico and Venezuela and Costa Rica and West Germany and the Soviet Union and East Germany and Sweden and Japan and Canada and France in offering the people of El Salvador and Nicaragua the plural sources of aid they need to reconstruct their shattered economies.

What we expect of the United States is a shift in its attention away from the sterility of East-West confrontation and toward the fertility of global economic negotiations.

What we expect from the United States is as little and as much as Roosevelt gave Cárdenas: American faith and trust in itself as a democratic polity, and an understanding that by respecting self-determination in Latin America, by understanding change, upheaval, and even violence in Latin America instead of stopping change, adding to violence, and creating its own counterrevolutionary havoc, by accepting the universal right to revolution even when it hurts U.S. private interests, the United States is most loyal to itself as a community founded on revolution, and most consonant with its self-interest when it does not permit marginal and private interests to set themselves above the meaning, the attraction, the truth of this great nation.

SELECTED BIBLIOGRAPHY

T. D. Allman, "Rising to Rebellion," *Harper's* [New York], March 1981.

Stephen E. Ambrose, *Rise to Globalism: American Foreign Policy, 1938–1980* [Pelican History of the United States, vol. 8., Robert A. Divine, ed.] (Harmondsworth, England: Penguin Books, 1980).

Amnesty International, *Guatemala: A Government Program of Political Murder* (New York: Amnesty International, 1981).

Thomas P. Anderson, *Matanza: El Salvador's Communist Revolt of 1932* (Lincoln, Neb.: Univ. of Nebraska Press, 1971).

Cynthia Arnson, "Cold War in the Caribbean," *Inquiry* [San Francisco], December 10, 1979.

Richard J. Barnet, *Intervention and Revolution: America's Confrontation with Insurgent Movements Around the World* (New York: New American Library, 1968).

——, *Real Security: Restoring American Power in a Dangerous Decade* (New York: Simon and Schuster, 1981).

Joseph Baylen, "Sandino: Patriot or Bandit?", *Hispanic-American Historical Review* [Durham, N.C.], XXXI (August, 1951).

Raymond Bonner, "The Agony of El Salvador," *The New York Times Magazine* [New York], February 22, 1981.

David Browning, *El Salvador: Landscape and Society* (London: Clarendon/Oxford University Press, 1971).

Marco V. Carías, *Análisis Sobre el Conflicto entre Honduras y El Salvador* (Tegucigalpa, Hond.: Universidad Nacional Autónoma, 1969).

James Chace, *Solvency: The Price of Survival: An Essay on American Foreign Policy* (New York: Random House, 1981).

Roy A. Childs, Jr., "El Salvador: The Roots of Conflict," *Libertarian Review* [Washington, D.C.], X, 1, April 1981.

Alexander Cockburn and James Ridgeway, "El Salvador: Reagan's War," *The Village Voice* [New York], March 4, 1981.

Abel Cuenca, *El Salvador: Una Democracia Cafetalera* (Mexico City: ARR-Centro Editorial, 1932).

Karen De Young, "White Hand of Terror: How the Peace Was Lost in El Salvador," *Mother Jones* [San Francisco], June 1981.

Robert V. Elam, "Appeal to Arms: The Army and Politics in El Salvador, 1931–1964" (Ph.D. thesis, University of New Mexico, 1968).

El Salvador: Another Vietnam—a film by Catalyst Media available from Icarus Films, 200 Park Ave. South, New York, N.Y. 10003

Plácido Erdozain, *Archbishop Romero: Martyr of Salvador* (New York: Orbis Books, 1981).

Richard R. Fagen, *The Nicaraguan Revolution: A Personal Report* (Washington, D.C., Institute for Policy Studies, 1981).

James Fallows, *National Defense* (New York; Random House, 1981).

Roger Fontaine, Cleto DiGiovanni, Jr., and Alexander Kruger, "Castro's Specter," *The Washington Quarterly* [Washington, D.C.], Autumn 1980.

John Gerassi, *The Great Fear in Latin America* (New York: Macmillan, 1965).

——, Ed., *Revolutionary Priest: The Complete Writings and Messages of Camilo Torres* (New York: Vintage, 1971).

E. O. Guerrant, "The Recognition of El Salvador in 1934: An Alteration in the Foreign Policy of the United States," *The Historian* [Wichita, Kansas], VI (Autumn, 1943).

Gustavo Gutiérrez, *A Theology of Liberation* (New York: Orbis Books, 1977).

Fred Kaplan, *Dubious Specter: A Skeptical Look at the Soviet Nuclear Threat* (Washington, D.C.: Institute for Policy Studies, 1980).

George F. Kennan, "Cease this Madness," *The Atlantic* [Boston], January 1981.

Michael T. Klare and Cynthia Arnson, *Supplying Repression: U.S. Support for Authoritarian Regimes Abroad* (Washington, D.C.: Institute for Policy Studies, 1981).

Stewart Klepper, "The United States in El Salvador," *Covert Action Information Bulletin* [Washington, D.C.], April 1981.

Latin America Weekly Report and *Latin America Regional Report* [90-93 Cowcross Street, London EC 1M 6BL, England].

David Lena, "Análisis de una Dictatura Fascista Latino-Americana: Maximiliano Hernández Martínez," *La Universidad* [San Salvador], XCIV (September–October, 1969).

Penny Lernoux, *Cry of the People: United States Involvement in the Rise of Fascism, Torture, and Murder and the Persecution of the Catholic Church in Latin America* (New York: Doubleday, 1980).

Alejandro D. Marroquín, *Latin America and the Caribbean: A Handbook*, Claudio Véliz, ed. (Belfast, Ireland: Anthony Blound, 1968).

Percy F. Martin, *Salvador of the Twentieth Century* (London: Edward Arnold, 1911).

John D. Martz, *Central America: The Crisis and the Challenge* (Chapel Hill, N.C.: Univ. of North Carolina Press, 1959).

Rafael Menjivar, *El Salvador: El eslabón mas pequeño* (Costa Rica: Editorial Universitaria Centroamericana, 1980).

Dana G. Munro, *The Five Republics of Central America: Their Political and Economic Development and their Relations with the United States* (New York: Oxford Univ. Press, 1918).

——*Intervention and Dollar Diplomacy in the Caribbean, 1900–1921* (Princeton, N.J.: Princeton Univ. Press, 1964).

National Lawyers Guild, *Guatemala: Repression and Resistance* (NLG, 1980).

North American Congress on Latin America (NACLA), "El Salvador: Why Revolution?" (New York: *NACLA Report,* Jan.–Feb. 1981); "El Salvador: A Revolution Brews" *(NACLA Report,* March–April 1981), "Central America: No Road Back" *(NACLA Report,* May–June 1981). *Guatemala* (New York: NACLA, 1981).

Franklin D. Parker, *The Central American Republics* (London: Oxford Univ. Press, 1964).

James Petras, *Class, State and Power in the Third World: With Case Studies of Class Conflict in Latin America* [with A. Eugene Havens, Morris H. Morley and Peter De Witt], (Montclair, N.J.: Allanheld, Osmun, 1981).

James Petras and Maurice Zeitlin, eds., *Latin America: Reform or Revolution?* ["Political Perspectives," Marvin E. Gettleman, ed.] (New York: Fawcett: 1968).

David R. Raynolds, *Rapid Development in Small Economies: The Example of El Salvador* (New York: Praeger, 1967).

J. Fred Rippy, *Latin America: A Modern History*, Revised ed. [University of Michigan, "History of the Modern World," Allan Nevins and Howard M. Ehrmann, eds.] (Ann Arbor, Mich.: Univ. of Michigan Press, 1968).

O. Rodríguez [pseud.?] "The Uprising in Salvador," *The Communist* [New York], XI (March, 1932).

William O. Scroggs, *Filibusters and Financiers: The Story of William Walker and his Associates* (New York: Macmillan, 1916).

Holly Sklar and Robert Lawrence, "Who's Who in the Reagan Administration?" [Poster, with glossary and references.] (Boston: South End Press, 1981).

Daniel and Ester Slutsky, "El Salvador: Estructura de la explotación cafetalera," *Estudios Sociales Centro-Americanos* [San José, Costa Rica], I (May–August, 1971).

U.S. Central Intelligence Agency, Foreign Broadcast Information Service, Daily Reports [Latin American Series] (1942–), daily.

Alastair White, *El Salvador* ["Nations of the Modern World"] (London: Ernest Benn, 1973).

William Appleman Williams, *Empire as a Way of Life* (New York: Oxford Univ. Press, 1980).

Everett A. Wilson, "The Crisis of National Integration in El Salvador, 1919–1935" (Ph.D. thesis, Stanford University, 1969).

Alan Wolfe, *The Rise and Fall of the "Soviet Threat": Domestic Sources of the Cold War Consensus* (Washington, D.C.: Institute for Policy Studies, 1980).

RESOURCES

Some Organizations Concerned about El Salvador and U.S. Foreign Policy

Ad Hoc Committee of Scholars/El Salvador, 21 Washington Place, P.O. Box 138, New York, NY 10003

American Friends Service Committee, 1501 Cherry St., Philadelphia, PA 19102

Americans for Democratic Action, 1411 K St. NW, Washington, DC 20005

Amnesty International, 304 West 58th St., New York, NY 10019

Campus Outreach Committee, Mobilization for Survival, 135 West 4th St., New York, NY 10012

Center for Defense Information, 122 Maryland Ave., NE, Washington, DC 20002

Clergy and Laity Concerned, 198 Broadway, New York, NY 10007

Coalition for a New Foreign and Military Policy, 120 Maryland Ave., NE, Washington, DC 20002

Committee for Medical Aid to El Salvador, P.O. Box 384, Planetarium Station, New York, NY 10042

Committee in Solidarity with the People of El Salvador [CISPES], 853 Broadway, New York, NY 10003

Council on Hemispheric Affairs, 30 Fifth Ave. New York, NY 10011

Democratic Socialist Organizing Committee, 853 Broadway, New York, NY 10003

Ecumenical Program for Inter-American Communication and Action [EPICA], 1470 Irving St., NW, Washington, DC 20010

Fellowship of Reconciliation, Box 271, Nyack, NY 10960

Friends Committee on National Legislation, 245 Second St., NE, Washington, DC 20002

Institute for Policy Studies, 1901 Q St., NW, Washington, DC 20009

Interreligious Task Force on El Salvador, 1747 Connecticut Ave., NW, Washington, DC 20009

Labor Committee in Support of Democracy & Human Rights in El Salvador, Local 169 ACTWU, 33 West 14th St., New York, NY 10003

Mobilization for Survival, 3601 Locust Walk, Philadelphia, PA 19104

National Council of Churches (Human Rights Office), 475 Riverside Drive, New York, NY 10027

National Lawyers Guild, 853 Broadway, New York, NY 10003

New American Movement, 3244 N. Clark Street, Chicago, IL 60657
North American Congress on Latin America [NACLA], 151 W. 19th St.,
  New York, NY 10011
SANE, 514 C St. NE, Washington, DC 20002
War Resisters League, 339 Lafayette St., New York, NY 10012
Washington Office on Latin America, 110 Maryland Ave., NE, Washington,
  DC 20002

Some Alternative Publications With Regular Coverage of Latin America and U.S. Foreign Policy

Caribbean Review, Florida International University, Miami, Fl. 33199.
  Quarterly.
Christianity and Crisis, 537 W. 121 St., New York, N.Y. 10027. Bimonthly.
Guardian, 33 West 17th St., New York, NY 10003. Weekly.
Inquiry, 747 Front St., San Francisco, CA 94111. Monthly.
In These Times, 1509 North Milwaukee Ave., Chicago, IL 60622. Weekly.
Latin American Perspectives, Box 792, Riverside CA 92502.
  Quarterly.
Maryknoll Magazine, Maryknoll, NY 10545. Monthly.
Monthly Review, 62 West 14th St., New York, NY 10011. Monthly.
Mother Jones, 625 Third St., San Francisco, CA 94107. Monthly.
NACLA Report, 151 W. 19th St., New York, NY 10011. Bimonthly.
The Nation, 72 Fifth Ave., New York, NY 10011. Weekly.
The New Republic, 1220 19th St., NW, Washington, DC 20036. Weekly.
The Progressive, 408 West Gorham, Madison, WI 53703. Monthly.
Socialist Review, 4228 Telegraph Ave., Oakland, CA 94609. Bimonthly.
Washington Office on Latin America, *Newsletter*, 110 Maryland Ave., NE,
  Washington, DC 20002. Monthly.
WIN Magazine, 326 Livingston St., Brooklyn, NY 11217. Biweekly.

INDEX

This is a selective index containing significant names and subjects that cannot be readily found in the table of contents. —Editors.